The Glannon Guide to Sales

The Glannon Guide to Sales

Learning Sales Through Multiple-Choice Questions and Analysis

Second Edition

Scott J. Burnham

Frederick N. and Barbara T. Curley Professor of Law
Gonzaga University School of Law

Wolters Kluwer
Law & Business

Published by Wolters Kluwer Law & Business in New York.

Wolters Kluwer Law & Business serves customers worldwide with CCH, Aspen Publishers, and Kluwer Law International products. (www.wolterskluwerlb.com)

To contact Customer Service, e-mail customer.service@wolterskluwer.com, call 1-800-234-1660, fax 1-800-901-9075, or mail correspondence to:

> Wolters Kluwer Law & Business
> Attn: Order Department
> PO Box 990
> Frederick, MD 21705

Printed in the United States of America.

1 2 3 4 5 6 7 8 9 0

ISBN 978-0-7355-0966-5

Library of Congress Cataloging-in-Publication Data

Burnham, Scott J.
    The Glannon guide to sales : learning sales through multiple-choice questions and analysis / Scott J. Burnham. — 2nd ed.
      p. cm.
    Includes index.
    ISBN 978-0-7355-0966-5
    1. Sales—United States. 2. Leases—United States. 3. Commercial law—United States. 4. Sales—United States—Problems, exercises, etc. 5. Leases—United States—Problems, exercises, etc. 6. Commercial law—United States—Problems, exercises, etc. I. Title.

KF915.B875 2012
346.7307'2—dc23   2012013607

About Wolters Kluwer Law & Business

Wolters Kluwer Law & Business is a leading global provider of intelligent information and digital solutions for legal and business professionals in key specialty areas, and respected educational resources for professors and law students. Wolters Kluwer Law & Business connects legal and business professionals as well as those in the education market with timely, specialized authoritative content and information-enabled solutions to support success through productivity, accuracy and mobility.

Serving customers worldwide, Wolters Kluwer Law & Business products include those under the Aspen Publishers, CCH, Kluwer Law International, Loislaw, Best Case, ftwilliam. com and MediRegs family of products.

CCH products have been a trusted resource since 1913, and are highly regarded resources for legal, securities, antitrust and trade regulation, government contracting, banking, pension, payroll, employment and labor, and healthcare reimbursement and compliance professionals.

Aspen Publishers products provide essential information to attorneys, business professionals and law students. Written by preeminent authorities, the product line offers analytical and practical information in a range of specialty practice areas from securities law and intellectual property to mergers and acquisitions and pension/benefits. Aspen's trusted legal education resources provide professors and students with high-quality, up-to-date and effective resources for successful instruction and study in all areas of the law.

Kluwer Law International products provide the global business community with reliable international legal information in English. Legal practitioners, corporate counsel and business executives around the world rely on Kluwer Law journals, looseleafs, books, and electronic products for comprehensive information in many areas of international legal practice.

Loislaw is a comprehensive online legal research product providing legal content to law firm practitioners of various specializations. Loislaw provides attorneys with the ability to quickly and efficiently find the necessary legal information they need, when and where they need it, by facilitating access to primary law as well as state-specific law, records, forms and treatises.

Best Case Solutions is the leading bankruptcy software product to the bankruptcy industry. It provides software and workflow tools to flawlessly streamline petition preparation and the electronic filing process, while timely incorporating ever-changing court requirements.

ftwilliam.com offers employee benefits professionals the highest quality plan documents (retirement, welfare and non-qualified) and government forms (5500/PBGC, 1099 and IRS) software at highly competitive prices.

MediRegs products provide integrated health care compliance content and software solutions for professionals in healthcare, higher education and life sciences, including professionals in accounting, law and consulting.

Wolters Kluwer Law & Business, a division of Wolters Kluwer, is headquartered in New York. Wolters Kluwer is a market-leading global information services company focused on professionals.

There is something special about UCC Article 2 that reveals itself to those who work with it. I would like to dedicate this work to all those who have contributed to the Code, from the great Karl Llewellyn to the late Richard Speidel.

Contents

Acknowledgments

I am indebted to my former law school, The University of Montana School of Law, and especially to my colleague Professor Kristen Juras; to the University of Nevada, Las Vegas, Boyd School of Law, where I worked on this project as a visitor; and to my present law school, Gonzaga University School of Law, for their support of this project.

I also wish to thank Amy Lord and David Lord, former students at The University of Montana School of Law, for their indexing; and Emily Reed, a former student at the University of Nevada, Las Vegas, Boyd School of Law, and Erik Kukuk, a former student at Gonzaga University School of Law, for their research assistance.

I gratefully acknowledge the permission granted by the American Law Institute (ALI) and the Uniform Law Commission (ULC) to reprint portions of the Uniform Commercial Code. Copyright 2002.

Finally, I am grateful to all those involved in the editorial process at Aspen Publishers, including the anonymous reviewers, who made this a better book.

1

A Very Short Introduction

A. Introduction to sales and leases
B. Answering multiple-choice questions
C. How to use this book

A. Introduction to sales and leases

This book has three goals: (1) to provide you with a concise overview of Sales and Leases that will prove helpful whether you are taking the course or preparing for the bar, (2) to use multiple-choice questions to assess your understanding of the material and to improve your multiple choice exam-taking skills, and (3) to develop your skills of statutory analysis and interpretation.

Sales and Leases is a cumulative subject. You have to begin by learning some basic concepts and vocabulary, and then use those concepts and vocabulary to build your understanding of the subject. If you are working with the book as you take the course, you might find that the order of topics differs from the order in your class. Don't be concerned about that. As long as you see how all the pieces fit together, the order doesn't really matter. I believe, however, that I have designed a sequence that flows logically, allowing you to learn in a coherent fashion. If you are reading the book for a final course review or for bar review, I think you will find it helpful to see the topics arranged from another perspective. This book emphasizes the main contours of the topics, but it is not a detailed treatise. If you use the book to prepare for the bar exam, I think you will find that it addresses the main points that are more likely to appear on the exam.

You don't know whether you understand a concept until you are asked to apply it to a particular fact situation. You will find at least one multiple-choice question at the end of each section that asks you to apply your knowledge of the material in order to solve problems. In the analysis that follows each question, you will find not only which response is better than the others, but also the reasoning process that leads to that conclusion. The analysis will discuss the rules, which are usually found in the statutes, in the context of particular facts. Because you are learning skills of legal analysis, the questions and analysis are beneficial for both multiple-choice and essay exams.

Sales and Leases is a statutory course, requiring you to become familiar with Articles 2 and 2A of the Uniform Commercial Code (UCC or Code). Unless you are a very unusual person, reading statutes is probably not one of your favorite things. However, because the answers to most Sales and Leases questions are found in the Code, you must develop the habit of reading the relevant Code sections, particularly when answering the multiple-choice questions. Although many individual sections are laid out in the reading, it will be helpful if you have a copy of the complete Code handy to see the big picture and to consult other sections that are referenced.

Don't be concerned if you are not seeing a lot of references to leases, the subject of Article 2A. We initially make sure you understand what leases are and how to distinguish a sales transaction from a lease transaction, but we won't mention leases much after that until the end of the book. Because Article 2A is closely modeled on Article 2, if you understand how the concepts apply to sales, you should be able to transfer that understanding to the subject of leases. We then have a chapter dedicated to leases (Chapter 21) that indicates the similarities and the differences.

B.   Answering multiple-choice questions

The answer to a legal question is a function of both the facts and the rules. To properly analyze the question, you need to appreciate the facts, knowing which ones are important, and you need to be able to apply the correct rule in the particular factual situation. Multiple-choice questions can help you develop and improve your legal analysis skills.

The following section is designed to assist you in answering multiple-choice questions. A multiple-choice question consists of a fact pattern that ends with a *question*. Following the question is a series of *options* or *responses*, one of which is correct, and the rest of which (sometimes called the *distractors*) are incorrect. Sometimes two responses may appear to be correct, but one is usually the *best* response.

As with any exam, follow instructions. If your score is simply the sum of the right answers, and there is no penalty for guessing incorrectly, don't leave any blanks. If there is only one correct response, don't choose two responses. As with any exam, pay attention to the "call of the question," which means answering the question that is asked. For example, suppose the question asks:

Which of the following is not within the Article 2 definition of goods?

Here, the question asks you to do the opposite of what you normally do: It asks that you choose the *wrong* response rather than the right response. If you miss a little word like *not* when you read the call of the question, you are likely to go astray.

Some multiple-choice questions simply ask you to recall information, such as the following example:

> In the absence of agreement by the parties, what is the Code rule on the place of delivery?
>
> **A.** Seller's place of business.
> **B.** Buyer's place of business.
> **C.** A reasonable place.
> **D.** There is no Code rule on this point.

These questions require that you know the rule, and little analytical reasoning is involved. These questions may reward those who have learned the rules. Your instructor may give an open-book exam, perhaps limiting the allowed materials to a copy of the Code. In that case, you can verify the answer by finding the relevant statute. The question then rewards those who are familiar with the Code, who know where to find things so they are not doing original research.

Other questions may draw on the materials used in class, asking you to recall what you read or discussed, as in this example:

> The holding of *Neri v. Retail Marine Corp.* is
>
> **A.** A down payment may be retained as liquidated damages.
> **B.** A seller may recover as damages the difference between the contract price and the resale price.
> **C.** Lost profits may be awarded as a remedy.
> **D.** A seller may not recover consequential damages.

These questions reward students who have read the material and paid attention in class. If you don't know the answer, there is no logical way to figure it out, and even in an open-book exam, there might not be time to find the answer.

Most multiple-choice questions, however, require analysis. Your approach to these questions should employ the traditional approach used on essay examinations known by the acronym IRAC: Issue, Rule, Analysis or Application, and Conclusion. On an essay examination, you are given the facts. You then deduce the *issue* that is raised by these facts in your response. You then recall the appropriate *rule* that applies to the issue. Finally, you *analyze* or *apply* the rule to the facts to come to a *conclusion*.

A multiple-choice question similarly begins with facts from which you must determine the issue. This task can be easier with multiple-choice questions because the facts for an essay can be complex, raising many issues, whereas a multiple-choice question is usually narrow, raising only a single issue. It can be difficult to spot issues, but familiarity with the table of contents of the course material can help, as you can use the contents as a checklist for the topical areas in which issues may arise. Except for Chapter 24, which contains review questions, this book will be less helpful in developing your broad issue-spotting skills because the questions are already placed in the section that covers the relevant topic.

The facts will suggest the relevant issue. Ask yourself why the author included certain facts in the question. It was probably to raise a certain issue. For example, a question begins with these facts:

> Trying to sell his Rembrandt painting, a rich individual made a telephone call to a museum. During the call, the museum agreed to buy the painting for $5,000,000....

Although you won't know if it is relevant until you have read the entire item, a light should go on when you read the fact that the individual "made a telephone call" to the museum. Why did the drafter of the question include that particular fact, instead of just stating that the parties made an agreement? A good working hypothesis is that it is a significant fact that this transaction was *oral*, suggesting that the issue might involve the enforceability of an oral agreement. Look for words or phrases that trigger particular issues.

Once you have determined the issue, you will need to employ the relevant rule. In the area of Sales, the relevant rule will usually be found in a statute from UCC Article 2. Your familiarity with the organization of Article 2 will help you find the relevant rule. You can then apply the facts to the rule and come to a conclusion. On an essay exam, you would explain all of your reasoning, but on a multiple-choice exam, it is simply a matter of selecting the correct response.

Sometimes the responses offered contain only conclusions, but other times they contain both a conclusion and analysis, such as the reason for the conclusion. Consider this example:

A contract between a buyer and a seller of goods is silent on the recovery of consequential damages and attorney's fees incurred in the event of breach. On Seller's default, Buyer incurs consequential damages that were reasonably foreseeable to Seller in the amount of $1,000 and reasonable attorney's fees of $2,000. Buyer may recover

A. Neither the consequential damages nor the attorney's fees, because neither is permitted by the statute.
B. The consequential damages only, because the statute permits consequential damages but permits attorney's fees only if provided for by agreement.

C. The attorney's fees only, because the statute permits attorney's fees but permits consequential damages only if provided for by agreement.
D. Both the consequential damages and the attorney's fees, because both are permitted by the statute.

Alternatively, the responses following the same question might look like this:

A. $0.
B. $1,000.
C. $2,000.
D. $3,000.

These two sets of responses, although different, are functionally equivalent. The first set of responses contains a conclusion and also analysis, the reason for the conclusion. The second set of responses contains only the conclusion and omits the analysis required to reach that conclusion. Because the consequential damages are $1,000 and the attorney's fees are $2,000, you will quickly see that the response "$1,000" is the same as saying "the consequential damages only." To respond to this question, you would need to know the appropriate rules and then apply them to the facts.

You will often be able to eliminate two responses as erroneous or irrelevant, thereby narrowing the field to two responses that both seem correct. To distinguish between those two responses, you might employ some of the following techniques:

- Review the facts to determine whether you are being tested on a factual distinction. One response might be correct when the contract is *oral,* another when the contract is *written.* Or one response might be correct when the seller is a *merchant,* another when the seller is a *nonmerchant.*
- Make sure you are applying the right rule. Rule A might lead you to one response, whereas Rule B might lead you to another.
- Check whether you are being tested on the exception to a rule. The rule might lead you to one response, but the exception might lead you to another.

In this book, a question will sometimes be designated a *statute reader* when the question focuses on your ability to read the text of a statute, and the analysis following the question will sometimes include a *Note on test taking* that points out some of these techniques.

C.   How to use this book

There are two beneficial ways to use this book. One approach is to read the material in each section and then take the multiple-choice assessment. With this approach, you are trying to master the material and then determine whether you have understood it. Alternatively, you could take the assessment first. If the analysis seems familiar, you probably have an understanding of the material and can move on to the next section. If the analysis does not seem familiar, you should read the material that preceded the assessment. This approach might work well if you are looking for multiple-choice questions with which to practice.

If you have any comments about the book, positive or negative, do not hesitate to get in touch with me at sburnham@lawschool.gonzaga.edu.

2

Working with the Uniform Commercial Code

A. Introduction

What is Sales and Leases all about? It all begins with contracts. In first-year Contracts, you were probably told that in the Anglo-American system, the study of contracts is a common law subject. Although that is true, it is true only because so many areas of law have been codified and spun off from the central core of contracts, leaving what one authority called "the law of leftovers." Sales and Leases are two of the subjects that have been codified and stand apart from the general study of contracts. Of course, when there is a gap in the codified law, we draw from the general principles of contract law to fill it.

Article 2 of the Uniform Commercial Code (UCC or Code) deals with the sale of goods, whereas Article 2A deals with leases of goods. Before we get into the details of Articles 2 and 2A, let's look at them against the more general backdrop of the UCC. Where does the UCC come from? It is a project of the Uniform Law Commission (ULC), also known as the National Conference of Commissioners on Uniform State Law (NCCUSL), with the assistance of the American Law Institute (ALI), the folks who bring us the *Restatements of Law*. The ULC is a private, nonprofit group that attempts to draft model codes that (1) get the law right, and (2) are enactable. The UCC is the most successful of the uniform laws promulgated by the ULC; most of it has been enacted in all 50 states and the District of Columbia. Louisiana is the only state that has not enacted Articles 2 and 2A.

In working with the UCC, however, remember that

- It is not uniform.
- It is not commercial.
- It is not a code.

1. *It is not uniform*

Section 1-103(a) states the purposes of the Uniform Commercial Code:

> **§ 1-103. Construction of [Act] to Promote its Purposes and Policies; Applicability of Supplemental Principles of Law.**
>
>   (a) [The Uniform Commercial Code] must be liberally construed and applied to promote its underlying purposes and policies, which are:
>
>   (1) to simplify, clarify, and modernize the law governing commercial transactions;
>
>   (2) to permit the continued expansion of commercial practices through custom, usage, and agreement of the parties; and
>
>   (3) to make uniform the law among the various jurisdictions.

In spite of the fact that one of the purposes is "to make uniform the law among the various jurisdictions," this goal has not been accomplished. A Uniform Law is, of course, just a model. It has no mandatory authority until it has been enacted through a state's legislative process. States are free to create their own local variations, and in fact, they often do. Furthermore, after the initial enactment, revisions of a Uniform Law are sometimes proposed by the ULC. You will therefore find that like other Uniform Laws, there are variations in Articles 2 and 2A from jurisdiction to jurisdiction, depending on how many local changes the legislature has made, and whether the legislature has kept current with proposed revisions.

A major revision of Article 2 was undertaken that culminated in a 1999 draft, but the ULC ultimately decided not to support it. An attempt was then made to address issues of information transactions that are not covered by Articles 2 and 2A. The ULC promulgated the Uniform Computer Information Transactions Act (UCITA) in 2002, but after it was adopted by only two states, the ULC withdrew its support for UCITA and it is unlikely to gain momentum. In 2002, the ULC promulgated an amended version of Article 2 (called, not surprisingly, Amended Article 2) that was much more modest in scope than the earlier revision. Amended Article 2 failed to gain any traction and was withdrawn from consideration by the states in 2011. Amended Article 2 has some value for us, however, as the goals of the drafters included resolving ambiguities in the existing Article 2 and updating it to expressly apply to electronic commerce. Therefore, even though it has no mandatory authority, Amended Article 2 can help us see how enacted Article 2 could be interpreted and modernized, so we will be citing it from time to time. Always remember, however, that its authority is merely persuasive.

After it has become law, the Code is then codified in the statutes of the enacting jurisdiction. Many jurisdictions use different numbering systems for the Code, but that is a superficial distinction. For example, the uniform version of § 2-204(1) was codified in Montana as § 30-2-204(1) and in Oregon as § 72.2040(1), but the text is the same. You might think Article 2A was not enacted in California until you discover that it was enacted as Article 10, or more specifically as Division 10 of the California Commercial Code, § 10101 et seq. When you cite a uniform Code section as authority, or when you cite a case from another jurisdiction that construes a Code section, you must find the comparable section in your jurisdiction and check to be sure the text is the same as the text of the section as enacted in your jurisdiction.

You will recall from your study of other commercial courses that the concepts and definitions in UCC Article 1 apply throughout the Code, including Articles 2 and 2A. To complicate matters, a Revised Article 1 has been approved by the ALI and the ULC, but it has not been enacted in every state, and the states that have enacted it have not enacted it in its uniform version. Nevertheless, because Revised Article 1 will become the norm, it is the version of Article 1 that is cited in this book. Here is a table indicating where the corresponding sections that we will be working with can be found in Revised Article 1 and in pre-Revision Article 1:

Revised Article 1	Pre-Revision Article 1
1-103	1-102, 1-103
1-201(b)(20)	1-201(19)
1-201(b)(37)	1-201(39)
1-201(b)(43)	1-201(46)
1-203	1-201(37)
1-205	1-204(2), (3)
1-301	1-105
1-302(a), (b)	1-102(3)
1-302(c)	1-102(4)
1-303	1-205, 2-208
1-305	1-106
1-306	1-107
1-308	1-207

> **QUESTION 1.** The Uniform Law Commission (ULC) promulgates the UCC. Is the same version of UCC Article 2 found in every state?
>
> A. Yes, because as federal law, it is uniform throughout the states.
> B. Yes, because each state has enacted the uniform version.
> C. No, because some states have enacted Revised Article 2.
> D. No, because many state legislatures make changes to the uniform version.

ANALYSIS.   The uniform version of Article 2 is promulgated by the ULC, but to become law, it must be enacted in each state. Therefore, **A** is an incorrect response, because the UCC is state law, not federal law. Revised Article 2 has been enacted by no states; therefore **C** is not correct. Even though the ULC doesn't like it, each state usually makes some changes to the uniform version. Therefore, **B** is not a correct response. **D** is the correct response.

2. *It is not commercial*

The word *commercial* is often used to distinguish a transaction between two businesses from a *consumer* transaction. For purposes of the Code, however, *commercial* is used in the broad sense of *involving commerce,* so a consumer transaction is just one kind of commercial transaction. The Code governs both kinds of transactions and, most of the time, does not distinguish between them. Article 2 applies to *all* sales of goods, whether the transaction is the sale of 50,000 pens from the Bic Company to IBM, the sale of a pen from The Office Supply Company to you, or the sale of my pen to you.

Even though Article 2 applies to both merchants and nonmerchants, there are number of occasions (14 to be exact) where Article 2 tells us that a particular rule applies only to "a merchant," or only "between merchants." We spend more time in Chapter 4.B on the meaning of *merchant,* but it should be apparent that the distinction is between one who has experience with sales and one who does not. These rules, therefore, apply only to sophisticated parties.

Article 2A expressly distinguishes between a *lease* and a *consumer lease.* Although Article 2 makes no express reference to consumers (and only one reference to "consumer goods"), a panoply of other state and federal law kicks in when there is a sale of consumer goods or when there is a consumer transaction, which is a transaction entered into for personal, family, or household purposes. When deciding cases, courts often find the sophistication of the parties to be an important factor. Therefore, even if the Code appears to treat them the same, you will find it helpful to distinguish between a consumer transaction and a commercial transaction.

> **QUESTION 2.** Section 2-314 provides that "[u]nless excluded or modified (Section 2-316), a warranty that the goods shall be merchantable is implied in a contract for their sale if the seller is a merchant with respect to goods of that kind." I (a law professor) buy a new car and sell my old car to you (a law student). Do I give you a warranty of merchantability?
>
> A. No, because Article 2 does not apply to this transaction.
> B. No, because the seller is not a merchant.
> C. No, because there is no warranty of merchantability in the sale of used goods.
> D. Yes, because the statute provides that "a warranty that the goods shall be merchantable is implied."

ANALYSIS. We know that **A** is not a correct response because Article 2 applies to the sale of goods, and the transaction involves a car, which is a good. According to § 2-102, Article 2 applies to transactions in goods, and for that purpose, it does not matter whether a party is a merchant or not. Once we are within Article 2, however, the applicability of certain provisions may turn on the status of the parties. Section 2-314 is such a provision. We know that **C** is not correct because there is nothing in the statute that says it does not apply to used goods. The statute provides that the warranty is given "if the seller is a merchant with respect to goods of that kind." Because I am not a regular seller of cars, I am not a merchant, so I do not give the warranty. Response **D** is not correct because the quoted language is qualified by the words, "if the seller is a merchant." Therefore, the correct response is **B**.

3. It is not a code

We generally use the word *code* in contrast to the common law as a source of law. Codes generally represent the exclusive law in the area. The UCC, however, has been called a "common law code" because of the extent to which it is supplemented by the common law. Section 1-103(b), one of the most important provisions in the Code, expressly provides for this supplementation:

> Unless displaced by the particular provisions of [the Uniform Commercial Code], the principles of law and equity, including the law merchant and the law relative to capacity to contract, principal and agent, estoppel, fraud, misrepresentation, duress, coercion, mistake, bankruptcy, and other validating or invalidating cause supplement its provisions.

For example, § 2-205 deals with a "firm offer," but the Code does not define the term *offer*. We would supplement the Code rule with the concept of offer from general principles of contract law. A firm offer, then, has to be an offer as understood at common law before it can be a firm offer under the Code.

Recall also that the Code generally provides default rules for a transaction while enabling the parties to vary the provisions, thus preserving freedom of contract. Section 1-302 provides in part:

> ### § 1-302. Variation by Agreement.
>
> (a) Except as otherwise provided in subsection (b) or elsewhere in [the Uniform Commercial Code], the effect of provisions of [the Uniform Commercial Code] may be varied by agreement.
>
> (b) The obligations of good faith, diligence, reasonableness, and care prescribed by [the Uniform Commercial Code] may not be disclaimed by agreement. The parties, by agreement, may determine the standards by which the performance of those obligations is to be measured if those standards are not manifestly unreasonable.

Parties are therefore generally free to change the default rules of the Code, with the exceptions enumerated in § 1-302(b). Working with the Code can be difficult, however, because there are other "immutable rules" that the parties are unable to change, and the Code does not label them as such. Part of our job in understanding the Code is to identify these provisions.

Furthermore, Article 2 is supplemented by many other statutes. Frequently, finding your way around the Code is necessary but not sufficient to resolve all the issues raised in a sales transaction. As state law, Article 2 is subject to both other state law regulating the transaction and preemption by federal law. The fact that you have determined the result under Article 2 does not mean you have found all the relevant law. That other relevant law, some of which is discussed in this book, includes the federal Magnuson-Moss Warranty Act and state Consumer Protection Acts.

QUESTION 3. A supplier sells microwave ovens to be used by consumers. The oven is sold with a written warranty in which the supplier promises that the oven will be defect-free for a period of one year. In addition, the warranty states, "There are no warranties which extend beyond the description on the face hereof." Here are the applicable statutes:

UCC § 2-316. Exclusion or Modification of Warranties.

(2) [T]o exclude or modify the implied warranty of merchantability or any part of it the language must mention merchantability and in case of a writing must be conspicuous, and to exclude or modify any implied warranty of fitness the exclusion must be by a writing and conspicuous. Language to exclude all implied warranties of fitness is sufficient if it states, for example, that "There are no warranties which extend beyond the description on the face hereof."

> **Federal Magnuson-Moss Warranty Act. 15 U.S.C. § 2308. Implied Warranties.**
>
>   a. Restrictions on disclaimers or modifications. No supplier may disclaim or modify . . . any implied warranty to a consumer with respect to such consumer product if
>   (1) such supplier makes any written warranty to the consumer with respect to such consumer product.
>
> Based only on what you read in those statutes, is the language used by the supplier sufficient to disclaim the implied warranty of fitness?
>
> **A.** Yes, because the UCC provides that the quoted language is sufficient.
> **B.** Yes, because the U.S. Code provides that a supplier may disclaim any implied warranty.
> **C.** No, because the UCC provides that a supplier may not disclaim any implied warranty to a consumer if it has made a written warranty.
> **D.** No, because the U.S. Code provides that a supplier may not disclaim any implied warranty to a consumer if it has made a written warranty.

ANALYSIS.   Responses **B** and **C** cannot be correct because they do not correctly state the rules found in the statutes. Response **A** does correctly state the UCC rule and **D** does correctly state the U.S. Code rule. The problem is that these rules are contradictory. The UCC rule states that the implied warranty can be disclaimed (technically it says "excluded," but it is fair to assume that is the same thing), and the U.S. Code rule says that it can't be excluded if a written warranty is made. Which one governs? When there is both a federal rule and a state rule on point, the federal rule generally preempts the state rule. So **D**, the federal rule, is the correct response. As we will see in Chapter 9.F, the Magnuson-Moss Act was enacted by Congress with the intention of supplementing the relevant state law of warranties.

B.   Working with the Code

What sources assist you in trying to comprehend a Code section? Remember the first rule of statutory interpretation: Read the statute. You will find that in most statutory compilations, the Code section is followed by Official Comments. Remember that the Official Comments are not enacted by the legislature, so they do not have the force of law; they are merely persuasive. Speaking of persuasive authority, you might also want to become familiar with the treatise by Summers and White, *Uniform Commercial Code.* There are other sources on the Code, some of them very good, but the work by Summers and White seems to be the source most frequently cited by courts.

QUESTION 4. The sections of UCC Article 2 are followed by Official Comments. What is the legal significance of the Official Comments to the sections?

A. They are part of the statute that is enacted into law in every state.
B. They are mandatory authority in states that have enacted the Code.
C. They are highly persuasive authority in states that have enacted the Code.
D. They have no more persuasive authority than any other secondary source on the Code.

ANALYSIS.   When the ULC promulgates a Uniform Law, it often promulgates Official Comments as well. However, because the state legislatures do not enact the Official Comments, **A** is not correct. Similarly, the only authority that is "mandatory" is authority enacted by the legislature, so **B** cannot be correct. The Official Comments are only "persuasive" authority. However, because the Official Comments express the views of the drafters of the Code, they are close to the source and are considered highly persuasive, so **C** is a better response than **D** and is the correct response.

C.   Closers

QUESTION 5. Which of the following statements about the sale of goods is true?

A. Provisions in Article 2 may be varied by the parties' agreement and may be supplemented by the common law.
B. The law of sales of goods is primarily found in federal law.
C. Article 2 applies only to commercial transactions and not to consumer transactions.
D. All the law governing a sale of goods can be found in UCC Article 2.

ANALYSIS.   The law of sales of goods is primarily found in UCC Article 2, which is state law, so **B** is not true. However, not all the law governing a sale of goods can be found in Article 2. Because other law must be consulted, **D** is not correct. Article 2 applies to consumer transactions as well as commercial transactions, so **C** is not correct. According to § 1-302, parties have some freedom of contract to vary Code provisions, and § 1-103(b) provides that the Code is supplemented by principles of law and equity, so **A** is the best response.

> **QUESTION 6.** You are litigating a case in Oklahoma. You find that the section of Article 2 that is in issue has not been addressed by the Oklahoma Supreme Court, but it has been addressed by courts in other jurisdictions. Should the Oklahoma Supreme Court give deference to the decisions of other jurisdictions on the issue?
>
> A. Yes, but it should give more weight to decisions from other states in the 10th Circuit.
> B. Yes, because uniformity is important in Code jurisprudence.
> C. No, because Article 2 is entirely a matter of state law.
> D. No, because the other jurisdictions are likely to have different laws.

ANALYSIS.   When doing research, remember that each state's enactment of the Code may be different. You will want to be sure to check whether the wording of the statute in issue is the same in both states. Nevertheless, because most of the statutes are uniform, **D** is not a correct response. Response **C** may appear to be correct. However, the fact that the Code is state law is tempered by the purpose expressly stated in § 1-103(a)(3): "to make uniform the law among the various jurisdictions." In keeping with that purpose, the supreme court of a state should give deference to the decisions of other jurisdictions to keep the law uniform. The best response is **B**. Response **A** is not correct. Because Article 2 is state law, it does not matter what federal circuit a state is in. Be careful of that when you do research. You might find, for example, a decision of the 10th Circuit on point. Because the UCC is state law, however, the federal court probably obtained jurisdiction because of diversity, so you have to ask which state's law was applied by the circuit court. If the 10th Circuit applied Colorado law in a particular case, then that case is only persuasive authority in Oklahoma. In fact, even if the 10th Circuit applied Oklahoma law, it is not mandatory that an Oklahoma state court follow that decision, because it is not the decision of a higher court.

 # Burnham's picks

Question 1	**D**
Question 2	**B**
Question 3	**D**
Question 4	**C**
Question 5	**A**
Question 6	**B**

3

The Scope of Article 2

A. Transactions in goods

This book focuses on Article 2 as dealing with the sale of goods, even though it might initially appear that the scope of the article is broader than that. Section 2-102 provides:

> Unless the context otherwise requires, this Article applies to transactions in goods; it does not apply to any transaction which although in the form of an unconditional contract to sell or present sale is intended to operate only as a security transaction nor does this Article impair or repeal any statute regulating sales to consumers, farmers or other specified classes of buyers.

What is a "transaction in goods"? The following might all be included:

- Sale of goods
- Lease of goods
- Security interest in goods
- Gift of goods

In spite of this apparently broad scope, in context, most of the provisions of Article 2 refer to a "buyer" or a "seller," or to a "contract" for the sale of goods. For example, you may wonder if a barter transaction is within the scope of Article 2. Section 2-304(1) specifically addresses this situation. It provides:

§ 2-304. Price Payable in Money, Goods, Realty, or Otherwise.
(1) The price can be made payable in money or otherwise. If it is payable in whole or in part in goods each party is a seller of the goods which he is to transfer.

So the answer is yes, it does apply to a barter transaction, but each party is referred to as a seller of goods.

Let's first examine what the Code means by a *contract*. The Code is careful to distinguish between a *contract* and an *agreement*. The term *agreement* is defined at § 1-201(b)(3):

> (3) "Agreement," as distinguished from "contract," means the bargain of the parties in fact, as found in their language or inferred from other circumstances, including course of performance, course of dealing, or usage of trade as provided in Section 1-303.

The agreement starts with the bargain the parties in fact made, which could come from their words, their conduct, and the circumstances. In addition, the agreement includes any course of performance, course of dealing, or usage of trade. We look more closely at the meaning of those terms in Chapter 7.C. In § 1-201(b)(12), *contract* is defined:

> (12) "Contract," as distinguished from "agreement," means the total legal obligation that results from the parties' agreement as determined by [the Uniform Commercial Code] as supplemented by any other applicable laws. (Compare "Agreement.")

Essentially the agreement is what the parties agreed to, whereas the contract is the legal effect of that agreement. As stated in the Official Comment to the definition of *agreement*, "[w]hether an agreement has legal consequences is determined by applicable provisions of the Uniform Commercial Code and, to the extent provided in Section 1-103, by the law of contracts." As we will see, the parties are likely to leave many terms out of the agreement, but those terms are supplied by contract law. Furthermore, contract law will determine the extent to which the agreement is enforceable. For example, the parties may make an *agreement* to perform an illegal act, but they have not made a *contract* because they have not created any legal obligation.

In § 2-103(1)(a), "buyer" is defined as "a person who buys or contracts to buy goods," and § 2-103(1)(d) defines "seller" as "a person who sells or contracts to sell goods." What is the difference between buying and selling and contracting to buy and sell? The definitions in § 2-106(1) provide:

> (1) In this Article unless the context otherwise requires "contract" and "agreement" are limited to those relating to the present or future sale of goods. "Contract for sale" includes both a present sale of goods and a contract to sell goods at a future time. A "sale" consists in the passing of title from the seller to the buyer for a price (Section 2-401). A "present sale" means a sale which is accomplished by the making of the contract.

We could diagram the definition of *sale* as follows:

To have a sale, there must be:

- A passing of title
- From the seller to the buyer
- For a price

Whether that sale is a present sale or a contract to sell goods at a future time is simply a matter of timing. When I go to the grocery store and tender money for the groceries, I am entering into a contract for sale. It is a present sale of goods because at the same moment the contract is formed, the title to those groceries passes. Alternatively, suppose the grocery store is out of my favorite beer. The grocer says, "We will have some in on Monday." I say, "Good. Set aside two cases for me and I will pick them up on Tuesday." The grocer says, "It's a deal." Do we have a contract for sale? Yes, we do. We do not have a present sale, because title has not yet transferred to me, but we have a contract to sell and buy the goods at a future time. When you think about it, most of the contracts you studied in the basic Contracts class were not present sales, but would occur in the future.

Let me ask you something that is a preview of things to come: Did it bother you that § 2-106(1) defined a sale as a passing of title "for a price," but in my hypothetical, no price was mentioned for the beer? It shouldn't have bothered you. It is clear from the context that the grocer was not making a gift of the beer. Therefore, there was a contract with an open price term. The rule of § 2-305(1) is that "[t]he parties if they so intend can conclude a contract for sale even though the price is not settled." In such a case, the price is a reasonable price, which in this context would be the retail price of the beer. This is an example of the "gap filler" function of Code provisions. If the parties leave a gap in their agreement, the Code frequently provides a way to fill that gap to make the contract enforceable.

Putting this all together, we can see that the scope of Article 2 is narrower than we may have initially thought from reading § 2-102. It generally applies to contracts for the sale of goods. As we will see, Article 2A applies to the lease of goods, and as you may know, Article 9 applies to security interests in goods. Gifts of goods are a property transaction and may be covered in a course in property law.

We will look at some study aids that will help you in your exploration of Article 2 before looking more closely at the definition of *goods* in the next chapter.

QUESTION 1. A borrower goes to a lender to borrow money. The lender says, "We will lend you $5,000 if you promise to pay it back with interest. In addition, you will have to turn over the title to your car to us. If you default on your payments, then we may keep the title to your car." The borrower agrees and a contract is drawn up containing these terms. Is this an Article 2 transaction?

A. Yes, because there is a present passing of title to the car.
B. Yes, because there may be a future passing of title to the car.
C. No, because there is no contract for sale.
D. No, because a car is not goods.

ANALYSIS. Even though title to the car is transferred, it is not transferred from a seller to a buyer. That is, the purpose of the transaction is not to sell the car. The purpose of the transaction is to create a security interest in the car so that it secures the loan. Part of § 2-102 that we did not examine provides:

> . . . [Article 2] does not apply to any transaction which although in the form of an unconditional contract to sell or present sale is intended to operate only as a security transaction nor does this Article impair or repeal any statute regulating sales to consumers, farmers or other specified classes of buyers.

If a person transfers ownership only for purposes of security, it is not an Article 2 transaction. Therefore, the correct response is **C**.

QUESTION 2. In the business that seller and buyer are part of, it is customary to allow the parties to terminate an agreement on 30 days' written notice. When making a deal, the buyer and seller included a term that provides that either party may terminate the agreement on 30 days' written notice to the other. The buyer then exercised its power under this provision. As the terms are defined in the Code, was this power found in the agreement or in the contract?

A. Agreement, because it was part of the parties' language.
B. Agreement, because it is supplied by trade usage.
C. Contract, because the buyer had a contractual right to do it.
D. Contract, because the power to do it was supplied by law.

ANALYSIS. As the terms are used in the Code, this provision was part of the parties' agreement because it was part of their "bargain in fact" as found in the language they used. The correct response is **A**. Note that even if the parties had not referred to this term in the language of their agreement, it still would be part of their agreement because it would be inferred from trade usage. The term *agreement* is defined at § 1-201(b)(3):

> (3) "Agreement," as distinguished from "contract," means the bargain of the parties in fact, as found in their language or inferred from other circumstances, including course of performance, course of dealing, or usage of trade as provided in Section 1-303.

B.   Study aids

1. A road map of Article 2

Article 2 is divided into seven sections, called *parts*:

> PART 1. SHORT TITLE, GENERAL CONSTRUCTION AND SUBJECT MATTER
>
> PART 2. FORM, FORMATION AND READJUSTMENT OF CONTRACT
>
> PART 3. GENERAL OBLIGATION AND CONSTRUCTION OF CONTRACT
>
> PART 4. TITLE, CREDITORS, AND GOOD FAITH PURCHASERS
>
> PART 5. PERFORMANCE
>
> PART 6. BREACH, REPUDIATION AND EXCUSE
>
> PART 7. REMEDIES

These parts provide a logical organization for our study because they mirror the stages in the life of a contract. While this chapter examines the scope of Article 2, Chapter 4 looks at some key definitions and concepts used in the Code. Some of these definitions and concepts are found in Part 1 of Article 2, whereas others are found in Article 1, which, you may recall, applies throughout the Code. Chapter 5 includes matters of formation of contract that are covered in Part 2, as well as an introduction to the gap fillers from Part 3. Once the contract is formed, we look into other issues surrounding formation, such as the parol evidence rule (Chapter 6) and the interpretation and modification of the contract (Chapter 7). In Chapter 8, we look at the Statute of Frauds, where we discuss the issue of whether an oral contract is enforceable.

Part 3 introduces the important concept of default rules—the terms that are implied in the contract in the absence of the parties' agreement. Chapters 9, 10, and 11 each explore an aspect of the warranty term, which is often supplied by default.

The rules in Part 4, relating to the passing of title, are integrated into the discussion of the material on performance of the contract, as that is when issues involving the passage of title become significant. Part 5 involves the performance of the contract and is explored in Chapters 12 and 13. Part 6 includes issues of breach. In Chapter 14 we look at whether a party's nonperformance is breach or whether it is excused by the circumstances. A similar issue of nonperformance is explored in Chapter 15, where we look at whether a party has the right to cancel a contract because of concerns about the other party's prospective performance.

The all-important issue of remedies in the event of breach is the subject of Part 7, and is explored in Chapters 16, 17, and 18. Chapter 19 is devoted to issues involving assignment and delegation, which are actually in Part 2 of Article 2, but which seem to be more naturally discussed toward the conclusion of our study. Finally, we end the discussion of Article 2 with an exploration of the statute of limitations (Chapter 20).

After we have completed our exploration of the sale of goods in Article 2, Chapter 21 compares and contrasts those rules with the rules for the lease of goods in Article 2A. Chapter 22 explores the rules applicable to a software transaction, which has many things in common with a goods transaction, and Chapter 23 explores the international sale of goods. We conclude with a series of review questions in Chapter 24. That chapter has a novel format, as we introduce a contract for the sale of goods and base the questions around your analysis of that contract.

QUESTION 3. In what part of Article 2 are you likely to find the rule on when a party can obtain specific performance?

A. Part 4. Title, Creditors, and Good Faith Purchasers
B. Part 5. Performance
C. Part 6. Breach, Repudiation and Excuse
D. Part 7. Remedies

ANALYSIS.   Did you get tricked into choosing response **B** because the subject of that part is performance? I hope not. That part deals with performance of the contract. Specific performance is a remedy that a party seeks when it wants the thing itself that was promised rather than money damages. Because specific performance is a remedy, it is found in Part 7 of Article 2—§ 2-716 to be precise. The correct response is **D**.

2. Reading a statute

Sales and Leases is a Code course, which means you must not only know your way around the Code, but you need to be able to read particular sections. In the version of the Code promulgated by the Uniform Law Commission (ULC), each section is supplemented by material that is not part of the statute because it is not enacted by a legislature. For example, § 2-106 is followed by the following commentary:

> **Official Comment § 2-106**
> **Prior Uniform Statutory Provision:** Subsection (1)—Section 1(1) and (2), Uniform Sales Act; Subsection (2)—none, but subsection generally continues policy of Sections 11, 44 and 69, Uniform Sales Act; Subsections (3) and (4)—none.
> **Changes:** Completely rewritten.
> **Purposes of Changes and New Matter:**
>   1. Subsection (1): "Contract for sale" is used as a general concept throughout this Article, but the rights of the parties do not vary according

to whether the transaction is a present sale or a contract to sell unless the Article expressly so provides.

   2. Subsection (2): It is in general intended to continue the policy of requiring exact performance by the seller of his obligations as a condition to his right to require acceptance. However, the seller is in part safeguarded against surprise as a result of sudden technicality on the buyer's part by the provisions of Section 2-508 on seller's cure of improper tender or delivery. Moreover usage of trade frequently permits commercial leeways in performance and the language of the agreement itself must be read in the light of such custom or usage and also, prior course of dealing, and in a long term contract, the course of performance.

   3. Subsections (3) and (4): These subsections are intended to make clear the distinction carried forward throughout this Article between termination and cancellation.

Cross References:
Point 2: Sections 1-203, 1-205, 2-208 and 2-508.
Definitional Cross References:
"Agreement." Section 1-201.
"Buyer." Section 2-103.
"Contract." Section 1-201.
"Goods." Section 2-105.
"Party." Section 1-201.
"Remedy." Section 1-201.
"Rights." Section 1-201.
"Seller." Section 2-103.

The Prior Uniform Statutory Provision is now of largely historical interest. When Article 2 replaced the Uniform Sales Act, it was important to educate those who knew the earlier act, but this is no longer significant. You will find a similar section in the Official Comments to Amended Article 2. Even though Amended Article 2 has been withdrawn, it is a valuable source for indicating where the drafters believed reform of Article 2 was needed. In the case of an ambiguity in present Article 2, for example, you could argue that the way Amended Article 2 resolves the problem is persuasive authority for your position.

   The Purposes of Changes and New Matter contain the Official Comments on the text. These Comments are an excellent source for determining the meaning of the text. Remember, however, that with the rarest of exceptions, these Official Comments are not enacted by the legislature of a state that enacts the statute. When you are citing authority, it is better to cite the text itself, which is mandatory authority, rather than the Official Comments, which are merely persuasive authority.

   You will find the Cross References and Definitional Cross References to be a useful tool. Because we are dealing with a code, each provision cannot be looked at in isolation. Each provision is often related to another provision.

Most important, if you want to know what a word means in the Code, it is essential that you first check to see if it is defined in the Code, as that is the best evidence of its meaning. Unfortunately, the defined terms are sometimes omitted from the Definitional Cross References, so get in the habit of flipping through the Code to find related sections and definitions.

QUESTION 4. Section 2-611 provides in part: "Until the repudiating party's next performance is due he can retract his repudiation unless the aggrieved party has since the repudiation cancelled or materially changed his position." To further pursue the meaning of "cancelled" in this provision, where would you go first?

A. An ordinary dictionary.
B. Black's Law Dictionary.
C. Definitions in Article 1.
D. Definitions in Article 2.

ANALYSIS.   To discover the meaning of a word used in the Code, you should first determine whether it is defined in the Code. Therefore, responses **C** and **D** are better than responses **A** and **B**. Within the Code, Article 1 contains many definitions that are used throughout the Code. If a word is used in Article 2, you first want to check whether there is a meaning established in that part of the Code. Therefore, **D** is a better response than **C**. In fact, if you look at the Official Comments to § 2-611, you will find the following Definitional Cross Reference: "'Cancellation.' Section 2-106."

3. How to diagram

Let's explore how to diagram a Code provision. You might want to try these techniques to better understand the Code sections you are working with by breaking the section down into its individual elements. The techniques are, of course, applicable to any statute. We will practice on § 2-106(1), which provides:

> (1) In this Article unless the context otherwise requires "**contract**" and "**agreement**" are limited to those relating to the present or future sale of goods. "**Contract for sale**" includes both a present sale of goods and a contract to sell goods at a future time. A "**sale**" consists in the passing of title from the seller to the buyer for a price (Section 2-401). A "**present sale**" means a sale which is accomplished by the making of the contract.

A good way to start is to use your word processing program to break up the text into its natural components without making any changes to the language. In this case, we get four sentences:

In this Article unless the context otherwise requires "**contract**" and "**agreement**" are limited to those relating to the present or future sale of goods.

"**Contract for sale**" includes both a present sale of goods and a contract to sell goods at a future time.

A "**sale**" consists in the passing of title from the seller to the buyer for a price (Section 2-401).

A "**present sale**" means a sale which is accomplished by the making of the contract.

The first and fourth sentences are pretty simple declarations that we can't do much with. Let's initially work with the second sentence. Again, the first step is to break it down into its component parts to reveal its structure without making any changes:

> "**Contract for sale**" includes both
>> a present sale of goods and
>> a contract to sell goods at a future time.

Although that may be all we need to do to reveal the meaning more clearly, we could take further steps to diagram the provision. The first approach is simply to bullet each enumerated item. I'm also going to add punctuation: both a colon to announce the list, and a comma to separate the enumerated items.

> "**Contract for sale**" includes both:
> - a present sale of goods, and
> - a contract to sell goods at a future time.

A second approach is to create an "if . . . then" statement. This approach works best with rules. With a rule, if all the elements are present, then the rule is satisfied. We can do it in this case, but we have to be careful because the "and" is not conjunctive, indicating that we need both elements to satisfy the rule, but disjunctive, indicating that either element will satisfy the rule. We have to change it to an "or." Our statement might look something like this:

> IF there
>> is a present sale of goods, OR
>> a contract to sell goods at a future time,
> THEN there is a "**Contract for sale**."

A third approach is to create a flow chart. Our flow chart might look something like this:

> Is there a present sale of goods?
>> If YES, there is a "**Contract for sale**"
>> If NO, is there a contract to sell goods at a future time?
>>> If YES, there is a "**Contract for sale**"
>>> If NO, there is not a "**Contract for sale**"

Let's now try this with the third sentence. Don't worry if your diagrams don't look exactly like mine; there is no single way to achieve the result. That sentence provides:

A "**sale**" consists in the passing of title from the seller to the buyer for a price.

We can break this sentence down into three enumerated items:

A "**sale**" consists in
    the passing of title
    from the seller to the buyer
    for a price.

This statement can be thought of as a rule where the outcome is satisfied by the three elements:

To have a sale, there has to be:

- a passing of title
- from the seller to the buyer
- for a price

As an if . . . then statement, it might look like this:

IF there is:
    the passing of title
    from the seller to the buyer
    for a price
THEN there is a sale

Finally, here is the provision as a flow chart:

Did title pass?
    If NO, there is no sale
    If YES, did it pass from the seller to the buyer?
      If NO, there is no sale
      If YES, did it pass for a price?
        If NO, there is no sale
        If YES, there is a sale

C. Closers

QUESTION 5. Section 2-725 provides for a four-year statute of limitations. Amended Article 2 adds this sentence to existing § 2-725: "However, in a consumer contract, the period of limitation may not be reduced." You are representing a consumer in a contract dispute in which the consumer agreed to a statute of limitations of one year. Can you use the provision from Amended Article 2 to support an argument that the agreed-upon statute of limitations is not enforceable?

A. No, because Amended Article 2 is not enacted law.

B. No, because present Article 2 does not apply to consumers.

C. Yes, because Amended Article 2 changes the law to make a one-year statute of limitations illegal.

D. Yes, because the fact that the drafters of Amended Article 2 recommended this rule for consumers supports an argument that it is an unconscionable or unfair practice.

ANALYSIS. Both **B** and **C** are clearly incorrect responses. Present Article 2 does apply to consumers, and Amended Article 2 is not enacted law anywhere. Even if it is not enacted law, however, it can be used to indicate a trend. Many provisions in Amended Article 2 offer more protection to consumers than is provided under present Article 2. That trend can be used as persuasive authority to show that the drafters may have considered some of the provisions of existing Article 2 to be unfair to consumers. Therefore, the best response is **D**. In this book, we occasionally look at the proposals for revision in Amended Article 2, for the revisions often illuminate the present text.

QUESTION 6. A hired hand offers to work for a farmer, and the farmer tells him that if he helps harvest the crop, the farmer will give him a calf, which is presently unborn. The hired hand agrees. Is this transaction within Article 2? (*Hint:* Find the governing provision and then use the Definitional Cross References to find the terms defined in that provision.)

A. Yes, because it involves a sale of goods.

B. No, because it does not involve a sale of goods.

C. No, because it does involve a sale, but not of goods.

D. No, because it does involve goods, but is not a sale.

ANALYSIS. Because no cash is exchanging hands, we should recognize that this is a barter transaction as described in § 2-304:

§ 2-304. Price Payable in Money, Goods, Realty, or Otherwise.

(1) The price can be made payable in money or otherwise. If it is payable in whole or in part in goods each party is a seller of the goods which he is to transfer.

It may initially appear that there is no sale here, because the hired hand has exchanged his services for the right to receive something that is not movable. However, the Definitional Cross References following the section inform us that there is a definition of *seller* in § 2-103(1)(d). That section provides that "'seller' means a person that sells or contracts to sell goods." Therefore, the farmer is a seller if what he has contracted to sell is goods. The Definitional Cross References also lead us to the definition of *goods* in § 2-105(1):

> (1) "Goods" means all things (including specially manufactured goods) which are movable at the time of identification to the contract for sale other than the money in which the price is to be paid, investment securities (Article 8) and things in action. "Goods" also includes the unborn young of animals and growing crops and other identified things attached to realty as described in the section on goods to be severed from realty (Section 2-107).

Although goods are generally movables, the definition specifically states that goods "includes the unborn young of animals." Because the farmer is a seller of goods, this is a transaction within Article 2. The correct response is **A**.

 # Burnham's picks

Question 1	**C**
Question 2	**A**
Question 3	**D**
Question 4	**D**
Question 5	**D**
Question 6	**A**

4

Some Key Concepts: Goods, Merchants, Good Faith, and Policing the Agreement

A. Goods

1. What are goods?

We have seen in the previous chapter that Article 2 governs contracts for the sale of goods. But what are *goods?* Section 2-105(1) supplies the following definition:

(1) "Goods" means all things (including specially manufactured goods) which are movable at the time of identification to the contract for sale other than the money in which the price is to be paid, investment securities (Article 8) and things in action. "Goods" also includes the unborn young of animals and growing crops and other identified things attached to realty as described in the section on goods to be severed from realty (Section 2-107).

There are many specific exceptions and inclusions in that definition, but the general rule is that goods are "things . . . which are movable at the time of identification to the contract for sale." The universe of movable things is very large and obviously excludes things like services and real property. Specific exclusions include:

- The money in which the price is to be paid.
- Investment securities.
- Things in action.

The Code does not define "things in action" (also known as *choses in action*). A thing in action is best thought of as a claim or right. If you owe me $5,000, then I have a claim against you that can be bought and sold, but that sale would not be an Article 2 transaction.

The first parenthetical in the definition indicates that the sale of specially manufactured goods is also within the definition of goods. If instead of buying a suit off the rack, I order it to be tailor-made, that transaction is a sale of goods within Article 2 even though a substantial part of what I have purchased is the services of making the goods. Also within the definition of goods for purposes of Article 2 is "the unborn young of animals and growing crops." If prior to harvesting it, a farmer sells his wheat crop to Cargill, that transaction is a sale of goods even though the crop is not movable "at the time of identification to the contract for sale."

The final specific inclusion in § 2-105(1) is "other identified things attached to realty as described in Section 2-107." That provision is complex, because it is close to describing interests in real property, and real property is not within the scope of Article 2. The first transaction is a sale of "minerals or the like (including oil and gas) or a structure or its materials to be removed from realty." This transaction is within Article 2 only if the property is severed from the real property *by the seller.* Official Comment 1 explains that "[i]f the buyer is to sever, such transactions are considered contracts affecting land." The second transaction within Article 2 is a sale of timber or "growing crops or other things attached to realty and capable of severance without material harm thereto." Property in this category includes *fixtures*, although Article 2 consciously avoids that term, according to Official Comment 2. Transactions involving these things are included within Article 2 whether the property is removed by the buyer or by the seller.

QUESTION 1. Which of the following transactions is a sale of goods under Article 2?

    I. The sale of $10,000 in Confederate money for $100.
    II. The sale of a claim to a rare vase for $10,000.
    III. The sale of a ton of coal for $500 to be removed from seller's property by buyer.

A. I only.
B. III only.
C. I and II.
D. Neither I, II, or III.

ANALYSIS. *Note on test taking.* You may occasionally encounter this kind of multiple-choice question in which more than one response may be correct. The best approach is to determine whether each enumerated item is a correct answer and then find the matching response.

Item I involves the sale of money. The definition of goods in § 2-105(1) excludes "the money in which the price is to be paid," but, as explained in Official Comment 1, "Goods is intended to cover the sale of money when money is being treated as a commodity but not to include it when money is the medium of payment." Because the Confederate money is the commodity sold, this transaction involves the sale of goods. Item II involves the sale of a claim to the vase, not the sale of the vase itself. The sale of a claim is a *chose in action*, which is expressly excluded from the definition of goods. Item III involves minerals being severed from realty, but because the minerals are being severed by the buyer rather than by the seller, under § 2-107(1) this is not the sale of goods for purposes of Article 2. The only transaction that involves the sale of goods is Item I, so the correct response is **A**.

2. Applying Article 2 by analogy

Sometimes a court has to wrestle with a case in which the transaction does not appear to involve goods as defined in the Code, but Article 2 seems to be a helpful body of law to apply to the transaction. A good example is the sale of electricity. When faced with this situation, a court sometimes acknowledges that Article 2 does not expressly apply, but then states that it is applying Article 2 by analogy. For example, in *Norcon Power Partners, L.P. v. Niagara Mohawk Power Corp.*, 92 N.Y.2d 458 (1998), the New York Court of Appeals applied Article 2 by analogy to the sale of electricity:

> A useful analogy can be drawn between the contract at issue and a contract for the sale of goods. If the contract here was in all respects the same, except that it was for the sale of oil or some other tangible commodity instead of the sale of electricity, the parties would unquestionably be governed by [the UCC].

You might use the same method in your analysis of a particular transaction—but be sure to first analyze whether Article 2 is applicable to the transaction and, only if it is not, then state that you are applying it by analogy.

Another area where the issue of the applicability of Article 2 arises is with the sale or licensing of software. Software is probably not movable, and therefore not a *good* according to the Article 2 definition, but the sellers or licensors of software often model their contracts, particularly the warranty provisions, on contracts for the sale of goods, so it seems sensible to apply Article 2 to the transaction. Many courts have done so, either expressly or by analogy. The folks at the Uniform Law Commission (ULC), who are responsible for drafting and revising the Uniform Laws, at one time thought of redrafting Article 2 to incorporate software, and at another time drafted the Uniform Computer Information Transactions Act (UCITA) to address these transactions. The first did not happen, and the second is dead (except in the states of Maryland and Virginia, which are the only jurisdictions that have enacted UCITA). Chapter 22 looks at software transactions in greater detail.

QUESTION 2. Certain tax preparation software can be downloaded from the Internet. The terms and conditions state that it is sold with a one-year warranty against defects, but with a disclaimer of consequential damages. A purchaser claims that he suffered consequential damages, but the seller claims that the particular loss is not within the meaning of consequential damages. To resolve the issue, would it be appropriate for a court to look to cases arising under Article 2 that discuss what losses are within the scope of consequential damages?

A. Yes, because this is a transaction in goods.
B. Yes, but the court should make clear that it is applying Article 2 by analogy.
C. No, because Article 2 does not apply to computer information.
D. No, because computer information is not a good and the analogy is not apt.

ANALYSIS.   There is some authority for response **A**. As an example, see *Advent Systems Ltd. v. Unisys Corp.*, 925 F.2d 670 (3d Cir. 1991), where the court stated:

> Applying the U.C.C. to computer software transactions offers substantial benefits to litigants and the courts. The Code offers a uniform body of law on a wide range of questions likely to arise in computer software disputes: implied warranties, consequential damages, disclaimers of liability, the statute of limitations, to name a few.
>
> The importance of software to the commercial world and the advantages to be gained by the uniformity inherent in the U.C.C. are strong policy

arguments favoring inclusion. The contrary arguments are not persuasive, and we hold that software is a "good" within the definition in the Code.

However, I have trouble thinking of an intangible as "movable," and the fact that other courts disagree with the result in *Advent Systems* makes this an overly broad response. Nevertheless, it is possible to acknowledge that computer information is not a good while applying the Code by analogy. It then comes down to a policy question, and although there is some debate, I think that the better policy is to treat the analogy as appropriate, so the best response is **B**.

3. Mixed transactions

Frequently a transaction involves the sale of goods, but there is also a non-goods component. Does Article 2 apply to a mixed transaction? Not surprisingly, courts are all over the board on this issue. The most popular approach is the *predominant factor test,* which requires a determination as to whether the sale of goods is the predominant factor in the transaction. If it is, then Article 2 is applied. In the case of *Bonebrake v. Cox,* 499 F.2d 951 (8th Cir. 1974), the court explained:

> The test for inclusion or exclusion is not whether they are mixed, but, granting that they are mixed, whether their predominant factor, their thrust, their purpose, reasonably stated, is the rendition of service, with goods incidentally involved (e.g., contract with artist for painting) or is a transaction of sale, with labor incidentally involved (e.g., installation of a water heater in a bathroom).

The issue under the predominant factor test is whether the transaction is predominantly a sale of goods with services attached or predominantly a service transaction with the sale of goods attached. Note that in measuring the predominant factor, the value of the goods is not necessarily the most important factor. For example, a dentist installs a crown in a patient's mouth. The charge is $1,200, of which $800 is the cost of the gold crown and $400 the cost of the service of installing it. Even though the more substantial part of the price was the cost of the gold crown, it seems unlikely that this can be viewed as a transaction to buy a lump of gold to which dental services were incidentally attached. The better view is that it was a transaction to buy dental services, and the gold crown was an incidental part of the transaction. So a court applying the predominant factor test would probably consider this a non-UCC transaction.

Another approach, called the *gravamen test,* looks to the source of the dispute. In *Anthony Pools v. Sheehan,* 455 A.2d 434 (Md. 1983), the court cited W. Hawkland, *Uniform Commercial Code Series* (1982), § 2-102:04, on this test:

> Unless uniformity would be impaired thereby, it might be more sensible and facilitate administration, at least in this grey area, to abandon the "predominant factor" test and focus instead on whether the gravamen of the action

involves goods or services. For example, in *Worrell v. Barnes,* if the gas escaped because of a defective fitting or connector, the case might be characterized as one involving the sale of goods. On the other hand, if the gas escaped because of poor work by Barnes the case might be characterized as one involving services, outside the scope of the UCC.

In our dentist example, if the patient sues, complaining that the crown was not properly made, then the UCC would apply under the gravamen test. However, if the patient complains that the crown was not properly installed, then the UCC would not apply. This test has the advantage of ease of application, but it has not gained much traction. Another approach, somewhat similar, is to bifurcate the transaction, applying the UCC to the goods part and other law to the non-goods part. This approach is rarely used. For example, if a farmer buys for $500,000 a farm that includes an above-ground irrigation system, a court using the bifurcated approach would apply Article 2 to the irrigation system part of the transaction, and real property law to the real property part of the transaction.

QUESTION 3. A patient went to a hospital for a blood transfusion. The patient sued the hospital, alleging that the blood was contaminated and the patient was seriously injured. If the court applied the gravamen test, would Article 2 apply?

A. Yes, because the complaint alleged that the blood was contaminated and blood is a good.

B. No, because the complaint alleged that the transfusion services were performed negligently and this is a service.

C. Yes, because the predominant factor was to buy blood, and the transfusion services were incidental.

D. No, because the predominant factor was to obtain a transfusion, and the buying of the blood was incidental.

ANALYSIS. Responses **C** and **D** refer to the predominant factor test, but the "call of the question" asked you to apply the gravamen test, so **C** and **D** are not correct responses. Note that in a jurisdiction that applied the predominant factor test, this could be a difficult question to resolve. Responses **A** and **B** refer to the allegations in the complaint, which is where you would look under the gravamen test. Because the allegation was that the blood was contaminated, then Article 2 would apply, so **A** is the correct response.

Because hospitals can be found liable without evidence of negligence in this situation when the UCC is applied, a number of jurisdictions have enacted statutes that expressly provide that the furnishing of blood is a service and not a sale of goods. For example, California Health & Safety Code § 1606 provides:

The procurement, processing, distribution, or use of whole blood, plasma, blood products, and blood derivatives for the purpose of injecting or transfusing the same, or any of them, into the human body shall be construed to be, and is declared to be, for all purposes whatsoever, the rendition of a service by each and every person, firm, or corporation participating therein, and shall not be construed to be, and is declared not to be, a sale of such whole blood, plasma, blood products, or blood derivatives, for any purpose or purposes whatsoever.

4. Why does it matter?

You might wonder why it matters whether Article 2 or some other body of law applies to the transaction or to a part of the transaction. This is a good question, but answering it requires us to look ahead to some issues that will be discussed later in the book. These include:

- Battle of the Forms
- Statute of Frauds
- Statute of limitations
- Strict liability
- Standard of performance

Although Article 2 changed a number of the common law rules on contract formation, no change is as dramatic as the rules of §§ 2-206 and 2-207, which provide that in some circumstances the acceptance does not have to match the offer. Article 2 has a Statute of Frauds provision that requires contracts for the sale of goods for $500 or more to be evidenced by a writing in order to be enforceable. See § 2-201. Outside of the UCC, there is no Statute of Frauds based on the dollar value of the transaction. Also, Article 2 has a statute of limitations of four years. See § 2-725. Tort statutes of limitations tend to be shorter, whereas contracts statutes tend to be longer. A party who misses the statute of limitations in tort might characterize the claim as arising under Article 2 to get the benefit of the longer statute.

A significant reason for making a claim under Article 2 is that § 2-314 provides that a seller who is a merchant with respect to goods of that kind gives the buyer a warranty of merchantability. As we have seen in the example involving the sale of blood, this claim has a strict liability component, which can be easier to prove than negligence. Assume, for example, a plumber installs pipe that leaks, damaging the owner's property. In tort, the owner would have to prove that the plumber acted negligently. Under Article 2, however, the owner would only have to prove that ordinary pipe does not leak, which is a much easier burden to prove. Also, the Article 2 claim is against the seller, who might not have had any control over the defective goods, rather than against the manufacturer. For example, if a person buys a candy bar from a store and injures her teeth when she bites into it, she can sue the store for breach of warranty instead of suing the manufacturer for negligence. Finally, under the *perfect tender* rule of § 2-601, a buyer may reject a shipment for any breach; the common law generally requires a material breach to cancel the contract. In situations involving these rules, the parties may find it advantageous to argue that either Article 2 applies or does not apply.

QUESTION 4.   A farmer buys a hay baler. While attempting to remove some hay that is stuck in the chute, the farmer injures his arm. Three-and-a-half years later, the farmer sues the seller of the hay baler, claiming that the baler was not merchantable. The seller seeks to have the claim dismissed on the grounds that the statute of limitations for negligence claims is three years. Should the claim be dismissed?

A.   Yes, because the statute of limitations for negligence has run.
B.   Yes, because the statute of limitations for the sale of goods has run.
C.   No, because the farmer brought the claim under Article 2.
D.   No, because the statute of limitations for negligence has not run.

ANALYSIS.   The hay baler is goods, so Article 2 applies to the transaction. Under § 2-725, a party has four years to bring a claim under Article 2. This claim could be brought for breach of warranty. Therefore, **C** is the best response. Sometimes, cases that you would expect to be brought as negligence claims are brought under Article 2; frequently, the reason is that the statute of limitations in tort has run. See, e.g., *Schlenz v. John Deere Co.,* 511 F. Supp. 224 (D. Mont. 1981). Note also that the claim can be brought against the *seller* under Article 2, even though the seller is unlikely to have been negligent. Because the seller gets the same Article 2 warranty from its seller, the claim will work its way up the chain until it reaches the responsible party.

B.   Merchants

1. *What is a merchant?*

We saw in Chapter 3.A that Article 2 applies to all sales of goods, and it generally does not matter how we characterize the buyer and the seller. They might be two giant businesses, a business and an individual, or two ordinary individuals. In general, the same Article 2 rules apply to each of these situations, although these rules might be supplemented by the common law and other statutes, such as consumer protection law, that could alter the outcome under the Code. On a few occasions (14 to be exact), however, Article 2 states that a rule applies only to "a merchant" or only "between merchants." Not surprisingly, these rules are often referred to as the "merchant rules." To better understand the merchant rules, we need to know what a merchant is for purposes of Article 2.

The definition of *merchant* in § 2-104(1) provides:

> (1) "Merchant" means a person who deals in goods of the kind or otherwise by his occupation holds himself out as having knowledge or skill peculiar to the practices or goods involved in the transaction or to whom such knowledge or skill may be attributed by his employment of an agent or broker or other intermediary who by his occupation holds himself out as having such knowledge or skill.

If we use the techniques we learned in Chapter 3.B to diagram this definition, we see that there are three ways to be deemed a merchant:

"Merchant" means a person who

1. deals in goods of the kind or
2. otherwise by his occupation holds himself out as having knowledge or skill peculiar to the practices or goods involved in the transaction or
3. to whom such knowledge or skill may be attributed by his employment of an agent or broker or other intermediary who by his occupation holds himself out as having such knowledge or skill.

Obviously, the policy here is that merchants are held to a higher standard because they have superior knowledge. The first way to be considered a merchant describes a *goods merchant* who has superior knowledge because of frequent dealings with the goods involved in the transaction. For example, if John goes to buy a car from a dealership, the dealership would be such a merchant with respect to cars. The second way describes a *practices merchant*, who might not deal in the particular goods, but is familiar with the practices of buying and selling. For example, the purchasing department of a university may be ordering a gidget for the first time; the university may never have dealt with gidgets, but it is familiar with purchasing practices in general. It is therefore a practices merchant rather than a goods merchant with respect to the gidget. The third way will only arise when a party uses an agent who has the knowledge. For example, John, our car buyer, has heard that there are techniques a person can use to get a better deal, but he thinks he would be unable to successfully employ those techniques He hires Mary, who is in the business of assisting car buyers, to negotiate the deal for him. For Article 2 purposes, John is a merchant because his agent has superior knowledge in this transaction.

The distinction between a merchant who is familiar with the practices and a merchant who is familiar with the goods becomes significant in a number of Article 2 provisions. For example, the following rules apply only to a goods merchant:

- § 2-314 provides that "a warranty that the goods shall be merchantable is implied in a contract for their sale *if the seller is a merchant with respect to goods of that kind.*" So the warranty of merchantability is given only by a goods merchant, and not by a practices merchant.

- § 2-312(3) provides that "*a seller who is a merchant regularly dealing in goods of the kind* warrants that the goods shall be delivered free of the rightful claim of any third person by way of infringement or the like." So the warranty against infringement is given only by a goods merchant, and not by a practices merchant.
- § 2-403(2) provides that "[a]ny entrusting of possession of goods *to a merchant who deals in goods of that kind* gives him power to transfer all rights of the entruster to a buyer in ordinary course of business." If you entrust your ring to a jeweler, the jeweler can transfer all rights because it is a merchant who deals in goods of the kind; if you entrust your ring to a car dealer, the car dealer cannot transfer all rights because the car dealer is not a merchant who deals in goods of the kind.

On the other hand, the default rule of § 2-509(3) with respect to when risk of loss passes makes a distinction not between the classes of merchants, but between a merchant and a nonmerchant:

> (3) In any case not within subsection (1) or (2), the risk of loss passes to the buyer on his receipt of the goods *if the seller is a merchant;* otherwise the risk passes to the buyer on tender of delivery.

For this purpose, it does not matter whether the merchant is a goods merchant or a practices merchant.

The policy behind the different categories of merchants is explained in Official Comment 2 to § 2-104:

> 2. The term "merchant" as defined here roots in the "law merchant" concept of a professional in business. The professional status under the definition may be based upon specialized knowledge as to the goods, specialized knowledge as to business practices, or specialized knowledge as to both and which kind of specialized knowledge may be sufficient to establish the merchant status is indicated by the nature of the provisions.
>
> The special provisions as to merchants appear only in this Article and they are of three kinds. Sections 2-201(2), 2-205, 2-207 and 2-209 dealing with the statute of frauds, firm offers, confirmatory memoranda and modification rest on normal business practices which are or ought to be typical of and familiar to any person in business. For purposes of these sections almost every person in business would, therefore, be deemed to be a "merchant" under the language "who . . . by his occupation holds himself out as having knowledge or skill peculiar to the practices . . . involved in the transaction . . . " since the practices involved in the transaction are non-specialized business practices such as answering mail. In this type of provision, banks or even universities, for example, well may be "merchants." But even these sections only apply to a merchant in his mercantile capacity; a lawyer or bank president buying fishing tackle for his own use is not a merchant.

On the other hand, in Section 2-314 on the warranty of merchantability, such warranty is implied only "if the seller is a merchant with respect to goods of that kind." Obviously this qualification restricts the implied warranty to a much smaller group than everyone who is engaged in business and requires a professional status as to particular kinds of goods. The exception in Section 2-402(2) for retention of possession by a merchant-seller falls in the same class; as does Section 2-403(2) on entrusting of possession to a merchant "who deals in goods of that kind."

QUESTION 5. Doris, who is the purchasing agent for a university, buys a CD player for her living room from Best Buy. Is Doris a merchant for purposes of this transaction?

A. Yes, because Best Buy is a goods merchant.
B. Yes, because Doris is a practices merchant.
C. No, because Doris is not acting on behalf of the university.
D. No, because a CD player is consumer goods.

ANALYSIS. Although they did not expressly state this understanding in the statute, the drafters of Article 2 intended that examination of the context of the transaction would determine the applicability of the merchant rules. Official Comment 2 states that "these sections only apply to a merchant in his mercantile capacity; a lawyer or bank president buying fishing tackle for his own use is not a merchant." Technically, it is the university and not Doris personally that has the expertise of a merchant. The best response is **C**.

QUESTION 6. As a new promotion, a car dealer offered ten pounds of beef with every car purchase. John bought a car, got the beef, and came down with food poisoning when he ate the beef. Is he likely to be successful if he brings a claim for breach of the warranty of merchantability under § 2-314 against the car dealership?

A. Yes, because the car dealer is a merchant.
B. Yes, because the car dealer is familiar with the practices involved in the transaction.
C. No, because the car dealer is not a merchant with respect to food.
D. No, because John is not a merchant.

ANALYSIS. Section 2-314 provides that "a warranty that the goods shall be merchantable is implied in a contract for their sale *if the seller is a merchant with respect to goods of that kind.*" The car dealer is a merchant with respect to cars, but not a merchant with respect to food. The correct response is **C**. Official Comment 2 to § 2-104 explains that "this qualification restricts the implied warranty to a much smaller group than everyone who is engaged in business and requires a professional status as to particular kinds of goods."

2. Transactions "between merchants"

On occasion, the Code makes a distinction between transactions where both parties are merchants and transactions where only one party is a merchant. For example, the confirmation exception to the Statute of Frauds in § 2-201(2) provides that it applies "between merchants." When a large agricultural company sends a confirmation to a farmer, the issue frequently arises as to whether the farmer is a merchant for this purpose. If the farmer were not a merchant, then the rule would not apply. Other rules that apply between merchants are

- § 2-207(2), the Battle of the Forms, provides that "[b]etween merchants [additional] terms become part of the contract."
- § 2-209(2), the oral modification rule, provides that "except as between merchants such a requirement [a no oral modification clause] on a form supplied by the merchant must be separately signed by the other party."

> **QUESTION 7.** A firm offer is sent by a merchant seller to a buyer who is not a merchant. Does this offer qualify as a firm offer under § 2-205? The statute provides in pertinent part:
>
> > An offer by a merchant to buy or sell goods in a signed writing which by its terms gives assurance that it will be held open is not revocable, for lack of consideration, during the time stated.
>
> **A.** Yes, because only the party making the offer must be a merchant.
> **B.** Yes, because either party must be a merchant.
> **C.** No, because both the buyer and the seller must be merchants.
> **D.** No, because the party receiving the offer must be a merchant.

ANALYSIS.   This statute applies to "an offer by a merchant." Only the offeror must be a merchant, whether the offer is an offer to buy or an offer to sell, and the offeree is not required to be a merchant. Here, the offeror is a merchant and the offeree is not. Therefore, the correct response is **A**.

C.   Good faith

The concept of good faith pervades the Code. It is expressly found in § 1-304:

> **§ 1-304. Obligation of Good Faith**. Every contract or duty within [the Uniform Commercial Code] imposes an obligation of good faith in its performance and enforcement.

Good faith is defined in Revised § 1-201(b)(20):

> (20) "Good faith," except as otherwise provided in Article 5, means honesty in fact and the observance of reasonable commercial standards of fair dealing.

Under this definition there are two requirements of good faith, which can be described as subjective and objective. The subjective requirement of "honesty in fact" goes to a person's motive, whether the person is acting honestly or not. Obviously, it can be hard to prove what a person's motives are, so it can be difficult for a plaintiff to prove breach of this standard. The objective requirement of "the observance of reasonable commercial standards of fair dealing" may require a party to establish what the reasonable standards are in a particular business. For example, assume a seller had the right under a contract to raise its prices if the cost of power becomes excessive. The seller raises its prices and the buyer claims that the price increase was not justified. Under the subjective test, the buyer would have to prove that the seller raised its prices not because of the cost of power but for some other reason. Under the objective test, the buyer would have to prove that a reasonable seller in this business would not have raised its prices.

In the jurisdictions that have not enacted Revised Article 1, which are a minority, the definition of *good faith* varies depending on whether the party is a merchant or not. In those jurisdictions, § 1-201(19) defines *good faith* as "honesty in fact." Therefore, all parties are required to be honest. However, in those jurisdictions § 2-103(1)(b) provides that "[i]n this Article . . . in the case of a merchant, good faith includes observance of reasonable commercial standards of fair dealing in the trade." In those jurisdictions, that Article 2 standard is applicable only to merchants. Recall that the provisions found in Article 1 apply throughout the Code, including Article 2. In those jurisdictions, therefore, in an Article 2 transaction, the good faith standard applicable to nonmerchants is "honesty in fact," whereas the standard applicable to merchants is "honesty in fact" *and* the "observance of reasonable commercial standards of fair dealing in the trade."

Jurisdictions that have enacted Revised Article 1 repealed § 2-103(1)(b). That is because Revised § 1-201(b)(20) provides that "'[g]ood faith' . . . means honesty in fact and the observance of reasonable commercial standards of fair dealing." In those jurisdictions, then, the same standard is applicable to both merchants and nonmerchants in Article 2. Of course, it is likely that a nonmerchant is not familiar with "reasonable commercial standards." It would seem logical in that event not to hold the nonmerchant to those standards. Section 1-201(a) acknowledges that problem when introducing the definitions, for it provides:

> (a) *Unless the context otherwise requires,* words or phrases defined in this section, or in the additional definitions contained in other articles of [the Uniform Commercial Code] that apply to particular articles or parts thereof, have the meanings stated.

A nonmerchant can argue that in a particular case, "the context otherwise requires," and therefore the nonmerchant should not be held to "the observance of reasonable commercial standards."

QUESTION 8. A buyer of potatoes uses the potatoes to make potato chips. A clause in the contract between the buyer and the seller states that the potatoes must "chip to buyer's satisfaction." After the buyer contracts to buy potatoes for $2.00 per hundredweight, the market price falls to $1.00 and the buyer refuses to buy from this seller, claiming that the potatoes did not chip satisfactorily. The buyer tells the seller, "Why should I buy from you when I can buy potatoes all day for $1.00?" The seller has the potatoes tested by an independent agency, which confirms that they are good for chipping. Has the buyer breached the obligation of good faith?

A. Yes, both the subjective and objective standards.
B. Yes, the subjective standard only.
C. Yes, the objective standard only.
D. No.

ANALYSIS.   These facts are based on the case of *Neumiller Farms, Inc. v. Cornett*, 368 So. 2d 272 (Ala. 1979). Note that it does not matter whether this hypothetical is set in a jurisdiction that has enacted Revised Article 1 or not. If it took place in a jurisdiction that has enacted Revised Article 1, then under § 1-201(b)(20), "'[g]ood faith' . . . means honesty in fact and the observance of reasonable commercial standards of fair dealing," so all parties are subject to both the subjective and objective standard of good faith. If it took place in a jurisdiction that has not enacted Revised Article 1, then under § 1-201(19), good faith means "honesty in fact" and under § 2-103(1)(b), "in the case of a merchant, good faith includes observance of reasonable commercial standards of fair dealing in the trade." Because the buyer of potatoes is a merchant, it is subject to both the subjective and objective standard of good faith.

Under the facts, the buyer said, "Why should I buy from you when I can buy potatoes all day for $1.00?" That is pretty good evidence that the reason the buyer rejected the potatoes was the price, not the chipping quality. That shows he was not honest in fact. The fact that the independent agency confirmed that the potatoes were good for chipping shows that the buyer did not observe reasonable commercial standards in the trade. Therefore, he has breached both the subjective and objective standards. The correct response is **A**.

By the way, the fact that the buyer breached the duty of good faith does not in any way enhance the breach of contract. There is no independent cause of action for breach of this duty. As explained in the Official Comment to § 1-304:

> This section does not support an independent cause of action for failure to perform or enforce in good faith. Rather, this section means that a failure to perform or enforce, in good faith, a specific duty or obligation under the contract, constitutes a breach of that contract or makes unavailable, under the particular circumstances, a remedial right or power. This distinction makes it clear that the doctrine of good faith merely directs a court towards interpreting contracts within the commercial context in which they are created, performed, and enforced, and does not create a separate duty of fairness and reasonableness which can be independently breached.

Furthermore, as with any other breach under the Code, punitive damages and attorney's fees may not be recovered.

QUESTION 9. John was given a widget. He had no use for it, so he sold it to Mary at a yard sale. Mary later complained that the widget did not include a widget cap, without which it was inoperable. John said, "I'm sorry, but I don't think I'm responsible for that." Mary said, "Any widget seller will tell you that it is not reasonable to sell one without a cap." In a jurisdiction that has enacted Revised Article 1, has John breached the duty of good faith?

A. Yes, because the sale makes him a merchant, so he must observe reasonable commercial standards of fair dealing.

B. Yes, even though he is not a merchant, he must observe reasonable commercial standards of fair dealing.

C. No, because he is not a merchant, he is not required to observe reasonable commercial standards of fair dealing.

D. No, even though nonmerchants must generally observe reasonable commercial standards of fair dealing, in this context he should not be held to that standard.

ANALYSIS. Under the facts, John is not a widget merchant. However, Revised § 1-201(b)(20) provides that "'[g]ood faith' . . . means honesty in fact and the observance of reasonable commercial standards of fair dealing," and this standard is applicable to all parties under Article 2. However, the definition applies, according to § 1-201(a) "[u]nless the context otherwise requires." Here, in a context where a party is not a merchant and would have no knowledge of commercial standards of fair dealing, it seems unreasonable to hold him to that standard. The best response is **D.**

D.   Policing the agreement

At common law, courts had the power to police agreements and refuse to enforce all of an agreement or part of it in the name of public policy. Today, two concepts are important aspects of this police power, particularly with respect to contracts of adhesion: unconscionability and reasonable expectations.

1. *Unconscionability*

Section 2-302 gives the court the power to police the contract, striking all of it or any part of it that the court finds to be "unconscionable." It provides:

> **§ 2-302. Unconscionable Contract or Clause.**
>
> (1) If the court as a matter of law finds the contract or any clause of the contract to have been unconscionable at the time it was made the court may refuse to enforce the contract, or it may enforce the remainder of the contract without the unconscionable clause, or it may so limit the application of any unconscionable clause as to avoid any unconscionable result.

The term *unconscionable* is not defined in the Code, probably on the theory that defining it might limit it, and the Code wants to grant courts a great deal of flexibility in this area. Some guidance is provided in Official Comment 1, although even this explanation becomes circular, defining unconscionable terms as unconscionable:

> The basic test is whether, in the light of the general commercial background and the commercial needs of the particular trade or case, the clauses involved are so one-sided as to be unconscionable under the circumstances existing at the time of the making of the contract.

You may recall the case of *Williams v. Walker-Thomas Furniture Co.*, 350 F.2d 445 (D.C. Cir. 1965), in which the plaintiff claimed that a "cross-collateralization" clause in a credit agreement was unconscionable. Judge Skelly Wright gave courts some guidance in resolving issues of unconscionability: "Unconscionability has generally been recognized to include an absence of meaningful choice on the part of one of the parties together with contract terms which are unreasonably favorable to the other party." The first element— "an absence of meaningful choice on the part of one of the parties"—characterizes a contract of adhesion. Although a contract of adhesion is a necessary element of unconscionability, it is not sufficient, for there is nothing wrong with a contract of adhesion as such. The second element—"contract terms which are unreasonably favorable to the other party"—indicates that the party with the bargaining power used that power to force unfair terms on the other party. Note that the second element is not sufficient either, for it would not behoove a party to a negotiated contract to claim that it was the victim of an unconscionable term. For this reason, unconscionability cases tend to arise in a consumer context, where there is often no negotiation, rather than a commercial context. This is not to say that there can be no unconscionability in the commercial arena, but when it is found in a business context, it is usually in a relationship such as a franchise that is characterized by an absence of meaningful choice.

When a claim of unconscionability arises, § 2-302(2) takes the familiar Code approach of directing the fact-finder to look at the situation in its commercial context:

> (2) When it is claimed or appears to the court that the contract or any clause thereof may be unconscionable the parties shall be afforded a reasonable opportunity to present evidence as to its commercial setting, purpose and effect to aid the court in making the determination.

For example, in a case like *Williams*, the defendant would be given an opportunity to prove that its credit practices were not unreasonable under the facts and circumstances of its particular situation.

QUESTION 10. John buys a TV from Megalo Mart. When he wants to return the TV, Megalo Mart points out that the contract provides for a charge of 30% of the price as a "restocking fee." John claims the term is unconscionable. Which fact will help Megalo Mart the most in its defense?

A. Before the sale, John read the contract and was aware of the term.
B. Megalo Mart put the term in bold print on the front of the contract.
C. Many other stores have the same policy.
D. The charge is reasonable in its commercial setting.

ANALYSIS. Response **C** is not a good response. The fact that others are doing it may suggest that there is a widespread unconscionable practice. Courts have sometimes raised the argument made in responses **A** and **B** in connection with a claim of unconscionability. I must say that doesn't make sense to me. If a term is so outrageous that it does not belong in a contract, then it should not matter that a party was actually aware of it because they read it, or objectively aware of it because it was in bold print. On the other hand, the defense in response **D** is specifically mentioned in § 2-302(2). **D** is the best response.

2. Reasonable expectations

A concept that is not expressly mentioned in the Code but that is becoming significant in contract law is the doctrine of *reasonable expectations*. It can be found in Restatement (Second) of Contracts § 211(3):

(3) Where the other party has reason to believe that the party manifesting such assent would not do so if he knew that the writing contained a particular term, the term is not part of the agreement.

A Comment to the Restatement section explains:

> [A] party who adheres to the other party's standard terms does not assent to a term if the other party has reason to believe that the adhering party would not have accepted the agreement if he had known that the agreement contained the particular term. Such a belief or assumption may be shown by the prior negotiations or inferred from the circumstances. Reason to believe may be inferred from the fact that the term is bizarre or oppressive, from the fact that it eviscerates the non-standard terms explicitly agreed to, or from the fact that it eliminates the dominant purpose of the transaction. The inference is reinforced if the adhering party never had an opportunity to read the term, or if it is illegible or otherwise hidden from view. This rule is closely related to the policy against unconscionable terms and the rule of interpretation against the draftsman.

The concept again relates to contracts of adhesion. It assumes that it is not efficient for a party to read a contract of adhesion because (1) the party thinks it knows what terms the contract contains, and (2) if it contains terms the party doesn't like, the party can't do anything about it because the contract is not negotiable anyway. In that context, if there is a term that the offeror knows the offeree would not reasonably expect, then the offeror has an obligation to call it to the offeree's attention, for example, by highlighting it or having that provision separately signed. On the Internet, where the offeree rarely reads the terms and conditions, it may mean making that term more conspicuous, perhaps asking the offeree to check it off individually. Note that these techniques would be less likely to save an unconscionable provision, for if a term is so outrageous, one would think it would not be any the less so for being highlighted.

QUESTION 11. A wholesale chicken seller contracts with a number of farms to produce chickens. Each year the wholesaler sends the farmer a form contract stating the price the wholesaler will pay and the farmer signs and returns the form. Because of pressure from consumers, the wholesaler decides it will sell chickens that are free of growth hormones. It inserts in the middle of the contract a provision that the farmer promises not to use growth hormones. A number of farmers nevertheless use growth hormones and the wholesaler refuses to purchase their chickens. Is the wholesaler's refusal justified?

A. Yes, because it was the duty of the farmers to read the contract.
B. No, because the wholesaler defrauded the farmers.
C. No, because the provision is unconscionable.
D. No, because the provision was not within the farmers' reasonable expectations.

ANALYSIS.   It is technically true that a person has a duty to read a contract and is objectively bound by what he signs. Nevertheless, in this context, the wholesaler would not reasonably expect the farmers to know the provision was in the contract. On the other hand, there is nothing unfair about the provision, so it is not unconscionable. The best way to strike a balance between the interests of the parties would be to require the wholesaler, if it was including in the form contract a term that the farmer was not reasonably expecting, to call the term to the farmer's attention. Such an action would satisfy the doctrine of reasonable expectations. The best response is **D**.

E.   Closers

QUESTION 12. A consumer sees a television set for sale at a retail store with a price of $800. After she buys the set, she discovers that another store is selling the same set for a price of $400. She complains, but the store refuses to do anything. What is the consumer's best argument to avoid this contract?

A. The seller did not act in good faith in setting a price twice as high as the market price.
B. It is unconscionable to sell a television set at a price twice as high as others are selling it for.
C. The price was not within the consumer's reasonable expectations.
D. None of the above is a good argument.

ANALYSIS.   Price unconscionability has been rare, because the price is a term that is clearly available and the consumer is free to shop for a better price. Generally a consumer has been successful in claiming price unconscionability only when the contract was entered into in an unconscionable manner (sometimes called *procedural unconscionability*) so that in the circumstances the consumer was not aware of the price. Similarly, because price is a conspicuous term, it is within reasonable expectations. Nor is it considered a breach of the duty of good faith and fair dealing for a seller to establish a higher than normal price term. The consumer does not have a good claim under these facts, so the best response is **D**.

QUESTION 13. Two sophisticated parties are entering into a contract for the sale of computer hardware, software, and installation and repair services. They reside in a jurisdiction that uses the predominant factor test to determine whether Article 2 applies to a transaction. They are unable to predict, however, how the jurisdiction would view this transaction under that test. They would like to specify in the contract that the UCC applies to all claims relating to the goods, and other law applies to other claims. Is such a provision likely to be enforceable?

A. No, because the enacted law of the jurisdiction is Article 2.
B. No, because a court will want to make that decision.
C. Yes, because parties generally have freedom of contract under the Code.
D. Yes, because that reflects the outcome under the predominant factor test.

ANALYSIS. Businesses like predictability, and in a situation like this they are faced with the unpredictable. Although some courts may want to make the decision, I would think most courts would be glad to leave this to the parties. The best response is **C**. An example of the Code expressly encouraging this behavior by contracting parties can be found in Article 2A. We will see in Chapter 21 that Article 2A applies to the lease of goods. However, parties involved in other transactions might want this body of law to apply to their transaction. The Official Comment to § 2A-102 endorses this approach:

> Further, parties to a transaction creating a lease of personal property other than goods, or a bailment of personal property may provide by agreement that this Article applies. Upholding the parties' choice is consistent with the spirit of this Article.

 # Burnham's picks

Question 1	A
Question 2	B
Question 3	A
Question 4	C
Question 5	C
Question 6	C
Question 7	A

Question 8   **A**
Question 9   **D**
Question 10   **D**
Question 11   **D**
Question 12   **D**
Question 13   **C**

5

Formation

A.   Introduction

I am going to assume that you are familiar with the common law rules of contract formation that you studied in the basic Contracts class. Our approach to the formation of contracts under Article 2 will demonstrate how the drafters changed those basic rules when they thought the changes would serve a useful purpose. We explore the following:

- Firm offers (§ 2-205)
- Unilateral contracts (§ 2-206)
- Gap fillers (§ 2-204)
- The Battle of the Forms (§ 2-207)

B.   Firm offers: § 2-205

The common law rule is that the offeror can revoke an offer any time before acceptance. Under the common law, assume a seller wrote to a buyer, "I'll sell you a type X widget for $1,000. This offer is open for ten days." The seller is nevertheless free to revoke the offer at any time before the offeree effectively accepts. An exception would arise if the offeree paid a consideration to have the offer held open. In that event there would be an option contract. So if the offeree said, "I'll pay you $1 to keep that offer open for ten days," and the offeror agreed, then the offeror would lose the ability to effectively revoke the offer for ten days.

A good example of how the Code changes the common law is the merchant's firm offer rule in § 2-205:

§ 2-205. Firm Offers.
An offer by a merchant to buy or sell goods in a signed writing which by its terms gives assurance that it will be held open is not revocable, for lack of consideration, during the time stated or if no time is stated for a reasonable time, but in no event may such period of irrevocability exceed three months; but any such term of assurance on a form supplied by the offeree must be separately signed by the offeror.

Let's diagram this provision using the skills we learned in Chapter 3.B.3:

An offer
by a merchant
to buy or sell goods
in a signed writing which by its terms gives assurance that it will be held
    open
is not revocable, for lack of consideration, during the time stated or if no
    time is stated for a reasonable time, but in no event may such period
    of irrevocability exceed three months; but any such term of assurance
    on a form supplied by the offeree must be separately signed by the
    offeror.

The first element is that there is an offer. *Offer* is not defined in Article 2, so according to the basic rule of § 1-103(b), we would look to the common law for the rule. Under the common law, an offer is a promise to do or not to do something conditional on getting something requested in return. The second element is that the rule of § 2-205 only applies to an offer by a merchant. *Merchant* is defined in § 2-104(1). As we saw in Chapter 4.B, when the Code states that a rule is applicable only to a merchant or only between merchants (recall that these rules are collectively called the "merchant rules"), it generally means that the party is expected to have some sophistication. We can therefore assume that the firm offer rule will have some ramifications that might not be appreciated by an unsophisticated party. The third element is that the offer has to be "to buy or sell goods," which shouldn't surprise us, as this is Article 2. The fourth element is that the offer has to be "in a signed writing which by its terms gives assurance that it will be held open." The fact that it has to be in a signed writing is an indication that something serious is going on because, as we shall see, signed writings are often substitutes for consideration. This particular signed writing has to inform the offeree that it will be held open, stating something to the effect of "This offer is open for 14 days" or "This offer is firm."

If those elements are satisfied, the consequence is that the offer "is not revocable, for lack of consideration, during the time stated." Do I hear the common law rolling over in its grave? The legislature in its wisdom has just done away with the common law rule that an offer is revocable by the offeror unless there is some consideration paid. Under the Code rule, if all the elements are satisfied, the offer is irrevocable even though no consideration has been paid. Note that other defenses to formation remain available—the offer is not revocable for lack of consideration, but it might be revocable for other reasons. Why would the drafters of the Code create such a rule? The reason is that the Code tries not to be *prescriptive*, telling buyers and sellers what the rules should be, but *descriptive*, capturing common business practices. Therefore, if in business an offeree expects such an offer to be binding, the Code reflects that practice.

The rest of the section deals with how long the offer remains open. As is often the case under the Code, the default rule is a reasonable time. However, the offeror has freedom of contract to change the default rule by stating a time that the offer remains open. Even that time can't exceed three months, though, so there is a regulatory aspect to the provision. The last sentence—"any such term of assurance on a form supplied by the offeree must be separately signed by the offeror"—is confusing but not very important. It is intended to keep the offeror from being surprised to find that it made a firm offer; if the term is found in a form supplied by the offeree, the offeree must call it to the offeror's attention and have the offeror sign that term. This is a good example of the doctrine of *reasonable expectations* that we discussed in Chapter 4.D.2. Under that doctrine, if a term might take a party by surprise, the term is enforceable only if a reasonable party would have known it was in the contract.

QUESTION 1. A department store runs an ad in a local newspaper that states, "Black lapin stoles. $100. This sale price is effective for the next 10 days." The department store then decides to stop this sale and the next day it runs an ad in the newspaper that states, "Effective at the close of business today, black lapin stoles are no longer available at the sale price. We regret any inconvenience this may cause." Is the sale price for the stoles still effective the next day?

A. Yes, because it was a merchant's firm offer that is not revocable during the time stated.

B. Yes, because the method of revocation through the newspaper was not effective.

C. No, because the newspaper advertisement was not an offer.

D. No, because the offer was not a firm offer because it was made to the general public, not to merchants.

ANALYSIS. This is a bit tricky—you might even say it was a trick question. When we work through the elements of § 2-205 to see if they are satisfied, the first element is that there is "an offer." You may recall from Contracts (and I gave you a hint by using a hypothetical involving the sale of black lapin stoles, the subject matter of the case of *Lefkowitz v. Great Minneapolis Surplus Store*, 86 N.W.2d 689 (Minn. 1957)) that an advertisement is generally not an offer, and this one does not have the earmarks of an offer. Therefore, if it isn't an offer, it cannot be a firm offer, so the correct response is **C**. Note that response **B** is not correct because in general an offer can be effectively revoked in a medium similar to the medium in which it was made. Response **D** is not correct because, although a firm offer can only be made *by* a merchant, it does not have to be made *to* a merchant.

QUESTION 2. A seller of electrical supplies wrote on stationery that had his letterhead at the top, "I am offering 100-watt Luminex bulbs for 10 cents each while my supplies last." Without signing the letter, he sent it to his best customers. Is this a § 2-205 firm offer?

A. Yes, but it will remain open for no more than three months.
B. Yes, and it will remain open until all the lightbulbs are sold.
C. No, because it is not made in a signed writing.
D. No, because it does not state that it will remain open for a time stated.

ANALYSIS. This is clearly an offer by a merchant to sell goods. Is it made in a signed writing? The definition of *writing* in § 1-201(b)(46) provides that "'[w]riting' includes printing, typewriting, or any other intentional reduction to tangible form." It would seem that the seller's printed stationery would constitute a writing. And the definition of *signed* in § 1-201(b)(37) states that it "includes any symbol executed or adopted with present intention to adopt or accept a writing." It would seem that the seller's letterhead was adopted with the intention to indicate that the offer came from him. The Official Comment to that section elaborates:

> The symbol may be printed, stamped or written; it may be by initials or by thumbprint. It may be on any part of the document and in appropriate cases may be found in a billhead or letterhead. No catalog of possible situations can be complete and the court must use common sense and commercial experience in passing upon these matters. The question always is whether the symbol was executed or adopted by the party with present intention to adopt or accept the writing.

Do its terms give assurance that it will be held open? I think that can be implied by the statement that the offer is open "while my supplies last." There is no time stated, but the Code would supply a reasonable time, and the Code also says that the time cannot exceed three months. Therefore, the best response is **A**.

C.   Unilateral contracts: § 2-206

Another common law contracts rule you learned concerned the manner of acceptance. An offer can be accepted either by (1) promise, (2) performance, or (3) promise or performance. Which manner is appropriate can be stated by the offeror, but if it is not specified, then the manner is whatever is reasonable in the circumstances. These rules, with an interesting twist, are found in Article 2 at § 2-206:

§ 2-206. Offer and Acceptance in Formation of Contract.

(1) Unless otherwise unambiguously indicated by the language or circumstances

(a) an offer to make a contract shall be construed as inviting acceptance in any manner and by any medium reasonable in the circumstances;

(b) an order or other offer to buy goods for prompt or current shipment shall be construed as inviting acceptance either by a prompt promise to ship or by the prompt or current shipment of conforming or non-conforming goods, but such a shipment of non- conforming goods does not constitute an acceptance if the seller seasonably notifies the buyer that the shipment is offered only as an accommodation to the buyer.

(2) Where the beginning of a requested performance is a reasonable mode of acceptance an offeror who is not notified of acceptance within a reasonable time may treat the offer as having lapsed before acceptance.

Subsections (1)(a) and (2) pretty much restate the common law and don't contain any surprises. The prefatory language—"[u]nless otherwise unambiguously indicated by the language or circumstances"—is a useful reminder that the rules are flexible. The rules are to be applied in particular circumstances and the parties are generally free to change them in their contract. The "manner" of acceptance referred to in subsection (1)(a) refers to either acceptance by promise (bilateral contract) or acceptance by performance (unilateral contract) or by either method where reasonable. Subsection (2) is a reminder that when the manner of acceptance is by performance, the offeror might not reasonably know that the offeree has accepted. The burden is placed on the offeree to notify the offeror of its acceptance; if the offeree does not do so in a reasonable time, the offeror can assume that the offer has lapsed.

The "medium" of acceptance referred to in subsection (1)(a) is the medium used for communication. There is no requirement that the same medium be used in both the offer and the acceptance, as long as the medium is reasonable in the circumstances. For example, if an offer is received by letter, it is probably reasonable to accept that offer by fax even though fax is technically a different medium. The policy behind this provision is to provide for flexibility.

The provision that changes the common law is subsection (1)(b), which begins as follows:

> (b) an order or other offer to buy goods for prompt or current shipment shall be construed as inviting acceptance either by a prompt promise to ship or by the prompt or current shipment of conforming or nonconforming goods, . . .

This provision seems to start by reiterating the rule of subsection (1)(a) that an offer to buy can be accepted either by a promise to ship or by the performance of shipping the goods. Let's look at an example. An office sends a fax to a beer distributor that states, "Please ship ten cases of Beck's for our Christmas party on December 23." Without further communication, the distributor ships ten cases of Budweiser. Under the *common law* rule, is the distributor in breach? The defense of the distributor goes like this: "Your offer was to ship Beck's. Under the common law, an acceptance must be the mirror image of the offer, or it is not an acceptance. I shipped Budweiser. What I sent you was not the mirror image of what you requested in your offer. Therefore, it was not an acceptance. If there is not an acceptance, there is not a contract. And if there is not a contract, there is no claim for breach of contract." The distributor is unfortunately correct and gets away with sending the wrong goods. The office is, of course, free to reject the goods, but it may prefer to have Budweiser rather than no beer at all. If it accepts the goods that were shipped, it has accepted a counteroffer so there is no breach.

The drafters of Article 2 don't let the offeree get away with what has been called the "unilateral contract trick." The Code states that "an order or other offer to buy goods for prompt or current shipment shall be construed as inviting acceptance either by a prompt promise to ship or by the prompt or current shipment *of conforming or non-conforming goods.*" In other words, the shipment is an acceptance even if the goods shipped don't conform to the terms of the offer. If there is an acceptance, then there is a contract. If the goods don't conform to the terms of the contract, then there is a breach. So the distributor, by sending the wrong goods, has both accepted the offer and breached the contract! We see again how the Code in its wisdom made some changes in the common law rules.

The last clause of subsection (1)(b) is also interesting because it shows how flexible and practical the Code is when it states the following:

> . . . but such a shipment of non-conforming goods does not constitute an acceptance if the seller seasonably notifies the buyer that the shipment is offered only as an accommodation to the buyer.

Suppose the distributor in my hypothetical was not trying to take advantage of the offeror. On the contrary, he didn't have any Beck's and he thought the office would rather have Budweiser than no beer at all. The Code says that in that case, all he has to do is send a note saying that he is sending the nonconforming goods as an accommodation. In that case, shipping them would not be an acceptance. It would be a counteroffer, which the office would be free to accept or reject. The note must be sent "seasonably." What does *seasonably* mean? Section 1-205(b) provides that "[a]n action is taken seasonably if it is taken at or within the time agreed or, if no time is agreed, at or within a reasonable time." Here, there is no time stated, and in this context I would think a reasonable time would be any time up to and including the time of delivery. At that time, the offeror would need to know the consequences of accepting or rejecting the shipment.

QUESTION 3. A coal-fired power station became short of fuel and sent a fax to a number of coal companies that said, "We are offering to buy 100 tons of coal that contains at least 80% carbon at market price."
The Carbon County Coal Company replied by email, "We accept your offer. The coal will be shipped tomorrow." Carbon County only had coal that contained 75% carbon, so when it shipped the coal it notified the buyer that it was sending the coal as an accommodation. Is Carbon County in breach?

A. Yes, because a contract was formed when it accepted the offer and it then shipped nonconforming goods.
B. Yes, because a contract was formed when it shipped nonconforming goods.
C. No, because its reply by email did not constitute an acceptance.
D. No, because it offered the nonconforming goods as an accommodation.

ANALYSIS. When an offer is made by fax, email seems to be a reasonable medium of acceptance, so **C** is not a correct response. The solution to this problem is to determine whether the acceptance was by promise or performance. Although the offer invited either method of acceptance, when Carbon County sent its email, it appears that the language of the email constituted an acceptance by promise. Therefore, **B** is not a correct response because there was acceptance by promise rather than by performance. Even though Carbon County notified the buyer that it was shipping nonconforming goods as an accommodation, this fact is irrelevant because it had already accepted by promise. The best response is **A**. Had the acceptance been by performance, **D** would have been the correct response.

D.   Gap fillers: § 2-204

The flexibility of Article 2 is indicated by the formation rules in § 2-204:

§ 2-204. Formation in General.

(1) A contract for sale of goods may be made in any manner sufficient to show agreement, including conduct by both parties which recognizes the existence of such a contract.

(2) An agreement sufficient to constitute a contract for sale may be found even though the moment of its making is undetermined.

(3) Even though one or more terms are left open a contract for sale does not fail for indefiniteness if the parties have intended to make a contract and there is a reasonably certain basis for giving an appropriate remedy.

The rule of subsection (3) reflects the common law principle that you may recall from the case of *Wood v. Lucy, Lady Duff-Gordon,* 118 N.E. 214 (N.Y. 1917). The law is concerned with substance rather than form; if it appears that both parties intended to make a contract, then the law will assist them by making clear the terms that they may have drafted carelessly. For example, if John and Mary sign an agreement that states, "John hereby sells his 2005 Toyota Corolla to Mary for $5,000," Mary won't have much luck if she complains that the contract doesn't expressly say that she agreed to buy the car. That promise will be reasonably implied from the facts and circumstances.

The task of filling in the gaps in an indefinite contract is made considerably easier by the gap-filling or default provisions of the Code that supply the terms in the absence of the parties' agreement. For example, § 2-305(1) provides a default rule for price. Not surprisingly, it is a "reasonable price." So if a buyer and a seller agree on the sale of 1,000 widgets, the absence of a price is not fatal to their agreement if there is a reasonable way of establishing price, such as an objective market price.

One gap that often cannot be filled, however, is the quantity term. If no quantity is stated, and there is no objective basis for supplying a quantity, then no contract is formed. This is what § 2-204(3) means when it says that an agreement does not fail for indefiniteness if "there is a reasonably certain basis for giving an appropriate remedy." Assume, for example, a buyer and a seller agree on the sale of "widgets" for $10 each. The seller then breaches and the buyer has to pay $12 for widgets. If there is no way to determine the quantity of widgets that the buyer had agreed to buy, then there is no way to determine the remedy to which the buyer is entitled.

An exception to the rule that quantity must be stated or an agreement fails for indefiniteness is found in § 2-306(1):

§ 2-306. Output, Requirements and Exclusive Dealings.

(1) A term which measures the quantity by the output of the seller or the requirements of the buyer means such actual output or requirements

as may occur in good faith, except that no quantity unreasonably dispro-portionate to any stated estimate or in the absence of a stated estimate to any normal or otherwise comparable prior output or requirements may be tendered or demanded.

Under this provision, the quantity is stated in terms of the output of the seller or the requirements of the buyer. At common law, this was fatal. Because the seller did not promise to have an output and the buyer didn't promise to have requirements, it was claimed that there was no consideration—the party was not committed to doing anything. However, the Code recognizes that there is an objective measure for determining the quantity in estimates or in prior outputs and requirements. The obligation of good faith provides a further check on a party's behavior under an output or requirements contract. Official Comment 2 states in part:

> (2) Under this Article, a contract for output or requirements is not too indefinite since it is held to mean the actual good faith output or requirements of the particular party. Nor does such a contract lack mutu-ality of obligation since, under this section, the party who will determine quantity is required to operate his plant or conduct his business in good faith and according to commercial standards of fair dealing in the trade so that his output or requirements will approximate a reasonably foreseeable figure. Reasonable elasticity in the requirements is expressly envisaged by this section and good faith variations from prior requirements are per-mitted even when the variation may be such as to result in discontinu-ance. A shut-down by a requirements buyer for lack of orders might be permissible when a shut-down merely to curtail losses would not. The essential test is whether the party is acting in good faith.

QUESTION 4. A seller agrees to sell a television set to a buyer for $1,000. After the deal was completed, the buyer discovers that other sellers in the area were selling the same television set for $750. The buyer claims that he is entitled to rescind the contract because under § 2-305 the price must be reasonable. Is the buyer correct?

A. Yes, because the purpose of the statute is to ensure that prices are reasonable.

B. Yes, because the market price is the reasonable price and this price was above market.

C. No, because the reasonable price rule only applies when nothing is said as to price.

D. No, because freedom of contract allows a buyer to agree to pay an unreasonable price.

ANALYSIS. A careful reading of the statute indicates that "the price is a reasonable price" only if "nothing is said as to price." Here, there was an agreed-upon price, so the correct response is **C**. Although **D** is a true statement, it is not responsive to the call of the question. The question asked whether the buyer was correct in claiming that the price had to be reasonable under § 2-305.

QUESTION 5. In a jurisdiction that applies Article 2 to the sale of electricity, an electric co-op in a small city agreed to buy "all the electricity it requires" from a supplier at a fixed price. When the market price of electricity went up in a nearby state, the co-op ordered enough electricity at the contract price so that it could satisfy its customers' needs and ship surplus electricity to that state. Is a court likely to find that the co-op was in breach of its agreement?

A. No, because freedom of contract is an important principle in the Code.
B. No, because no limit on requirements was stated in the contract.
C. Yes, because it could only order the same amount it had ordered in previous years.
D. Yes, because a reasonable measure of its requirements was the needs of its customers.

ANALYSIS. The requirements of the buyer would probably be objectively measured by the amount needed to satisfy its customers. This is not exactly the same thing stated in response **C**. Although prior purchases can represent an objective measure of requirements, in this case the needs of the customers is probably a better measure. It appears here that the co-op's purchase of additional electricity was not driven by the needs of customers but was an attempt to take advantage of the market, which was not in good faith. The best response is **D**.

Two other default rules, § 2-308 and § 2-309, relate to the place and time for delivery. You will not be surprised to learn that in the absence of the parties' agreement, the time for delivery is a reasonable time. The place for delivery is more specific, however—it is the seller's place of business. This is obviously an important rule, because when it comes to terms like who bears the cost of shipping and who bears the risk of loss, we must always remember the starting point: In the absence of agreement, it is the buyer's responsibility to get the goods from the seller. We explore the delivery terms in greater detail in Chapter 13. There are also default rules for warranties, which we explore in Chapter 9.

E.   The Battle of the Forms: § 2-207

1. Introduction

Section 2-207 is one of the most difficult provisions in the Code to understand, which means that we will be even more rewarded for our efforts at parsing it. Fasten your seat belts and get ready for the ride. It provides:

§ 2-207. Additional Terms in Acceptance or Confirmation.

(1) A definite and seasonable expression of acceptance or a written confirmation which is sent within a reasonable time operates as an acceptance even though it states terms additional to or different from those offered or agreed upon, unless acceptance is expressly made conditional on assent to the additional or different terms.

(2) The additional terms are to be construed as proposals for addition to the contract. Between merchants such terms become part of the contract unless:

(a) the offer expressly limits acceptance to the terms of the offer;

(b) they materially alter it; or

(c) notification of objection to them has already been given or is given within a reasonable time after notice of them is received.

(3) Conduct by both parties which recognizes the existence of a contract is sufficient to establish a contract for sale although the writings of the parties do not otherwise establish a contract. In such case the terms of the particular contract consist of those terms on which the writings of the parties agree, together with any supplementary terms incorporated under any other provisions of this Act.

Like a number of other Code provisions, § 2-207 is best understood against the background of how the drafters were trying to change the common law. Let's think about how contracts are formed. In the classic model, one side makes an offer and the other side proposes additional or different terms— that is, terms addressing matters that aren't in the offer, or terms addressing matters that are in the offer, but that are substantively different. The two sides negotiate, and if they come to terms, they sign a single document that embodies their agreement. In terms of offer and acceptance, it could be said that the first to sign the document is the offeror, and the second to sign is the offeree. This usually insignificant matter became significant in an episode of the television show *Deadwood* when, as a matter of pride, each party refused to be the first to sign because that would mean he was making an offer to the other and would lose face by doing so. The solution? At an appointed signal, they signed conforming copies simultaneously.

In another model, the party with the most bargaining power drafts the contract. The other party may have no opportunity to negotiate, or its attempts to negotiate are spurned; the offeror tells the offeree to "take it or leave it." This model of contract we call a *contract of adhesion*. The result again is a single document that embodies the agreement of the parties. As we saw in Chapter 4.D.1 when we looked at unconscionability, there is nothing wrong with this kind of contract as such; in fact, most modern contracts fit this model.

There is another model of contract formation. In this model, one of the parties, who may be either the buyer or the seller, sends an offer to the other party on a form prepared by its office. On the front page of the form, at the top, are the "dickered" provisions that contain essential information such as a description of the goods, quantity, price, and delivery terms. The remaining part of the form is "boilerplate" that generally does not change from transaction to transaction. When the offeree receives the form, it reads over the dickered terms and decides that it will conclude a deal based on those terms. It copies the terms into its own printed form and returns the form. At this point, one party has completed a document such as a purchase order and the other party has completed a document such as an acknowledgment. The dickered terms are the same in the two documents, but the boilerplate terms are not. The seller then ships the goods and the buyer pays for them. Everyone is happy until a problem with performance of the contract arises. Each party then retrieves its "contract" to see how it addresses the problem that has arisen.

The dilemma is that in this situation, unlike the other models for contract formation, there is no single document that embodies the contract. The buyer believes the terms are found in its form, and the seller believes the terms are found in its form. The "Battle of the Forms" begins, and the result of the battle determines which party's contract terms govern. At common law, the solution was fairly easy. If the offeree sent a form that differed from the offeror's form, then under the "mirror-image rule," the offeree was not giving its acceptance but was making a counteroffer. If, after receiving the counteroffer, the other party performed by shipping the goods or by paying for them, then there was acceptance of the counteroffer by conduct. Therefore under the common law scheme, the offeree generally got its terms.

The drafters of the Code didn't think the common law result made sense. After all, the offeror is supposed to be the "master of the offer," and yet the offeror easily lost control. It could certainly be said that instead of performing, all the offeror had to do when it got the offeree's form was to initiate negotiations with the other party until they reached agreement. Although that makes sense in theory, the Code is always realistic. The drafters knew that in practice it is not cost effective for the parties to custom-make every contract they enter into because there will probably not be a problem with the vast majority of them. The solution was to balance the interests of the offeror and the offeree so that a contract that more realistically reflected the parties' expectations would emerge from the contrasting forms. And, as with much of the Code, there had to be default rules that could be changed by the parties.

We will now see how these common law rules were changed by the Code. Keep in mind, however, that they generally remain the rule outside of transactions for the sale of goods.

QUESTION 6. A contractor sends a company its bid on a construction job. The bid consists of specifications and prices, followed by a number of boilerplate provisions. The company responds by writing up the price and specifications on its own form, which it sends to the contractor. The contractor completes the project and the company inspects it after 25 days. The company finds some unfinished work and demands payment for it. The contractor claims that he is not responsible for the unfinished work because the form he sent says that inspection must be completed within 20 days after construction, and the company did not timely inspect. However, the company's form indicates that it has 30 days after completion to inspect. Who is responsible for the unfinished work?

A. The owner, because the contractor's form governs.
B. The contractor, because the company's form governs.
C. Neither, because there is no agreement on this term.
D. Both terms are knocked out and the party who would be responsible is supplied by trade usage or by a court.

ANALYSIS. This problem involves construction services rather than the sale of goods. Therefore, the common law rather than Article 2 applies. Under the common law mirror-image rule, if the acceptance does not match the offer, then it is a counteroffer. Here, the contractor's bid was an offer, and the company's response with different terms was a counteroffer. The contractor accepted those terms by conduct when it completed the project. Although I am not completely confident in this outcome, I think most courts would conclude that the correct response is **B**.

2. Acceptance that states additional or different terms

The first part of the first sentence of § 2-207(1) contains the most dramatic change to the common law rules:

> A definite and seasonable expression of acceptance . . . which is sent within a reasonable time operates as an acceptance even though it states terms additional to or different from those offered. . . .

With the first few words, we run into our first unresolved question under § 2-207. What is a "definite and seasonable expression of acceptance"? The interpretation that I think makes sense is that there has to be agreement on the essential or "dickered" terms in order for § 2-207 to apply. For example, if one party's form contains an order for "1,000 widgets at $1 each to be delivered by April 1," and the responding form acknowledges an order for "1,000 widgets at $1 each to be delivered by April 1," then the Battle of the Forms can be used to resolve the differences in the boilerplate. But if one party's form contains an order for "1,000 widgets at $1 each to be delivered by April 1," and the responding form acknowledges an order for "1 widget at $1,000 each to be delivered by April 1," then the forms do not contain sufficient agreement to make a contract. We assume in our examples that the additional or different terms are in the boilerplate and not in the essential terms.

In the remainder of the above-quoted sentence, the drafters say that if a response that is definite and seasonable states terms that are additional or different from those in the offer, then it is still an acceptance. Think about that: Although the terms do not mirror those of the offer, it is still an acceptance! Do I hear the common law rolling over in its grave? If there is an offer and an acceptance (and we can assume that there is consideration in the promises of each party), then there is a contract. So these two differing forms comprise not an offer and a counteroffer, but a contract.

This approach to contract formation is revolutionary—and it doesn't quite make sense yet, because we still have to figure out where the contract is found. Is it in the terms of the buyer, the terms of the seller, some combination of the two, or neither? I know you can't stand the suspense, but before we answer that question we are going to look at an exception to the rule that the differing forms make a contract.

QUESTION 7. A buyer sent an order form to a seller, offering to buy 100 widgets for $10 each, with delivery on April 1 and payment 30 days after delivery. The seller sent back an acknowledgment form to the buyer, stating that it is selling ten widgets for $100 each, with delivery on April 1 and payment 30 days after delivery. Shortly after that, the seller shipped the ten widgets to the buyer, who promptly put them to use. The buyer's payment department then discovered the problem and asked for your advice about how much it has to pay. How would you best analyze the problem?

A. The forms constitute an offer and an acceptance, and therefore there is a contract. The different terms would be analyzed under the rules of the jurisdiction to determine which terms are part of the contract.

B. The forms constitute an offer and an acceptance, and therefore there is a contract, and the additional terms would be analyzed under § 2-207(2) to determine which terms are part of the contract.

> **C.** The forms do not form a contract under the common law mirror-image rule. The seller made a counteroffer, which the buyer accepted by conduct, so there is a contract on the seller's terms.
>
> **D.** The writings of the parties do not constitute a contract, but there is a contract by conduct under § 2-207(3). The terms are the terms the forms did agree on, and where they did not agree, the UCC supplies the terms, such as a reasonable price under § 2-305 for the ten widgets the buyer accepted.

ANALYSIS. I don't think it makes any sense to analyze this problem as involving different terms under § 2-207(1). Even though the forms contain different terms, they contain different essential or "dickered" terms, and I think § 2-207 was designed to deal only with conflicting terms in the boilerplate. There is support for this position in the language of § 2-207(1) that says that "a definite . . . expression of acceptance . . . operates as an acceptance." Because the seller did not give a definite expression of acceptance, I would reject both responses **A** and **B**. While it is true that the exchange of forms did not constitute a contract under the common law, we should not use the common law if there is an applicable statute. Because § 2-207(3) speaks to this situation, I would look to it rather than to the common law, so **C** is incorrect. This is a situation where the writings do not establish a contract under § 2-207(1). However, conduct under § 2-207(3) establishes a contract for ten widgets because the seller shipped those goods and the buyer accepted them. The writings did not agree on price, but when the parties do not agree on price, § 2-305 states that the price is a reasonable price. Therefore, while there may be some debate, I think **D** is the best response.

3. Acceptance conditional on assent to additional or different terms

The first sentence of § 2-207(1) ends with this exception after the comma:

> . . . unless acceptance is expressly made conditional on assent to the additional or different terms.

We started with a rule that a response that contains additional or different terms is an acceptance, and therefore forms a contract. However, a party can contract around that default rule by providing that "acceptance is expressly made conditional on assent to the additional or different terms." If the party effectively does that, its response is not an acceptance and there is no contract. One issue that has perplexed courts faced with interpreting § 2-207 is to determine what language is sufficient to satisfy that statutory requirement. Because the party is effectively saying, "If you don't agree to my terms, then we don't have a contract," the best answer is that the language would have to be very strong to communicate that intention. I would recommend that a drafter satisfy the statutory requirement by simply adopting the statutory language and stating in the contract, "Acceptance is expressly made conditional on assent to the additional or different terms."

What happens if a drafter effectively incorporates that language in its form? Because this language creates an exception to the rule that there is acceptance in spite of additional or different terms, the answer must be that there is not an acceptance, and if there is not an acceptance, then there is not a contract. If after the exchange of forms containing that language, the goods are shipped and the buyer refuses to accept them, then there is no breach of contract because there is no contract to breach. Unfortunately, that is not what usually happens. Just as a party doesn't bother to negotiate when the other party's form contains additional or different terms, a party usually continues to deal with the other even though its form states that it won't make a deal unless the other party accepts the additional or different terms. Instead or refusing to perform, the seller ships the goods and the buyer pays for them.

What happens when a problem arises after the goods have been shipped and accepted when that conditional language is found in one of the forms? Even though according to the forms there is no contract, subsection (3) says there is a contract:

> (3) Conduct by both parties which recognizes the existence of a contract is sufficient to establish a contract for sale although the writings of the parties do not otherwise establish a contract. In such case the terms of the particular contract consist of those terms on which the writings of the parties agree, together with any supplementary terms incorporated under any other provisions of this Act.

In this case, because one party said it would not agree to a contract unless there was assent to its additional or different terms, then the writings of the parties do not establish a contract. However, a contract has been recognized by their conduct. Because the seller voluntarily shipped the goods and the buyer accepted and paid for them, that conduct speaks louder than the words on their forms. When the parties have recognized the existence of a contract by their conduct, where are the terms found? The last sentence of subsection (3) tells us that the terms are found in the terms on which their forms agree, and where the forms do not agree, both parties' terms are "knocked out" and we read in the default provisions of the Code (which may be a common law rule under § 1-103(b) if the Code is silent on the point). So the curious result is that a party who refuses to contract unless it gets its terms, but then goes ahead and deals anyway, doesn't get its terms. It gets the terms of the Code.

QUESTION 8. A buyer of goods sends a purchase order to a seller on its form. The seller responds with an acknowledgment form that has additional and different terms. In addition, the seller's form states, "Acceptance is expressly made conditional on assent to the additional or different terms in this acknowledgment." When it receives the form, the buyer refuses to go through with the deal. Is the buyer in breach?

A. No, because under the common law there was a counteroffer that was not acted on.

B. No, because the Code says there was no acceptance, and therefore no contract.

C. Yes, because the Code says there is an acceptance and therefore a contract.

D. Yes, because there was acceptance by conduct.

ANALYSIS. Under the Code, the language employed by the seller satisfies the requirement of § 2-207(1) after the comma ("unless acceptance is expressly made conditional on assent to the additional or different terms"). That language prevents seller's form from being an acceptance. Because there was no acceptance of buyer's offer, buyer cannot be in breach of contract. The correct response is **B**.

QUESTION 9. A buyer of goods sends a purchase order to a seller on its form. The boilerplate on the form states that the seller is liable for consequential damages. The seller responds with an acknowledgment form that contains boilerplate that states that the seller is not liable for consequential damages. In addition, the seller's form states, "Acceptance is expressly made conditional on assent to the additional or different terms in this acknowledgment." After the forms are exchanged, the seller ships the goods and the buyer pays for them. The buyer then suffers consequential damages because of a breach by the seller. Is the seller liable for consequential damages?

A. No, because there is no contract between the parties.

B. No, because the seller's form governs.

C. Yes, because the buyer's form governs.

D. Yes, because the Code provides for consequential damages in § 2-714(3).

ANALYSIS. The language employed by the seller satisfies the requirement of § 2-207(1) after the comma ("unless acceptance is expressly made conditional on assent to the additional or different terms"). That language prevents seller's form from being an acceptance. Under § 2-207(3), however, there has been a contract formed by conduct. In that event, because the parties' writings did not agree on the consequential damages term, both parties' terms on that issue are knocked out and the consequential damages term is supplied by the Code. Therefore, the correct response is **D**.

4. Additional or different terms

Now that we have finished with the exception, let's go back to the general rule. The general rule states that when there are additional or different terms in the responding form, there is an acceptance and therefore a contract. But we still have to find the terms of that contract. For that purpose we look to subsection (2). That subsection begins by stating, "The additional terms are to be construed as proposals for addition to the contract." Because that language refers only to *additional* terms, we immediately wonder what becomes of the *different* terms. Unfortunately, the Code does not tell us, and courts have come up with three different solutions to fill this gap. The most popular is the *knockout rule*, under which both parties' different terms are knocked out and we read in the default rule from the Code. Another approach is to assume that the offeror would have objected to a different term, so the offeree's term is out and the offeror's term governs.

A third approach, which I think is the best approach, is to treat different terms the same as additional terms, as if the Code said, "The additional *or different* terms are to be construed as proposals for addition to the contract." This reading gains some support from Official Comment 3, which begins by stating, "Whether or not *additional or different* terms will become part of the agreement depends upon the provisions of subsection (2)." This view also makes sense because it can be difficult to tell the difference between an additional term and a different term. Suppose, for example, a buyer's form is silent on the issue of consequential damages. The seller's form states, "Seller is not liable for consequential damages." Is this an additional term? It would appear so, because no term on consequential damages is stated in buyer's form. But isn't it nevertheless one of the buyer's terms, because when a contract is silent on a term, we read in the default rules of the UCC, and the Code provides that a seller is liable for consequential damages? See §§ 2-712 to 2-714. If that term is impliedly present in buyer's form, then the terms in the two forms are different rather than additional. I don't seem to be winning that argument, so I won't belabor it.

We now explore what happens when there are *additional* terms in the acceptance, and if you accept the third view, this is also what happens when there are *different* terms in the acceptance. Under subsection (2), "[t]he additional terms are to be construed as proposals for addition to the contract." That is, the offeree is in effect saying to the offeror, "I propose that we make the terms I have added a part of the contract." Is that proposal accepted by the offeror? It depends. The next sentence states the general rule: "Between merchants such terms become part of the contract." So we have to determine if both parties are merchants. If they are, then the terms proposed by the offeree are presumptively part of the contract. What happens if both parties are *not* merchants? The Code does not tell us, but a logical implication is that if between merchants the proposed terms are presumptively part of the contract, then not between merchants the proposed terms are *not* presumptively part of the contract. This implication makes sense if we again think of why the Code sometimes has merchant rules. Merchants are sophisticated parties who are held to a higher standard. Therefore, the acceptance of a proposal that is automatic in the case of a merchant might reasonably require an affirmative assent if a nonmerchant were involved.

Assuming both parties are merchants, the proposed additional terms are presumptively part of the contract. However, the Code gives the offeror three chances to rebut this presumption and reject the offeree's proposed terms. The subsection goes on to say that the proposed terms become part of the contract unless

(a) the offer expressly limits acceptance to the terms of the offer;
(b) they materially alter it; or
(c) notification of objection to them has already been given or is given within a reasonable time after notice of them is received.

Under subsection (2)(a), the offeror's first opportunity to reject the proposed terms is when drafting the offer. Again, the prudent drafter will track the language of the statute, stating something like "this offer expressly limits acceptance to the terms of the offer." The offeror has a second opportunity under subsection (2)(c) to object to them when the acceptance is received. As a practical matter, however, offerors rarely do either of these things. Nevertheless, even if an offeror doesn't affirmatively act, it is deemed to have rejected a proposed term under subsection (2)(b) if the term proposed by the offeree "materially alters" the offeror's term.

Sometimes there is confusion about what you are examining to determine whether there is a material alteration. Do not look at the offeree's proposed terms *in toto* but look at each term individually; some may be in, supplementing the offeror's terms, and some may be out. Some examples of terms that materially alter and do not materially alter the offeror's terms are found in Official Comments 4 and 5. The intention of the drafters of the Code appears to be to prevent the offeror from being unreasonably surprised to find that the terms of the offer have dramatically changed. So, to use our example, if the buyer's offer was silent on consequential damages, and the additional term proposed by the seller stated that the buyer would recover no consequential damages, this is a dramatic difference. Because that proposed term materially alters the terms of the offer, the proposal would be deemed rejected, and the term in the offer would be the contract term between the parties. This analysis would then be repeated for each proposed term.

> **QUESTION 10.** In a contract for the sale of goods, a merchant offeror's form states, "This contract is governed by the law of Texas." The merchant offeree's form states, "This contract is governed by the law of Vermont." In a jurisdiction that employs the knockout rule, which jurisdiction supplies the governing law?
>
> A. Texas, because the offeror should be able to choose the applicable law.
> B. Texas, because Vermont is materially different.
> C. Vermont, because it is not materially different from Texas.
> D. Whichever state prevails when the Code choice of law rules are applied.

ANALYSIS. These are different terms, and under the knockout rule, both are out and the term supplied by the Code is in. The choice of law rule supplied by the Code is found in § 1-301. Under that rule, if the parties have not agreed on the governing law, "this Act applies to transactions bearing an appropriate relation to this state." Application of that rule would determine which state prevails. The correct response is **D**.

> **QUESTION 11.** In a contract for the sale of goods, a merchant offeror's form states, "This contract is governed by the law of Texas." The merchant offeree's form states, "This contract is governed by the law of Vermont." In a jurisdiction that treats different terms the same as additional terms, which jurisdiction supplies the governing law?
>
> A. Texas, because the offeror should be able to choose the applicable law.
> B. Texas, because Vermont is materially different.
> C. Vermont, because it is not materially different from Texas.
> D. Whichever state prevails when choice of law rules are applied.

ANALYSIS. *Note on test taking:* The responses to this question are identical to those of the previous question, so the correct response is likely to turn on a difference in facts. The difference is that the previous question asked us to apply the knockout rule, and this question asks us to treat different terms the same as additional terms.

Because we are treating different terms like additional terms, § 2-207(2) tells us that the different term (Vermont law) in the offeree's form is being proposed as an addition to the contract. Because both parties are merchants, the term presumptively becomes part of the contract unless it is eliminated in one of the three ways. Subsections (a) and (c) are not satisfied by the facts, so under subsection (b) it turns on whether Vermont choice of law materially alters Texas choice of law. Initially, one might think the two terms are materially different, but note that the issue is whose law will apply—and in both states the applicable law is the UCC, which by definition is unlikely to be materially different in Vermont (although it could be argued that a particular provision at issue in the case was materially different). So if the offeree's different term does not materially alter the offeror's term, then the offeree's term, Vermont law, is in the contract, and the offeror's term, Texas law, is out. The best response is **C**.

5. *Confirmation*

The reference to a "confirmation" in the first sentence of § 2-207(1) suggests another way in which contracts are formed that we should explore. Often the parties enter into an oral agreement, perhaps by telephone, and then one party confirms the oral agreement by sending a form to the other. We would have to look to a number of circumstances, including trade practice and course of dealing, to determine when a contract was formed. For example, the parties might be expressly or impliedly saying, "We don't have a contract until we have a written agreement." In that event, if they don't reach the point of having a single, signed document, then we would use our § 2-207(2) analysis to find the terms of the contract.

The other possibility is that they did make an oral agreement. It is likely that they discussed only the dickered terms orally, leaving the details to the confirmation. In that event, even though § 2-207(1) says that "a written confirmation . . . operates as an acceptance," it isn't really an acceptance because a contract has already been formed. Subsection 2-207(3) would not be relevant here because the contract is not established by their conduct; it is established orally.

Therefore, the written confirmation must be a proposal for additional terms under subsection (2). If both parties submit confirmations and each contains an additional term but states it differently, one approach would be to apply a knockout rule and knock them both out. This approach is supported by Official Comment 6. Some authorities find support in this Comment for the knockout rule in the case of different terms, but the Comment clearly applies only to confirmations. Another approach would be to examine each proposed term in the light of the three ways a term can be excluded from the contract under subsection (2). The method stated in subsection (2)(a) is unlikely to be applicable because the oral agreement probably did not contain any limitations. The method in subsection (2)(c) can be used, but as a practical matter parties usually do not do this. So it will come down to the issue stated in subsection (2)(b), whether the additional term materially alters the contract. Because the term is unlikely to be expressly stated in the oral agreement, the issue would be whether it materially alters the course of dealing, trade usage, or gap filling default rule that would be read into the oral agreement.

Sometimes only one party submits a written confirmation—usually a business that sends a confirmation to a consumer who has called up to order goods over the phone. Courts have analyzed this problem differently. Some courts have found that the parties had agreed to a "rolling contract," in which some of the terms were supplied during the telephone call and the remainder were supplied by the confirmation that arrived later. Others have analyzed the problem under § 2-207 and found that the merchant had proposed the additional terms to the consumer, and because the consumer is not a merchant, the terms did not become part of the contract because they were not affirmatively accepted. Compare *Hill v. Gateway 2000, Inc.*, 105 F.3d 1147 (7th Cir. 1997), with *Klocek v. Gateway, Inc.*, 104 F. Supp. 2d 1332 (D. Kan. 2000). The issue is largely moot because now the consumer would order the goods over the Internet and click to indicate agreement with the seller's terms—a practice that raises its own issues.

QUESTION 12. A merchant buyer calls a seller with whom she has not previously dealt and orders 10,000 widgets. The parties discuss the description of the goods, the price, and the delivery terms. The seller puts that information on a sales confirmation and sends it to the buyer. The buyer checks that the information is correct. When the goods arrive, the buyer claims that they are defective, but the seller disputes the claim. The buyer sues the seller, but the seller asks the court to dismiss the suit because the confirmation has an arbitration clause, requiring that the parties bring all claims to arbitration. Is the arbitration clause part of the parties' agreement?

A. Yes, because the agreement between the parties is found in the seller's confirmation.

B. Yes, because the seller's confirmation proposes arbitration as an additional term and between merchants such terms become part of the contract.

C. No, because the agreement between the parties is found in their oral conversation.

D. No, because arbitration materially alters the term agreed to in the oral conversation.

ANALYSIS. The parties reached an oral agreement that was then confirmed by the seller's confirmation. According to § 2-207(2), the additional term (arbitration) in the confirmation is a proposal for addition to the contract. Between merchants, the proposal becomes part of the contract unless it materially alters it. The default rule is that parties have a right to go to court and cannot be compelled to arbitrate unless they agree to arbitration, so that rule is implied as part of the oral agreement. Arbitration has been found to be materially different from use of the court system, so the seller's proposed term materially alters the terms of the oral agreement and is not part of the contract. The correct response is **D**. Response **C** is not correct because, although the oral agreement is a starting point, it would be supplemented by additional terms in the confirmation that do not materially alter it.

6. Conclusion

Let's step back and see if we can see the big picture that emerges from this analysis of the Battle of the Forms. Remember that at common law, the offeree's form was a counteroffer, so if the offeror did not protest, the offeree ended up getting all of its terms. But the bottom line under § 2-207 is that only minor terms in the offeree's form that don't change the offeror's terms significantly are going to end up as terms of the agreement. The offeree cannot rely on subterfuge to sneak significant changes in the offered terms past the offeror; if it wants materially different terms, it must bargain for them. The statute has returned the terms of the offeror to their preeminent position, so that once again "the offeror is the master of the offer."

It may be that the Battle of the Forms will soon be only a (fond) memory. With the rise of the Internet as a place where commerce takes place, a buyer must generally go to the seller's Web site and place its order on the seller's terms. We are back to the contract in a single document (or *record* as it is called in electronic commerce) and, except in the case of buyers with significant bargaining power, it is likely to be a contract of adhesion.

F.   Closers

> **QUESTION 13.** In a contract for the sale of goods, a merchant offeror's form states, "This contract is governed by the law of Texas." The merchant offeree's form states, "This contract is governed by the law of Vermont." In a jurisdiction that treats the offeror as having objected to different terms, which jurisdiction supplies the governing law?
>
> **A.** Texas, because the offeror should be able to choose the applicable law.
> **B.** Texas, because Vermont is materially different.
> **C.** Vermont, because it is not materially different.
> **D.** Whichever state prevails when choice of law rules are applied.

ANALYSIS. In this hypothetical, the offeree's form contains a different term. The Code in § 2-207(2) does not tell us what to do with different terms. In a jurisdiction that treats the offeror as having objected to different terms, the offeror's term would govern. The correct response is **A**. Note that the correct response is not **B**, because we are not determining the governing term under § 2-207(2)(b). Under this approach, the offeror gets its term whether the offeree's term is materially different or not.

QUESTION 14. A consumer calls a computer seller to purchase a computer. The essential terms, such as the description of the goods and the purchase price are discussed. When the computer arrives, the consumer finds a form purporting to be a contract. The contract contains some terms that are onerous, but not unconscionable. Is the consumer bound by them?

A. No. Because the contract is a confirmation, the terms are binding only if they do not materially alter the terms that would be implied by the default rules.

B. Yes, because as a practical matter the seller could not discuss all the terms over the telephone, the consumer should have expected additional terms to follow.

C. Yes, but as with all consumer contracts, the buyer has a three-day "cooling-off period" to decide whether to keep the goods.

D. It depends on the jurisdiction. Some would go with response A and others response B.

ANALYSIS. Response **C** is incorrect, although it is a popular myth. Consumer protection statutes that provide a three-day "cooling-off period" generally apply only to door-to-door sales and telephone solicitation sales initiated by the seller. This is law, so "it depends on the jurisdiction" is a pretty reliable answer. Response **A** represents the holding in *Klocek v. Gateway, Inc.*, 104 F. Supp. 2d 1332 (D. Kan. 2000). Response **B** represents the holding in *Hill v. Gateway 2000, Inc.*, 105 F.3d 1147 (7th Cir. 1997). The correct response is **D**.

QUESTION 15. A consumer wishing to purchase a computer goes to the seller's Web site to place an order. The buyer fills in the blanks that describe the goods and the quantity. The buyer is given an opportunity to read the terms and conditions, but without reading them, he clicks the button labeled "I accept." What are the terms of the contract that has been formed?

> **A.** The terms in seller's terms and conditions.
> **B.** The terms in the buyer's counteroffer.
> **C.** We would have to perform an analysis of the additional and different terms under § 2-207 to answer the question.
> **D.** Where the parties' terms don't agree, the terms are the default terms of the UCC.

ANALYSIS. Under these facts, the buyer has agreed to the terms offered by the seller, so the best response is **A**. Because the buyer does not have an opportunity to bargain for terms, this transaction represents the modern contract of adhesion. The buyer has no opportunity to negotiate for terms prior to entering the contract. After formation, if the buyer objects to a term, it may argue that the term is unconscionable or contrary to the buyer's reasonable expectations. Note that this is becoming the prevailing method by which goods are bought and sold, so the issue raised in Question 14 may soon be moot.

 # Burnham's picks

Question 1	C
Question 2	A
Question 3	A
Question 4	C
Question 5	D
Question 6	B
Question 7	D
Question 8	B
Question 9	D
Question 10	D
Question 11	C
Question 12	D
Question 13	A
Question 14	D
Question 15	A

6

The Parol Evidence Rule

A. Introduction

The parol evidence rule is complex, but probably not as hard to understand as it is sometimes made out to be. Most of the time it arises when there is a signed, written agreement between the parties. Then one party offers evidence of a promise or agreement that is not found in that written agreement and claims that it should be considered along with the writing. Such evidence is called *parol evidence* or *extrinsic evidence,* meaning it is found outside the writing itself. A useful first step is to ask for what purpose the evidence is being offered. It might be offered for any of the following reasons:

- To supplement or contradict the terms of the written agreement
- To prove that there has been an additional agreement supported by consideration
- To show that the agreement is not effective
- To show that performance is not due
- To prove that there has been a modification of the agreement
- To explain or interpret the terms of the written agreement
- To offer evidence of course of performance, course of dealing, or trade usage

It is only in connection with the first of these purposes that the parol evidence rule applies. In other words, in all of these situations there may be an offer of *parol evidence,* but that does not mean the *parol evidence rule* applies. We will look first at the application of the rule, and then return to those situations where the rule does not apply.

B. The parol evidence rule

1. Background

One authority said of the parol evidence rule, "There are few things darker or more full of subtle difficulties." But it isn't really all that hard. What we are trying to do is find the contract. You might think it is easy to find the contract. If the parties make an oral agreement, like John selling his Ted Williams autographed baseball to Mary for $400, part of the contract resides in the memories of the parties and any witnesses. There may be a fact question as to exactly what they said, but as a matter of law it is not too hard to find the agreement. That oral agreement will, of course, be supplemented by the gap fillers.

On the other hand, John and Mary might write down their agreement. There might then be less of a fact question as to what the terms of their agreement were. But what if they wrote it down and when John tendered the ball, Mary said, "Wait a minute, you said you would include a picture of Ted Williams with it." Two questions might arise. First is the fact question. John might deny he ever said that. Even if he admits he said it, however, he might still raise an issue. He might say, "Sure I said it. But I said lots of things. We talked about the weather and the latest baseball scores, but the things that counted, the things that we wanted to include in our agreement, we wrote down. Anything we didn't write down isn't part of the agreement."

If John makes this argument, then we have a parol evidence rule issue. The question is, where do we find the contract—is it found just in the writing, or is it found in the writing plus other agreements or representations that may have been made, usually orally? As we further explore in Chapter 8, with the exception of the Statute of Frauds, there is no requirement that a contract or the terms of a contract be written. To some extent, therefore, it makes sense to admit the parol evidence as a matter of law, and then argue whether as a matter of fact the statement was made. On the other hand, business practices and business relationships favor having the agreement in writing. For example, even though a salesperson told the buyer of a used car, "You can bring it in for the next 30 days and we'll fix anything that goes wrong," the business itself might not want to stand behind that representation. It wants to administer the contract based on what is written in its standard form without having to worry about different terms created by each salesperson. The sanctity of the writing is particularly important when contracts are bought and sold. We discuss this topic in Chapter 19. The buyer of the contract wants to know by looking at it the extent of its obligations; it would not be efficient for the buyer to have to inquire about and keep track of oral understandings. Moreover, there is a danger of perjury if a party could readily claim the existence of additional terms.

It is against this background that we explore the parol evidence rule. The rule is not saying that an agreement can't be found partly in writing and partly in oral statements. Rather, it is saying that where it is found is a question of the parties' intent—and finding the intent of the parties is always problematic. Here is the rule as found in § 2-202:

> **§ 2-202. Final Written Expression: Parol or Extrinsic Evidence.**
>
> Terms with respect to which the confirmatory memoranda of the parties agree or which are otherwise set forth in a writing intended by the parties as a final expression of their agreement with respect to such terms as are included therein may not be contradicted by evidence of any prior agreement or of a contemporaneous oral agreement but may be explained or supplemented
>
> (a) by course of performance, course of dealing, or usage of trade (Section 1-303), and
>
> (b) by evidence of consistent additional terms unless the court finds the writing to have been intended also as a complete and exclusive statement of the terms of the agreement.

2. Partial integration

Let's work through the language of this section. Most of the time, after the parties negotiate, they set forth their agreement in a writing. According to the Code provision, if they do so, and if their writing is intended as a "final expression of their agreement," then they cannot offer evidence to contradict the terms that are included. The fact that it is final means that negotiations are over and the deal is concluded. A writing signed by the parties when negotiations are over is at a minimum a *partial integration,* for the writing is considered to be a final integration of the parties' understandings with respect to the terms it contains. This is not to say, however, that their agreement does not contain other terms. For example, if the writing between John and Mary for the sale of the baseball stated, "No picture is included," then parol evidence of a promised picture of Ted Williams would be excluded. The burden is on the parties to make sure that if oral statements are made that contradict the writing, those changes are made on the face of the written agreement so that it reflects that understanding.

Suppose the writing said nothing about a picture. Now the offered evidence does not contradict the writing; it supplements it. If the agreement is found partly in the writing and partly in the oral understanding, then these two parts can coexist. The parol evidence rule would not exclude admission of this evidence.

QUESTION 1. During negotiations, the seller of a boat promises the buyer that the engine will be warranted to be free of defects for a period of two years. The parties then sign a written agreement that contains a warranty term with standard disclaimers of express and implied warranties, followed by language stating that "seller warrants that the engine will be free of defects for a period of one year." After 14 months, the engine develops problems because of a defect. A court finds that the writing is not the complete and exclusive statement of the terms of the agreement. Is the seller liable under the warranty?

A. Yes, because the parties did not intend their writing to be final as to the warranty.
B. Yes, because the oral promise does not contradict the terms of the writing.
C. No, because the writing was a final expression of their agreement as to the warranty.
D. No, because the buyer would have a claim even under the written warranty.

ANALYSIS. The parties had completed their negotiations and signed a written agreement. Such an agreement is considered final as to the terms that are incorporated therein. Here, that would include the one-year warranty term. The buyer is offering evidence of an oral understanding that contradicts a term in the writing. This evidence is excluded under the parol evidence rule. Note that it does not matter whether, as a matter of fact, the promise was actually made, for it is excluded as a matter of law. Therefore, the term in the writing supplies the warranty and under that term, the seller is not liable. The correct response is **C**.

QUESTION 2. During negotiations between two friends over the sale of a boat, the seller tells the buyer that the engine will be warranted to be free of defects for a period of two years. The parties finally sign a written agreement that contains no warranty terms. After 14 months, the engine develops problems because of a defect. A court finds that the writing is a partial integration and that the promise was actually made. Is the seller liable under the warranty?

A. Yes, because the gap fillers will supply an implied warranty.
B. Yes, because the oral promise does not contradict the terms of the writing.
C. No, because the writing was a final expression of their agreement as to the warranty.
D. No, because the buyer would have a claim even under the written warranty.

ANALYSIS. The parties had completed their negotiations and signed a written agreement. Such an agreement is considered final as to the terms that are incorporated therein. Because the agreement is only a partial integration, however, the writing is not complete and there may be other terms that are not found in the writing. In that event, the terms are admissible if they do not contradict the writing. Here, the alleged oral term does not contradict the writing, so it is admissible under the parol evidence rule. That only means that as a matter of law it cannot be excluded as evidence. The party who offered the evidence still needs to prove as a matter of fact that the statement was made, but you are told that the court did find that the promise was actually made. Therefore, the oral term supplies the warranty and under that term, the seller is liable. The correct response is **B**.

As we will see in the next section, the hard part is making the determination of whether a writing is final and complete. One test, articulated in Official Comment 4, is that "[i]f the additional terms are such that, if agreed upon, they would certainly have been included in the document," then they must be excluded. Here, the court might have determined that because the parties were friends, they would not certainly have included the term in the writing.

3. *Complete integration*

We have just seen that if the writing is a partial integration of the parties' agreement, then it "may be . . . supplemented . . . (b) by evidence of consistent additional terms." But there is an exception stated in § 2-202(b). In fact, the exception tends to swallow up the rule, for the exception states that the writing may be supplemented "unless the court finds the writing to have been intended also as a complete and exclusive statement of the terms of the agreement." Under the exception, even terms that supplement the agreement are not admissible if the court finds that the writing was intended to be "complete and exclusive." Such a writing is known as a *full integration.*

If a writing is a full integration, the writing is considered the last word as to the agreement the parties made, and evidence of any extrinsic promises or agreed terms, even those that do not contradict the terms of the writing, will be excluded. Although this rule is generally accepted, it begs the question, for the difficult issue is to determine whether or not the writing is a full integration. The Code says that depends on what was "intended." But that answer is not satisfactory, for now the question becomes, how do we determine the intent of the parties? Most authorities agree that only objective evidence of intent may be offered. For example, a party may not testify, "This is what I had in mind when I signed the agreement." Nevertheless, there is still an issue as to what objective evidence may be considered.

The first place to look in determining whether the writing is a full integration is to the writing itself. One thing to look for is a *merger clause* or *integration clause.* Just like it sounds, this is a term that states that the parties intend the writing to be a complete and exclusive statement of their understanding. Here is an example of a merger clause:

> **Parol evidence**. This writing is intended by the parties as a final expression of their agreement and is intended also as a complete and exclusive statement of the terms of their agreement.

Nevertheless, many authorities say that the presence of a merger clause is not conclusive on the issue of integration. If it is found buried in boilerplate text at the end of a consumer contract, for example, it does not seem to be good evidence of the parties' intentions. Another thing to look for is whether the agreement appears to be carefully negotiated and drafted. If it was, then even if it lacks a merger clause, it was probably the parties' intention to include their final and complete agreement in the writing. A court is very likely to find that a writing that resulted from negotiation between sophisticated parties was intended to be their complete and exclusive agreement; it is less likely to draw the same conclusion when the writing is a contract of adhesion signed by a consumer. To many courts, therefore, the presence of a merger clause is a factor to consider, but it is not determinative. Official Comment 3 to Amended Article 2 provides:

> 3. Whether a writing is final, and whether a final writing is also complete, are issues for the court. This section rejects any assumption that because a record has been worked out which is final on some matters, it is to be taken as including all the matters agreed upon. If the additional terms are those that, if agreed upon, would certainly have been included in the document in the view of the court, then evidence of their alleged making must be kept from the trier of fact. *This section is not intended to suggest what should be the evidentiary strength of a merger clause as evidence of the mutual intent that the record be final and complete. That determination depends upon the particular circumstances of each case.*

A final objective test is to ask, in the words of Official Comment 3 to § 2-202, whether "the additional terms are such that, if agreed upon, they would certainly have been included in the document in the view of the court." For example, the buyer and seller of a widget have signed a writing that exhaustively provides the terms of their agreement. The buyer claims that there is an additional warranty term that is not included in the writing.

A court might find that reasonable parties who exhaustively detailed their agreement would have certainly included a warranty term in it. Note that this is an objective test. The inquiry is not whether these parties actually made the agreement, but whether reasonable parties in their circumstances would have done so.

QUESTION 3. ABC Corp. and XYZ Corp. negotiated a detailed multi-page agreement over a period of weeks that did not contain a merger clause. After the agreement was signed, seller sought to admit evidence of a term that supplemented the agreement. Should the evidence be barred by the parol evidence rule?

A. Yes, because the writing was intended to be a complete and exclusive statement of the terms of the agreement.

B. Yes, because the evidence contradicts the writing.

C. No, because there is no merger clause in the agreement.

D. No, because the writing was not intended to be a final expression of their agreement.

ANALYSIS. Recall that the intention of the parties is the key factor in determining whether a writing is intended to be complete and exclusive. Often, a merger clause is evidence of that the intent, but here there is no merger clause. On the other hand, we are told that this was a detailed agreement negotiated over a period of weeks by two corporations. It seems to me that those facts and circumstances indicate the intent of the parties was to embody their agreement in the writing. The presence or absence of a merger clause may be a strong factor in ascertaining the intent, but it is not determinative. See, e.g., *Arb, Inc. v. E-Systems, Inc.*, 663 F.2d 189 (D.C. Cir. 1980), in which the court stated:

> Here, the bulk of the evidence suggests that the parties intended the written contract to be the complete and exclusive statement of the terms of their agreement. The length of the contract, its exhaustive detail, and the prolonged period of negotiation preceding its signing, collectively considered, support this conclusion.

The best response is **A.**

QUESTION 4. During negotiations, the seller of a boat promised the buyer that the engine was warranted to be free of defects for a period of two years. The parties eventually signed a written agreement that contained no express warranty terms. Fourteen months after the purchase, the engine developed problems because of a defect. A court found that the writing is a complete and exclusive statement of the terms of the agreement. Is the seller liable under the oral warranty?

A. It remains to be determined as a question of fact whether the promise was made.

B. Yes, because the oral promise does not contradict the terms of the writing.

C. No, because the writing was a complete and exclusive expression of their agreement.

D. No, because the buyer would have a claim even under the written warranty.

ANALYSIS. The court has determined that the agreement is a full integration. Therefore, no evidence may be offered to contradict or to supplement it. Here, even though the evidence supplements, it is excluded. If it is excluded as a matter of law, then it doesn't matter whether, as a question of fact, the agreement was actually made. The correct response is **C**. Some say that in cases like this the parol evidence rule elevates efficiency at the expense of truth.

4. Exceptions

We have seen that a parol evidence rule issue arises when the extrinsic evidence is offered for the purpose of supplementing or contradicting the terms of the written agreement. The rule then determines whether that evidence is admissible. If extrinsic evidence is offered for other purposes, the rule does not apply. These purposes include the following:

- To prove that there has been an additional agreement supported by consideration
- To show that the agreement is not effective
- To show that performance is not due
- To prove that there has been a modification of the agreement
- To explain or interpret the terms of the written agreement
- To offer evidence of course of performance, course of dealing, or trade usage

a. Additional agreement.   There is nothing wrong with parties having two contracts, one oral and one written. Assume, for example, that when John and Mary were discussing the sale of the baseball, Mary asked for a picture of Ted Williams. John said, "I'll include that for another five dollars," and Mary agreed. They then wrote up an agreement for the sale of the baseball that did not mention the picture. Mary should be able to prove the existence of the picture agreement because there is nothing wrong with their having made two agreements: a written agreement for the sale of a baseball for $400, and an oral agreement for the sale of a picture for $5.

Now, assume instead that when John and Mary were discussing the sale of the baseball, Mary asked for a picture of Ted Williams. John said, "No problem. I'll include that at no additional charge." They then wrote up an agreement for the sale of the baseball that did not mention the picture. Now the promise of the picture does not stand by itself, for it lacks consideration. The only chance Mary has of enforcing it is to prove that it was part of the deal—that she was paying a $400 consideration for a baseball and a picture. This is now a true parol evidence rule issue because the case will turn on whether the written agreement was intended to be "complete and exclusive." If it was complete and exclusive, Mary will lose, but if it was not complete and exclusive, then evidence of supplementary terms is admissible.

b. Formation issue.   If a written contract stated, "No one held a gun to my head and made me sign this contract," that term would obviously not bar the person from offering evidence that the other party held a gun to his head and made him sign the contract. Duress—like other formation defenses, such as fraud, mistake, unconscionability, lack of capacity, and lack of consideration—may be offered even if an agreement was intended to be final and exclusive. The reason is that in these cases, the evidence is offered not to prove a term of the contract, but to prove that there was a vitiating factor that prevented formation of a contract. The formation issue that most frequently arises is fraud. To prove fraud, a party often introduces the promise, not to show that it is part of the agreement but to show that it induced him to make the agreement. This can be problematic when the subject matter of the fraud is itself addressed in the contract. This is because one of the elements of fraud is reasonable reliance on the representation. It can be argued that a person should not reasonably rely on a representation that differs from the express language of the contract.

c. Condition.   Sometimes parties have an understanding that the contract will not be performed unless and until some event occurs, and that condition is sometimes omitted from the contract. For example, the seller of a car may agree to sell her car to the buyer only after she gets a new car. Even though the condition is not stated in the contract, courts usually admit this evidence, for it shows that the parties did not intend their performances to become due unless some event occurred first. This rule is found in Restatement § 217:

> Where the parties to a written agreement agree orally that performance of the agreement is subject to the occurrence of a stated condition, the agreement is not integrated with respect to the oral condition.

d. Modification.   Many times parties will put a term in a contract that states, "Modifications are not binding unless in a signed writing. Oral modifications are not enforceable." Such a *no oral modification clause* (see § 2-209(2)) serves a function similar to that of the parol evidence rule in that it channels the parties' behavior so they are encouraged to put everything in writing. However, the question of whether evidence of an oral modification is admissible is not a parol evidence rule issue because of the timing. With the parol evidence rule we are trying to find the agreement of the parties. Therefore, the rule excludes agreements that were made prior to the parties' entering into the written agreement. (The statute also refers to "contemporaneous agreements," but these are rare.) A modification is an agreement that is made *after* the parties entered into the written agreement. Such an agreement raises modification issues; it does not raise parol evidence rule issues. We examine modification in Chapter 7.

e. Interpretation.   Once we have used the parol evidence rule to find the agreement of the parties, questions often arise as to what the language in that agreement means. An agreement has to be found before it can be interpreted. The issue of interpretation might, for example, relate to the oral part of an agreement that is not fully integrated. Interpretation issues arise when language is *ambiguous,* meaning it is susceptible to more than one meaning. All courts agree that parol evidence should be admitted for the purpose of resolving an ambiguity in language. They disagree about whether parol evidence should be admitted for the purpose of determining whether there is an ambiguity. Some courts believe they can determine whether language is ambiguous merely by looking at the language. This approach is often called the *plain meaning test.* Other courts believe that they must admit parol evidence for the purpose of determining whether language is ambiguous. This approach is often called the *context test* because it presumes that language has meaning only in context, and the extrinsic evidence can show the context. We address other aspects of interpretation in the next chapter. Although these questions involve the admissibility of *parol evidence,* they do not invoke the *parol evidence rule,* for the rule determines whether a term is part of the agreement, which is a different question from the meaning of terms that are part of the agreement.

f. Course of performance, course of dealing, or trade usage.   Subsection (a) of § 2-202 expressly states that evidence of course of performance, course of dealing, and trade usage to supplement the agreement should not be barred even if the parties intended the agreement to be final and complete. Official Comment 2 states:

> 2. Paragraph (a) makes admissible evidence of course of dealing, usage of trade and course of performance to explain or supplement the terms of any writing stating the agreement of the parties in order that the true understanding of the parties as to the agreement may be reached. Such writings are to be read on the assumption that the course of prior dealings between the parties and the usages of trade were taken for granted when the document was phrased. Unless carefully negated they have become an element of the meaning of the words used. Similarly, the course of actual performance by the parties is considered the best indication of what they intended the writing to mean.

This Comment makes sense, because parties in a trade or accustomed to dealing with each other probably make unconscious assumptions that the practices they are familiar with will be incorporated in the contract. Employing freedom of contract, the parties are free to provide that course of performance, course of dealing, and trade usage shall *not* be read into their contract, but it would be unwise for them to do so because parties are often unconscious of the fact that their agreement implicitly incorporates familiar usages. We look more closely at evidence of course of performance, course of dealing, and trade usage in the next chapter.

QUESTION 5. A widget seller negotiates with a buyer for the purchase of 100 widgets for $10,000, with delivery 30 days from the signing of the agreement. After the parties sign the agreement, which contains a merger clause, the buyer asks the seller if delivery could be in 20 days and the seller says, "Yes, I promise we will do that." The seller does not deliver until 30 days from signing. The buyer sues the seller and the seller seeks to bar the evidence that the seller promised delivery in 20 days. Will the evidence be excluded under the parol evidence rule?

A. Yes, because it contradicts a term of the written agreement.
B. Yes, because it supplements a written agreement that is complete and exclusive.
C. No, because it is offered for the purpose of interpreting the writing.
D. No, because it is offered on an issue of modification.

ANALYSIS. The key here is the fact that "[a]fter the parties sign the agreement . . . the buyer asks the seller. . . ." When the issue is parol evidence, there is always an understanding that is "prior or contemporaneous" to the signing of the agreement. Here, the understanding came *after* the signing of the agreement. Therefore it is not a parol evidence rule issue but a modification issue. The correct response is **D.**

QUESTION 6. A business has ordered a new delivery truck and puts its old truck up for sale. The parties agree on all the terms of the sale, but the seller says, "We need this truck until our new one comes, so we won't give you delivery until then." The buyer says, "No problem." They both sign a writing that contains the complete and exclusive statement of the terms of their agreement. The buyer then demands immediate delivery of the truck. The seller reminds the buyer of their oral understanding and the buyer says, "Ha Ha! I don't see that in the contract." Is the evidence of the oral understanding admissible?

A. No, because the writing is a complete and exclusive statement of the terms of their agreement.
B. No, because reasonable parties would have included this understanding in the writing.
C. Yes, because the evidence shows that performance is subject to an oral condition.
D. Yes, because the evidence shows a defense to contract formation.

ANALYSIS. You may agree with response **B.** That response is subsumed in response **A,** however, because **B** is merely evidence of **A.** Nevertheless, in this case the parol evidence is offered for the purpose of proving a condition, and most courts will admit evidence of a condition even if the writing is a complete and exclusive statement of the terms of the parties' agreement. The correct response is **C.** Note that UCC § 2-202 does not address this issue. Under § 1-103(b), however, the Code is supplemented by the common law, and this is a common law rule, as stated in Restatement § 217.

C.   Closers

> **QUESTION 7.** ABC Corp. and XYZ Corp. negotiated a multi-page agreement over a period of weeks that contained a merger clause. During negotiations, ABC said, "We won't agree to this deal unless you agree to the language we have proposed in Paragraph 13. This is a deal-breaker." XYZ reluctantly agreed to include the language proposed in ABC's Paragraph 13. When the final agreement was typed up, though, the typist inadvertently left out that language and both sides signed, not realizing it was not there. After the agreement was signed, ABC discovered the problem and asked XYZ to include the language in the agreement. XYZ refused to include it, citing the parol evidence rule. Is the admission of this evidence barred by the parol evidence rule?
>
> **A.** Yes, because it would supplement the terms of an agreement that was complete and exclusive.
> **B.** No, because it is offered for the purpose of modifying the agreement.
> **C.** No, because it evidences a mistake in formation.
> **D.** No, because it evidences duress on the part of ABC.

ANALYSIS. The evidence is offered on a formation issue. ABC is attempting to show that the agreement the parties signed is not the one they agreed to and should be reformed to conform to their agreement. This is an issue of mistake, called mistake in integration, and courts do allow the evidence to come in for this purpose. The correct response is **C**.

> **QUESTION 8.** Buyer and seller negotiated a detailed multi-page agreement over a period of weeks that contained a merger clause. After the agreement was signed, the seller discovered that the agreement stated, "Delivery shall begin in days." Seller claimed that during negotiations, the parties had talked about delivery in 60 days but the buyer claimed the discussion involved 30 days. Is evidence of the parties' negotiations admissible?
>
> **A.** Yes, because the writing was not intended to be a complete and final expression of their agreement as to the delivery date.
> **B.** Yes, because the issue is one of interpretation of an ambiguous term.
> **C.** No, because the agreement was intended to be complete and exclusive.
> **D.** No, because the evidence would contradict a term of the writing.

ANALYSIS. It seems to me that this agreement cannot be final on the delivery term because it is clear from the face of the agreement that the parties did not reach agreement on that term. Therefore, the written agreement is only a partial integration. It may be final and complete on everything else, but not on delivery, so evidence can be admitted on that issue. The best response is **A**.

QUESTION 9. A consumer is test driving a car of a used car dealership. She hears a sound under the car and asks the salesperson about it. The salesperson says, "Don't worry about that. We stand behind the cars we sell. If anything goes wrong in the next 60 days, we will fix it free of charge." Relieved, the consumer agrees to buy the car. Two days later, the transmission fails. She brings it back to the dealer and tells the manager what the salesperson said. The manager tells her that the salespeople aren't allowed to negotiate terms and all the terms are found in the writing. He points out that the writing effectively disclaims all warranties and conspicuously states that the car is sold "AS IS." He also points out a merger clause that states that there are no promises or understandings other than those found in the writing. Is the consumer likely to recover?

A. Yes, because the evidence does not contradict the writing.
B. Yes, because the parol evidence rule does not apply to consumers.
C. No, because the writing is a partial integration and the evidence does not contradict the writing.
D. No, because the writing is a full integration.

ANALYSIS. This is a very common sad story. A court must first determine whether the agreement is fully integrated in the writing. The writing contains a merger clause and extensive language concerning warranty, so in context it appears to be complete and exclusive. The best response is **D**. It is true that a court might find that the boilerplate language is not determinative on the issue of integration. Even if the consumer overcomes that hurdle, however, and the agreement is found to be only partially integrated, a court will still not admit evidence that contradicts the writing, and here it contradicts the writing. So in most courts, the consumer will not prevail.

The buyer might also claim fraud. The salesperson made a statement that was not true in order to induce the buyer to purchase the car. In many jurisdictions this claim will not be successful because one of the elements of fraud is reasonable reliance on the statement. If the consumer planned to rely on the statement, why didn't she get it included in the written contract? Note that if fraud is successful, the result is that no contract is formed. That would be fine with the buyer in this case, but in many cases the buyer does not want to rescind the contract, but wants the spoken promise to be enforced as part of the deal.

A number of years ago the Federal Trade Commission conducted a study of the practices of used car dealers and found that making this kind of statement was a common practice. The result was a regulation requiring that a "Buyers Guide" sticker be attached to the side rear window of the car being sold. Among other things, the sticker states whether the car is sold with a warranty or not and contains this warning: "IMPORTANT. Spoken promises are difficult to enforce. Ask the dealer to put all promises in writing." Although this language may help the consumer who reads it and acts accordingly, it will probably work against the consumer who does not heed it and then seeks to introduce parol evidence. It appears to me that the language enhances the dealer's argument that a reasonable customer would have understood that the writing contained the complete and exclusive agreement of the parties. The burden is on the party to whom such statements are made to get them in the riting.

 # Burnham's picks

Question 1	**C**
Question 2	**B**
Question 3	**A**
Question 4	**C**
Question 5	**D**
Question 6	**C**
Question 7	**C**
Question 8	**A**
Question 9	**D**

7

Interpretation and Modification

A. Introduction

We saw in Chapter 6.A that extrinsic evidence (evidence outside the writing) is offered for many purposes. The parol evidence rule applies only when a party offers a term that was agreed to before (or at the same time) the agreement was signed for the purpose of proving that that term is part of the agreement. However, we saw in that chapter that extrinsic evidence may be offered for other purposes. We now look more closely at some of these other purposes. Frequently, evidence is offered to interpret the terms of the agreement. Also, evidence is offered of course of performance, course of dealing, or usage of trade. Furthermore, after they have executed their agreement, the parties are free to change it. If a party offers evidence of a change that was made after the agreement was signed, then we have a modification issue.

B. Interpretation

As we saw in Chapter 6, the parol evidence rule does not generally bar evidence when offered for the purpose of interpreting the agreement. We use the parol evidence rule to determine whether the agreement is found only in the writing or is found in the writing plus other understandings. Once we have made that determination, questions may arise as to what the language in that agreement means. The principal goal of interpretation is to carry out the intention of the parties. It therefore does not make sense to impose a meaning on them, even if that meaning comes from an objective source such as a dictionary. Nor does it make sense to impose a meaning that one of the parties had in mind when the agreement was signed. Rather, the meaning should be determined on the basis of the language the parties used in the commercial context in which they used it. Official Comment 1 to § 1-303 explains:

> 1. The Uniform Commercial Code rejects both the "lay-dictionary" and the "conveyancer's" reading of a commercial agreement. Instead the meaning of the agreement of the parties is to be determined by the language used by them and by their action, read and interpreted in the light of commercial practices and other surrounding circumstances. The measure and background for interpretation are set by the commercial context, which may explain and supplement even the language of a formal or final writing.

Frequently, that commercial context is found in course of performance, course of dealing, or usage of trade. We now look at these concepts in detail.

QUESTION 1. A buyer and a seller of widgets have entered into a written contract that was prepared by the buyer and is the complete and exclusive statement of the terms of their agreement. The buyer claims that a term in the agreement is ambiguous and wants to offer evidence to prove its meaning. The seller claims that the term is not ambiguous and resists the buyer's offer of evidence. What should the court do?

A. Exclude the evidence because the writing is complete and exclusive.
B. Determine whether the term is ambiguous.
C. Admit the evidence for the purpose of determining the meaning as a question of fact.
D. Interpret the term against the buyer, as the buyer was the drafter.

ANALYSIS. Response **A** is not correct because when we say that the writing is "complete and exclusive," we are saying that all the terms are found in the writing. However, that says nothing about the meaning of those terms. To resolve an issue of interpretation, the court will first determine as a matter of law whether the term is ambiguous. Therefore, the correct response is **B**. Note that I have bypassed the issue of what test will be used to determine whether the term is ambiguous because that differs from state to state. If the court determines that the term is ambiguous as a matter of law, then evidence may come in to prove its meaning as a question of fact. Response **C** is incorrect because it represents the second step in the process. One consideration in determining that fact question is which party drafted the agreement. Response **D** is incorrect because before the evidence comes in to determine what the meaning is as a question of fact, it must be determined whether the language is ambiguous as a matter of law.

QUESTION 2. A buyer and a seller entered into a fully integrated contract for the sale of "1,000 red pens." The seller tendered pens that had a silver body but wrote with red ink. The buyer claimed that the parties intended that the contract called for pens with a red body. Which of the following facts should be determinative of the outcome in the case?

A. The seller had in mind pens that wrote with red ink when the contract was signed.
B. In the pen business, the color generally describes the color of the ink.
C. The contract was fully integrated.
D. During pre-contract negotiations, the seller had sent the buyer a color photograph of the pen.

ANALYSIS.   Interpretation issues arise when language is *ambiguous,* meaning it is susceptible to more than one meaning. Here the language can reasonably be interpreted either way. Even though the contract was fully integrated, it makes no sense to refuse to admit evidence for the purpose of resolving an ambiguity in language, so **C** is not a correct response. Response **A** describes subjective evidence. It is not reliable, and it does not indicate that the parties agreed on that meaning. Response **B** describes trade usage. It is reliable, and in the absence of agreement by the parties, would probably be the best response. However, when there is objective evidence that indicates what the parties have intended the language to mean, that evidence should be given greater weight. The best response is **D**.

C.   The Code hierarchy of interpretation

We saw in Chapter 6 that, according to § 2-202(a), the written agreement "may be explained or supplemented (a) by course of performance, course of dealing, or usage of trade (Section 1-303)." It is important to understand the meaning of the Code concepts of course of performance, course of dealing, and usage of trade, and how the concepts interrelate. Let's first look at the definitions as found in § 1-303(a)–(d):

§ 1-303. Course of Performance, Course of Dealing, and Usage of Trade.

(a) A "course of performance" is a sequence of conduct between the parties to a particular transaction that exists if:

(1) the agreement of the parties with respect to the transaction involves repeated occasions for performance by a party; and

(2) the other party, with knowledge of the nature of the performance and opportunity for objection to it, accepts the performance or acquiesces in it without objection.

(b) A "course of dealing" is a sequence of conduct concerning previous transactions between the parties to a particular transaction that is fairly to be regarded as establishing a common basis of understanding for interpreting their expressions and other conduct.

(c) A "usage of trade" is any practice or method of dealing having such regularity of observance in a place, vocation, or trade as to justify an expectation that it will be observed with respect to the transaction in question. The existence and scope of such a usage are to be proved as facts. If it is established that such a usage is embodied in a trade code or similar record, the interpretation of the record is a question of law.

(d) A course of performance or course of dealing between the parties or usage of trade in the vocation or trade in which they are engaged or of which they are or should be aware is relevant in ascertaining the meaning of the parties' agreement, may give particular meaning to specific terms of the agreement, and may supplement or qualify the terms of the agreement. A usage of trade applicable in the place in which part of the performance under the agreement is to occur may be so utilized as to that part of the performance.

A "course of performance" under § 1-303(a) arises in a single transaction when there are repeated occasions for performance. The fact that one party repeatedly accepts a performance without objection leads the other party to believe that its performance is acceptable. For example, an installment sales agreement provides that "the buyer shall inspect each delivery within a reasonable time." The buyer inspects the first delivery on the ninth day after it is received, the second delivery on the eighth day, and the third delivery on the tenth day. When the buyer has not inspected the fourth delivery by the third day, the seller claims that the buyer is not inspecting within a reasonable time. However, the buyer's course of performance, in which the seller has acquiesced, has established the meaning of "reasonable time" under the contract. The seller will not be successful.

A "course of dealing" under § 1-303(b) arises when the same parties have had previous transactions with each other. It is assumed that understandings arrived at through the performance of those past agreements will carry over to the present agreement. For example, if the parties described in the previous paragraph enter into another agreement that contains the same term, it is presumed that the previous understanding—that the buyer has eight to ten days to inspect—will carry over. If the seller doesn't agree with that understanding, he is free to bargain for an express term in the new agreement that provides something like "buyer must complete inspection within three days from delivery."

A "usage of trade" arises under § 1-303(c) when a practice is so common in a particular place or particular trade that it is presumed to be part of the agreement. For example, if buyers and sellers in this business generally allow seven to ten days for the buyer to inspect, then it will be assumed that that term is part of the contract. Of course, a party may claim it is not familiar with the trade or may contest the usage. For that reason, § 1-303(g) provides that notice must be given that evidence of trade usage will be presented:

> (g) Evidence of a relevant usage of trade offered by one party is not admissible unless that party has given the other party notice that the court finds sufficient to prevent unfair surprise to the other party.

These sources of meaning are always admissible to supplement or explain the terms of the writing, even if the agreement is fully integrated. Let's apply these concepts in the context of the case of *Frigaliment Importing Co. v. B.N.S. International Sales Corp.*, 190 F. Supp. 116 (S.D.N.Y. 1960), the notorious "chicken" case, which you probably remember from first-year Contracts. The buyer and seller disputed the meaning of *chicken*, a term that was used but was not expressly defined in their contract. The buyer then offered evidence of usage of trade to show that among those in the poultry trade, *chicken* meant *broiler*. You may recall that the seller countered by arguing that because it was new to the business, trade usage was not binding on it. The court responded that even so, a trade usage would be binding if (1) there was actual knowledge, or (2) there was imputed knowledge because the usage was so common. Both sides then presented evidence on whether the usages were so common that everyone knew them.

There was no previous contract between the parties in *Frigaliment*, but let's assume there was. If that previous contract also used the term *chicken*, and in performing that contract the seller had shipped broilers without objection, then a course of dealing would have been established and we would presume that *chicken* meant *broilers* under the new contract as well.

A course of performance arises when there is more than one performance under the contract. This situation did arise in *Frigaliment*, because the seller made an initial shipment of stewing chicken that the buyer accepted. The seller argued that this gave rise to a course of performance that established the meaning of *chicken* as *stewers*. This would be a good argument, except that the concept of course of performance provides that it is established only if the other party "accepts the performance or acquiesces in it without objection," in the words of § 1-303(a)(2). In the case, the buyer claimed that it did object by sending cables to that effect. Furthermore, in the usual case, one occasion does not establish a course of performance.

You may have noticed that things can get complicated if more than one of these sources of evidence of meaning is available. To resolve that situation, the code establishes a hierarchy in § 1-303(e):

> (e) Except as otherwise provided in subsection (f), the express terms of an agreement and any applicable course of performance, course of dealing, or usage of trade must be construed whenever reasonable as consistent with each other. If such a construction is unreasonable:
>> (1) express terms prevail over course of performance, course of dealing, and usage of trade;
>> (2) course of performance prevails over course of dealing and usage of trade; and
>> (3) course of dealing prevails over usage of trade.

The hierarchy of interpretation provides that the best source of meaning is the one closest to the parties' transaction, so if there is evidence from more than one of these areas, the order in which it prevails is as follows, with the best source at the top:

- express terms
- course of performance
- course of dealing
- trade usage

In *Frigaliment,* the parties could have resolved all issues by stating in the contract, "Seller shall deliver broiling chicken," or "Seller shall deliver stewing chicken." It then would not matter what the course of performance, course of dealing, or usage of trade was. The hierarchy makes this clear by providing in subsection (e)(1) that "express terms prevail over course of performance, course of dealing, and usage of trade." However, failure of a party to follow the express term is not necessarily breach. For example, assume that in our example of course of performance, there was a term in the agreement that stated, "buyer must complete inspection within three days from delivery." Because the parties addressed this subject with an express term, we assume that they intended to displace any trade usage or prior course of dealing. If, in spite of this express term, the buyer repeatedly took more time to inspect and the seller acquiesced, it might be held that this course of performance constituted a waiver by the seller of its right to insist on the express term. See § 1-303(f), which provides:

> (f) Subject to Section 2-209 and Section 2A-208, a course of performance is relevant to show a waiver or modification of any term inconsistent with the course of performance.

A waiver is a relinquishment of a known right. Even though the seller had the right to object when the buyer took more than three days to inspect, he lulled the buyer into thinking that he would not object. The waiver does not necessarily result in the express term being permanently displaced, however. The seller can probably make clear that even though it has waived its rights in the past, it will not do so in the future. Such a retraction of a waiver will probably have the effect of re-establishing the primacy of the express term. That is the key difference between a waiver and a modification, which we address shortly. A waiver arises by conduct, and can be retracted, whereas a modification represents the parties' agreement to change the contract terms.

QUESTION 3. A seller sells a machine to a buyer. The contract provides that the seller will service it "every week" for three years. After delivery, the seller finds out that in the trade, these machines are only serviced monthly, so the seller insists that it only has to service the machine monthly. Is the seller right?

A. Yes, because the trade usage is monthly.
B. Yes, because the course of dealing is monthly.
C. No, because the express term is weekly.
D. No, because the course of performance is weekly.

ANALYSIS.   The important facts are that the express term of the agreement is "every week" and the trade usage is monthly. In the Code hierarchy of interpretation, express terms govern over trade usage. Therefore, the express term, "every week," governs. The correct response is **C**.

QUESTION 4. A seller sells a machine to a buyer. The contract provides that the seller will service it "regularly" for three years. For a year, the seller services it every week. Then the seller finds out that in the trade, these machines are only serviced monthly, so the seller insists that he only has to service the machine monthly. Is the seller right?

A. Yes, because the trade usage is monthly.
B. Yes, because the course of dealing is monthly.
C. No, because the express term is weekly.
D. No, because the course of performance is weekly.

ANALYSIS.   *Note on test taking.* When you see a question that is very similar to a previous question, identify the factual differences. The assessor probably intends different facts to lead to a different conclusion.

The important facts are that the express term of the agreement is "regularly," which is an undefined term, the course of performance is weekly, and the trade usage is monthly. In the Code hierarchy of interpretation, course of performance governs over trade usage. Therefore, the correct response is **D**.

> **QUESTION 5.** Assume in the *Frigaliment* case that the buyer offered evidence that in the poultry business, *chicken* meant *broilers,* and the seller offered evidence that in a previous contract between the parties, the buyer accepted stewing chicken without objection. Which meaning would govern?
>
> **A.** Broilers, because trade usage prevails over course of performance.
> **B.** Broilers, because trade usage prevails over course of dealing.
> **C.** Stewers, because course of performance prevails over trade usage.
> **D.** Stewers, because course of dealing prevails over trade usage.

ANALYSIS.   First, let's characterize the evidence. The buyer's evidence of meaning in the poultry business is trade usage; the seller's evidence from a previous contract between the parties is course of dealing. According to § 1-303(e)(3), "course of dealing prevails over usage of trade." Therefore, response **D** is correct.

D.   Modification

1. The general rule

Historically, the issue of modification has been problematic. The common law regarded a modification as similar to the formation of a new contract. A modification was considered to be a new exchange of promises, and for an exchange of promises to be binding, there has to be consideration. Often, however, when the parties are making a modification, one party does not supply any new consideration. The common law dealt with this situation by invoking the pre-existing duty rule: It is not consideration if a party merely promises to do what it was already bound to do. Assume, for example, a painter had agreed to paint a house for $5,000. In the middle of performance, the painter justifiably says that he underbid the job and a more reasonable price would be $6,000. The owner agrees to give him $5,800. When the job is complete, the owner gives the painter $5,000, claiming that the modification did not count. At common law, the owner would be right, because in return for her promise of an additional $800, the owner got nothing from the painter. The painter was already obligated to paint the house; that was his pre-existing duty.

Although the requirement of consideration makes formalistic sense, the modern view is that the parties should be free to modify their agreement as they see fit. It is a "snare and delusion" for one party to agree to a modification and then hold the other to the original agreement, making him a fool for thinking the modification was meaningful. The modern rule, found in

Restatement § 89, provides that a modification is enforceable if it is "fair and equitable in view of circumstances not anticipated by the parties."

Article 2 takes the more straightforward view of dispensing with the requirement of consideration for a modification. Section 2-209(1) provides:

§ 2-209. Modification, Rescission and Waiver.

(1) An agreement modifying a contract within this Article needs no consideration to be binding.

For example, a brickyard promises to deliver a load of bricks to a buyer for $5,000. Later, the seller tells the buyer that the cost of making bricks has gone up dramatically since the contract was made and a more reasonable price would be $6,000. The buyer agrees to pay $5,800. When the delivery is complete, the buyer gives the seller $5,000 and claims that the modification is not enforceable. Under the Code, the buyer would be in breach, because the modification is enforceable in spite of the absence of consideration.

Note the key role played by *good faith* in this transaction. There is a duty of good faith in all Code transactions. See § 1-304, discussed in Chapter 4.C. Therefore, not all modifications without consideration are enforceable, but only those entered into in good faith. It should be noted, however, that there is no requirement that a party agree to a modification. The buyer in our example is free to say, "The cost of brick-making is a risk you took when you entered the contract. I refuse to make any adjustment."

QUESTION 6. A brickyard entered into a contract to deliver a load of bricks for $5,000. Just before delivery, the buyer tells the seller, "I sure was lucky to get that order of bricks in when I did. There is suddenly a shortage of bricks on the market and if I didn't have them I'd be way behind on my building project." The seller responds, "Since you need them so bad, the price has just gone up to $6,000." The buyer agrees to pay the higher price. Is the agreement to pay a $6,000 price enforceable?

A. Yes, because the modification was freely made.
B. Yes, but the buyer has a remedy for any losses that he suffered.
C. No, because there is no consideration for the additional $1,000.
D. No, because the modification was not entered in good faith.

ANALYSIS. The seller has clearly engaged in opportunistic behavior. There is no good reason for the demanded increase other than to take advantage of the buyer's situation. Even if it is not duress on the part of the seller, the behavior demonstrates a lack of good faith. The correct response is **D**. The modification is not enforceable, so the price remains $5,000.

> **QUESTION 7.** A buyer orders ten widgets for future delivery. In between the time the contract is made and the time for performance, the cost of widget-making increases substantially. The seller asks the buyer if it would agree to pay an additional 5% to reduce the seller's loss. The buyer agrees. After delivery, the buyer refuses to pay more than the original contract price, claiming the modification is not enforceable. Is it enforceable?
>
> **A.** No, because there was no consideration for the promise to pay more.
> **B.** No, because the agreement was not in writing.
> **C.** Yes, because the modification does not require consideration.
> **D.** Yes, because the modification was fair and equitable in view of the circumstances.

ANALYSIS.   Response **D** states the general rule from the Restatement, but this contract is for the sale of goods, so the Article 2 rule is applicable. There is no general requirement that a modification be in writing. Under § 2-209(1), there is no requirement of consideration for a modification. There are no facts suggesting that the modification was not made in good faith. Therefore, **C** is the correct response.

2. The Statute of Frauds and "no oral modification" clauses

There is no general requirement that a modification be in writing as a matter of law. However, there are two aspects of modifications that impact the writing requirement. The first is the inadequately drafted § 2-209(3). It provides:

> (3) The requirements of the statute of frauds section of this Article (Section 2-201) must be satisfied if the contract as modified is within its provisions.

We know that § 2-201 provides that a contract is within the Statute of Frauds if the price of the goods is $500 or more (see Chapter 8.A), but what does it mean that "the contract as modified is within its provisions"? White and Summers, *Uniform Commercial Code* § 1-6, say there are at least five interpretations of this language. A harmless interpretation would be that a writing is required when the initial contract is not within the Statute of Frauds; for example, there is an oral agreement for the sale of a baseball for $400, but a modification brings it into the Statute of Frauds by changing the price to $600. The most troublesome interpretation is the most obvious—a modification of a contract that is initially within the Statute of Frauds must itself be evidenced by a writing. For example, in a writing, a seller agrees to sell a buyer a truckload of bricks for $1,000 in 30 days. The parties then orally agree that delivery will be in 60 days. When the seller does not deliver in 30 days, the buyer claims breach because the contract as modified—a contract for $1,000 worth of bricks delivered in 60 days—is within the statute, and therefore not enforceable. A troubling aspect of that argument is that the Statute of Frauds does not require the contract to be written; it only requires that the contract be *evidenced by* a writing. Under the Statute of Frauds, there would be nothing wrong with a contract for the sale of $1,000 worth of bricks to be delivered in 60 days evidenced by a writing that left out the delivery date.

Even under this interpretation, however, the party who claimed the modification was effective might find relief in the doctrine of waiver. Subsection (4) provides:

> (4) Although an attempt at modification or rescission does not satisfy the requirements of subsection (2) or (3) it can operate as a waiver.

Under the doctrine of waiver, the conduct of one party that led the other to believe the modification was effective could estop that party from denying the effectiveness of the modification. In our hypothetical, if the seller acted in reliance on the modification to 60 days, the buyer would be held to have waived its right to deny the effectiveness of the modification.

Greater mischief is caused by subsection (2):

> (2) A signed agreement which excludes modification or rescission except by a signed writing cannot be otherwise modified or rescinded, but except as between merchants such a requirement on a form supplied by the merchant must be separately signed by the other party.

Because there may be questions of fact as to whether a modification was made, and what exactly it said, parties rightly believe it may be a good idea to put the modification in writing. To that end, the boilerplate of a contract usually contains a *no oral modification* (NOM) clause that states that a modification is not enforceable unless it is in writing. The language before the comma in subsection (2) is straightforward, granting the parties the power to adopt a NOM clause. The second half of that subsection has proven to be of little importance, but essentially it says that a merchant dealing with a nonmerchant must get the nonmerchant to affirmatively acknowledge the NOM clause. This is a good example of the doctrine of *reasonable expectations* that we discussed in Chapter 4.D.2; the term is not enforceable unless reasonably called to the attention of the other party. The rule does not apply to merchants, who are held to the higher standard of knowing what terms the agreement contains.

Although that private Statute of Frauds may have the salutary effect of channeling the parties' behavior into writing down their modifications, the fact is that parties notoriously include that provision in their boilerplate and then go ahead and make an oral modification anyway. The issue then becomes whether the oral modification is enforceable. This situation is so common that the practical-minded drafters of Article 2 anticipated the problems and addressed them in subsections (4) and (5) of § 2-209, which provide as follows:

> (4) Although an attempt at modification or rescission does not satisfy the requirements of subsection (2) or (3) it can operate as a waiver.
>
> (5) A party who has made a waiver affecting an executory portion of the contract may retract the waiver by reasonable notification received by the other party that strict performance will be required of any term waived, unless the retraction would be unjust in view of a material change of position in reliance on the waiver.

Subsection (4) undermines most of subsection (2) by telling us that if an oral modification is made in the face of a NOM clause, the oral modification may still be enforceable because of the doctrine of waiver. Subsection (4) provides:

> (4) Although an attempt at modification or rescission does not satisfy the requirements of subsection (2) or (3) it can operate as a waiver.

Under this provision, a party may have had the right to insist on a written modification, but by agreeing to an oral modification, the party may be held to have waived that right. Some drafters try to contract around this requirement by including in the contract a "no waiver" clause that states that rights are not waived merely by conduct. However, most courts hold that a party who agreed to an oral modification also waived the effect of the "no waiver" clause.

Does that mean that NOM clauses are of no effect whatever? Not quite. For one thing, the provision does serve the channeling function; it reminds the parties to get modifications in writing to better preserve proof of their agreement. Also, subsection (5) makes clear that a party may retract a waiver unless the other party has relied on it:

> (5) A party who has made a waiver affecting an executory portion of the contract may retract the waiver by reasonable notification received by the other party that strict performance will be required of any term waived, unless the retraction would be unjust in view of a material change of position in reliance on the waiver.

Contrast these hypotheticals. In the first, a buyer and a seller enter into a written contract that contains a NOM clause under which the seller agrees to sell goods for a certain price. The parties nevertheless enter into an oral modification that the price will be increased. The seller delivers the goods and the buyer pays the increased price. The buyer then claims that she only owed the original price because the increase was not in writing as required by the contract. Under the Code, a court will hold that the parties waived the NOM when they entered into the modification and, because the contract has been executed, it is too late for the buyer to retract her waiver. In the second, the facts are the same except immediately after entering into the oral modification, the buyer changes her mind and insists on the original price. Because the contract is executory (hasn't been performed) and the seller has not changed his position in reliance on the waiver, the buyer is permitted to retract it.

> **QUESTION 8.** A buyer and a seller entered into a written agreement for the delivery of a truckload of bricks in 30 days. The contract contained a no oral modification clause. Shortly after the agreement was made, the buyer asked the seller if it could deliver in 20 days and the seller responded that that would not be a problem. The buyer then hired a crew of bricklayers to begin work in 20 days. The next day the seller told the buyer that he changed his mind, and he insisted on the 30-day delivery date as specified in the written agreement. Is the oral modification to 20 days effective?
>
> **A.** Yes, because NOM clauses are not enforceable.
> **B.** Yes, because the buyer relied on the modification.
> **C.** No, because the NOM clause is enforceable.
> **D.** No, because the seller retracted his waiver within a reasonable time.

ANALYSIS.   This is a typical situation. Even though the agreement contained an enforceable NOM clause, the parties waived their right to insist on it when they made an oral modification. The seller could retract his waiver, but not after the buyer had relied on it. The best response is **B**. Sometimes a contract includes not only a NOM clause, but a "no waiver" clause providing that waivers are not effective unless written. Courts will generally disregard this provision, finding that parties are free to change their minds and that the no waiver clause was waived along with the NOM clause.

> **QUESTION 9.** A contract that contains a NOM clause allows the seller 20 days to deliver the goods. The seller calls the buyer and asks if he may instead have 30 days and the buyer agrees. Immediately after agreeing, the buyer calls the seller back and says, "I changed my mind. That modification is not enforceable because it is not in writing." Is the modification enforceable?
>
> **A.** No, because there is a NOM clause.
> **B.** No, because the buyer retracted his waiver before the seller could rely on it.
> **C.** Yes, because the buyer waived his right to insist on the NOM clause by making an oral modification.
> **D.** Yes, because under the Code an NOM clause is not effective.

ANALYSIS.   Under the rule of § 2-209(4), the buyer has waived the right to insist that the oral modification is not enforceable because of the NOM clause. But if the buyer reaches the seller before the seller has taken action in reliance on the oral agreement, then pursuant to subsection (5), the buyer can retract the waiver. The correct response is **B**.

E.   Closers

QUESTION 10. A doughnut manufacturer contracts with a bakery to deliver "ten dozen" assorted doughnuts to the bakery each day. The contract contains a merger clause and is fully integrated. On the first day, the manufacturer delivers 120 doughnuts. The bakery claims that the manufacturer should have delivered 130 doughnuts because there are 13 doughnuts in a baker's dozen. If the matter went to court, would the evidence that there are 13 doughnuts in a baker's dozen be admissible?

A. Yes, because evidence of trade usage is admissible to explain the meaning of a term in an agreement, even if it is fully integrated.

B. Yes, because evidence of course of dealing is admissible to explain the meaning of a term in an agreement, even if it is fully integrated.

C. No, because parol evidence is not admissible to supplement the terms of a fully integrated agreement.

D. No, because the parties expressly contracted around the admissibility of trade usage evidence.

ANALYSIS.   The evidence that there are 13 doughnuts in a baker's dozen is trade usage. Therefore, response **B** is incorrect. It is offered to prove the meaning of the term "ten dozen" in the contract, so this is an issue of interpretation. According to § 2-202(a), such evidence is admissible to explain the meaning of a term in the agreement even if the contract is fully integrated. Unlike other kinds of evidence of meaning, evidence of course of performance, course of dealing, and trade usage are admissible without any initial proof that the term is ambiguous as a matter of law. Official Comment 1(c) provides:

> 1. This section definitely rejects: . . .
>   (c) The requirement that a condition precedent to the admissibility of the type of evidence specified in paragraph (a) is an original determination by the court that the language used is ambiguous.

Therefore, response **C** is incorrect. As suggested by response **D**, the parties are free to contract around this rule, and prohibit evidence of course of performance, course of dealing, and trade usage, but it would be unwise for them to do so. Official Comment 2 explains:

2. Paragraph (a) makes admissible evidence of course of dealing, usage of trade and course of performance to explain or supplement the terms of any writing stating the agreement of the parties in order that the true understanding of the parties as to the agreement may be reached. Such writings are to be read on the assumption that the course of prior dealings between the parties and the usages of trade were taken for granted when the document was phrased. Unless carefully negated they have become an element of the meaning of the words used. Similarly, the course of actual performance by the parties is considered the best indication of what they intended the writing to mean.

In any event, there is no evidence that they did so here, so the correct response is **A**.

QUESTION 11. A buyer orders a widget for $100. When she goes to pick it up, she tells the seller, "I am so lucky to get that widget. It is the last one available in town and I need it to keep my machine going." The seller's eyes light up and he says, "The price just went up to $200." The buyer reluctantly agrees to pay, but then sues to get the additional $100 back. Is the modification enforceable?

A. Yes, because the modification does not require consideration.
B. Yes, because the buyer was free not to agree to it.
C. No, because there was no consideration for the promise to pay more.
D. No, because the seller did not act in good faith.

ANALYSIS.   Article 2 does not require consideration to support a modification, but that does not mean that all modifications entered into without consideration are enforceable. As stated in § 1-304, the obligation of good faith is found in every contract. The request for a modification can sometimes come from a chiseler, as it did here. The best response is **D**. Official Comment 2 to § 2-209 states:

However, modifications made [under subsection (1)] must meet the test of good faith imposed by this Act. The effective use of bad faith to escape performance on the original contract terms is barred, and the extortion of a "modification" without legitimate commercial reason is ineffective as a violation of the duty of good faith.

QUESTION 12. A buyer orders ten widgets for future delivery. In between the time the contract is made and the time for performance, the cost of widget-making increases substantially. The seller asks the buyer if it would agree to pay an additional 5% to reduce the seller's loss. The buyer refuses. The seller delivers, but then claims that the buyer is in breach of the duty of good faith for failing to agree to the modification. Is the buyer in breach?

A. No, because there is no requirement that a party agree to a modification.
B. No, because the Code does not require a party to act in good faith.
C. Yes, because the buyer took advantage of the seller's situation.
D. Yes, because the request for a modification was fair and equitable in view of the circumstances.

ANALYSIS.   I included this question to make sure you don't take the notion of good faith too far. The fact that there is a reasonable request for a modification does not require the other party to agree to it. If you "just say no," that is not lack of good faith. It is simply insisting on the benefit of the bargain you made. The correct response is **A**.

QUESTION 13. A long-term contract between a buyer and a seller provides that "Seller retains the right to modify the agreement on ten days' written notice to Buyer." After the agreement has been in effect for two years, the seller notified the buyer that pursuant to this provision, "the price of the goods in the next delivery will increase by 7% to reflect an increase in the cost of raw materials, and any disputes will be resolved by arbitration pursuant to the rules of the American Arbitration Association." Which of the modifications is a court likely to enforce?

A. Both the price increase and the arbitration provision.
B. The price increase, but not the arbitration provision.
C. The arbitration provision, but not the price increase.
D. Neither the price increase nor the arbitration provision.

ANALYSIS.   Provisions such as this are beginning to appear in many consumer contracts. Even though a court might be more likely to enforce it in a negotiated contract, I have concerns about it. If taken literally, the provision gives the seller the power to rewrite the contract, which would make the initial agreement illusory and meaningless. On the other hand, parties should be able to plan to alter their agreement to address future situations. I think a fair compromise would be to allow the seller to make modifications that reflect an objective change in the parties' situation. For example, it is reasonable to allow the seller to reset the price based on changing circumstances. However, it seems unreasonable to allow the seller to use this power to obtain advantages that it did not initially bargain for, such as using arbitration as a forum. While the law on this matter is uncertain, I think the best response is **B**.

Burnham's picks

Question 1	**B**
Question 2	**D**
Question 3	**C**
Question 4	**D**
Question 5	**D**
Question 6	**D**
Question 7	**C**
Question 8	**B**
Question 9	**B**
Question 10	**A**
Question 11	**D**
Question 12	**A**
Question 13	**B**

8

The Statute of Frauds

A.   The Statute of Frauds—the general rule

When we refer to the Statute of Frauds, we mean any statute that provides that a certain type of contract is not enforceable unless evidenced by a writing. When a transaction is subject to the Statute of Frauds, we say that the agreement is "within" the Statute. Incidentally, in connection with the Statute, I make an effort not to refer to *verbal* agreements. The word *verbal* can mean "using words" as well as "oral," so technically, a verbal agreement can be in writing. To avoid any ambiguity, I use the word *oral* to refer to agreements that may be within the Statute.

The Statute of Frauds that is applicable to the sale of goods is found at § 2-201(1):

§ 2-201. Formal Requirements; Statute of Frauds.

(1) Except as otherwise provided in this section a contract for the sale of goods for the price of $500 or more is not enforceable by way of action or defense unless there is some writing sufficient to indicate that a contract for sale has been made between the parties and signed by the party against whom enforcement is sought or by his authorized agent or broker. A writing is not insufficient because it omits or incorrectly states a term agreed upon but the contract is not enforceable under this paragraph beyond the quantity of goods shown in such writing.

According to this statute, "a contract for the sale of goods for the price of $500 or more" is within the Statute, so it must be evidenced by a writing. By the way, don't fall into the trap of thinking that Article 2 doesn't apply if the sale price is under $500. Of course it applies. As we saw in Chapter 3.A, Article 2 applies to all transactions in goods. This provision is merely saying that transactions for a price of under $500 don't have to be evidenced by a writing to be enforceable.

Note that we didn't say that to be enforceable, the contract has to *be* in writing. It doesn't. It only has to be *evidenced by* a writing. Don't make the writing do too much work. According to subsection (1), the writing only needs to be "sufficient to indicate that a contract for sale has been made between the parties and signed by the party against whom enforcement is sought." Let's look at that last requirement of the writing first. When the Code says the writing must be "signed by the party against whom enforcement is sought," it means signed by the person who denies the enforceability of the agreement. So if John and Mary make an oral agreement for the sale of a Ted Williams autographed baseball for $1,000, and John denies that the agreement is enforceable, then Mary will have to produce a writing signed by John; if Mary denies that the agreement is enforceable, then John will have to produce a writing signed by Mary. This makes sense, for if the purpose of the statute is to prevent fraud, then the person who admits entering the agreement is not being defrauded.

The next requirement is that the writing be "signed." What constitutes a signed writing? Again, don't ask the writing to do too much work; the Code and the courts are very liberal in accepting evidence that satisfies the Statute of Frauds. Let's look at the applicable definitions in § 1-201(b):

> (37) "Signed" includes using any symbol executed or adopted with present intention to adopt or accept a writing.
> (43) "Writing" includes printing, typewriting, or any other intentional reduction to tangible form. "Written" has a corresponding meaning.

If the name of a corporation were printed on the letterhead of a document that otherwise evidenced the transaction, this would probably constitute a signed writing, for the letterhead is a symbol adopted by the corporation with the intention of showing that the writing came from that corporation. Don't look for formality. If John wrote an email to his mother that stated, "I just sold that Ted Williams autographed baseball I've had lying around to Mary for $1,000," the email indicating that the sender was John would probably constitute a signed writing.

The final requirement is that the writing "indicate that a contract for sale has been made between the parties." The writing does not have to contain all the terms of the agreement. This makes sense, for the terms can be provided by other evidence and by the gap fillers. Official Comment 1 provides:

1. The required writing need not contain all the material terms of the contract and such material terms as are stated need not be precisely stated. All that is required is that the writing afford a basis for believing that the offered oral evidence rests on a real transaction. It may be written in lead pencil on a scratch pad. It need not indicate which party is the buyer and which the seller. The only term which must appear is the quantity term which need not be accurately stated but recovery is limited to the amount stated. The price, time and place of payment or delivery, the general quality of the goods, or any particular warranties may all be omitted.

There is some dispute over whether the writing has to contain the quantity term in order to be sufficient. The statute contains the somewhat ambiguous statement that "[a] writing is not insufficient because it omits or incorrectly states a term agreed upon but the contract is not enforceable under this paragraph beyond the quantity of goods shown in such writing." This language could mean two things. It could mean that if quantity is not mentioned in the writing, then the oral agreement is not enforceable. Or it could mean that *when* quantity is mentioned, then the agreement is not enforceable beyond the quantity mentioned in the writing. Official Comment 1 resolves this ambiguity by stating that "the only term which must appear is the quantity term." Even though the Official Comments are merely persuasive, most authorities agree that the absence of the quantity term is fatal to the sufficiency of the writing.

QUESTION 1. John and Mary agreed on the telephone that John would buy Mary's Ted Williams autographed baseball for $400. Mary later told him, "Ha, Ha. I got a better offer for that ball, and all I had with you was a verbal agreement, so that doesn't count." Is there an enforceable contract between John and Mary?

A. Yes, because oral agreements for the sale of goods for less than $500 are enforceable.

B. Yes, because the UCC does not apply to this agreement because John and Mary are not merchants.

C. Yes, because Mary admitted making the agreement.

D. No, because there is no writing signed by Mary.

ANALYSIS. Of course, we know that Mary meant to say, "all I had with you was an *oral* agreement." Because this is a transaction in goods, the UCC applies. Under § 2-201(1), this agreement does not need to be evidenced by a writing because it is not "a contract for the sale of goods for the price of $500 or more." Therefore, response **A** is correct.

> **QUESTION 2.** John agreed to sell his car to Mary for $25,000. John then went to his lawyer's office, but his lawyer was not there, so he left a note for her that said: "I've just sold my car to Mary for $25,000. What documents do I need to complete the transaction? s/John" That night, John got a better offer for the car and told Mary the agreement was not enforceable because it was oral. Is there an enforceable agreement between John and Mary?
>
> A. No, because serious agreements for large amounts of money must always be reduced to writing.
> B. No, because there is no sufficient writing signed by Mary.
> C. Yes, because it is unethical for John to try to refuse enforcement of this contract.
> D. Yes, because there is a sufficient writing signed by John.

ANALYSIS. Response **A** suggests one of the policy reasons behind the Statute of Frauds—it is a reminder to a person that this is a serious matter and serious matters should be reduced to writing. This is sometimes called the *channeling* function—it channels our behavior into a more desirable pattern. Nevertheless, there is no such general rule. Similarly, Response **C** suggests one of the policy reasons behind enforcing oral agreements—if the purpose of the Statute is to prevent fraud, how is that purpose served when people refuse to honor agreements that they really made? Nevertheless, a person is free to raise the defense even if the person made the contract, subject to an exception we look at shortly. Because this agreement is within the Statute of Frauds, it needs to be evidenced by a writing signed by John, the party against whom enforcement is sought. The note to his attorney satisfies the requirement of a "writing sufficient to indicate that a contract for sale has been made between the parties and signed by the party against whom enforcement is sought." Therefore, **D** is the correct response. You might wonder as a practical matter how Mary could enforce the agreement, but if a suit were brought, the memorandum would probably be discoverable.

B. Exceptions

The remaining subsections of § 2-201 contain exceptions to the general rule; that is, they represent situations in which an oral agreement for the sale of goods for $500 or more is enforceable even without a sufficient signed writing. These exceptions are:

- Confirmation
- Specially manufactured goods

- Admission
- Performance

1. Confirmation

The confirmation exception in subsection (2) is a good one to break down into its elements. The subsection provides:

> (2) Between merchants if within a reasonable time a writing in confirmation of the contract and sufficient against the sender is received and the party receiving it has reason to know its contents, it satisfies the requirements of subsection (1) against such party unless written notice of objection to its contents is given within 10 days after it is received.

The subsection could be converted to an IF/THEN statement as follows:

If

> two merchants make an oral agreement,
> and
> one party sends a written confirmation within a reasonable time,
> and
> the writing is sufficient against the sender,
> and
> the other party receives it and has reason to know its contents,
> and
> the party receiving it does not give written notice of objection to its
>   contents within 10 days after it is received,

then

> the confirmation satisfies the requirements of the statute of frauds
> against the party who received it.

This provision would be a little easier to understand if it avoided the passive voice so that it was clearer who was doing what. It should be clear, though, that if after an oral agreement is made, one party sends a confirmation and the receiving party has reason to know its contents but does not object to it, then a confirmation that is a sufficient writing operates as if it were a writing signed by the receiving party. Even if the sender has satisfied the Statute of Frauds, however, the sender is not home free; the sender must still prove that there was a contract and what its terms were.

   This might be a good time to review the various concepts of notice that appear in this provision, for it uses the terms *sender, received, reason to know,* and *notice.* The term *sender* is not defined, but presumably it means one who sends, and *send* is defined in § 1-201(b)(36):

(36) "Send" in connection with a writing, record, or notice means:

    (A) to deposit in the mail or deliver for transmission by any other usual means of communication with postage or cost of transmission provided for and properly addressed and, in the case of an instrument, to an address specified thereon or otherwise agreed, or if there be none to any address reasonable under the circumstances; or

    (B) in any other way to cause to be received any record or notice within the time it would have arrived if properly sent.

Note that under this definition, to *send* is to deposit or deliver the communication, whether or not it is received. This usage is consistent with the definition of *notifies* in § 1-202(d), which expressly provides that a person can notify or give notice even if the other party does not actually come to know of it:

    (d) A person "notifies" or "gives" a notice or notification to another by taking such steps as may be reasonably required to inform the other in ordinary course, whether or not the other person actually comes to know of it.

Subsection (2) of § 2-201, however, requires that the notice is "received." That definition is found in § 1-202(e):

    (e) Subject to subsection (f), a person "receives" a notice or notification when:

        (1) it comes to that person's attention; or

        (2) it is duly delivered in a form reasonable under the circumstances at the place of business through which the contract was made or at another location held out by that person as the place for receipt of such communications.

Note that under subsection (2) of this definition, a notice can be received when it is delivered at the person's place of business. Again, it does not matter whether the person actually comes to know of it. However, § 2-201(2) contains the further requirement that the recipient "has reason to know its contents." Section 1-202(b) provides that "'[k]nowledge' means actual knowledge. 'Knows' has a corresponding meaning." Therefore, if a person *knows* of the contents of a letter, the person has actual knowledge of it. Here, however, the requirement is short of actual knowledge, for the statute uses the term "reason to know." It seems to me this means that a reasonable person would have known the contents even if this particular person did not. For example, if the recipient got the confirmation, but threw it away thinking it was junk mail, then the recipient would have "reason to know" the contents. It is obvious that a drafter must use these words with precision.

    In a typical situation that arises under subsection (2), a representative of a major grain company visits with farmers, orally agreeing with each that the grain company will purchase the crop of the farmer when it is harvested. When he gets back to headquarters, the representative sends each farmer a confirmation of the oral agreement. When harvest time comes, the farmers find they can get a higher price for the crop and claim that the oral agreement with the grain company is not enforceable. Note that in this situation, the agreement would not be enforceable under § 2-201(1) because there is no writing signed by the farmer, the party against whom enforcement is sought. The issue is whether the confirmation that is not objected to substitutes for that writing.

The grain company claims that the exception applies. The grain company sent a writing to confirm the oral contract, it was a writing sufficient to satisfy the statute, it was sent within a reasonable time, the farmer had reason to know what was in it, and the farmer did not object to it within ten days of receipt. Because all these elements are satisfied, it looks pretty good for the grain company. However, there is one more element—this is one of the provisions of Article 2 that applies only "between merchants." See § 2-104(3). Is the farmer a merchant? This issue has been frequently litigated. It provides us with a good opportunity to reflect on the issue we first addressed in Chapter 4.B: why some Article 2 provisions apply only to merchants or only between merchants.

Obviously the policy is that merchants are held to a higher standard because they have superior knowledge or experience. In the context of the confirmation, the parties who send and receive these documents are held to a higher standard of knowing what they may be getting into. If a nonmerchant received a confirmation, the nonmerchant might not be aware of its legal import. However, a merchant receiving a confirmation should know that this is serious business and must take steps to object to its contents where appropriate. Here, the rule applies to all merchants, so it doesn't matter whether the merchant is a goods merchant or a practices merchant. (Review Chapter 4.B if you do not recall the distinction.) Because farmers frequently buy and sell goods, such as their crops, one would think a farmer would be considered a merchant for this purpose.

QUESTION 3. A contract for the sale of goods between parties who work out of their residences provides that one party has ten days to act after receiving written notice from the other party. The seller deposits a notice in the mailbox on March 1. It arrives at the home of the buyer on March 4. The buyer, however, is away on vacation and returns on March 10. On March 12, the buyer goes through the mail and reads the notice. Under these facts, when was notice *received*?

A. March 1.
B. March 4.
C. March 10.
D. March 12.

ANALYSIS.   According to § 1-202(e):

> (e) Subject to subsection (f), a person "receives" a notice or notification when:
>> (1) it comes to that person's attention; or
>> (2) it is duly delivered in a form reasonable under the circumstances at the place of business through which the contract was made or at another location held out by that person as the place for receipt of such communications.

Under these facts, it would appear that the buyer received the notice on March 4, when it was duly delivered at the buyer's place of business. The correct response is **B**. Under these facts, the notice was given on March 1, and the buyer had reason to know of it on March 10 and knowledge of it on March 12. Note that § 1-202(f) realistically cuts some slack for an organization that requires time to get the notice from the office that receives mail to the office of the person who is responsible for the transaction:

> (f) Notice, knowledge, or a notice or notification received by an organization is effective for a particular transaction from the time it is brought to the attention of the individual conducting that transaction and, in any event, from the time it would have been brought to the individual's attention if the organization had exercised due diligence. An organization exercises due diligence if it maintains reasonable routines for communicating significant information to the person conducting the transaction and there is reasonable compliance with the routines. Due diligence does not require an individual acting for the organization to communicate information unless the communication is part of the individual's regular duties or the individual has reason to know of the transaction and that the transaction would be materially affected by the information.

QUESTION 4. On a Friday, a customer who rarely purchased art walked into an art gallery and saw a painting displayed that he liked. He said to the manager, "I'll give you $5,000 for that painting." The manager said, "It's a deal." The customer then explained that he would return with the money on Monday and the manager said, "That won't be a problem. I'll hold the painting for you in the back." The customer then said, "Not that I don't trust you, but I'm going to confirm our deal so there is some evidence of it." He wrote on a piece of paper, "John Smith agreed to purchase the Picasso painting La Reve from the Gilderson Gallery on March 1." He signed the paper and handed it to the manager. When the customer returned on Monday with the money, the manager apologetically explained that the painting had inadvertently been sold to someone else. The customer insisted that they had an enforceable contract. Did they?

A. No, because the confirmation was not sufficient.
B. No, because both parties were not merchants.
C. Yes, because there was a writing signed by the party against whom enforcement is sought.
D. Yes, because there is a confirmation that was sufficient.

ANALYSIS.   Under subsection (1), there is not a writing signed by the art gallery, which is the party against whom enforcement is sought. Is the gallery bound under the confirmation exception? The confirmation here sufficiently described the transaction. The price was missing, but that can be supplied by evidence of the commercial setting in which the transaction was made. The problem is that the purchaser is not a merchant. Therefore, subsection (2) is not satisfied. The best response is **B**.

2. Specially manufactured goods

Another exception to the rule that a contract within the Statute is not enforceable unless evidenced by a writing is found in § 2-201(3)(a), which concerns specially manufactured goods. It provides:

> (3) A contract which does not satisfy the requirements of subsection (1) but which is valid in other respects is enforceable
>> (a) if the goods are to be specially manufactured for the buyer and are not suitable for sale to others in the ordinary course of the seller's business and the seller, before notice of repudiation is received and under circumstances which reasonably indicate that the goods are for the buyer, has made either a substantial beginning of their manufacture or commitments for their procurement . . .

This exception is based on reliance. If Joe's Bar and Grill orally orders a neon sign from a sign manufacturer and then Joe changes his mind, the sign manufacturer would be stuck with a useless sign. It is only fair to enforce the contract. In keeping with this reasoning, note that this exception to the rule does not apply if the goods are suitable for sale to others, or if the manufacturer has not substantially begun performance of the contract.

3. Admission

The admission exception in subsection (3)(b) is an interesting one. It provides:

> (3) A contract which does not satisfy the requirements of subsection (1) but which is valid in other respects is enforceable . . .
>> (b) if the party against whom enforcement is sought admits in his pleading, testimony or otherwise in court that a contract for

sale was made, but the contract is not enforceable under this provision beyond the quantity of goods admitted . . . .

Let's go back to our hypothetical of John agreeing to sell Mary an autographed Ted Williams baseball for $1,000. Mary then refuses to go through with the transaction and John sells the ball to another buyer for $800. John is unable to produce a writing signed by Mary, so it looks like he cannot satisfy the statute, but he sues her anyway. In his complaint, he alleges:

1. I offered to sell an autographed Ted Williams baseball to Mary for $1,000.
2. Mary accepted the offer.
3. I tendered the ball, but Mary refused to perform.
4. I sold the ball to Fred for $800.
5. I was damaged in the amount of $200.

When Mary truthfully answers this complaint, she responds to each allegation:

1. Admit.
2. Admit.
3. Admit.
4. Lack knowledge or information sufficient to answer.
5. Lack knowledge or information sufficient to answer.
6. Affirmative defense: Statute of Frauds.

Even though Mary has raised the defense of the Statute of Frauds, she loses! The reason is because according to subsection (3)(b), by admitting allegations 1, 2, and 3, she has admitted that she made the contract. This result is appropriate, because the purpose of the Statute of Frauds is to give people a shield to protect themselves if someone falsely claims they entered into a contract. It is not intended to give people a sword to get out of contracts that they really made. Note that under this provision, the admission must be "in his pleading, testimony or otherwise in court," so it must be made under oath. A casual admission might not be sufficient. This provision raises an interesting ethical dilemma, for the admission exception only arises when the defendant, like Mary, honestly admits that the contract was formed. It may lead the defendant to undertake procedural efforts to avoid answering the complaint.

4. Performance

The final exception involves completed performance. Subsection (3)(c) provides:

> (3) A contract which does not satisfy the requirements of subsection (1) but which is valid in other respects is enforceable . . .
>
> (c) with respect to goods for which payment has been made and accepted or which have been received and accepted (Sec. 2-606).

Suppose John orally agrees to sell Mary an autographed Ted Williams baseball for $1,000. He gives her the ball and she gives him the $1,000. She then says, "I want to avoid this contract. It is within the Statute of Frauds." She will not be able to avoid it. Contracts within the Statute are not voidable; they are unenforceable. By performing, a party has effectively waived its right to claim the benefit of the Statute of Frauds.

A more complex issue arises when there is partial performance. Suppose, for example, that Mary gave John a $100 cash deposit toward the baseball and then John claimed that the agreement was not enforceable. When the Code provides "payment has been made and accepted," does it mean full payment or partial payment? Courts are divided on this issue, but they are more inclined to find a deposit sufficient when enforcement is sought against the seller rather than against the buyer.

> **QUESTION 5.** Mary and John agree that John will sell Mary an autographed Ted Williams baseball for $1,000. John then emails a friend with a copy to Mary: "I just agreed to sell that autographed Ted Williams baseball to Mary for $1,000." Before the exchange, Mary says to John, "I admit I made that agreement with you, but I changed my mind. I am not going to buy it." Is the agreement enforceable?
>
> **A.** Yes, because John's email to the friend evidences it.
> **B.** Yes, because John's sending a copy of the email to Mary acts as a confirmation.
> **C.** Yes, because Mary admitted making it.
> **D.** No, because there is no writing signed by the party against whom enforcement is sought and no exception applies.

ANALYSIS.   John's email to the friend would probably be sufficient against John, but he is not the party against whom enforcement is sought. There is no writing signed by Mary. The confirmation exception does not apply because it appears that John and Mary are not merchants. The admission exception does not apply because the admission was not in a "pleading, testimony or otherwise in court." Because no exception applies, the correct response is **D**.

C.   Are the Code provisions exclusive?

Sometimes a situation arises that invokes an element of the Statute of Frauds that is not addressed in the Code. For example, in most jurisdictions, the non-Code Statute of Frauds provides that a contract that by its terms cannot be performed within a year from the time of its making is within the Statute. Assume that on October 1, 2012, John orally agrees with Mary that he will sell his Ted Williams autographed baseball to her for $400 on November 1, 2013. Is the agreement within the Statute of Frauds? It is not within the UCC statute, for the sale is for a price under $500, but it is within the one-year statute. However, it is not clear that the one-year statute applies to transactions for the sale of goods. One argument is that the UCC statute is the exclusive source of the Statute of Frauds for the sale of goods, in which case the one-year rule would not apply. This is the approach used in Amended § 2-201, which specifically addressed the issue in a new subsection (4):

> (4) A contract that is enforceable under this section is not unenforceable merely because it is not capable of being performed within one year or any other period after its making.

We reiterate that Amended Article 2 has been withdrawn, but it does indicate that the drafters wanted to resolve this ambiguity by excluding the one-year rule from the UCC Statute of Frauds. It seems to me this would be persuasive authority.

A similar issue arises with respect to the estoppel exception. Even though there is no express exception in § 2-201 for estoppel, some cases have held that a party's conduct may estop it from denying enforcement of the oral agreement. For example, in *Northwest Potato Sales, Inc. v. Beck*, 678 P.2d 1138 (Mont. 1984), the defendant farmer orally agreed to sell more than $500 worth of potatoes to plaintiff buyer. After the agreement was made, the buyer visited the farm to examine the crop and told the seller that he had committed to sell the potatoes to a third party. When the market price went up, the seller refused to perform, claiming that § 2-201, the exclusive source of the Statute of Frauds in the Code, did not mention estoppel as an exception to the statute. But the court found that estoppel is expressly recognized in § 1-103(b) as one of the principles that supplement the Code, and that the obligation of good faith further supported the plaintiff's case.

QUESTION 6. A nonmerchant buyer talks with a nonmerchant seller on the phone, and agrees to buy the seller's Frank Lloyd Wright chair for $60,000. The seller then changes her mind and refuses to sell. The buyer sues the seller. When the buyer takes the seller's deposition, the seller testifies that she did in fact agree to sell the chair for $60,000, but her lawyer told her that there was a Statute of Frauds for her protection. It gave her a chance to reflect on the transaction before writing anything down, and she had changed her mind before committing the agreement to writing. Is the agreement enforceable?

A. No, because there is no writing signed by the seller, the party against whom enforcement is sought.

B. No, because one of the purposes of the Statute of Frauds is the cautionary function, that makes people consider serious transactions.

C. Yes, because she admitted it in her deposition.
D. Yes, because oral contracts between nonmerchants are enforceable even if the amount is more than $500.

ANALYSIS. It is often said that one of the purposes of the Statute of Frauds is its cautionary function. However, the drafters of the Code apparently thought that it would do little harm to enforce agreements that the parties actually made. They therefore created the admission exception in § 2-201(3)(c). Here, the deposition satisfies that exception, for a deposition is testimony under oath. The correct response is **C**. For Judge Richard Posner's take on whether a party who claims the benefit of the statute can be compelled to submit to a deposition, see *DF Activities Corp. v. Brown*, 851 F.2d 920 (7th Cir. 1988). Judge Posner said, "if defendant swears in an affidavit that there was no contract, we see no point in keeping the lawsuit alive; although defendant may blurt out an admission in a deposition, . . . this is hardly likely."

D. Closers

QUESTION 7. Mary Jones called John Smith and ordered 1,000 red widgets at a price of $1 each. Smith wrote on a notepad that was headed "From the desk of John Smith," these notes: "8/29/12 sold red widgets $1 each Mary Jones." Smith later could not find the notes and did not place the order. Did the parties have an enforceable contract?

A. Yes, because the writing requirement was satisfied.
B. No, because Smith did not sign the writing.
C. No, because the writing lacked an essential term.
D. No, because the writing could not be found.

ANALYSIS. The definition of "signed" in § 1-201(b)(39) provides that "'Signed' includes any symbol executed or adopted with present intention to adopt or accept a writing." The notepad contained the heading "From the desk of John Smith," which seems to indicate that it was adopted as a writing of Smith's. Therefore, **B** is not a correct response. Curiously, cases have held that it is sufficient that there has been a writing that evidenced the agreement even if the writing was lost. Therefore, **D** is not a correct response. However, the writing is lacking a quantity term, which the weight of authority holds makes the writing insufficient to evidence the agreement. Therefore, **A** is not a correct response and **C** is the correct response.

> **QUESTION 8.** A seller entered into an oral agreement with a buyer for the sale of a widget for $10,000. Shortly thereafter, the seller sent the buyer a written confirmation, confirming the sale of a widget from the seller to the buyer for $10,000. The buyer received the confirmation and did not object to it. At the time for performance, the seller tendered the widget and the buyer refused to accept it. What is the buyer's best defense to a claim that it is in breach for refusing to accept the widget?
>
> **A.** There is no writing signed by the buyer.
> **B.** The confirmation was not sent within a reasonable time.
> **C.** The confirmation was not sufficient against the sender.
> **D.** Both parties are not merchants.

ANALYSIS.   These facts invoke the confirmation exception of § 2-201(2). Response **A** is true, but it is not the best response because the point of the subsection is to provide an exception to the rule that a writing signed by the party against whom enforcement is sought is required to make a contract within the Statute of Frauds enforceable. If the writing is sufficient against the sender, then it is sufficient against the receiving party. The other responses indicate elements that have to be satisfied to come within the confirmation exception. There are facts indicating that **B** and **C** are satisfied, for the facts state that the confirmation was sent "shortly thereafter," which is probably within a reasonable time, and that the confirmation stated that a contract for sale had been made between the parties, which would be sufficient against the seller. Other terms of the agreement can be supplied. There are no facts, however, indicating that both parties are merchants, so **D** is the best response.

Burnham's picks

Question 1	**A**
Question 2	**D**
Question 3	**B**
Question 4	**B**
Question 5	**D**
Question 6	**C**
Question 7	**C**
Question 8	**D**

9

Warranties

A.   Introduction

The purpose of warranty law, according to Official Comment 4 to § 2-313, is "to determine what it is that the seller has in essence agreed to sell." The warranty provisions of the Code are a good example of the interplay of the default rules and freedom of contract. Historically, warranties in the "law merchant" developed to inform parties what quality they could expect in the goods they purchased, but the parties also had the ability to contract around those expectations. Because of the different expectations and sophistication of merchants and nonmerchants, some rules may apply only to merchants. The UCC provides for a number of warranties, including:

- Express warranty: § 2-313
- Implied warranty of title: § 2-312
- Implied warranty of merchantability: § 2-314
- Implied warranty of fitness for a particular purpose: § 2-315

Recall that states are free to enact variations of the uniform Code provisions. This seems to happen frequently in the area of warranty. For example, a number of states prohibit the disclaimer of implied warranties in the sale of consumer goods. In that event, because this is a regulatory rule, it might be a breach of a consumer protection act to disclaim the warranties. Also, a number of states exclude implied warranties in the sale of plants or livestock. In that event, the state is merely changing the default rule rather than regulating the transaction. The attorney for the buyer of plants or livestock is free to negotiate for an express warranty from the seller that would change the rule.

B. Express warranty: § 2-313

Express warranties are easy to make. They require no magic words and no intention on the part of the seller to make them. As with all breaches, however, § 2-607(4) provides that "[t]he burden is on the buyer to establish any breach with respect to the goods accepted." Therefore, it is up to the buyer to prove that the seller both gave a warranty and breached it.

Section 2-313 provides:

> **§ 2-313. Express Warranties by Affirmation, Promise, Description, Sample.**
>
> (1) Express warranties by the seller are created as follows:
>
> (a) Any affirmation of fact or promise made by the seller to the buyer which relates to the goods and becomes part of the basis of the bargain creates an express warranty that the goods shall conform to the affirmation or promise.
>
> (b) Any description of the goods which is made part of the basis of the bargain creates an express warranty that the goods shall conform to the description.
>
> (c) Any sample or model which is made part of the basis of the bargain creates an express warranty that the whole of the goods shall conform to the sample or model.
>
> (2) It is not necessary to the creation of an express warranty that the seller use formal words such as "warrant" or "guarantee" or that he have a specific intention to make a warranty, but an affirmation merely of the value of the goods or a statement purporting to be merely the seller's opinion or commendation of the goods does not create a warranty.

Express warranties may arise from the following:

- Oral representations
- Written representations
- Description of goods
- Any sample or model shown
- Plans or blueprints
- Technical specifications
- Reference to a market or official standard
- Quality of goods sent to the buyer in the past
- Brochures and advertisements

Warranties are affirmations of fact or promises, not opinions or statements of value. A great deal of litigation has ensued over whether the statements of a salesperson are statements of fact or merely "puffing." For example, in the course of selling her car to Barney, Sally tells Barney the car is a 2002 Toyota Corolla. Has Sally given Barney any express warranties? Yes! She has affirmed as a fact that the car is made by Toyota, that it is the Corolla model, and that it is a 2002 model. In addition, when describing the car, she makes the statements, "This car is a real bargain," and "This car gets great gas mileage." Are these statements warranties? Probably not. They are puffing or opinion. Although it can sometimes be difficult to draw the line between affirmations of fact and puffing, a good test would be to imagine the buyer suing for breach of warranty and claiming damages. As we will see in § 2-714(2), "[t]he measure of damages for breach of warranty is the difference at the time and place of acceptance between the value of the goods accepted and the value they would have had if they had been as warranted." It does not seem possible for Barney to prove to a reasonable certainty what the difference is between the value of the goods as delivered and the value of the goods as promised based on these statements. On the other hand, if Sally had told him, "This car gets at least 25 miles to the gallon around town," and it only got 20 miles to the gallon, then he might be able to establish a claim because she has made a statement of fact that is verifiable and it is possible to compute damages.

Another issue that may arise is whether the express warranty is, in the words of § 2-313, part of the "basis of the bargain." It is not entirely clear what those words mean. It might be a matter of timing. Representations that are made during negotiations but are not included in the written contract may be excluded because of the parol evidence rule (see Chapter 6). Others may be excluded because they were not made at a time that is deemed to constitute the bargain. For example, a customer purchases a television set from a retailer and receives a receipt that describes the goods but contains no other express warranty. At home, the customer opens the box and finds an express warranty inside the box. It is most likely that the warranties found in the box are part of the basis of the bargain even though they did not appear to be part of the transaction at the time it was formed. We return to the subject of express warranties after we have examined implied warranties and exclusion of warranties.

Most authorities hold that "basis of the bargain" means that the buyer must have relied on the warranty. Sometimes a court denies a claim for breach of express warranty because the buyer never knew there was a warranty. Therefore, she could not have relied on it in making the purchase. This view has some support in Official Comment 1 to § 2-313, which states that "'express' warranties rest on 'dickered' aspects of the individual bargain." However, these words may simply suggest that express warranties arise from the agreement of the parties and not as a matter of law. Official Comment 3 goes on to say that "[i]n actual practice affirmations of fact made by the seller about the goods during a bargain are regarded as part of the description of those goods; hence no particular reliance on such statements need be shown in order to weave them into the fabric of the agreement." This statement reflects the practical view that many buyers do not know what express warranties they received at the time they entered the contract.

QUESTION 1. A producer of cherries offers his crop to a fruit wholesaler. The producer shows the wholesaler sample cherries from his crop and, in a written agreement, the wholesaler agrees to buy the entire cherry crop for a certain price. When the cherries arrive, most of them are less plump and less ripe than the ones the producer had shown to the wholesaler. Does the wholesaler have a claim for breach of warranty?

A. Yes, because the producer told the wholesaler the cherries would be plump and ripe.
B. Yes, because the sample created an express warranty that the goods would conform to that sample.
C. No, because no warranty was in writing.
D. No, because the wholesaler bore the risk that the goods did not conform to the sample.

ANALYSIS.   This is a good example of how express warranties may be created. When the seller shows the buyer a sample, he is in effect promising that the goods will conform to the sample. Section 2-313(1)(c) provides:

> (c) Any sample or model which is made part of the basis of the bargain creates an express warranty that the whole of the goods shall conform to the sample or model.

The correct response is **B**.

C.   Implied warranty of title and against infringement: § 2-312

The implied warranty of title and against infringement is found in § 2-312:

§ 2-312. Warranty of Title and Against Infringement; Buyer's Obligation Against Infringement.
(1) Subject to subsection (2) there is in a contract for sale a warranty by the seller that

      (a) the title conveyed shall be good, and its transfer rightful; and

      (b) the goods shall be delivered free from any security interest or other lien or encumbrance of which the buyer at the time of contracting has no knowledge.

    . . . .

    (3) Unless otherwise agreed a seller who is a merchant regularly dealing in goods of the kind warrants that the goods shall be delivered free of the rightful claim of any third person by way of infringement or the like but a buyer who furnishes specifications to the seller must hold the seller harmless against any such claim which arises out of compliance with the specifications.

Even though I am describing the § 2-312 warranties as "implied warranties," note that the Code does not use that term in referring to them. This omission by the Code drafters might not appear to make sense, because the language does say that the warranty is given even if not expressly part of the contract. So for most purposes, these are implied warranties. However, we will see later that the Code describes methods for disclaiming implied warranties. It is for this purpose that the Code does not describe the § 2-312 warranties as implied warranties, because they cannot be disclaimed the way other implied warranties are disclaimed. To put it all together, these warranties are given like implied warranties but cannot be disclaimed like implied warranties.

    Subsection (1)(a) reflects the property notion that a buyer can't get good title from a thief. When you buy something, it is implied that the seller has the right to convey title to you. Note that the seller is also promising in subsection (1)(b) that there are no undisclosed liens on the property. If you have studied Article 9, you know that debtors sometimes give creditors a security interest in their property. In that event, when the debtor defaults, the creditor may take possession of the property, in some cases even taking it from someone who has purchased it from the debtor. For example, if a business sells its equipment (as opposed to selling inventory) and there is a filed security interest covering those goods, then the buyer takes subject to that security interest. In that event, the secured party would have a claim against the buyer under Article 9 and the buyer would have a claim against the seller under § 2-312(1)(b). Note that the seller only gives this warranty if the buyer "has no knowledge" of the lien. Does the buyer have knowledge of a security interest if it is recorded in a filing that is available to the buyer? Recall from Chapter 8.A that "knowledge" is defined in § 1-202(b) as "actual knowledge." A filing would be imputed knowledge rather than actual knowledge, so it would not prevent the buyer from having a claim under this warranty. Sometimes the problem with title is a threatened claim rather than an actual lien or encumbrance. The authorities are split as to whether the seller has warranted that there is no such "cloud" on the title.

Unlike the warranty of title in subsection (1), the warranty against infringement in subsection (3) is given only by a merchant who regularly deals in goods of the kind. This warranty states that the goods shall be delivered free of claims of infringement. This warranty is of increasing importance because "smart goods" frequently contain intellectual property. Sometimes the owner of a patent, trademark, or copyright is able to obtain relief that makes the use of the goods problematic. In that event, the buyer of the goods would have a claim against the seller for breach of the § 2-312(3) warranty.

QUESTION 2. A buyer purchases a Gizmo GPS system from a retail store. After the purchase, a third party wins a patent infringement suit against Gizmo and, because of the ensuing injunction, the system ceases to function. Does the buyer have a warranty claim against the retail store?

A. Yes, because as a matter of law, the seller gave a warranty that the goods were free of infringement claims.

B. Yes, because the seller gave an express warranty that the goods were free of infringement claims.

C. No, because the claim for breach of warranty must be brought against Gizmo, the party who infringed, and not against the seller.

D. No, because unless the buyer gets a warranty in writing, there is no warranty that the goods are free of infringement claims.

ANALYSIS. The Code does not describe the § 2-312(3) warranty as an implied warranty; nevertheless it comes automatically with the sale. Note also that under the Code, warranties are given by the seller, not by the manufacturer. In this case it was the retail store that gave the buyer a warranty that the goods were free of infringement claims, and it gave that warranty as a matter of law rather than expressly. The correct response is **A.** Under the Code scheme, if a buyer brought a claim against the seller, the seller would implead the manufacturer, who would ultimately be responsible. See § 2-607(3)–(6).

QUESTION 3. A buyer is considering buying a car from a friend. The seller shows the buyer the title to the car, which states on its face that First Bank has a lien on the title. The parties agree on a price of $10,000 for the car, and the seller signs the title over to the buyer. Shortly thereafter, First Bank repossesses the car from the buyer because the seller was in default on his loan. Does the buyer have a claim against the seller?

A. Yes, because the seller gave an implied warranty that the goods were free of liens.

B. Yes, because the seller gave an implied warranty that the goods were free of infringement claims.

C. No, because the implied warranty of good title is given only by merchant sellers.

D. No, because the buyer had knowledge of the lien.

ANALYSIS. The warranty of good title is given by all sellers, not just merchants. However, § 2-312(1)(a) provides that the seller warrants that the goods are free from liens "of which the buyer at the time of contracting has no knowledge." Here, the buyer had actual knowledge of the lien because it appeared on the face of the title. In that situation, presumably the parties adjust the purchase price to account for the lien. The correct response is **D**.

D.   Implied warranty of merchantability: § 2-314

Section 2-314(1) provides in part:

> Unless excluded or modified (Section 2-316), a warranty that the goods shall be merchantable is implied in a contract for their sale if the seller is a merchant with respect to goods of that kind.

Note that this warranty is implied by law only if the seller is a "merchant with respect to goods of that kind." If the seller is a *practices merchant* rather than a *goods merchant,* then it does not give this warranty. This warranty determines the quality of the goods unless the parties effectively disclaim this warranty. The warranty provides that the goods must be "merchantable" as defined in § 2-314(2):

> (2) Goods to be merchantable must be at least such as
>
> (a) pass without objection in the trade under the contract description; and
>
> (b) in the case of fungible goods, are of fair average quality within the description; and
>
> (c) are fit for the ordinary purposes for which such goods are used; and
>
> (d) run, within the variations permitted by the agreement, of even kind, quality and quantity within each unit and among all units involved; and
>
> (e) are adequately contained, packaged, and labeled as the agreement may require; and
>
> (f) conform to the promise or affirmations of fact made on the container or label if any.

The most common meaning of *merchantable* is found in § 2-314(2)(c): "Goods to be merchantable must be at least such as . . . are fit for the ordinary purposes for which such goods are used." In other words, the buyer can reasonably expect a certain level of performance from the goods. If the buyer purchases a car, it has to perform as a car, and not as 4,000 pounds of steel and plastic. What if it is a used car? An implied warranty of merchantability is given with used goods, but the buyer can only reasonably expect that it is fit for the ordinary purposes of a car of that age.

Section 2-314(3) provides that "[u]nless excluded or modified (Section 2-316) other implied warranties may arise from course of dealing or usage of trade." This rule is consistent with the Code methodology we examined when we looked at course of dealing and usage of trade in Chapter 7.C. If, for example, a farm implement dealership has always sold its used tractors with the understanding that it would repair any defects that arose within 30 days of the sale, then that warranty becomes part of the bargain because of course of dealing. Similarly, it may be understood in a certain trade that goods must live up to a certain level of performance. Of course, the parties to a particular transaction are free to contract around these implied warranties.

QUESTION 4. A car dealer sells a used car with 50,000 miles on it to a buyer. Shortly thereafter, the transmission fails. Did the seller breach the implied warranty of merchantability?

A. No, because used car dealers don't give a warranty of merchantability.
B. No, because the implied warranty of merchantability is not given in the sale of used goods.
C. Yes, because the seller has impliedly promised that the car will function properly.
D. It depends whether an automobile transmission is ordinarily fit to last more than 50,000 miles.

ANALYSIS.   A merchant seller gives an implied warranty of merchantability when it sells goods, and it does not matter that the goods are used. Therefore, responses **A** and **B** cannot be correct. However, the warranty does not promise that the goods will perform perfectly. It promises only that the goods "are fit for the ordinary purposes for which such goods are used." So we would have to determine whether the car is fit for the purposes of a vehicle that has 50,000 miles on it. The best response is **D**.

E. Implied warranty of fitness for a particular purpose: § 2-315

Section 2-315 provides:

> Where the seller at the time of contracting has reason to know any particular purpose for which the goods are required and that the buyer is relying on the seller's skill or judgment to select or furnish suitable goods, there is unless excluded or modified under the next section an implied warranty that the goods shall be fit for such purpose.

The warranty of fitness for a particular purpose does not arise often. It is implied by law only when the seller has reason to know any particular purpose for which the buyer requires the goods and the buyer relies on the seller's skill or judgment in selecting the goods. It is given by sellers who are not merchants as well as by merchant sellers. For example, a customer in a shoe store expresses a need for a good mountain climbing shoe. The salesperson recommends a particular shoe and the customer buys it. Note the distinction between this warranty and the implied warranty of merchantability. When the seller selects suitable goods to suit the purposes of the buyer, it is impliedly promising that the goods are fit not just for the ordinary purposes for which the goods are used, but for the particular purpose communicated by the buyer. In our hypothetical, the shoes must not only be fit for the ordinary purposes of shoes, but also for mountain climbing.

QUESTION 5. Both Brenda and Sarah are law students. Brenda tells Sarah that she needs word processing software to write her law review article. Sarah says, "I just bought new software, so I'll sell you my old software." Brenda buys the software and discovers that although it otherwise works perfectly well, it does not create footnotes and is therefore not useful for writing her law review article. Assuming that Article 2 applies to this transaction, has Sarah breached the implied warranty of fitness for a particular purpose?

A. Yes, because she impliedly promised that the software would create footnotes.
B. Yes, because the software is not fit for the ordinary purpose of word processing.
C. No, because neither party is a merchant.
D. No, because no warranty was given in writing.

ANALYSIS. No warranty of merchantability is given here, because that warranty is only given by a goods merchant; and even if it were given, it was not breached because the software is fit for ordinary purposes. The elements of an implied warranty of fitness are satisfied here because the seller knew the buyer's purposes and directed her to particular goods that would satisfy that purpose. There is no requirement that the seller be a merchant or that the warranty be in writing; in fact, the warranty of fitness for a particular purpose almost always arises from the circumstances. The correct response is **A**.

F.   The Magnuson-Moss Warranty Act

The Magnuson-Moss Warranty Federal Trade Commission Improvement Act was designed to protect consumers from deceptive warranty practices. It supplements UCC warranty law. As stated in the report of a House committee:

> The paper with the filigree border bearing the bold caption "Warranty" or "Guarantee" was often of no greater worth than the paper it was printed on. Indeed, in many cases where a warranty or guarantee was ostensibly given the old saying applied: "The bold print giveth and the fine print taketh away." For the paper operated to take away from the consumer the implied warranties of merchantability and fitness arising by operation of law leaving little in its stead.

Magnuson-Moss gives consumers a federal cause of action for breach of warranty, including the possibility of recovering costs and attorneys' fees for breach of warranty. There are, however, a number of differences between UCC warranty law and Magnuson-Moss. Magnuson-Moss applies only to warrantors of consumer products. Magnuson-Moss regulates only written warranties. "Written warranty" is a term of art under Magnuson-Moss, which does not employ the UCC definition of warranty. Magnuson-Moss defines *written warranty* in 15 U.S.C. § 2301(6) as follows:

> (A) any written affirmation of fact or written promise made in connection with the sale of a consumer product by a supplier to a buyer which relates to the nature of the material or workmanship and affirms or promises that such material or workmanship is defect free or will meet a specified level of performance over a specified period of time, or
> (B) any undertaking in writing in connection with the sale by a supplier of a consumer product to refund, repair, replace, or take other remedial action with respect to such product in the event that such product fails to meet the specifications set forth in the undertaking, which written affirmation, promise, or undertaking becomes part of the basis of the bargain between a supplier and a buyer for purposes other than resale of such product.

Because of the difference in definition, a warranty for purposes of the UCC might not be a warranty for purposes of Magnuson-Moss. For example, if a sweater contains a label that states, "100% Cotton," that is a UCC express warranty but not a Magnuson-Moss warranty, for it does not pass the tests for a written warranty under the Act.

Magnuson-Moss makes few substantive changes in warranty law. It does not require a seller to give any warranty, but a seller who does give a written warranty must make certain disclosures. The seller must designate the warranty as either "full" or "limited." A warrantor who gives a full warranty may not disclaim or limit the duration of implied warranties. A warrantor who gives a limited warranty may not disclaim the implied warranties, but may limit them to the duration of a written warranty of reasonable duration.

Magnuson-Moss was supposed to work not by regulating warranties but by using the power of the market to improve warranties. The theory was that if the warranty terms were clearly disclosed, then consumers would shop for the best warranties just as they shop for the best price. Their task would be made easier because presumably they would prefer full warranties to limited warranties, so sellers would compete to provide the most attractive warranty. Has it worked? I'll let you be the judge.

> **QUESTION 6.** Consider the following situations:
>
> 1. A seller of a machine tool writes on a statement to a manufacturer who buys the tool: "We will repair any defects that show up in the next 30 days."
> 2. A seller sells a microwave oven that has a one-year warranty to Cisco Systems for use in the employee cafeteria.
>
> In both of these cases, the seller has given a UCC warranty. Has it given a Magnuson-Moss warranty?
>
> **A.** Yes, for the machine tool; yes, for the microwave oven.
> **B.** Yes, for the machine tool; no, for the microwave oven.
> **C.** No, for the machine tool; yes, for the microwave oven.
> **D.** No, for the machine tool; no, for the microwave oven.

ANALYSIS.   This is a bit tricky, as it requires careful reading of Magnuson-Moss. The machine tool does not have a Magnuson-Moss warranty, for the transaction does not involve a consumer product. The microwave oven does have a Magnuson-Moss warranty; although Cisco Systems is not a consumer, the microwave is a consumer product, and it is "consumer products" that are warranted under Magnuson-Moss. The correct response is **C**.

> **QUESTION 7.** A seller of consumer goods conspicuously states on the goods, "These goods are sold 'AS IS.' There are no warranties, express or implied, INCLUDING THE IMPLIED WARRANTY OF MERCHANTABILITY." Is this a legal warranty under Magnuson-Moss?

A. Yes, because Magnuson-Moss does not require sellers to give warranties.

B. No, because a Magnuson-Moss warranty cannot use the term "as is."

C. No, because it disclaims the implied warranty of merchantability.

D. No, because a Magnuson-Moss warranty must promise that the goods will be defect-free for a certain period of time.

ANALYSIS. The correct response is **A**. Magnuson-Moss does not require sellers to give warranties but only to disclose the warranty terms clearly.

G.   Closers

QUESTION 8. A consumer goes to a jewelry store and points out to the clerk a particular watch on display that he wishes to purchase. The clerk goes to the back of the store and emerges with a watch that he briefly shows to the consumer before wrapping it. The consumer buys the watch. When he gets home, the consumer discovers that the watch he purchased differs from the one that he pointed out in the display. Does the consumer have a claim for breach of warranty?

A. Yes, because an express warranty was created by affirmation of fact or promise.

B. Yes, because an express warranty was created by sample or model.

C. No, because he had an opportunity to inspect the goods before purchase.

D. No, because there was no language of warranty.

ANALYSIS.   Response **D** is not correct. Section 2-313(2) states in part that "[i]t is not necessary to the creation of an express warranty that the seller use formal words such as 'warrant' or 'guarantee' or that he have a specific intention to make a warranty." As we will see in the next chapter, there is some support for a disclaimer of implied warranty under § 2-316(3)(b) when the buyer has an opportunity to inspect the goods for defects. This provision does not specifically apply to express warranties. An express warranty probably requires a stronger fact situation to indicate that the parties' conduct constituted a disclaimer of the warranty, so response **C** is not correct. Under these facts, there was no affirmation of fact or promise by the seller, so response **A** is not correct. However, under § 2-313(1)(c):

> (c) Any sample or model which is made part of the basis of the bargain creates an express warranty that the whole of the goods shall conform to the sample or model.

Here, the conduct of the buyer in indicating the model of watch that he desired and the conduct of the seller in apparently finding one that conformed to that model created an express warranty that the watch sold was the same model as the watch displayed. The correct response is **B**.

QUESTION 9. A consumer buys a candy bar from a grocery store, bites into it, and breaks a tooth. Does the consumer have a claim for breach of warranty against the store?

A. Yes, because a candy bar that breaks a tooth is probably not merchantable.
B. Yes, because Magnuson-Moss provides a warranty of this consumer product.
C. No, because if anyone is to blame, it is the manufacturer and not the seller.
D. No, because no promises were made about the candy bar.

ANALYSIS.   There is no Magnuson-Moss claim because there is no "written warranty" under that statute. However, under § 2-314, the seller who is a goods merchant warrants that the goods are merchantable. Therefore, it appears that the buyer has a claim if he can show that a merchantable candy bar does not break teeth. The best response is **A**. It may indeed be the manufacturer who is to blame, but that does not bar the buyer's claim against the store since implied warranties are given by sellers. The store as a buyer of the candy bar would also have a claim against its seller for breach of warranty, so eventually the trail would lead to the manufacturer as the responsible party. We often think of this kind of case as a negligence claim, but there are many advantages to bringing it as a breach of warranty claim. For one, the claim is against the seller, which might prove more convenient. For another, it is a matter of strict liability; the plaintiff does not have to prove negligence. On the other hand, although the plaintiff can claim direct and consequential damages for breach of warranty, punitive damages and damages for "pain and suffering" cannot be recovered.

 # Burnham's picks

Question 1	**B**
Question 2	**A**
Question 3	**D**
Question 4	**D**

Question 5	**A**
Question 6	**C**
Question 7	**A**
Question 8	**B**
Question 9	**A**

10

Disclaimer of Warranties

A.   Introduction

The first rule of warranty law is: "The bold print giveth and the fine print taketh away." That is a bit of an exaggeration, but it could accurately be said that the law giveth and freedom of contract taketh away. Just as warranties are easily made by the seller and impliedly given by the Code, the Code also provides the means for the seller to disclaim or limit them. To explore the disclaimer of warranties under the Code, we will look at the following:

- Disclaimer of express warranties: § 2-316(1)
- Disclaimer of implied warranties: § 2-316(2) and (3)
- The "conspicuousness" requirement: § 1-201(b)(10)
- Disclaimer of the warranty of title and the warranty against infringement: § 2-312(2)
- Limitation of remedies: § 2-719

B.   Disclaimer of express warranties: § 2-316(1)

Express warranties that are part of the basis of the bargain are hard to disclaim. The first issue is whether the warranty was made. If an affirmation of fact or a promise is made during negotiations and the parties omit it when they reduce their agreement to a writing that they intend to be "a complete and exclusive statement of the terms of the agreement," in the words of § 2-202(b), then the express warranty is not part of the contract because of the parol evidence rule (see Chapter 6). This rule protects the seller against the buyer's fraudulent claims and against the statements of its own overzealous salespersons. If it is established that the express warranty was made, the next issue is to determine whether it is effectively disclaimed. Section 2-316(1) provides:

> Words or conduct relevant to the creation of an express warranty and words or conduct tending to negate or limit warranty shall be construed wherever reasonable as consistent with each other; but subject to the provisions of this chapter on parol or extrinsic evidence (§ 2-202) negation or limitation is inoperative to the extent that such construction is unreasonable.

If an express warranty is admissible under the parol evidence rule because the writing was not a full integration, the warranty might nevertheless be effectively disclaimed if the disclaimer limited the warranties to those given in the writing.

What happens when the writing both gives warranties and disclaims them? The reason express warranties are hard to disclaim is that the typical warranty of a seller or manufacturer starts by disclaiming all warranties, both express and implied. It then gives the buyer certain express warranties. Because the seller in that warranty package intends to give some express warranties, it would not make sense to say that the language of disclaimer disclaims all warranties. Instead, § 2-316(1) says that the language creating warranties and the language disclaiming warranties is to be read as consistent with each other, but where that is unreasonable, the disclaimer is not effective. For example, the manufacturer of an automobile provides the following warranty terms:

> THERE ARE NO WARRANTIES EXPRESS OR IMPLIED, INCLUDING BUT NOT LIMITED TO THE IMPLIED WARRANTY OF MERCHANTABILITY. For the first three years or 36,000 miles, whichever comes first, we will repair or replace any defective parts.

The manufacturer has both disclaimed express warranties ("THERE ARE NO WARRANTIES EXPRESS OR IMPLIED") and given an express warranty ("For the first three years or 36,000 miles, whichever comes first, we will repair or replace any defective parts"). It is not reasonable to read the two terms as consistent. Therefore, the language of disclaimer is not effective to disclaim the express warranties that were given. This is a reasonable interpretation, for the manufacturer's intention was to say that there are no express warranties *other than* the "repair or replace" warranty. That express warranty will be given effect in spite of the disclaimer.

Express warranties may be disclaimed orally with a statement such as "There are no express warranties" or with a more formal written statement such as this:

> *Disclaimer of Express Warranties.* Seller warrants that the goods are as described in this agreement, but no other express warranty is made in respect to the goods. If any model or sample was shown Buyer, such model or sample was used merely to illustrate the general type and quality of the goods and not to represent that the goods would necessarily be of that type or nature.

QUESTION 1. John, a law student, is selling his car to Mary. He says, "This car will get 25 miles per gallon around town. I disclaim all express warranties." The parties then enter into a partially integrated agreement that makes no mention of warranties or warranty disclaimer. Has John given Mary a warranty that the car will get 25 miles per gallon around town?

A. No, because John is not a merchant seller.
B. No, because the statement is puffing and not an express warranty.
C. No, because all express warranties were disclaimed.
D. Yes.

ANALYSIS. An express warranty can be made by any seller, so response **A** is not correct. This statement is an affirmation of fact rather than puffing, because it can be objectively measured and a remedy for breach can be fashioned, so response **B** is not correct. The warranty has been both made and disclaimed. It is not possible to construe these statements as consistent with each other. Therefore, the warranty is given effect to protect the buyer. The correct response is **D**.

QUESTION 2. The buyer of a used car from a dealer signs a contract containing a merger clause that states that the writing constitutes the final expression of the parties. The agreement contains an effective disclaimer of "all warranties, express or implied, including the implied warranty of merchantability." The buyer claims that during negotiations, a salesman for the seller gave her an oral warranty against latent mechanical defects. If there were such a promise, is it excluded from the contract?

A. No, because an express warranty that is both made and disclaimed is given effect.
B. No, because it is part of the basis of the bargain.
C. Yes, because there is an effective disclaimer of express warranties.
D. Yes, because of the parol evidence rule.

ANALYSIS.   For a seller to give an express warranty, it has to make an affirmation of fact or promise that is part of the basis of the bargain. Here, the promise does not make it into the contract, not because of the disclaimer of warranties, but because of the parol evidence rule in § 2-202. This is exactly the kind of statement that the parol evidence rule is designed to exclude. The burden was on the buyer to ask that the statement be written into the contract before the contract was signed. Had it been written into the contract, it would have been given effect in spite of the disclaimer. The correct response is **D**.

Incidentally, a number of years ago the Federal Trade Commission conducted a study of used car dealers and found that the practice of making promises that did not end up in the written contract was pervasive. The resulting Used Motor Vehicle Trade Regulation Rule, which can be found at 16 C.F.R. § 455, made some efforts to resolve this problem. The merchant seller of a used car must put a sticker in the rear window of the car that states conspicuously whether the car comes with a warranty or not. The sticker also warns the buyer: "IMPORTANT. Spoken promises are difficult to enforce. Ask the dealer to put all promises in writing. Keep this form."

C.   Disclaimer of implied warranties: § 2-316(2) and (3)

Implied warranties can be disclaimed in a number of ways, including the following:

- Use of a specific disclaimer: § 2-316(2)
- Use of a general disclaimer: § 2-316(3)(a)
- When the seller requires the buyer to examine the product for defects, the seller effectively disclaims warranty for those defects that the buyer should have discovered: § 2-316(3)(b)
- By course of dealing, course of performance, or usage of trade: § 2-316(3)(c)

The disclaimers created under § 2-316(3)(b) and (c) do not raise many issues. These disclaimers, consistent with Code methodology, arise because of the parties' actions rather than their words. We saw in § 2-314(3) that warranties may be created by course of dealing or usage of trade. They may similarly be disclaimed. For example, it may be understood in the wholesale used widget business that the widgets do not come with any implied warranty of merchantability.

The most common way to disclaim the implied warranties is through the use of a specific disclaimer. Section 2-316(2) provides:

Subject to subsection (3), to exclude or modify the implied warranty of merchantability or any part of it the language must mention merchantability and in case of a writing must be conspicuous, and to exclude or modify any implied warranty of fitness the exclusion must be by a writing and conspicuous. Language to exclude all implied warranties of fitness is sufficient if it states, for example, that "There are no warranties which extend beyond the description on the face hereof."

According to the statute, to effectively disclaim the implied warranty of merchantability, the disclaimer must use the word *merchantability* and, if written, the disclaimer must be conspicuous. So it would appear that if a seller orally states as part of the basis of the bargain, "I am not giving you a warranty of merchantability with this purchase," then the warranty of merchantability is effectively disclaimed. As a practical matter, that does not usually happen. Usually the seller's form contains language like this:

> WARRANTY. Seller warrants that the products sold by it will, when delivered, or when installed, if this contract provides for installation by Seller, be free of defects in workmanship or material. Should any failure to conform to this warranty become apparent during a period of one (1) year after date of installation, and not more than two (2) years after date of delivery, Seller shall, upon prompt, written notice and compliance by the customer with such instructions as it shall give with respect to the return of defective products or parts, correct such nonconformity by repair or replacement, F.O.B. factory, of the defective part or parts. Correction in the manner provided above shall constitute a fulfillment of all liabilities of Seller with respect to the quality of the products. THE FOREGOING WARRANTY IS EXCLUSIVE AND IN LIEU OF ALL OTHER WARRANTIES OF QUALITY, WHETHER WRITTEN, ORAL OR IMPLIED (INCLUDING ANY WARRANTY OF MERCHANTABILITY).

The statute provides that to effectively disclaim the implied warranty of fitness for a particular purpose, the disclaimer must be in writing and conspicuous. Note, however, that although the seller must use the word *merchantability* to effectively disclaim the implied warranty of merchantability, the term *fitness for a particular purpose* need not be used to disclaim that implied warranty. Therefore, if the seller orally states as part of the basis of the bargain, "I am not giving you a warranty of fitness for a particular purpose with this purchase," then the disclaimer is not effective because it is not in writing. But if the seller provides in a conspicuous writing, "THERE ARE NO IMPLIED WARRANTIES WITH THIS PURCHASE," then the implied warranty of fitness for a particular purpose is effectively disclaimed even though the implied warranty of merchantability is not.

The other way to disclaim implied warranties is through the use of a general disclaimer. Section 2-316(3)(a) provides:

> Notwithstanding subsection (2):
> (a) unless the circumstances indicate otherwise, all implied warranties are excluded by expressions like "as is," "with all faults" or other language which in common understanding calls the buyer's

attention to the exclusion of warranties and makes plain that there is no implied warranty;

On the surface, use of this statutory provision makes it easy for a seller to disclaim implied warranties. The seller may use the phrases "as is," "with all faults," "as is, where is," or similar language. However, the general disclaimer is not effective if "the circumstances indicate otherwise." A court might find such circumstances in a consumer transaction in which the purchaser does not understand the meaning of the term or when the language is not conspicuous. Because of this danger, many drafters use the more complex disclaimer in § 2-316(2). Furthermore, although the term "as is" seems to be a safe harbor, effective to disclaim all implied warranties, courts are reluctant to recognize other language that makes plain that there is no implied warranty.

QUESTION 3. A seller's form states on the front page, "THERE ARE NO WARRANTIES, EXPRESS OR IMPLIED." Is that language sufficient to disclaim the implied warranty of fitness for a particular purpose?

A. No, because it does not use the words *fitness for a particular purpose.*
B. No, because it is not conspicuous.
C. No, because it is disclaimed only when the implied warranty of merchantability is disclaimed.
D. Yes, because the disclaimer is in writing and conspicuous.

ANALYSIS.   The only statutory requirements for disclaimer of the implied warranty of fitness for a particular purpose is that the language of exclusion is in writing and conspicuous. Even though it does not disclaim the implied warranty of merchantability because it fails to use the word *merchantability,* this disclaimer seems to satisfy the statutory requirements for disclaimer of the implied warranty of fitness for a particular purpose. The correct response is **D.**

QUESTION 4. A sales receipt given to a merchant states, "All goods sold AS IS." Are the implied warranties effectively disclaimed?

A. Yes, because all implied warranties are excluded by expressions like "as is."
B. Yes, because the language of a specific disclaimer has been used.
C. No, because in the circumstances a person would not expect to find a disclaimer on the sales receipt.
D. No, the implied warranty of merchantability is not disclaimed because the word *merchantability* is not used.

ANALYSIS. There is no language of specific disclaimer under § 2-316(2) here, but the words "as is" are effective language of general disclaimer under § 2-316(3) and the words are conspicuous. That provision, however, is prefaced by the ominous words, "unless the circumstances indicate otherwise." A case could be made that a reasonable person would not expect to find the terms of a contract on a sales receipt. However, this might be a better argument in the case of a consumer than in the case of a merchant. Although the issue is somewhat in doubt, I think the best response is **A.**

A study by the Federal Trade Commission found that buyers of used cars did not generally know what "as is" meant and sometimes car dealers misled them as to its meaning. The Federal Trade Commission Used Motor Vehicle Trade Regulation Rule requires a window sticker in which the merchant seller of a used vehicle must inform the buyer whether the car is purchased with or without a warranty. Under the box marked AS IS — NO WARRANTY, the sticker states, "YOU WILL PAY ALL COSTS FOR ANY REPAIRS. The dealer assumes no responsibility for any repairs regardless of any oral statements about the vehicle." In theory, the rule prevents any dispute about whether the purchaser saw the disclaimer and understood its meaning.

D. The requirement of "conspicuousness"

Section 2-316(2) requires that the disclaimer be "conspicuous." Although the statute does not expressly require it, most courts read the requirement of conspicuousness into § 2-316(3) as well. How is the requirement that a disclaimer of warranty be conspicuous satisfied? According to Official Comment 1, the intent of § 2-316 is "to protect a buyer from unexpected and unbargained language of disclaimer." In that context, consider the definition of *conspicuous* in § 1-201(b)(10):

> (10) "Conspicuous," with reference to a term, means so written, displayed, or presented that a reasonable person against which it is to operate ought to have noticed it. Whether a term is "conspicuous" or not is a decision for the court. Conspicuous terms include the following:
> (A) a heading in capitals equal to or greater in size than the surrounding text, or in contrasting type, font, or color to the surrounding text of the same or lesser size; and
> (B) language in the body of a record or display in larger type than the surrounding text, or in contrasting type, font, or color to the surrounding text of the same size, or set off from surrounding text of the same size by symbols or other marks that call attention to the language.

Many issues arise with respect to the conspicuousness requirement. It is interesting to note that although the statute requires the standard of "a reasonable person," that judgment is not made by a jury. The statute provides that "[w]hether a term is 'conspicuous' or not is a decision for the court," and courts have been all over the place in their decisions. For example, if the disclaimer is in capital letters, but all the text is in capital letters, then there is probably nothing conspicuous about the disclaimer. In an interesting case, the contract contained a term with the conspicuous heading "WARRANTY" followed by a disclaimer of warranty in ordinary font. The court held that the consumer would be misled into thinking it was getting a warranty rather than getting no warranty. A disclaimer in italics arguably complies with the statutory requirement of "contrasting type, font, or color," but some courts have found that insufficient. Even if a disclaimer is conspicuous in appearance, it could be held not to satisfy the requirement if it is buried in the body of the contract.

QUESTION 5. In a contract that otherwise uses nonitalicized text, is the following disclaimer conspicuous?

3. The parties agree that the implied warranties of merchantability and fitness for a particular purpose and all other warranties, express or implied, are excluded from this transaction and shall not apply to the goods sold.

A. Yes, because the italics contrast with the surrounding text.
B. Yes, because a reasonable person should notice it.
C. No, because every word is in the same type.
D. No, because it is not larger than the other type.

ANALYSIS.   I don't think this question is easily answered. The statute requires that "a reasonable person against which it is to operate ought to have noticed it." The statute then goes on to say that it is conspicuous if in "contrasting type." There is no requirement that the type has to be larger or that every word can't be emphasized. So it would appear that italics satisfy the requirements and the best response is **B**. However, a court that dealt with the issue disagreed. It said, "It appears to be a classic case of attempting barely to comply with the letter of the law while circumventing its spirit. [The disclaimer] is not bolder, larger or different color type. It is not . . . indented, underscored or highlighted in any manner. It is not preceded by a distinctive legend or statement signifying the importance of that particular passage." The court's language suggests ways that the disclaimer should be made more conspicuous. The prudent drafter would take steps to do so.

E. Disclaimer of the warranty of title and the warranty against infringement: § 2-312(2)

Recall that § 2-312(1) provides that by operation of law, the seller gives the buyer a warranty of good title. The methods we discussed for disclaiming the other implied warranties will not work to disclaim this warranty, because it is not described by the Code as an implied warranty even though it is implied in every sales contract. Section 2-312(2) provides a rule for the effective disclaimer of this warranty:

> (2) A warranty under subsection (1) will be excluded or modified only by specific language or by circumstances which give the buyer reason to know that the person selling does not claim title in himself or that he is purporting to sell only such right or title as he or a third person may have.

Curiously, this language does not refer to the warranty against infringement in § 2-312(3). The specific disclaimers of § 2-316(2) do not address this warranty, and it is probably not an implied warranty for purposes of § 2-316(3)(a), which states that "all *implied* warranties are excluded by expressions like 'as is.'" My guess is that this was an oversight on the part of the drafters, who probably intended the warranty against infringement to be excluded by specific language as provided in § 2-312(2). This was the view of the drafters of Amended Article 2, who switched subsections (2) and (3), and referred in subsection (3) to the disclaimer of "[a] warranty under this section" rather than "[a] warranty under subsection (1)." Although Amended Article 2 has been withdrawn, it can be cited as persuasive evidence of how an existing problem under Article 2 should be resolved.

F. Conflicts among warranties: § 2-317

Conflicts that arise when an express warranty is both given and disclaimed were discussed earlier in this chapter. If express and implied warranties conflict, the intention of the parties governs. Section 2-317 establishes rules for determining that intention:

> **§ 2-317. Cumulation and Conflict of Warranties Express or Implied.**
> Warranties whether express or implied shall be construed as consistent with each other and as cumulative, but if such construction is unreasonable the intention of the parties shall determine which warranty is dominant. In ascertaining that intention the following rules apply:
> (a) Exact or technical specifications displace an inconsistent sample or model or general language of description.

(b) A sample from an existing bulk displaces inconsistent general language of description.

(c) Express warranties displace inconsistent implied warranties other than an implied warranty of fitness for a particular purpose.

The subsections provide some hierarchies for resolving inconsistencies. For example, assume a seller of grapefruit showed a buyer a sample and provided in the agreement that the fruit would be no less than ten inches in circumference. The fruit as delivered was less than ten inches in circumference, but it turns out the model was less than ten inches in circumference as well. Which source provided the express warranty—the sample or the language providing the specifications? According to § 2-317(a), the exact specifications displace the sample, so the seller would be in breach.

QUESTION 6. A used car warranty states in full: "This vehicle is warranted to be free of defects for 2,000 miles or 2 months, whichever occurs first." A defect manifests itself at 2,500 miles. Does the purchaser have a claim for breach of warranty?

A. No, because the express warranty expired after 2,000 miles.
B. No, because there is no implied warranty of merchantability.
C. Yes, under the express warranty.
D. Yes, under the implied warranty of merchantability.

ANALYSIS.   The problem here is that although the seller gave an express warranty, the seller did not effectively disclaim the implied warranty of merchantability. Section 2-317(c) provides that "[e]xpress warranties displace inconsistent implied warranties." The issue then becomes whether in this case the express warranty displaced the implied warranty. Most courts have held that the express warranty is not inconsistent with the implied warranty and therefore does not displace it. The result would be the same if the seller attempted a disclaimer but the disclaimer was not effective. Therefore, in addition to the express warranty, the buyer got an implied warranty of merchantability, and is free to argue that the car was not merchantable. The best response is **D.**

G.   Limitation of remedies: § 2-719

Very often, a seller does not disclaim all warranties. Instead, the seller gives a warranty but limits the buyer's remedies under the warranty. In the absence of limitation, the remedies for breach of warranty are found in § 2-714(2) and (3):

(2) The measure of damages for breach of warranty is the difference at the time and place of acceptance between the value of the goods accepted and the value they would have had if they had been as warranted, unless special circumstances show proximate damages of a different amount.

(3) In a proper case any incidental and consequential damages under the next section may also be recovered.

We will further explore the limitation of remedies outside of the warranty context in Chapter 18. We will then see that many sellers limit the recovery under the warranty. They often exclude consequential damages entirely, or they limit recovery to a certain amount, such as the purchase price of the product. Section 2-719 places a number of restrictions on the seller who limits remedies. The section provides:

(1) Subject to the provisions of subsections (2) and (3) of this section and of the preceding section on liquidation and limitation of damages,

(a) the agreement may provide for remedies in addition to or in substitution for those provided in this chapter and may limit or alter the measure of damages recoverable under this chapter, as by limiting the buyer's remedies to return of the goods and repayment of the price or to repair and replacement of nonconforming goods or parts; and

(b) resort to a remedy as provided is optional unless the remedy is expressly agreed to be exclusive, in which case it is the sole remedy.

(2) Where circumstances cause an exclusive or limited remedy to fail of its essential purpose, remedy may be had as provided in this code.

(3) Consequential damages may be limited or excluded unless the limitation or exclusion is unconscionable. Limitation of consequential damages for injury to the person in the case of consumer goods is prima facie unconscionable but limitation of damages where the loss is commercial is not.

A remedy provided by the seller is optional unless it is expressly agreed to be exclusive. Subsection (2) provides that if the remedy fails of its essential purpose, the buyer has available the other remedies provided in the UCC. This remedy is akin to the "lemon laws" passed by states. Many sellers give an express "repair or replace" warranty that provides that instead of paying money damages, the seller will repair or replace any defective part for a certain period of time. Sometimes the product breaks down and the buyer takes it in for repair. When it repeatedly breaks down, and the seller fixes it each time, the seller claims it is living up to the warranty by repairing the product. But many courts have found that in such a case the limited remedy does not satisfy its essential purpose, which was to provide the buyer with a defect-free product. In such a case the buyer may have other remedies, such as revocation under § 2-608.

Under § 2-719(3), consequential damages may be limited or excluded unless unconscionable. In the case of consumer goods, limitation of consequential damages for personal injury is prima facie unconscionable. When a court determines that the limited remedy fails of its essential purpose and the court throws out the limited remedy, an issue often arises as to whether the court should throw out the exclusion or limitation of consequential damages as well. Courts are divided on this issue. In addition to all of these issues, there is an issue of whether the limitation of remedies must be conspicuous, and courts are also divided on that issue.

QUESTION 7. A manufacturer of a power saw sold to consumer buyers provides a warranty that contains the following provision:

> *Consequential Damages.* In the event of a breach or repudiation of this contract by Seller, Buyer shall not be entitled to any consequential damages in excess of $1,000.

The saw malfunctions and a purchaser is injured. Is the injured party likely to recover consequential damages in excess of $1,000?

A. Yes, because the limitation of consequential damages will be thrown out when the limited remedy fails of its essential purpose.

B. Yes, because the limitation of consequential damages is prima facie unconscionable.

C. No, because parties have freedom to contract around the default rules of the Code.

D. No, because the presumption of unconscionability can be rebutted.

ANALYSIS. Response **A** is not relevant because there is no fact indicating that a limited remedy fails of its essential purpose. Under § 2-719(3), "[l]imitation of consequential damages for injury to the person in the case of consumer goods is prima facie unconscionable." Although the presumption can be rebutted, there are no facts here to indicate that it should be. Parties can generally contract around the default rules, but this one is clearly a regulatory rule that cannot be changed by the parties. The best response is **B**.

H. Closers

Questions 8 through 10 are based on the following typical seller's warranty (I have divided the text into paragraphs and numbered the paragraphs for convenient reference):

   1. If within one year from the date of sale, any product sold under this purchase order, or any part thereof, shall prove to be defective in

material or workmanship upon examination by the Manufacturer, the Manufacturer will supply an identical or substantially similar replacement part f.o.b. the Manufacturer's factory, or the Manufacturer, at its option, will repair or allow credit for such part.

2. NO OTHER WARRANTY, EITHER EXPRESS OR IMPLIED AND INCLUDING A WARRANTY OF MERCHANTABILITY AND FITNESS FOR A PARTICULAR PURPOSE HAS BEEN OR WILL BE MADE BY OR ON BEHALF OF THE MANUFACTURER OR THE SELLER OR BY OPERATION OF LAW WITH RESPECT TO THE EQUIPMENT AND ACCESSORIES OR THEIR INSTALLATION, USE, OPERATION, REPLACEMENT OR REPAIR.

3. NEITHER THE MANUFACTURER NOR THE SELLER SHALL BE LIABLE BY VIRTUE OF THIS WARRANTY, OR OTHERWISE, FOR ANY SPECIAL OR CONSEQUENTIAL LOSS OR DAMAGE RESULTING FROM THE USE OR LOSS OF THE USE OF EQUIPMENT AND ACCESSORIES.

4. THE BUYER RECOGNIZES THAT THE EXPRESS WARRANTY SET FORTH ABOVE IS THE EXCLUSIVE REMEDY TO WHICH HE IS ENTITLED AND HE WAIVES ALL OTHER REMEDIES, STATUTORY OR OTHERWISE.

QUESTION 8. Which numbered paragraph serves each function described below?

A. Exclusive remedy
B. Disclaimer of implied warranties
C. Express warranty
D. Exclusion of consequential damages

ANALYSIS. This warranty begins in paragraph 1 by giving the buyer an express warranty under § 2-313. This is a typical "repair or replace" warranty, promising to repair or replace any defective parts for a period of time, here one year. So **C=1**. Note that because § 2-317 provides that warranties are cumulative, the mere fact that the seller has given an express warranty does not mean that it does not also give an implied warranty. Therefore, the seller here disclaims all warranties in the second paragraph, so **B=2**. The default rule of § 2-715 is that a buyer is entitled to consequential damages for breach of warranty, so the seller uses the power under § 2-719 to exclude consequential damages. Remember that according to § 2-719(3), "[l]imitation of consequential damages for injury to the person in the case of consumer goods is prima facie unconscionable." So **D=3**. Finally, according to § 2-719(1)(b), "resort to a remedy as provided is optional unless the remedy is expressly agreed to be exclusive, in which case it is the sole remedy." Here, the fourth paragraph constitutes the parties' agreement that the remedy is exclusive, so **A=4**.

> **QUESTION 9.** Does paragraph 2 effectively disclaim the implied warranty of merchantability?
>
> A. Yes, because it is conspicuous and uses the word *merchantability*.
> B. Yes, because it conspicuously states that "no other warranty . . . has been or will be made."
> C. No, because it does not use the term "as is."
> D. No, because it is unconscionable to disclaim the implied warranty of merchantability.

ANALYSIS. According to § 2-316(2), "to exclude or modify the implied warranty of merchantability or any part of it the language must mention merchantability and in case of a writing must be conspicuous." Here, paragraph 2 uses the word *merchantability*. According to § 1-201(b)(10)(B), the following language is conspicuous:

> (B) language in the body of a record or display in larger type than the surrounding text, or in contrasting type, font, or color to the surrounding text of the same size, or set off from surrounding text of the same size by symbols or other marks that call attention to the language.

Here, the language is in capital letters. There may be an issue as to whether this larger type is in contrasting type to the surrounding text. In other words, if the entire agreement were in capital letters, then this disclaimer would not stand out. I think we can infer from the fact that paragraph 1 is in lowercase that the rest of the agreement probably is. If that is the case, then this language would be conspicuous. The best response is **A**.

> **QUESTION 10.** Assume that a court throws out the limited remedy in paragraph 1 because it fails of its essential purpose. Will the court also throw out the exclusion of consequential damages in paragraph 3?
>
> A. Yes, because they are all part of the same warranty package.
> B. No, because they are in separate paragraphs.
> C. No, because they are different limitations of remedy.
> D. It depends on the jurisdiction.

ANALYSIS. According to § 2-719(2), "[w]here circumstances cause an exclusive remedy to fail of its essential purpose, remedy may be had as provided in this Act." As we have seen, this provision makes the repair or replace remedy exclusive. It could fail if the goods are a "lemon" and the seller is not able to make them work properly. In that event, all courts agree that other remedies are available, such as revocation of acceptance under § 2-608. However, not all courts agree that the exclusion of consequential damages is thrown out along with the exclusive repair or replace remedy. The best response is **D**.

 # Burnham's picks

Question 1	**D**
Question 2	**D**
Question 3	**D**
Question 4	**A**
Question 5	**B**
Question 6	**D**
Question 7	**B**
Question 8	**C=1, B=2, D=3, A=4**
Question 9	**A**
Question 10	**D**

11

Third-Party Beneficiaries

A. Vertical privity
B. Horizontal privity
C. Vertical and horizontal privity
D. Notice
E. Closers
 Burnham's picks

A. Vertical privity

Aclaim for breach of warranty is a contract claim. Under the common law principle of privity, only a party to the contract was allowed to bring a claim against the other party to the contract; the parties were said to be "in privity." Modern sales law, however, has diluted the concept of privity. We use the concept of *vertical privity* to describe the legal relationship between the parties to a chain of distribution, such as a manufacturer, a distributor, a retailer, and a buyer (sometimes called the *ultimate purchaser,* as there are others in the chain who are buyers). Each party in the chain has a contract only with the party on either side of it. We use the concept of *horizontal privity* to describe the legal relationship between a party and a nonparty, even though there is no contract between them. For example, the buyer of a candy bar at the bottom of our vertical chain is said to be in horizontal privity with the family member or guest to whom she offers the candy bar. The issue we are now faced with is whether the law permits a party to make a warranty claim against a party with which it is not in privity; for example, can the ultimate purchaser or the guest make a claim against the manufacturer?

We know from our study of warranties that the Code provides that the buyer obtains warranties from the seller and may have a claim against the seller for breach of warranty. For example, if a customer is injured by a foreign object in a candy bar purchased from Megalomart, the customer has a claim against Megalomart for breach of warranty. Megalomart can then make a claim against its seller, the distributor; and the distributor can make a claim against its seller, the manufacturer. In addition, the manufacturer might have a claim against the supplier that sold it the ingredient. In this way, the claim will ultimately be made against the party who is responsible for the defective product.

Note that in tort, the manufacturer or the supplier would be the likely defendants, for the distributor and retailer did not commit a wrong. An advantage of a warranty claim is that it allows a buyer to go after the buyer's immediate seller. The case for breach of warranty may also be easier to prove than the claim for negligence, for a warranty claim is one of strict liability. The plaintiff only needs to prove that the seller breached the warranty, for example, by selling goods that are not "fit for the ordinary purposes for which such goods are used." See § 2-314(2)(c). The plaintiff does not need to prove any "fault" or negligence of the seller. This is one of the reasons, as we explored in Chapter 4.A, that it might make a difference whether a transaction is within the scope of Article 2.

But can the customer sue the manufacturer, with which it is not in privity, for breach of warranty? Recall that under § 2-313, an express warranty consists of "any affirmation of fact or promise *made by the seller to the buyer.*" Technically the warranty has been given only to the seller's buyer (e.g., from the manufacturer to the distributor) and not to the customer, the ultimate purchaser. Also, to constitute an express warranty, the affirmation of fact or promise must become "part of the basis of the bargain." Many commentators believe that the "basis of the bargain" language creates a reliance requirement, and if a person was not aware of the seller's express warranty, then it was not possible for that person to rely on it. For these reasons, there is an argument that an ultimate purchaser should not be able to recover against a manufacturer for breach of an express warranty that was not given to the ultimate purchaser. Official Comment 2 to § 2-313, however, states:

> 2. Although this section is limited in its scope and direct purpose to warranties made by the seller to the buyer as part of a contract for sale, the warranty sections of this Article are not designed in any way to disturb those lines of case law growth which have recognized that warranties need not be confined either to sales contracts or to the direct parties to such a contract. They may arise in other appropriate circumstances such as in the case of bailments for hire, whether such bailment is itself the main contract or is merely a supplying of containers under a contract for the sale of their contents. The provisions of Section 2-318 on third party beneficiaries expressly recognize this case law development within one particular area. Beyond that, the matter is left to the case law with the intention that the policies of this Act may offer useful guidance in dealing with further cases as they arise.

The case law in most jurisdictions has developed to allow a claim by a third party against the manufacturer for breach of express warranties made by the manufacturer. Such a warranty might arise, for example, from the manufacturer's television advertising. Amended Article 2 proposed two new sections, 2-313A and 2-313B, that specifically recognized these warranties.

Fewer courts, however, allow remote purchasers to recover against manufacturers on a theory of breach of the implied warranty of merchantability. Courts may, however, be more willing to allow a claim against a manufacturer for personal injury rather than property damage or economic loss. Note that manufacturers, like other sellers, may be able to effectively disclaim the implied warranty of merchantability.

> **QUESTION 1.** John sees a TV commercial in which a certain car is driven across a shallow stream to get to a good fishing spot. He buys the car from the local dealership. A few days later, he drives the car across a stream and the engine is flooded and severely damaged. He brings a claim for breach of warranty against the manufacturer. What advice could you give him about this claim?
>
> **A.** In some jurisdictions, a claim for breach of implied warranty can be brought by a remote purchaser.
> **B.** He is out of luck because he is not in privity of contract with the manufacturer.
> **C.** In most jurisdictions, a claim for breach of express warranty can be brought by a remote purchaser.
> **D.** Amended Article 2 specifically recognizes this claim.

ANALYSIS. Although response **D** is correct, it is not the best answer. Amended Article 2 has not been enacted in any jurisdiction, so even though the advice is accurate, it will do the client little good. Response **B** is not a good response because the modern trend is away from a requirement of privity of contract. Although both responses **A** and **C** are correct, the content of the television advertisement would be an express warranty rather than an implied warranty, so **C** is the best response.

B.   Horizontal privity

Another privity issue is whether someone other than the buyer who ultimately uses the goods and suffers some loss may recover against the seller for breach of warranty. That person does not generally have a contractual relationship with the buyer. Therefore, if the concept of privity were strictly applied horizontally, such a person would not have a claim. However, an exception to the rule of privity is that a third-party beneficiary may be able to sue on the contract. For example, if the purchaser of a candy bar from Megalomart gives it to a guest in her house, and the guest is injured by a foreign object in the candy bar, the guest may be able to sue Megalomart for breach of warranty.

Section 2-318 was drafted to provide a breach of warranty claim to certain third-party beneficiaries of the warranty. Incidentally, it is interesting to note that the text of § 2-318 never mentions the term "third-party beneficiaries." That term, however, is found in the caption. Is it fair to use the caption of a statute to assist with the interpretation of the statute? With respect to most statutes, the answer is no. In the usual case, the legislature enacts the text of the statute and the caption is added later by an administrative body. Because it is not part of the law, the caption should not be used to interpret the law. However, the Uniform Commercial Code is an exception to that rule. The Uniform Law Commission (ULC) supplies the captions along with the text, and both are enacted by the legislature. This point is driven home by § 1-107, which provides in full:

§ 1-107. Section Captions.

Section captions are part of [the Uniform Commercial Code].

Section 2-318 is the only Article 2 provision that invites the adopting jurisdiction to enact one of three alternatives, each with a more liberal rule governing which third parties can sue a seller for breach of warranty and for what damages. The three alternatives are as follows:

§ 2-318. Third Party Beneficiaries of Warranties Express or Implied.
Alternative A

A seller's warranty whether express or implied extends to any natural person who is in the family or household of his buyer or who is a guest in his home if it is reasonable to expect that such person may use, consume or be affected by the goods and who is injured in person by breach of the warranty. A seller may not exclude or limit the operation of this section.

Alternative B

A seller's warranty whether express or implied extends to any natural person who may reasonably be expected to use, consume or be affected by the goods and who is injured in person by breach of the warranty. A seller may not exclude or limit the operation of this section.

Alternative C

A seller's warranty whether express or implied extends to any person who may reasonably be expected to use, consume or be affected by the goods and who is injured by breach of the warranty. A seller may not exclude or limit the operation of this section with respect to injury to the person of an individual to whom the warranty extends.

Under Alternative A, the most restrictive provision, the person bringing the claim must be a natural person in the buyer's family, household, or a guest in the buyer's home. It must be reasonable to expect that such a person might use the goods. The claim can only be for personal injury. The seller does not have freedom of contract to further restrict the class of protected beneficiaries or the type of injury protected against. Alternative B expands the class of protected persons to any natural person who may reasonably be expected to use the goods but is in all other respects similar to Alternative A. Alternative C, the most liberal provision, expands the class of protected parties to any person (including entities) who may reasonably be expected to use the goods. It covers any injury, including economic loss, but allows the seller to limit the protection to the personal injury of a natural person.

QUESTION 2. The coach of a Little League team buys candy bars at Megalomart and distributes them to team members on the field after a game. A member of the team is injured by a foreign object in the candy bar and makes a claim against Megalomart. In a jurisdiction that has enacted Alternative A, what is Megalomart's best defense?

A. The claimant is not a natural person.
B. The claimant is not in the buyer's family, household, or a guest in the buyer's home.
C. It is not reasonable to expect that the claimant might use the goods.
D. The claimant does not have a claim for personal injury.

ANALYSIS. All of the elements of Alternative A are satisfied, except that the claimant must be "in the family or household of his buyer or . . . a guest in his home." The correct response is **B**.

QUESTION 3. A landlord installs an air conditioner in a commercial space rented by Bookstore, Inc. The air conditioner leaks and damages the inventory of the bookstore. In which jurisdiction can Bookstore, Inc. bring a claim for breach of warranty against the seller of the air conditioner?

A. In a jurisdiction that has enacted Alternative A.
B. In a jurisdiction that has enacted Alternative B.
C. In a jurisdiction that has enacted Alternative C.
D. In none of these jurisdictions.

ANALYSIS. The claim is for economic loss rather than personal injury, so that eliminates a jurisdiction that has enacted Alternatives A and B. That leaves only Alternative C. The claimant is an entity rather than a natural person, but the warranty under Alternative C extends to "persons," which includes entities such as corporations. Because the bookstore would reasonably be expected to use the goods, all the elements of Alternative C are satisfied. The correct response is **C**.

C.   Vertical and horizontal privity

With the issue of horizontal privity resolved by § 2-318, we then have the additional question of the interplay of horizontal privity with vertical privity. For example, the issue might be whether the buyer's guest can sue the manufacturer of the candy bar for breach of warranty.

Whereas § 2-318 governs the horizontal privity analysis, common law governs the vertical privity analysis. The Official Comments to § 2-318 make clear that the Code intended to leave the question of vertical privity to common law development. Comment 3 states in part that "the section in this form is neutral and is not intended to enlarge or restrict the developing case law on whether the seller's warranties, given to his buyer who resells, extend to other persons in the distributive chain."

Not all jurisdictions permit a person in horizontal privity with the buyer to sue a person in vertical privity with the seller. Note, however, that whereas Alternative A refers to persons who are in privity with "a seller's . . . buyer," Alternatives B and C merely state to whom a seller's warranty extends. A remote purchaser in a jurisdiction that has enacted Alternative B or C could argue that because the manufacturer is a seller, its warranty is extended to remote purchasers by § 2-318. But the statute permits sellers to exclude or limit their liability, other than their liability for personal injury to natural persons.

QUESTION 4. A seller of trampolines distributes the manufacturer's brochures, which state that the trampoline is "tested to withstand a weight of 400 pounds," but the seller does not otherwise make any promises about the trampoline. John buys the trampoline. During his son's birthday party, three children, each weighing less than 100 pounds, are on the trampoline when it tears from the weight and one of the children is injured. Assume the trampoline is fit for the ordinary purposes of a trampoline. Does the injured child have a claim against the retail seller?

A. Yes, but only in a jurisdiction that has enacted Alternative B or C.
B. Yes, because there is a personal injury claim by a guest in the home that could reasonably be expected to use the trampoline.
C. Yes, but only if the jurisdiction recognizes vertical privity for personal injury claims.
D. No, because no warranty that extends to the injured child has been breached.

ANALYSIS.   It goes without saying that for a third-party beneficiary to have a claim, there must first be a breach of warranty. Here the manufacturer expressly warranted the trampoline to withstand a weight of 400 pounds. The retailer probably did not adopt that warranty merely by distributing the manufacturer's brochures. The retailer gave an implied warranty of merchantability, but the facts state that that warranty was not breached. Therefore, the child has no claim against the retailer. The correct response is **D**.

If the retailer had given a warranty that was breached, then response **A** would be incorrect because under all three alternatives a natural person who is a guest and who is personally injured would have a claim. Response **C** would also be incorrect because this is not a vertical privity issue; the question is whether the third party would have a claim against the buyer's immediate seller. Response **B** would be correct under those facts.

QUESTION 5. A seller of trampolines distributes the manufacturer's brochures, which state that the trampoline is "tested to withstand a weight of 400 pounds," but the seller does not otherwise make any promises about the trampoline. John buys the trampoline. During his son's birthday party, three children, each weighing less than 100 pounds, are on the trampoline when it tears from the weight and one of the children is injured. Assume the trampoline is fit for the ordinary purposes of a trampoline. Does the injured child have a claim against the manufacturer?

A. Yes, in every jurisdiction.
B. Yes, in a jurisdiction that has enacted Alternative B or C.
C. No, because even if there is horizontal privity, no jurisdiction recognizes vertical privity for breach of an express warranty.
D. No, because the manufacturer has given no warranty to the buyer.

ANALYSIS.   Response **D** is incorrect, because the manufacturer has made an express warranty that the trampoline is "tested to withstand a weight of 400 pounds," and that warranty extends to a buyer from the manufacturer. Response **A** is incorrect, because Alternative A states that a seller's warranty extends to the guests of the buyer. However, John is not the buyer from the manufacturer; the retailer is. Response **C** is also incorrect because many jurisdictions recognize vertical privity for breach of an express warranty. Response **B** represents the best answer, because Alternatives B and C provide that a seller's warranty extends to persons who may reasonably be expected to use the product. These alternatives do not limit the class of claimants to the family or guests of the buyer.

D.   Notice

When we look at remedies, we will see that § 2-607(3) requires that as a condition precedent to bringing a breach of warranty claim against a seller, the buyer must "within a reasonable time after he discovers or should have discovered any breach notify the seller of breach." Although it is clear that notice must be given to the immediate seller, there is a split of authority as to whether failure to give notice to a remote seller such as a manufacturer precludes the ultimate purchaser from bringing a claim against that party. It would seem that the better rule is not to require notice. The statute does not strictly require it. Because each seller has a claim against its seller, one might presume that the seller would have an interest in providing notice to the party above it in the chain.

These problems are all magnified when it is a third-party beneficiary, rather than the buyer, who brings the claim against the remote seller. Must the guest who is bringing a claim as a third-party beneficiary give notice before bringing a claim against a seller or manufacturer? Because the third party is not a buyer, many courts have not required the third-party beneficiary bringing a claim under § 2-318 to provide notice to the seller.

QUESTION 6. John buys a box of candy bars that are manufactured by Mars. He serves them at a weekly poker game at his house, and Jim breaks a tooth on one of the candy bars. Jim asks John where he got them, and John responds that it was at Megalomart. Jim complains to Megalomart and the negotiations become protracted. After a year, Jim becomes frustrated and sues both Megalomart and Mars. Which of the following statements most accurately describes Jim's legal situation?

A. Under the Code, he has no claim against Megalomart, and it is therefore unlikely he has a claim against Mars.

B. He has a claim against Megalomart under the Code, but in most jurisdictions he does not have a claim against Mars.

C. He has a claim against Megalomart under the Code, and in many jurisdictions he has a claim against Mars.

D. He has a claim against Megalomart under the Code, and in many jurisdictions he has a claim against Mars, but there is an issue as to whether he gave seasonable notice to Mars.

ANALYSIS. Even in a jurisdiction that has enacted the most restrictive Alternative A of § 2-318, Jim would have a claim as a third-party beneficiary against Megalomart. That resolves the horizontal privity issue. As to vertical privity, many jurisdictions allow a buyer to make a claim for breach of an implied warranty against a remote manufacturer, and they also allow the third-party beneficiary to make the claim. However, § 2-607(3) requires a buyer to give seasonable notice to the seller. The best response is **D**. In resolving that issue, by the way, many jurisdictions do not require the third party to give notice, and if they did have such a requirement, it might be satisfied by notice within one year of the injury. Official Comment 4 states that "the requirement of notification is meant to defeat commercial bad faith, not to deprive a good-faith consumer of a remedy."

E. Closers

Questions 7 and 8 are based on the following facts. A farmer bought Crown Quality Seed from Farmers Seed, a distributor of the product. The bag of seed, which the farmer did not see before the purchase, stated on the label: "This quality seed is protected by Heptachlor insecticide treatment to help ensure stronger stands, superior quality, and increased yields." When the seed did not grow, the farmer brought a claim against Crown Quality Seed for breach of this warranty.

QUESTION 7. How would you characterize this claim?

A. A claim in vertical privity for breach of an implied warranty.
B. A claim in vertical privity for breach of an express warranty.
C. A claim in horizontal privity for breach of an implied warranty.
D. A claim in horizontal privity for breach of an express warranty.

ANALYSIS. Under the facts, Crown Quality Seed sold the seed to Farmers Seed, which sold it to the farmer. The farmer as plaintiff is therefore suing the manufacturer who sold to his seller, so this is a case of vertical privity. Because the farmer is suing on the basis of the statement on the label, this is a claim for breach of express warranty. The correct response is **B**.

QUESTION 8. Is a court likely to allow the farmer to pursue this claim?

A. Yes, it is a straightforward claim for breach of express warranty.
B. Yes, because most jurisdictions allow a remote purchaser to sue a manufacturer for breach of an express warranty.
C. No, because most jurisdictions do not allow a remote purchaser to sue a manufacturer for breach of an express warranty.
D. No, because the farmer suffered no personal injury.

ANALYSIS. Most courts allow a remote purchaser to sue a manufacturer for breach of an express warranty. The correct response is **B**. For a case to the contrary, see the facts on which this question is based, *Schmaltz v. Nissen*, 431 N.W.2d 657 (S.D. 1988). In that case, the court found that the language of warranty was not part of the basis of the bargain because the plaintiff had not read it or known of it. White and Summers, *Uniform Commercial Code* § 9-5, approve of this result, asking, "Why should one who has not relied on the seller's statement have the right to sue? That plaintiff is asking for greater protection than he would get under the warranty of merchantability, far more than he bargained for." Another scholar responds, "Why should a seller be permitted to deny the validity of statements he has made in a sale context, whether or not the buyer has relied on them at the time of negotiation? To do so surely does not promote commercial honesty." Charles A. Heckman, *"Reliance" or "Common Honesty of Speech": The History and Interpretation of Section 2-313 of the Uniform Commercial Code,* 38 Case W. Res. L. Rev. 1 (1987-88). The debate goes on.

Although Amended § 2-313A directly addressed this situation, it is not clear that remote purchasers would have had a claim in this situation even under the amendments. Amended § 2-313A(3) stated that the warranty applies when "the seller reasonably expects the record to be, and the record is, furnished to the remote purchaser." This provision did not use the term *basis of the bargain.* Nevertheless, it could still be argued under this language that when the record containing the warranty is not furnished to the remote purchaser at the time of the transaction, then it is not part of the transaction.

There is probably a greater split on the issue of whether a remote purchaser may sue a manufacturer for breach of the implied warranty of merchantability, with more courts allowing the claim if there is a personal injury. See, e.g., *Peterson v. North American Plant Breeders,* 354 N.W.2d 625 (Neb. 1984).

 # Burnham's picks

Question 1	**C**
Question 2	**B**
Question 3	**C**
Question 4	**D**
Question 5	**B**
Question 6	**D**
Question 7	**B**
Question 8	**B**

12

The Code Scheme for Performance

A. Introduction

Let's look at the Code scheme for the exchange of performances. It can be diagrammed like this:

Seller tenders the goods (§ 2-601).
    Buyer inspects for nonconformity (§ 2-513(1), § 2-606(1)(b)).
        If a nonconformity is discovered:
            Buyer rejects (§ 2-602), or
                Seller has a limited right to cure (§ 2-508).
            Buyer accepts on the assumption it will be cured (§ 2-608(1)), or
            Buyer accepts (§ 2-606).
        If no nonconformity is discovered:
            Buyer accepts (§ 2-606) and pays K price (§ 2-607).
                If a nonconformity is discovered after acceptance:
                    Buyer revokes acceptance (§ 2-608), or
                    Buyer recovers for breach of contract or breach of warranty (§ 2-607, § 2-714, § 2-717).

We now examine this scheme in detail.

B.   The Code scheme

1. Seller tenders the goods and buyer inspects for nonconformity

We start with the seller's tender of the goods. Remember that *tender* means an offer to perform coupled with a present ability to perform. According to § 2-513(1), the buyer has a right to inspect the goods before accepting them. The buyer then makes an initial determination of whether—in the words of § 2-601—"the goods or the tender of delivery fail in any respect to conform to the contract." In the vocabulary of the Code, § 2-106(2) defines goods as "'conforming' . . . when they are in accordance with the obligations under the contract." Therefore, to determine whether the goods conform to the contract, a useful first step is to determine what was promised. Warranty law can help with that determination. If the goods were sold "as is," for example, then implied warranties are disclaimed, so the goods could not fail to conform to any level of quality that was implied. However, they still might fail to conform to the terms of an express warranty, such as a description, or to the promised quantity. If the goods were tendered in the wrong place or at the wrong time, then the tender might fail to conform to what was promised.

We next consider the alternatives that turn on whether or not a nonconformity is discovered during inspection.

2. If a nonconformity is discovered

a. Buyer rejects.   Let's first assume that during inspection a nonconformity is discovered. Section 2-601 provides, subject to a number of exceptions:

> . . . if the goods or the tender of delivery fail in any respect to conform to the contract, the buyer may
> > (a) reject the whole; or
> > (b) accept the whole; or
> > (c) accept any commercial unit or units and reject the rest.

This is one of the most controversial provisions in the Code. At common law, if there is an immaterial breach, then the nonbreaching party still has to accept performance from the breaching party; the remedy is to recover damages, not to withhold performance. It is only when there is a material breach that the nonbreaching party's remaining duties are discharged. It appears at first blush that the Code changes that rule, for it says that the buyer may reject if the goods or tender fail "in any respect"—not in a material respect, but in *any* respect. Because tender must be perfect, this rule has become known (not surprisingly) as the *perfect tender rule*. A buyer could easily take advantage of this situation. For example, if the market price went down after the contract was entered into, the buyer could find something wrong with the goods as tendered, reject them, and then buy the goods at the market price. However, such an action might constitute a breach of the duty of good faith. In fact, White and Summers, in *Uniform Commercial Code* § 8-3, express doubt that the perfect tender rule exists in practice:

> Section 2-601, the only section applicable to one-shot contracts, states a "perfect tender" rule; seller must conform perfectly to its obligation, for the buyer may reject any time "the goods or the tender of delivery fail *in any respect* to conform to the contract." We are skeptical of the real importance of the perfect tender rule. . . .
>
> We conclude, and the cases decided to date suggest, that the Code changes and the courts' manipulation have so eroded the perfect tender rule that the law would be little changed if 2-601 gave the right to reject only upon "substantial" non-conformity. Of the reported Code cases on rejection, none that we have found actually grants rejection on what could fairly be called an insubstantial non-conformity, despite language in some cases allowing such rejection.

In spite of this statement, there are a few cases that seem to honor the Code as written, so there seems to be some debate as to the extent to which there is a perfect tender rule. One of the tough things about being a commercial lawyer is that most of the time you will not face this issue when you are writing a brief for an appellate court. You will face it when your client calls and says that a shipment of goods has just arrived five hours late and he wants to know if he can reject it. Your answer of "it depends" is not going to cut it when he has to make a decision on the spot. Most attorneys, to the disappointment of many clients, will urge the client to take the prudent course and accept the goods when there is an immaterial breach (and I say that even though the Code purports not to recognize the concept of immaterial breach) rather than face the more dire consequences if it is later determined that the client wrongfully rejected the goods.

QUESTION 1. A farmer ordered a complex irrigation pump system from a seller. There was no disclaimer of the implied warranty of merchantability. When the pump arrived, the farmer installed it and found that it did not work properly. The farmer continued to try to get the pump to work and notified the seller of his efforts. Finally, after the farmer had the pump for two weeks, he returned it to the seller. The seller sued the farmer, claiming the attempted rejection was wrongful. Did the farmer wrongfully reject the pump?

A. Yes, because he had accepted it by keeping it for two weeks.
B. Yes, because the goods did not fail to conform to the contract.
C. No, because he had a reasonable period of time to inspect the goods.
D. No, because there was a material breach by the seller.

ANALYSIS. The facts of this question are based on *Steinmetz v. Robertus*, 637 P.2d 31 (Mont. 1981). The court held that the buyer's use of the pump was not an acceptance because he was still inspecting it, as he was entitled to under the Code. The best response is **C**. Response **B** is not correct because the goods did have a warranty of merchantability, so it was promised to be a working pump. Response **D** is not correct because under the perfect tender rule there is no requirement of a material breach for the buyer to reject the goods.

QUESTION 2. A buyer orders 100 widgets for $10,000. When the widgets arrive, he discovers that one of them is broken in the box. He has found another source that will sell him 100 widgets for $9,600, so he figures he can reject the widgets, buy them from the other source, and still come out ahead. He asks you for advice. Can he rightfully reject the widgets?

A. Yes, because the goods fail to conform to the contract.
B. Yes, because the seller has materially breached.
C. No, because the seller did not breach.
D. No, because his rejection would not be in good faith.

ANALYSIS. Although the perfect tender rule purports to allow the buyer to reject the goods if they fail "in any way" to conform to the contract, because the buyer is not acting in good faith, his rejection would probably be wrongful. The best response is **D**. Note that **C** is not a correct response because even though the breach is immaterial, it is still a breach and the seller is liable for damages.

We are now going to assume there is a nonconformity that permits the buyer to rightfully reject the goods under § 2-601. The seller has a limited right to cure the nonconformity under § 2-508. That section provides:

§ 2-508. Cure by Seller of Improper Tender or Delivery; Replacement.

(1) Where any tender or delivery by the seller is rejected because non-conforming and the time for performance has not yet expired, the seller may seasonably notify the buyer of his intention to cure and may then within the contract time make a conforming delivery.

(2) Where the buyer rejects a non-conforming tender which the seller had reasonable grounds to believe would be acceptable with or without money allowance the seller may if he seasonably notifies the buyer have a further reasonable time to substitute a conforming tender.

Note that the seller's right to cure under subsection (1) applies only when "the time for performance has not yet expired." This makes sense, as it does not prejudice the buyer if a conforming tender is made while the time for performance is still open. This situation frequently arises when the time for performance is the default "reasonable time" provided by § 2-309(1), because it is then easy to argue that the time for performance is still open. Subsection (2) addresses the situation where the buyer needs additional time to make a conforming tender. In that event, the seller may have the time only if "the seller had reasonable grounds to believe [the tender] would be acceptable with or without money allowance." That "money allowance" phrase means that the seller would have to reasonably believe that it would be acceptable to make a nonconforming delivery as long as he could offer the buyer money to compensate for it. What the seller would reasonably believe about what the buyer would accept is certainly difficult to determine in the absence of some course of performance or course of dealing. In fact, this provision was rewritten in Amended Article 2 as follows:

> [A] seller that has performed in good faith, upon seasonable notice to the buyer and at the seller's own expense, may cure the breach of contract, if the cure is appropriate and timely under the circumstances, by making a tender of conforming goods. The seller shall compensate the buyer for all of the buyer's reasonable expenses caused by the seller's breach of contract and subsequent cure.

Remember that the amended version has been withdrawn from consideration. However, it is nevertheless useful in suggesting to us (and we can then pass the suggestion on to the courts in framing an argument for our clients) how ambiguities in the enacted Code might be resolved. The advantage of the amended version is that it avoided any need to determine what another party would have believed. Although it is implied in the enacted Code section, the amended version emphasized that the seller must act in good faith. A seller would not, for example, be acting in good faith if it deliberately tendered the wrong goods on the delivery date in order to buy more time to perform and then claimed a right to cure.

QUESTION 3. A seller promises delivery of 100 type-X widgets by June 1. On May 25, the seller delivers 100 type-Y widgets and the buyer rejects them. The seller says that he has the type-X widgets in stock and promises to deliver them by June 1. The buyer says, "Don't bother to deliver them. You have proven to me that you are an unreliable supplier and I don't want anything more to do with you." The seller does not deliver the widgets. Who is in breach?

A. The seller because he did not deliver the proper widgets on May 25.
B. The seller because he never delivered the widgets.
C. The buyer because he wrongfully rejected the widgets on May 25.
D. The buyer because he wrongfully rejected the seller's offer to cure.

ANALYSIS.   There is no doubt that the buyer had a right to reject the widgets on May 25 as this was a material breach. However, the seller had a right to cure under § 2-508(1) because the time for performance had not yet expired. The buyer wrongfully repudiated the contract when it should have given the seller an opportunity to cure. The best response is **D**.

QUESTION 4. A seller promises delivery of 100 type-X widgets by June 1. From past dealings, the seller knows that the buyer keeps a stock of the widgets on hand to replace worn-out parts on its assembly line, and a typical supply lasts three months. On June 1, the seller delivers only 70 type-X widgets. The seller promises that it will have 30 more in three weeks and asks for the additional time, promising to pay for any losses the buyer incurs because of the delay. The buyer asks your advice. Does the buyer have to give the seller additional time?

A. Yes, because the time for performance has not yet expired.
B. Yes, because the seller would reasonably believe the offer of late tender would be acceptable.
C. No, because a seller is never entitled to cure after the time for performance has expired.
D. No, because the seller's breach was material.

ANALYSIS.   Because the time for performance expired on June 1, this question falls under § 2-508(2) and not § 2-508(1). Because of the past experience, it would seem that the seller had reasonable grounds to believe the nonconforming tender would be acceptable. It all turns on whether the additional three weeks the seller seeks is "a further reasonable time." It would appear that because the seller knows that the stock lasts for three months, the seller had reasonable grounds to believe that a three-week delay would be reasonable. The best response is **B**. Note that the analysis would be simpler under Amended § 2-508(2), for it would not turn on what the seller had reasonable grounds to believe.

b. Buyer accepts on the assumption the nonconformity will be cured. Sometimes a buyer accepts nonconforming goods on the assumption that the seller will cure the nonconformity, but the seller does not do so. Under the Code scheme, once the buyer has accepted the goods, it is too late to reject them. Nevertheless, the buyer may be able to revoke its acceptance pursuant to § 2-608. That section provides:

> **§ 2-608. Revocation of Acceptance in Whole or in Part.**
>   (1) The buyer may revoke his acceptance of a lot or commercial unit whose non-conformity substantially impairs its value to him if he has accepted it

(a) on the reasonable assumption that its non-conformity would be cured and it has not been seasonably cured; or

(b) without discovery of such non-conformity if his acceptance was reasonably induced either by the difficulty of discovery before acceptance or by the seller's assurances.

(2) Revocation of acceptance must occur within a reasonable time after the buyer discovers or should have discovered the ground for it and before any substantial change in condition of the goods which is not caused by their own defects. It is not effective until the buyer notifies the seller of it.

(3) A buyer who so revokes has the same rights and duties with regard to the goods involved as if he had rejected them.

One hurdle to the buyer's right of revocation is the requirement in subsection (1) that the nonconformity "substantially impairs its value to him." Note that unlike the perfect tender rule of § 2-601, this requirement involves substantial impairment, which might be considered the equivalent of material breach. Curiously, the requirement is stated subjectively in terms of the value "to him," the buyer. Official Comment 2 explains the meaning of this phrase as follows:

> For this purpose the test is not what the seller had reason to know at the time of contracting; the question is whether the non-conformity is such as will in fact cause a substantial impairment of value to the buyer though the seller had no advance knowledge as to the buyer's particular circumstances.

If the buyer can satisfy this requirement, and the revocation is timely, then the buyer may revoke acceptance by notifying the seller. According to § 2-608(3), the rights and duties of the buyer are the same as if he had rejected the goods.

QUESTION 5. A farmer orders a water pump that the seller promises will pump 1,000 gallons per minute. The farmer inspects the pump on arrival and finds that it will pump only 950 gallons per minute. The seller promises to make it work properly, so the farmer accepts it and pays for it. Later, it becomes clear that the seller cannot improve the pumping capacity but had hoped that the farmer would accept the slightly reduced capacity. In fact, unknown to the seller, the farmer requires the full capacity to fully irrigate his fields. Can the farmer revoke his acceptance?

A. Yes, because the nonconformity substantially impairs its value to him.
B. Yes, because he accepted it on the reasonable assumption that its nonconformity would be cured and it has not been seasonably cured.
C. Yes, because both elements described in responses A and B are satisfied.
D. No, because once there is acceptance it is too late to reject.

ANALYSIS.   Response **D** is true but not relevant because the buyer is not attempting to reject; he is attempting to revoke his acceptance. The applicable statute is § 2-608. One element is that "the nonconformity substantially impairs its value to him." In this situation, a reasonable seller might not know that a reduced capacity of only 10% would be a substantial impairment. But the test is not what the seller knew; rather it is whether the nonconformity impaired the value to the buyer, and here it did. But the buyer has to satisfy one of two more tests, one of which is that "he has accepted it . . . on the reasonable assumption that its nonconformity would be cured and it has not been seasonably cured." Because he can satisfy both elements, the buyer can revoke acceptance. The correct response is **C**.

c. Buyer accepts in spite of the nonconformity.   We have now walked through the alternatives where the buyer has discovered a nonconformity and either rejects the goods or accepts them and revokes his acceptance. Another possibility is that the buyer accepts the goods in spite of a nonconformity. Because of the acceptance, it is too late to reject. However, the fact that there has been acceptance does not preclude recovery if there has been breach. This sensible rule is found in § 2-607(2):

> (2) Acceptance of goods by the buyer precludes rejection of the goods accepted and if made with knowledge of a non-conformity cannot be revoked because of it unless the acceptance was on the reasonable assumption that the non-conformity would be seasonably cured *but acceptance does not of itself impair any other remedy provided by this Article for non-conformity.*

As provided in § 2-607(3)(a), to obtain a remedy, the buyer must notify the seller within a reasonable time:

> (3) Where a tender has been accepted
>   (a) the buyer must within a reasonable time after he discovers or should have discovered any breach notify the seller of breach or be barred from any remedy;

The remedies will usually be those provided in § 2-714(2). (See subsection 4 below.)

QUESTION 6.   A seller agrees to deliver 1,000 widgets by June 1. The widgets are not tendered until June 8. The buyer accepts delivery of the widgets and then informs the seller that it is seeking damages for the late delivery. Assuming the buyer suffered some loss, is the buyer entitled to damages?

A.   Yes, because the seller did not tender the widgets in conformity with the contract.

B. No, because the breach was immaterial.

C. No, because time is not of the essence.

D. No, because the buyer waived its rights by accepting the late delivery.

ANALYSIS. Because of the nonconformity in tender, the buyer might have had the right to reject the widgets under § 2-601. Because it accepted the goods, however, it is too late to reject. But acceptance does not waive the right to recover damages for breach. See § 2-607(2). The correct response is **A.**

3. If no nonconformity was discovered after inspection

We now go back to the inspection and assume that no nonconformity was discovered. In the usual situation, when the buyer inspects the goods and discovers no nonconformity, the buyer accepts the goods and pays the contract price. Under § 2-606, acceptance can occur affirmatively, or it can happen passively when the buyer fails to reject or performs an act inconsistent with the seller's ownership:

§ 2-606. **What Constitutes Acceptance of Goods.**

(1) Acceptance of goods occurs when the buyer

(a) after a reasonable opportunity to inspect the goods signifies to the seller that the goods are conforming or that he will take or retain them in spite of their non-conformity; or

(b) fails to make an effective rejection (subsection (1) of Section 2-602), but such acceptance does not occur until the buyer has had a reasonable opportunity to inspect them; or

(c) does any act inconsistent with the seller's ownership; but if such act is wrongful as against the seller it is an acceptance only if ratified by him.

(2) Acceptance of a part of any commercial unit is acceptance of that entire unit.

The default rule is that payment is due at the time of delivery, and each event is conditional on the other. That is, if delivery is not made, payment is not due; and if payment is not made, then delivery is not due. These rules are found in §§ 2-507(1) and 2-511(1), which provide:

§ 2-507. **Effect of Seller's Tender; Delivery on Condition.**

(1) Tender of delivery is a condition to the buyer's duty to accept the goods and, unless otherwise agreed, to his duty to pay for them. Tender entitles the seller to acceptance of the goods and to payment according to the contract.

§ 2-511. **Tender of Payment by Buyer; Payment by Check.**

(1) Unless otherwise agreed tender of payment is a condition to the seller's duty to tender and complete any delivery.

Of course, the parties are free to contract around this rule of concurrent conditions. Sometimes the buyer agrees to pay in advance of delivery, and sometimes the seller agrees to extend credit; for example, the seller may not require payment until 30 days after delivery. However, the basic rule is stated in § 2-607(1): "The buyer must pay at the contract rate for any goods accepted." The rule of § 2-511(2), which relates to the form in which the payment is made, is a good one for examining Code methodology:

> (2) Tender of payment is sufficient when made by any means or in any manner current in the ordinary course of business unless the seller demands payment in legal tender and gives any extension of time reasonably necessary to procure it.

The default rule is that tender of payment can be made "by any means or in any manner current in the ordinary course of business," but if a seller demands cash, and in the ordinary course of business checks are acceptable, then the buyer has been taken by surprise and will be given additional time to comply.

QUESTION 7. A commercial buyer receives a shipment of goods from a seller and stores them without inspecting them. Three months later, the buyer discovers a defect in the goods. The buyer immediately informs the seller that it is rejecting the goods and sends them back. Is the rejection a rightful rejection?

A. Yes, because the buyer had a reasonable time to conduct an inspection.
B. Yes, because the buyer could revoke its acceptance.
C. No, because the buyer had accepted the goods.
D. No, because the buyer has waived its right to recover damages from the seller.

ANALYSIS.   It seems that a reasonable time to conduct an inspection has long passed, so **A** is not a correct response. Whether the buyer can revoke acceptance is not the call of the question—you are asked about rejection—so **B** is not a correct response. **D** is not a correct response partly because it is not responsive to the call of the question and partly because it is not substantively correct. A buyer does not waive its rights to recover damages by accepting nonconforming goods. The correct response is **C**. Even though there is no affirmative act constituting acceptance, the buyer's retention of the goods for a substantial time amounts to an acceptance under § 2-606.

QUESTION 8.   A drug dealer tenders a buyer's weekly supply of cocaine and the buyer tenders a check. The dealer laughs and says that the buyer knows that it is a cash-only business. The buyer asks for more time to obtain cash and the dealer refuses. Assuming that this were a legal transaction, would the dealer have to give the buyer an extension of time to procure the cash?

A. Yes, because the buyer was taken by surprise by the demand for cash.
B. Yes, because it would not prejudice the seller to provide additional time.
C. No, because in the ordinary course of this business only cash is accepted.
D. No, because delivery is conditional on payment.

ANALYSIS.   I hope you are not offended by this question. I wanted to use an example in which everyone knows the business operates only on a cash basis (hopefully because they saw it in the movies). According to § 2-511(2), "tender of payment is sufficient when made by any means or in any manner current in the ordinary course of business." In this cash-only business, the tender was not sufficient and no additional time need be given. The best response is **C**. Response **D** is true but is not responsive to the call of the question, because the fact that delivery is conditional on payment does not explain why the buyer should not be given more time.

4. If a nonconformity is discovered after acceptance

a. Buyer revokes.   A nonconformity that is discovered after acceptance may give rise to a claim for revocation. In addition to the other § 2-608 requirements, revocation is permitted if the buyer has accepted the goods, in the words of § 2-608(1)(b), "without discovery of such non-conformity if his acceptance was reasonably induced either by the difficulty of discovery before acceptance or by the seller's assurances." This situation commonly arises when there is a latent defect in the goods that was difficult to discover on inspection.

b. Buyer recovers damages for breach.   Finally, assume the buyer has accepted the goods and discovers a nonconformity, but a claim for revocation is not available. The buyer may still have a claim for breach under § 2-607(2) or for breach of warranty. Section 2-714(2) provides:

> **§ 2-714. Buyer's Damages for Breach in Regard to Accepted Goods.**
> (2) The measure of damages for breach of warranty is the difference at the time and place of acceptance between the value of the goods accepted and the value they would have had if they had been as warranted, unless special circumstances show proximate damages of a different amount.

Whether in a consumer context or a commercial context, a breach of warranty claim arises when the buyer has accepted the goods but the goods do not conform to an affirmation of fact or promise that was made about them. We will look at the measure of damages for that claim in Chapter 17.C.

A simple self-help remedy applies when the seller is in breach and the buyer has accepted the goods. According to § 2-717, on notice to the seller, the buyer may deduct from the price the damages resulting from the breach:

§ 2-717. Deduction of Damages from the Price.

> The buyer on notifying the seller of his intention to do so may deduct all or any part of the damages resulting from any breach of the contract from any part of the price still due under the same contract.

QUESTION 9. A buyer purchases a machine "AS IS" for $1,000. When the machine arrives, the buyer inspects it and, finding no problems, accepts it. A week later, the machine fails to work and its value to the buyer is substantially impaired. Can the buyer revoke acceptance?

A. Yes, because the nonconformity substantially impairs its value to the buyer, and the buyer's acceptance was reasonably induced by the difficulty of discovery before acceptance.
B. Yes, because there is material breach by the seller.
C. No, because once there is acceptance, it is too late to revoke.
D. No, because there was no nonconformity.

ANALYSIS. This is a bit of a trick question. The key fact is that the machine was purchased "AS IS." According to § 2-316(3)(a), which we explored in Chapter 10.C, this language effectively disclaims the warranty of merchantability. Because the seller made no promise that the machine functions, the machine as delivered conforms to the contract. The correct response is **D**. If the facts were otherwise, and the seller had promised that the machine would function, then the correct response would be **A**. In those circumstances, revocation would be appropriate because a latent defect could not be discovered on inspection.

C. Closers

QUESTION 10. *Statute reader.* In which of the following situations is the buyer not entitled to revoke acceptance under § 2-608?

A. The seller tenders a complex machine that looks fine, but after the buyer sets it up, the machine does not work at all.

B. The seller tenders a complex machine. The buyer notices some defects in it on delivery, but the seller assures the buyer that she will repair the problems. The problems turn out to be serious and the seller does not fix them.

C. The seller tenders a complex machine and, before the buyer has a chance to accept it, the seller assures the buyer it is in good condition. It turns out to have serious problems.

D. The seller tenders a complex machine that looks fine, but after the buyer sets it up, the machine has a problem with a part that needs to be replaced.

ANALYSIS. Under § 2-608, the buyer may have a remedy if there is a "non-conformity [that] substantially impairs its value to him." This means that the goods do not conform to what was promised. Notice, however, that there are additional requirements. The buyer may revoke only if the goods were accepted:

(a) on the reasonable assumption that its non-conformity would be cured and it has not been seasonably cured; or

(b) without discovery of such non-conformity if his acceptance was reasonably induced either by the difficulty of discovery before acceptance or by the seller's assurances.

Response **A** sounds like the § 2-608(1)(b) situation where there is "difficulty of discovery before acceptance." Response **B** sounds like the § 2-608(1)(a) situation where the buyer reasonably assumed the nonconformity would be cured. Response **C** sounds like the § 2-608(1)(b) situation where the acceptance was induced by the seller's assurances. In response **D**, it does not sound like the nonconformity "substantially impairs the value" of the machine to the buyer. In that case, the § 2-608 remedy is not available. Therefore, **D** is the correct response.

QUESTION 11. For $1,000, payable 30 days after delivery, a buyer purchases a machine that has a one-year warranty against defects. During the first week of operation, a part fails. The buyer pays $100 for the replacement of the part. The buyer sends the seller $900 to pay for the machine, along with a note notifying the seller that he has deducted damages from the price. Did the buyer act properly?

A. No, because according to § 2-607, the buyer must pay at the contract rate for goods accepted.

B. No, because according to § 2-601, the buyer must reject defective goods.

C. Yes, because according to § 2-608, the buyer has the right to revoke acceptance.
D. Yes, because according to § 2-717, the buyer may deduct damages from the price due.

ANALYSIS.   Response **B** does not correctly state the rule. Even if the buyer discovered the defect during the period of inspection, he is free to accept the goods and seek damages. It appears that the buyer has no grounds for revocation of acceptance, so response **C** is not correct. The general rule that the buyer has an obligation to pay the price of goods accepted is correctly expressed in response **A**. However, the buyer also has a claim for damages for breach of warranty, and according to § 2-717, the buyer may deduct damages from the price due if he notifies the seller of his intention to do so. Therefore, **D** is the best response.

 # Burnham's picks

Question 1	C
Question 2	D
Question 3	D
Question 4	B
Question 5	C
Question 6	A
Question 7	C
Question 8	C
Question 9	D
Question 10	D
Question 11	D

13

Delivery and Shipment

A.   Introduction

A buyer and a seller agree that the buyer will buy certain goods from the seller. The parties' general obligations are set forth in § 2-301:

§ 2-301. General Obligations of Parties.
     The obligation of the seller is to transfer and deliver and that of the buyer is to accept and pay in accordance with the contract.

That is all well and good, but what are the seller's delivery obligations and what are the buyer's payment obligations? In addition to determining what these obligations are, it is also necessary to determine the point at which the risk of loss of the goods is transferred from the seller to the buyer. When the seller is responsible for risk of loss, then the seller may be liable for breach for nondelivery if the goods are lost (subject to the excuses for nonperformance discussed in Chapter 14). When the buyer is responsible for the risk of loss, then the buyer may have to pay for the goods if they are lost, even though the buyer never got them. As a practical matter, while the risk of loss is placed on a party, that party should obtain insurance coverage for the goods.
     Prior to the enactment of the UCC, the law looked to the moment when title passed to answer the question of when the risk of loss passed. As we will

see, this is no longer the rule, and the question of who has title is generally uncoupled from the question of who bears the risk of loss. More likely, the party who bears the risk of loss is the party who is in the best position to bear that risk, as by purchasing insurance to cover the risk. However, in other contexts it may be important to determine who has title, and what kind of title they have, so we explore that question as well.

B.   The default rules

The default rules for delivery are simple. If the parties do not otherwise agree, § 2-308(a) provides that "the place for delivery of goods is the seller's place of business or if he has none his residence." How does the seller tender delivery? Section 2-503 provides:

> **§ 2-503. Manner of Seller's Tender of Delivery.**
>
> (1) Tender of delivery requires that the seller put and hold conforming goods at the buyer's disposition and give the buyer any notification reasonably necessary to enable him to take delivery. The manner, time and place for tender are determined by the agreement and this Article, and in particular
>
> (a) tender must be at a reasonable hour, and if it is of goods they must be kept available for the period reasonably necessary to enable the buyer to take possession; but
>
> (b) unless otherwise agreed the buyer must furnish facilities reasonably suited to the receipt of the goods.

So the buyer has to come to the seller's place of business to get the goods, and the seller has to properly tender delivery. Does the seller have to tender the goods before the buyer pays for them, or does the buyer have to pay for them before the seller tenders them? As we saw in Chapter 12.B, in the absence of agreement by the parties, §§ 2-507(1) and 2-511(1) provide that the exchange is simultaneous. As a default rule, payment is made at the time of delivery and delivery is made at the time of payment.

What does *payment* mean? Section 2-511 provides:

> (2) Tender of payment is sufficient when made by any means or in any manner current in the ordinary course of business unless the seller demands payment in legal tender and gives any extension of time reasonably necessary to procure it.
>
> (3) Subject to the provisions of this Act on the effect of an instrument on an obligation (Section 3-802), payment by check is conditional and is defeated as between the parties by dishonor of the check on due presentment.

As discussed in Chapter 12.B, the general rule is that payment is made "by any means or in any manner current in the ordinary course of business." The means of payment will frequently be payment by check. Payment by check is considered a cash payment rather than a credit payment. If that is the case, has there been payment if three days after payment by check, the seller discovers that the buyer's check has bounced? No. Section 2-511(3) tells us that "payment by check is conditional." In other words, if the check is not good, then there has not been payment. Because delivery is conditional on payment, in that case delivery was not due; the buyer has "voidable" title and the seller has the right to recover the goods from the buyer.

One more wrinkle in this scheme is that unless the agreement or the circumstances require otherwise, all the goods are due in one delivery. Section 2-307 provides:

> **§ 2-307. Delivery in Single Lot or Several Lots.**
>
> Unless otherwise agreed all goods called for by a contract for sale must be tendered in a single delivery and payment is due only on such tender but where the circumstances give either party the right to make or demand delivery in lots the price if it can be apportioned may be demanded for each lot.

QUESTION 1. A law student walks into a bookstore and says, "I'm here to pick up that copy of *The Glannon Guide to Sales* I ordered." The clerk hands her *The Glannon Guide to Secured Transactions*. Has there been tender of delivery?

A. No, because this is not an Article 2 transaction as the law student is not a merchant.
B. No, because the goods are nonconforming.
C. No, because the time and place for tender have not been determined.
D. Yes, there has been a tender and there has also been a breach.

ANALYSIS. I hope you are still not being fooled by response **A**. If you are, please review Chapter 4.B. Here, the goods have been tendered at a reasonable time and place under § 2-503, so **C** is not a correct response. The reason tender of delivery is so important is because, according to § 2-507, once there has been tender and notice, then payment is due. But § 2-503(1) provides that "[t]ender of delivery requires that the seller put and hold *conforming goods* at the buyer's disposition." If the tender is of nonconforming goods, the buyer may prefer not to accept delivery rather than have a claim for breach. Here, there was not a tender of conforming goods, so the correct response is **B**.

QUESTION 2. A seller of bottled milk and a buyer agree that the buyer will pick up the milk at 10 P.M. after the seller's business has closed. The buyer arrives and the seller tenders the milk. The buyer complains that the seller has taken no steps to package the milk in a manner that will keep it cold for the buyer. The buyer refuses the tender. Is the seller in breach?

A. Yes, because the tender was not at a reasonable hour.
B. Yes, because the seller knew the milk had to be kept cold and did not properly package it.
C. No, because the seller may determine the time for delivery and the packaging.
D. No, because the buyer must furnish facilities reasonably suited to the receipt of the goods.

ANALYSIS. According to § 2-503(1)(a), the default rule is that tender must be at a reasonable hour, but here the parties agreed to the hour. Section 2-503(1)(b) provides that "unless otherwise agreed the buyer must furnish facilities reasonably suited to the receipt of the goods." Here, they did not otherwise agree, so it was up to the buyer to provide suitable facilities. The buyer did not do so. The correct response is **D**.

QUESTION 3. A seller agrees to sell 10,000 bricks to a buyer for $2,000 under a contract that states that payment is due on delivery. The buyer comes to the seller's place of business to get the bricks. The seller demands payment, but the buyer refuses to pay, claiming that it is customary in the trade that a buyer has 30 days after delivery to pay. The seller refuses to give the bricks to the buyer. Who is in breach?

A. The seller, because the rule is that delivery must be made before payment is made.
B. The seller, because the trade usage would be read into the contract.
C. The buyer, because the rule is that payment must be made before delivery is made.
D. The buyer, because the trade usage is trumped by an express term of the contract.

ANALYSIS. Responses **A** and **C** do not state the rule correctly. According to §§ 2-507 and 2-511, delivery and payment are conditional on each other, so they must be tendered simultaneously. As a general rule, according to § 1-303, usage of trade is read into the contract. However, the express terms of the contract prevail over the trade usage under § 1-303(e)(1). Here, the contract specifically states that payment is due on delivery. That express term is inconsistent with the trade usage, so it governs. The correct response is **D**.

When delivery is at the seller's place of business, according to § 2-509(3), "the risk of loss passes to the buyer on his receipt of the goods if the seller is a merchant; otherwise the risk passes to the buyer on tender of delivery." Recall that a *tender* is an offer to perform, whereas *receipt* of goods, according to § 2-103(1)(c), means "taking physical possession of them." So if the buyer is offered the goods, but decides to come back later to pick them up, there has been tender but not receipt.

QUESTION 4. Sarah, a law student, sells her car to Barney, another law student. Sarah signs over the title and gives Barney the keys. He tells her that he will pick it up from her house the next morning and she says it will be waiting for him. That night, a tree limb breaks off and damages the car, which is parked in Sarah's driveway. Who is responsible for the loss?

A. Sarah, because Barney did not have receipt of the car.
B. Sarah, because she had not tendered the car.
C. Barney, because Sarah had tendered the car.
D. Barney, because he had receipt of the car.

ANALYSIS.   Sarah is not a merchant. Therefore, according to § 2-509(3), "the risk passes to the buyer on tender of delivery." Sarah tendered delivery when she gave the title and the keys to Barney. Because the risk passed at that moment, Barney became responsible for the loss. The correct response is **C.** This seems to make sense as a matter of policy, for Sarah is likely to cancel her insurance after she has sold the car.

QUESTION 5. Barney, a law student, buys a used car from Bitterroot Motors, a car dealer. The dealer signs over the title and gives Barney the keys. Barney asks them if it would be all right if he picked up the car the next day and they tell him it is not a problem. That night, a tree limb breaks off and damages the car, which is parked at the dealership. Who is responsible for the loss?

A. Bitterroot Motors, because Barney did not have receipt of the car.
B. Bitterroot Motors, because it had not tendered the car.
C. Barney, because Bitterroot Motors had tendered the car.
D. Barney, because he had receipt of the car.

ANALYSIS.   Bitterroot Motors is a merchant. Therefore, according to § 2-509(3), "the risk of loss passes to the buyer on his receipt of the goods."

Receipt means physical possession. Even though Barney may have had constructive receipt because he had the title and the keys, he did not have physical possession. Therefore, the correct response is **A**. This seems to make sense as a matter of policy, because the merchant is in a better position to care for and insure the goods while they are under its control.

C.   The installment contract

Although the default rule, expressed in § 2-307, is that all the goods must be tendered in a single delivery, the parties are, of course free to change that rule. If they agree to delivery of the goods in separate lots, they have entered into an *installment contract,* as defined in § 2-612(1):

> **§ 2-612. "Installment contract"; Breach.**
>   (1) An "installment contract" is one which requires or authorizes the delivery of goods in separate lots to be separately accepted, even though the contract contains a clause "each delivery is a separate contract" or its equivalent.

Note that the installment contract is defined in terms of the delivery of the goods and not in terms of the payment. A contract would be an installment contract whether the payment was made entirely in advance, after delivery of each installment, or after delivery of all the installments. The installment contract under the Code is therefore not necessarily a *divisible* contract, for a divisible contract requires that the parties have agreed that a particular performance by one party is the equivalent of a particular performance by the other.

What happens if the seller makes a nonconforming delivery? The rule is very similar to the rule of § 2-601 as interpreted by the courts. The buyer may reject not in the literal words of § 2-601, "if the goods fail in any respect to conform to the contract," but only "if the non-conformity substantially impairs the value of that installment and cannot be cured," in the words of § 2-612(2). That section provides:

>   (2) The buyer may reject any installment which is non-conforming if the non-conformity substantially impairs the value of that installment and cannot be cured or if the non-conformity is a defect in the required documents; but if the non-conformity does not fall within subsection (3) and the seller gives adequate assurance of its cure the buyer must accept that installment.

It seems clear from this language that the Code wants to preserve the contract, for many breaches will not substantially impair the value of the installment and can be cured. This point is brought home by Official Comment 5:

5. Under subsection (2) an installment delivery must be accepted if the non-conformity is curable and the seller gives adequate assurance of cure. Cure of non-conformity of an installment in the first instance can usually be afforded by an allowance against the price, or in the case of reasonable discrepancies in quantity either by a further delivery or a partial rejection. This Article requires reasonable action by a buyer in regard to discrepant delivery and good faith requires that the buyer make any reasonable minor outlay of time or money necessary to cure an overshipment by severing out an acceptable percentage thereof. The seller must take over a cure which involves any material burden; the buyer's obligation reaches only to cooperation. Adequate assurance for purposes of subsection (2) is measured by the same standards as under the section on right to adequate assurance of performance.

If a breach does substantially impair the value of the installment and cannot be cured, then obviously the other party may reject the installment. The interesting question then arises as to whether the nonbreaching party can cancel the contract, refusing delivery of the remaining installments. It is natural for a party not to want to deal with another party who has proven to be unreliable, but this is not the way of the Code. The Code wants to help the parties make the relationship work, and subsection (3) limits the circumstances under which the nonbreaching party may cancel the entire contract:

> (3) Whenever non-conformity or default with respect to one or more installments substantially impairs the value of the whole contract there is a breach of the whole. But the aggrieved party reinstates the contract if he accepts a non-conforming installment without seasonably notifying of cancellation or if he brings an action with respect only to past installments or demands performance as to future installments.

Under this provision, there is breach of the whole contract only if the "non-conformity or default with respect to one or more installments substantially impairs the value of the whole contract." What does the phrase "substantially impairs the value of the whole contract" mean? Official Comment 6 is not exactly helpful. It explains:

> Whether the non-conformity in any given installment justifies cancellation as to the future depends, not on whether such non-conformity indicates an intent or likelihood that the future deliveries will also be defective, but whether the non-conformity substantially impairs the value of the whole contract.

Apparently it is not enough that there may be future defective breaches. Returning to subsection (2), each of these defective deliveries will probably not substantially impair the value even of the one installment, and therefore not of the whole. Suppose a buyer is late in paying for the first installment. That is a breach with respect to the first installment, but presumably not a breach that substantially impairs the value of the whole contract. But suppose the buyer cannot pay for the first installment because it is insolvent. That would indicate that the breach substantially impairs the value of the whole. How is the seller to know why payment is delayed? The seller can use the demand for assurances, described in Chapter 15.C, to find out the reasons for the other party's breach and the extent to which it will affect the whole contract.

QUESTION 6. A distributor of chickens orders frying chickens from a chicken processor. The chicken is to be delivered in five installments. For the first installment, the processor tenders stewing chicken. The distributor accepts the delivery under protest, for it feels it must provide chicken to its customers, even if it is not the right kind of chicken. The distributor finds, however, that its customers are unhappy with the chicken and refuse to buy any more from the distributor. The processor is willing and able to tender frying chicken for the next four installments. Can the distributor cancel the entire contract?

A. No, because the nonconformity in the first installment did not substantially impair the value of that installment.

B. No, because the nonconformity in the first installment did not substantially impair the value of the whole contract.

C. Yes, because the nonconformity in the first installment substantially impaired the value of that installment.

D. Yes, because the nonconformity in the first installment substantially impaired the value of the whole contract.

ANALYSIS.   I think these facts provide a good example of when the nonconformity in the first installment substantially impairs the value of the whole contract. Even though the seller is willing to make conforming deliveries in the future, those deliveries will be of no value to the distributor, because it has lost its customers. The best response is **D.**

D.   "Shipment" and "delivery" contracts

The default situation of delivery at the seller's place of business and payment on delivery often does not apply, because frequently the goods are shipped to the buyer and frequently the seller extends credit so that it is not paid on delivery. In the normal situation, the seller will agree that instead of the buyer picking up the goods, the seller will ship them. Nevertheless, the seller may be obligated to do a lot less than it might initially appear. The fact that the seller has agreed to ship the goods does not mean that the seller has agreed to pay for shipping. More important, it does not mean that the seller has agreed to deliver the goods to the buyer; it means that the seller has agreed to deliver them to a shipper who agrees to deliver them to the buyer. By making this arrangement, the seller has limited its risk of loss.

This arrangement, known as a *shipment contract,* is described in §§ 2-504 and 2-509(1)(a):

§ 2-504. Shipment by Seller.

Where the seller is required or authorized to send the goods to the buyer and the contract does not require him to deliver them at a particular destination, then unless otherwise agreed he must

(a) put the goods in the possession of such a carrier and make such a contract for their transportation as may be reasonable having regard to the nature of the goods and other circumstances of the case; and

(b) obtain and promptly deliver or tender in due form any document necessary to enable the buyer to obtain possession of the goods or otherwise required by the agreement or by usage of trade; and

(c) promptly notify the buyer of the shipment.

Failure to notify the buyer under paragraph (c) or to make a proper contract under paragraph (a) is a ground for rejection only if material delay or loss ensues.

§ 2-509. Risk of Loss in the Absence of Breach.

(1) Where the contract requires or authorizes the seller to ship the goods by carrier

(a) if it does not require him to deliver them at a particular destination, the risk of loss passes to the buyer when the goods are duly delivered to the carrier even though the shipment is under reservation (Section 2-505) . . .

The language of § 2-509(1)(a), providing that "it does not require him to deliver them at a particular destination," is a bit confusing. Suppose, for example, a seller in Seattle agrees to ship the goods via UPS to the buyer's factory in Boise. This is a shipment contract because it is the seller's responsibility to arrange for the shipping of the goods by UPS. A particular destination will always be named even in a shipment contract because it is necessary to identify the place to which the goods will be delivered. In spite of the fact that a particular destination is named, however, the seller is not required to deliver them there; the seller is required only to deliver them to UPS, the carrier.

Note that under a shipment contract, as between the buyer and the seller, the risk of loss passes to the buyer when the goods are duly delivered to the carrier. This sounds like bad news for the buyer. For example, in our previous example, the buyer bears the risk of loss if UPS loses the goods. But § 2-504(c) provides that it is also a duty of the seller to give the buyer notice of delivery.

If the buyer has not made an arrangement with the seller to do so, the buyer with notice can arrange for insurance through the carrier. Note also that the risk of loss passes under § 2-509 when the goods are "duly" delivered to the carrier. One of the obligations of the seller is to "make such a contract for their transportation as may be reasonable having regard to the nature of the goods and other circumstances of the case."

In our hypothetical, if the seller arranged for shipping via UPS, the risk of loss would pass to the buyer on delivery to the carrier, assuming the seller gave appropriate notice to the buyer. The seller frequently sends a postcard or email message informing the buyer that the goods have been shipped. This satisfies its notice obligation under § 2-504(c). If there has been proper shipment and notice, then there has been delivery, so the buyer is obligated to pay the seller even if the goods never reach the buyer.

If the seller does agree to deliver the goods to a particular destination, then the arrangement is known as a *destination contract,* which is described in § 2-509(1)(b):

> (b) if it does require him to deliver them at a particular destination and the goods are there duly tendered while in the possession of the carrier, the risk of loss passes to the buyer when the goods are there duly so tendered as to enable the buyer to take delivery.

It is important to note that as indicated in Official Comment 5 to § 2-503, "the 'shipment' contract is regarded as the normal one and the 'destination' contract as the variant type." Thus, the fact that the seller agrees to pay for shipping is not enough to make the contract a destination contract. It is only a destination contract if the seller has expressly agreed to *deliver* the goods to a particular destination. Between commercial parties, this is frequently accomplished with the designation F.O.B., meaning "free on board." According to § 2-319, if the contract term is "F.O.B. [seller's place of business]," then it is a shipment contract; if the contract term is "F.O.B. [buyer's place of business]," then it is a destination contract.

The shipping conventions used in international transactions make the responsibilities of each party even clearer. See the *incoterms* promulgated by the International Chamber of Commerce at *www.iccwbo.org/incoterms/.* For example, under the incoterms, DAT (Delivered at Terminal), followed by a named terminal at port or place of destination, is used with any mode of transportation. The seller pays for carriage to the terminal, except for costs related to import clearance, and assumes all risks up to the point that the goods are unloaded at the terminal. On the other hand, FOB (Free on Board), followed by a named port of shipment, is used for water transportation only, but not for shipment in containers. The seller must load the goods on board the vessel nominated by the buyer. Cost and risk are divided when the goods are actually on board of the vessel. The seller must clear the goods for export.

One more twist on these rules arises when the seller ships substantially nonconforming goods. Section 2-510 provides:

§ 2-510. Effect of Breach on Risk of Loss.

(1) Where a tender or delivery of goods so fails to conform to the contract as to give a right of rejection the risk of their loss remains on the seller until cure or acceptance.

(2) Where the buyer rightfully revokes acceptance he may to the extent of any deficiency in his effective insurance coverage treat the risk of loss as having rested on the seller from the beginning.

(3) Where the buyer as to conforming goods already identified to the contract for sale repudiates or is otherwise in breach before risk of their loss has passed to him, the seller may to the extent of any deficiency in his effective insurance coverage treat the risk of loss as resting on the buyer for a commercially reasonable time.

Under this provision, "the risk of loss remains on the seller if the tender or delivery of goods so fails to conform to the contract as to give a right of rejection." We have looked at the buyer's right of rejection under § 2-601, the so-called perfect tender rule, in Chapter 12.B. Let's assume an easy case where the seller has shipped goods that do not substantially conform to the contract under a shipment contract. If the goods are damaged during delivery, then under § 2-510 the risk of loss remains on the seller. This makes sense, because when the buyer is able to exercise its right of rejection, the buyer may return the goods to the seller.

QUESTION 7. An American importer contracted to buy 100 cases of wine from a German seller. The buyer agreed to pay for shipping. The seller arranged for shipment by ship from the port of Hamburg to the port of Wilmington, North Carolina, where the buyer was to receive it, but the seller did not notify the buyer. The ship sank en route and the buyer never received the wine. Which party is responsible for the risk of loss?

A. The seller, because this was a destination contract.
B. The seller, because even though this was a shipment contract, the seller failed to notify the buyer of the shipment.
C. The buyer, because this was a shipment contract.
D. The buyer, because it agreed to pay for shipping.

ANALYSIS. This was a shipment contract, because the seller agreed only to deliver the goods to the port and not to the buyer. In a shipment contract, according to § 2-509, "the risk of loss passes to the buyer when the goods are duly delivered to the carrier." Normally, therefore, the risk of loss would be on the buyer in this situation. However, the seller did not notify the buyer as required by § 2-504(c). Although failure to give notice is not material in all circumstances, under these facts, a court held that the risk of loss was on the seller. It stated, "The requirement of prompt notification by the seller, as used in [§ 2-504(c)], must be construed as taking into consideration the need of a buyer to be informed of the shipment in sufficient time for him to take action to protect himself from the risk of damage to or loss of the goods while in transit." See *Rheinberg-Kellerei GMBH v. Vineyard Wine Co., Inc.*, 281 S.E.2d 425 (N.C. App. 1981). The best response is **B**.

QUESTION 8. A seller sells 100 type-A widgets to a buyer and agrees to arrange for shipping to the buyer at the buyer's expense. The seller notifies the buyer that the goods have been shipped. While the goods are en route, they are hijacked and never found. As between the seller and the buyer, who is responsible for the loss?

A. The seller, because this was a destination contract.
B. The seller, because it was negligent in choosing the carrier.
C. The buyer, because the risk of loss passed when the goods were delivered to the carrier.
D. The buyer, because the shipment was at the buyer's expense.

ANALYSIS.   This is a shipment contract. Notice that the mere fact that the seller has arranged for shipment to the buyer does not make it a destination contract. Obviously, every shipping contract has to have a destination. In a shipment contract, under § 2-509(1)(a), "the risk of loss passes to the buyer when the goods are duly delivered to the carrier." The correct response is **C**.

QUESTION 9. A seller sells 100 type-A widgets to a buyer and agrees to arrange for shipping to the buyer at its own (the seller's) expense. The seller notifies the buyer that the goods have been shipped. The seller inadvertently loaded 100 type-B widgets. While the goods are en route, they are hijacked and never found. As between the seller and the buyer, who is responsible for the loss?

A. The seller, because its agreement to pay for the shipping made this a destination contract.
B. The seller, because the goods did not conform to the contract.
C. The buyer, because the risk of loss passed when the goods were delivered to the carrier.
D. The buyer, because it had a reasonable opportunity to obtain insurance after it was notified of the shipment.

ANALYSIS.   This is still a shipment contract. The fact that the seller has agreed to pay for shipping means just that, and does not alter the risk of loss.

As a general rule, in a shipment contract, under § 2-509(1)(a) "the risk of loss passes to the buyer when the goods are duly delivered to the carrier." However, the general rule is subject to an exception under § 2-510(1): "Where a tender or delivery of goods so fails to conform to the contract as to give a right of rejection the risk of their loss remains on the seller until cure or acceptance." Here, the seller shipped goods that did not conform to the contract. Therefore, the risk of loss remained on the seller during shipment. The correct response is **B**.

E.   Title

1. Passing of title between buyer and seller

We have discussed the rules involving shipment and delivery up to this point without mention of title. That is because it is not usually important to determine which party has title in order to determine the rights and remedies of buyer and seller. Section 2-401 tells us that "[e]ach provision of this Article with regard to the rights, obligations and remedies of the seller, the buyer, purchasers or other third parties applies irrespective of title to the goods except where the provision refers to such title." Nevertheless, there will be times when it is important to determine who has title to goods. Many of these situations involve the rights of a third party, for it may be necessary to determine what title the third party received. We now go over the rules regarding title, which are found in § 2-401:

> **§ 2-401. Passing of Title; Reservation for Security; Limited Application of This Section.**
>
> Each provision of this Article with regard to the rights, obligations and remedies of the seller, the buyer, purchasers or other third parties applies irrespective of title to the goods except where the provision refers to such title. Insofar as situations are not covered by the other provisions of this Article and matters concerning title become material the following rules apply:
>
> (1) Title to goods cannot pass under a contract for sale prior to their identification to the contract (Section 2-501), and unless otherwise explicitly agreed the buyer acquires by their identification a special property as limited by this Act. Any retention or reservation by the seller of the title (property) in goods shipped or delivered to the buyer is limited in effect to a reservation of a security interest. Subject to these provisions and to the provisions of the Article on Secured Transactions (Article 9), title to goods passes from the seller to the buyer in any manner and on any conditions explicitly agreed on by the parties.

(2) Unless otherwise explicitly agreed title passes to the buyer at the time and place at which the seller completes his performance with reference to the physical delivery of the goods, despite any reservation of a security interest and even though a document of title is to be delivered at a different time or place; and in particular and despite any reservation of a security interest by the bill of lading

(a) if the contract requires or authorizes the seller to send the goods to the buyer but does not require him to deliver them at destination, title passes to the buyer at the time and place of shipment; but

(b) if the contract requires delivery at destination, title passes on tender there.

(3) Unless otherwise explicitly agreed where delivery is to be made without moving the goods,

(a) if the seller is to deliver a document of title, title passes at the time when and the place where he delivers such documents; or

(b) if the goods are at the time of contracting already identified and no documents are to be delivered, title passes at the time and place of contracting.

(4) A rejection or other refusal by the buyer to receive or retain the goods, whether or not justified, or a justified revocation of acceptance revests title to the goods in the seller. Such revesting occurs by operation of law and is not a "sale."

According to § 2-401(2), "Unless otherwise explicitly agreed title passes to the buyer at the time and place at which the seller completes his performance with reference to the physical delivery of the goods." As with most provisions in the Code, the parties are free to contract around this one. If they don't, however, then with a shipment contract, title will pass when the seller delivers the goods to the carrier; with a delivery contract, title will pass when the seller delivers the goods to the buyer.

How early can title pass? According to § 2-401(1), "[t]itle to goods cannot pass under a contract for sale prior to their identification to the contract (Section 2-501)." What does *identification* mean? Section 2-501 provides in part:

§ 2-501. Insurable Interest in Goods; Manner of Identification of Goods.

(1) The buyer obtains a special property and an insurable interest in goods by identification of existing goods as goods to which the contract refers even though the goods so identified are non-conforming and he has an option to return or reject them. Such identification can be made at any time and in any manner explicitly agreed to by the parties. In the absence of explicit agreement identification occurs

(a) when the contract is made if it is for the sale of goods already existing and identified;

(b) if the contract is for the sale of future goods other than those described in paragraph (c), when goods are shipped, marked or otherwise designated by the seller as goods to which the contract refers;

(c) when the crops are planted or otherwise become growing crops or the young are conceived if the contract is for the sale of unborn young to be born within twelve months after contracting or for the sale of crops to be harvested within twelve months or the next normal harvest reason after contracting whichever is longer.

Because § 2-401(1) tells us that "[t]itle to goods cannot pass under a contract for sale prior to their identification to the contract," it will first be necessary to see when identification occurs. Section 2-501 tells us that identification occurs when the parties agree it occurs, and in the absence of their agreement, "when the contract is made if it is for the sale of goods already existing and identified." Don't you hate definitions that use the terms defined? The Code is here trying to distinguish between a *present sale* and a *sale of future goods*. To understand these terms, we have to go back to § 2-105(2) and 2-106(1), which provide:

§ 2-105(2) Goods must be both existing and identified before any interest in them can pass. Goods which are not both existing and identified are "future" goods. A purported present sale of future goods or of any interest therein operates as a contract to sell.

§ 2-106(1) In this Article unless the context otherwise requires "contract" and "agreement" are limited to those relating to the present or future sale of goods. "Contract for sale" includes both a present sale of goods and a contract to sell goods at a future time. A "sale" consists in the passing of title from the seller to the buyer for a price (Section 2-401). A "present sale" means a sale which is accomplished by the making of the contract.

Let's take the easy case first. Under § 2-501(1)(a), identification occurs "when the contract is made if it is for the sale of goods already existing and identified." In a typical situation, if you are buying goods from a store and you pick out what you want to buy, then the goods are "already existing and identified." When you pay the seller for them, the contract is made. That is a "present sale" as defined in § 2-106(1) and the goods have obviously been identified. But if you pick out a floor model and the store must get the goods from the warehouse for you, then the goods are not yet identified. Section 2-105(2) provides that "[g]oods which are not both existing and identified are 'future' goods." According to § 2-501(1)(b), identification occurs "if the contract is for the sale of future goods other than those described in paragraph (c), when goods are shipped, marked or otherwise designated by the seller as goods to which the contract refers." So in our hypothetical, the goods would be identified when the seller in some way indicated that the one it was getting from the warehouse was yours.

If a buyer ordered 100 widgets and seller's warehouse had 1,000 widgets in it, the goods would not yet be identified; if the seller then took 100 of them, put them in a box, and attached a shipping label in the name of buyer, then they would be identified. Note, however, that risk of loss would not yet pass to the buyer under § 2-509. Even though § 2-501 gives the buyer an insurable interest at that point, the seller is still in the best position to insure the goods.

QUESTION 10. A buyer and seller agree on terms for the purchase of 100 widgets. The contract provides that the seller will ship the goods via UPS and that "risk of loss passes to the buyer on identification of the goods." The seller takes 100 widgets from its stock of 1,000 widgets and puts them in a box with a shipping label addressed to buyer. That night there is a fire in the seller's warehouse and half the widgets in the warehouse are destroyed, including all of those in the box addressed to buyer. Who bears the risk of loss of the widgets in the box?

A. The buyer, because the Code provides that the risk of loss shifts to the buyer once the goods are identified as the buyer's.
B. The buyer, because the contract assigned the risk to the buyer once the goods had been identified.
C. The seller, because this was a shipment contract and seller bore the risk until the goods were delivered to the carrier.
D. Each bears half of the risk because the fire destroyed half the goods in the warehouse.

ANALYSIS. Under the default rule, this was a shipment contract, so **C** would normally be the correct response, with the seller bearing the risk until the goods were delivered to the carrier. See § 2-509(1)(a). Note that the mere fact that the goods had been identified is not enough to shift the risk to the buyer under the general rule. Therefore, **A** is not correct. However, according to § 2-509(4), the freedom of contract rule applies that "the provisions of this section are subject to contrary agreement of the parties." Here, the parties made a contrary agreement when they provided that "risk of loss passes to the buyer on identification of the goods." According to § 2-501(1)(b), identification occurs "when goods are shipped, marked or otherwise designated by the seller as goods to which the contract refers." Under the supplied facts, the goods were identified when the seller put them in a box with a shipping label addressed to the buyer. Therefore, the risk shifted to the buyer at that point. Response **B** is correct.

2. *Passing of title to a transferee*

You probably at some point learned property concepts such as "no one can give better title than he has," or "you can't get good title from a thief." These concepts relate to the ability of a party to transfer title. There are three kinds of title we discuss for this purpose: good title, void title, and voidable title. We start out with an initial owner who has good title to the property. *Good title* is not specifically defined in the Code, but historically it means a title free from all liens, encumbrances, and claims of third parties. If John owns a car free of any liens such as a security interest, he has good title. If John sells the car, his buyer also gets that good title. This might be a good time to review the Warranty of Title in § 2-312(1), discussed in Chapter 9.C. Recall that if John does not have good title, then his buyer has a claim against him for breach of warranty. Now suppose John's car is stolen by Jill. Jill obviously does not have any claim to title, which is called void title. A problem arises if Jill now sells the car to Tom, an innocent third party. Does Tom get good title from Jill? The answer has to be no, because a party with void title cannot pass on better title than the party has. John may recover the property from Tom, who has a claim against Jill for breach of warranty. Of course, the claim might not be worth much because often it is hard to recover from a thief.

Assume now that instead of taking the goods from John by theft, Jill induces John to transfer them fraudulently. A simple example would be Jill paying for them with a check that bounces. This is fraud because the buyer has represented that there are adequate funds in the account when in fact there are not. In this case, and in any other case where the transfer is voidable under contract law, the transferee does not get good title, but gets voidable title. As the name suggests, the seller has the power to avoid the contract and get the goods back.

A problem arises when the party with voidable title transfers the goods to a third party; for example, Jill fraudulently acquires the goods from John and then sells them to Tom. Does Tom get good title from Jill? The answer, perhaps surprisingly, may be yes. Section 2-403(1) provides that "[a] person with voidable title has power to transfer a good title to a good faith purchaser for value." The outcome turns on whether Tom was "a good faith purchaser for value." We know from Chapter 4.C what *good faith* is as defined in § 1-201(b)(20). *Value* is defined in § 1-204, and although the definition is complex, the pertinent part of the definition is that it is "consideration sufficient to support a simple contract."

The definition of *purchaser* may surprise you. Section 1-201(b)(30) defines it as "a person that takes by purchase." Well, I admit that probably did not surprise you. But when we go to the definition of *purchase* in § 1-201(b)(29), we see that it means "taking by sale, lease, discount, negotiation, mortgage, pledge, lien, security interest, issue or re-issue, gift, or any other voluntary transaction creating an interest in property." That description is much broader than one who thought that a purchaser was merely a buyer might assume. For example, if you make a gift of goods or grant a security interest in them, the transferee is a purchaser. Putting that all together, a good faith purchaser for value must have exchanged a consideration for the goods, and done so both honestly and reasonably.

QUESTION 11. Mary owns a work of art that is worth $20,000. John purchases the work for $19,000, giving Mary a check that bounces. Before Mary can do anything about it, John has sold the work out of the back of his truck to Arthur for $4,000. Does Mary have a claim against Arthur?

A. Yes, because Arthur is not a good faith purchaser for value.
B. Yes, because Arthur got only void title from John.
C. No, because Arthur is a good faith purchaser for value.
D. No, because John got good title and transferred good title to Arthur.

ANALYSIS. Because he paid with a bad check, John got only voidable title under § 2-403(1)(b). Therefore, responses **B** and **D** cannot be correct. The rule of § 2-403(1) is that "[a] person with voidable title has power to transfer a good title to a good faith purchaser for value." So the issue comes down to whether Arthur was a good faith purchaser for value. He was clearly a purchaser because he took by sale. And he purchased for value, as the law does not inquire into the adequacy of consideration, so $4,000 can be consideration for a $20,000 painting. However, it seems to me that a person does not act in good faith when he buys valuable goods off the back of a truck. In those circumstances, a reasonable purchaser would make further inquiry into the source of the goods. So I think the best response is **A**. See *Hollis v. Chamberlin*, 243 Ark. 201 (1967).

Extra credit: If Arthur loses to Mary, does Arthur have a claim against John? Sure. When John sold the goods to Arthur, he gave Arthur a warranty of title under § 2-312(1), so Arthur would have a claim against John for breach of that warranty.

3. Entrusting

Entrusting is an unusual situation that raises an interesting question. Assume you drop your skis off at a ski shop for waxing. That is the entrusting. An inexperienced clerk then sells the skis to a customer. Does the customer acquire good title? This question is resolved by § 2-403(2), which provides:

> (2) Any entrusting of possession of goods to a merchant who deals in goods of that kind gives him power to transfer all rights of the entruster to a buyer in ordinary course of business.

To determine whether good title has been transferred, we have to answer two questions: (1) is the seller "a merchant who deals in goods of that kind," and

(2) is the buyer "a buyer in ordinary course of business"? When you saw that first question, you immediately remembered that in Chapter 4.B we explored the Code definition of *merchant* in § 2-104(1) and saw that there are goods merchants, practice merchants, and merchants by agency. This section only applies to *goods merchants*—persons who deal in goods of the kind. This makes sense in the context of entrustment. For example, if a buyer saw a pair of skis for sale in a pet shop, the buyer should be tipped off that something unusual is going on. Note that the second question does not deal with a "good faith purchaser for value," but with a "buyer in ordinary course of business." This term is defined in § 1-201(b)(9) in part as "a person that buys goods in good faith, without knowledge that the sale violates the rights of another person in the goods, and in the ordinary course from a person, other than a pawnbroker, in the business of selling goods of that kind." There is a good faith requirement, but also an express requirement that this buyer buy from a seller "in the business of selling goods of that kind." Normally, a buyer in ordinary course of business will buy from inventory. Applying this definition to our hypothetical, if the buyer buys your skis from a business that has an inventory of skis, then the buyer got good title from you, the entruster. Notice that the merchant has the "power" to transfer title, but not the right. You obviously have a good claim against the merchant for conversion of your property.

QUESTION 12. John Smith takes his Rolex watch to be repaired by Alice's watch repair shop. After the watch has been repaired, it is inadvertently put in the display case until John can pick it up. There is a tag on it that says "John Smith $72," with the "$72" representing the cost of repair. An inexperienced clerk sells the watch, which is worth $2,000, to Martin for $72. Does Martin have good title in the watch?

A. Yes, because he is a good faith purchaser for value.
B. Yes, because he is a buyer in ordinary course of business.
C. No, because he should have known that the sale violates the rights of another person in the goods.
D. No, because he is not a buyer in ordinary course of business.

ANALYSIS. The combination of the name tag and the low price for a Rolex seem to me circumstances in which a reasonable person would not have assumed he was buying a watch out of the inventory of the seller. Although this may be a close case, I think the best response is **D**. If you do not agree, I hope you chose response **B**, because that is the standard applicable to a purchase from an entruster.

QUESTION 13. Hard up for money, Joe takes his laptop computer to a pawnshop. In the transaction with the pawnshop, Joe is loaned a certain amount of money and agrees that the laptop is to be security for the loan. Before the date on which Joe would be in default, Jan buys the laptop from the pawnshop. Did the pawnshop have the power to transfer title to Jan?

A. Yes, because she is a good faith purchaser for value.
B. Yes, because she is a buyer in ordinary course of business.
C. No, because she should have known that the sale violates the rights of another person in the goods.
D. No, because she is not a buyer in ordinary course of business.

ANALYSIS.   You would think the answer here would be **B**, because it is the ordinary course of a pawnshop's business to sell goods that once belonged to others. But if you carefully read the definition of "buyer in ordinary course of business" in § 1-201(b)(9), you noted that it refers to "a person that buys goods in good faith, without knowledge that the sale violates the rights of another person in the goods, and in the ordinary course from a person, *other than a pawnbroker,* in the business of selling goods of that kind." I can't explain the pawnbroker exception, other than to point out the obvious distinction between the inventory of a pawnshop and the inventory of other businesses to which one might entrust goods. Because she purchased from a pawnshop, Jan is not a buyer in ordinary course of business. The best response is **D**.

F.   Closers

QUESTION 14. A seller agrees to sell 10,000 bricks to a buyer for $2,000 under a contract that states that payment is due on delivery. The buyer comes to the seller's place of business to get the bricks. The buyer's truck will only hold 2,000 bricks. The seller demands payment of $400 for each truckload of 2,000 bricks and the buyer refuses to pay. The seller refuses to allow the buyer to take the bricks. Who is in breach?

A. The seller, because the goods must be tendered in a single delivery.
B. The seller, because it cannot demand payment until delivery is completed.
C. The buyer, because the circumstances gave the seller the right to make delivery in lots and to demand a portion of the price for each lot.
D. The buyer, because a buyer must pay when the seller makes any part of the delivery.

ANALYSIS. The general rule of § 2-307 is that the goods must be delivered in a single lot, with payment on delivery. This situation, however, seems to fit the exception: "where the circumstances give either party the right to make or demand delivery in lots the price if it can be apportioned may be demanded for each lot." Here, the seller had the right to deliver in lots; therefore, the seller also had the right to demand a portion of the price for each lot. The buyer was in breach for refusing to make the payment of $400 for 2,000 bricks, so **C** is correct.

QUESTION 15. In a contract dated March 22, a buyer in Omaha, Nebraska, purchased 100 identified head of cattle from a seller in Great Falls, Montana, who promised to ship them from Great Falls at its expense. The seller gathered the cattle in a pen near the railyard on March 23. The cattle were delivered to the railroad for shipping on March 25 and the seller duly notified the buyer of the shipment. When they arrived, the cattle were found to have a disease. Undisputed evidence shows that they contracted the disease while in the pen near the railyard. Who bore the risk of loss?

A. The seller, because under this destination contract, the seller assumes the risk of loss.

B. The seller, because the risk of loss did not pass until the cattle were delivered to the carrier.

C. The buyer, because under this shipment contract, the buyer assumes the risk of loss.

D. The buyer, because the risk of loss passed when the cattle were identified on March 22.

ANALYSIS. Note that the mere fact that goods are identified does not mean that the risk of loss passes at that point. See §§ 2-501 and 2-509. This makes sense, because the buyer does not necessarily know when identification takes place and is not in a position to cover the risk, such as by insuring the goods. Therefore, response **D** is incorrect. Here, the contract requires the seller to ship the goods by carrier. In such a situation, it is always necessary to determine whether it is a shipment contract or a destination contract. The mere fact that the seller has promised to ship them to a particular destination, even at its expense, does not make it a destination contract. The key is whether the seller has promised to *deliver* them to that destination. Here, the seller is only arranging for the shipment, which is probably not enough to rebut the presumption that this is a shipment contract. Therefore, response **A** is incorrect. Under a shipment contract, according to § 2-509(1)(a), "the risk of loss passes to the buyer when the goods are duly delivered to the carrier" and notice is given under § 2-504(c). Here, those events occurred on March 25. Because the facts say the cattle contracted the disease before that date, the correct response is **B**. See *S-Creek Ranch, Inc. v. Monier & Co.*, 509 P.2d 777 (Wyo. 1973).

 # Burnham's picks

Question 1	**B**
Question 2	**D**
Question 3	**D**
Question 4	**C**
Question 5	**A**
Question 6	**D**
Question 7	**B**
Question 8	**C**
Question 9	**B**
Question 10	**B**
Question 11	**A**
Question 12	**D**
Question 13	**D**
Question 14	**C**
Question 15	**B**

14

Excuse of Performance

A. Introduction

Even though it doesn't sound quite right, this chapter should be called "Excuse of *Nonperformance*." The issue arises when a party does not do what it promised to do. That seems to be the very definition of breach of contract. Sometimes, though, the party has a justifiable reason for not performing. In that event, we say that the party's nonperformance is excused; that is, even though the party did not perform, the nonperformance is not breach. This situation can arise when the party's performance is subject to a condition, either express or implied. According to Restatement (Second) of Contracts § 224, "[a] condition is an event, not certain to occur, which must occur, unless its non-occurrence is excused, before performance under a contract becomes due." Therefore, if the event on which performance is conditioned does not occur, then the performance is not due, so nonperformance is not breach.

Performance can be subject to an express condition. For example, a contract may provide that the buyer will buy the seller's potatoes "if the potatoes chip to buyer's satisfaction." If the buyer is in good faith not satisfied with the potatoes, then the event that had to occur before the buyer's performance was due has not occurred. The buyer did not buy the potatoes, but its nonperformance was excused by the failure of a condition to occur, so its nonperformance is not breach.

Performance can also be subject to an implied condition. For example, we saw in Chapter 12.B that under the Code, payment is conditional on delivery. If the seller does not deliver, then the buyer does not have to pay. The parties do not state this condition expressly in the contract, but it is implied as a matter of law. If there is part performance by one party, then factors similar to the analysis of material breach can be used to determine whether the part performance operates as failure to bring about the event, thereby excusing the other party from performing.

> **QUESTION 1.** A contract between a buyer and a seller provides that the seller will deliver the goods on March 1, but the contract is silent as to payment. The seller tenders the goods, but the buyer refuses to pay for them at that time, so the seller refuses to deliver them. How would you describe the legal situation?
>
> **A.** The seller is in breach, because it made an unconditional promise to deliver the goods on March 1 and failed to do so.
> **B.** Whether the seller's performance is excused depends on the materiality of the buyer's breach.
> **C.** The seller's performance is excused because of the buyer's failure to perform.
> **D.** Neither party is in breach because the seller's performance was excused when the buyer did not pay and the buyer's performance was excused when the seller did not deliver.

ANALYSIS.   When a contract is silent as to payment, then payment is due on delivery. See § 2-511(1), discussed in Chapter 12.B. Therefore, payment and delivery are implied conditions of each other. If the buyer does not tender payment, then the seller is justified in not tendering delivery of the goods. That is what happened here, so the seller's nonperformance was not breach. The correct response is **C**.

B. Excuse of nonperformance

Another source of excuse is an unanticipated event that is beyond the control of the parties. The Code deals with three situations in which a party seeks to have its nonperformance excused because of events that occur after the contract has been formed. The parties frequently address these situations in a contract provision frequently called a *force majeure clause* that identifies exactly which events excuse nonperformance. In the absence of such an agreement, the Code supplies the default rule. In working your way through these rules, it is helpful to be guided by the rule of reason: If reasonable parties had addressed this situation in their contract, what events would they have identified as excusing?

There are three types of excuse articulated in the Code:

- Loss of goods identified at the time the contract is made (§ 2-613)
- Nonperformance caused by a presupposed condition (§ 2-615)
- Failure of the manner of performance (§ 2-614)

We examine only the first two, as the third is not a common occurrence.

1. *Casualty to identified goods*

We discussed the process of identifying the goods in Chapter 13.E Section 2-501(1) describes when, in the absence of agreement of the parties, identification occurs. Section 2-613 provides for what happens if identified goods are lost:

> **§ 2-613. Casualty to Identified Goods.**
> Where the contract requires for its performance goods identified when the contract is made, and the goods suffer casualty without fault of either party before the risk of loss passes to the buyer, or in a proper case under a "no arrival, no sale" term (Section 2-324) then
>   (a) if the loss is total the contract is avoided; and
>   (b) if the loss is partial or the goods have so deteriorated as no longer to conform to the contract the buyer may nevertheless demand inspection and at his option either treat the contract as avoided or accept the goods with due allowance from the contract price for the deterioration or the deficiency in quantity but without further right against the seller.

Let's diagram the first part of this provision, changing the *where* into an *if* to make an if–then statement:

If
> the contract requires for its performance goods identified when the contract is made; and
> the goods suffer casualty
> without fault of either party
> before the risk of loss passes to the buyer, or in a proper case under a "no arrival, no sale" term (Section 2-324)

then
> (a) if the loss is total the contract is avoided

Once we have determined whether identification has occurred, application of the other elements is straightforward. If the loss is partial, things are a little more complicated under subsection (b). Let's diagram that provision:

If

the loss is partial or

the goods have so deteriorated as no longer to conform to the contract

then

the buyer may nevertheless demand inspection and at his option either

treat the contract as avoided or

accept the goods with due allowance from the contract price for the deterioration or the deficiency in quantity but without further right against the seller.

Section 2-613 is often relied on by farmers seeking excuse for failing to perform if the crops that they have contracted to sell are destroyed. The reality is that most crops are fungible and if the specific land on which they are to be grown is not identified with particularity in the contract, farmers may not take advantage of § 2-613. Let's see if we can apply these rules to solve some problems.

QUESTION 2. A seller has promised a buyer a unique machine to be shipped by truck on June 1 to the buyer. Before the machine is delivered, a fire in the seller's warehouse caused by defective wiring destroys the machine and the seller is unable to deliver it. Is the seller in breach?

A. Yes, because the goods had not been identified to the contract.
B. Yes, because the casualty was the fault of the seller.
C. No, because the risk of loss had passed to the buyer.
D. No, because all the elements of § 2-613 are satisfied.

ANALYSIS.   Under § 2-613, one element is that "the contract requires for its performance goods identified when the contract is made." Here the goods appear to be identified to the contract at the time it was made. Because they are unique, they are "otherwise designated by the seller as goods to which the contract refers," in the language of § 2-501(1)(b). If this was an ordinary machine that the seller produced rather than a unique one, this element would not be satisfied. They suffered a casualty that was not the fault of either party. This is a shipment contract (see Chapter 13.D), so the risk of loss had not yet passed to the buyer. The loss is total. The elements of § 2-613(a) are all satisfied, so the correct response is **D.**

QUESTION 3. A seller has promised a buyer a unique machine to be shipped by truck on June 1 to the buyer. Before the machine is delivered, a fire in the seller's warehouse caused by defective wiring damages the machine. What is the correct legal view of the situation?

> **A.** The seller is in breach.
> **B.** The seller is not in breach because the risk of loss passed to the buyer.
> **C.** The seller is not in breach because there was a casualty to the goods and the contract is terminated.
> **D.** The seller is not in breach because there was a casualty to the goods and the buyer has the choice of either treating the contract as terminated or accepting and paying for the damaged machine.

ANALYSIS. This question is similar to the previous question. All the elements for excuse in the main paragraph are satisfied, but we must also consider § 2-613(b) when "the loss is partial." Under that subsection, the buyer has a choice of either terminating the contract or accepting the goods and paying for them with an allowance for the damage. The correct response is **D**.

2. Excuse by failure of presupposed conditions

We focus here on the situation that arises when a seller claims that its performance is excused because of an event that is not mentioned in the contract. Often these are catastrophic events—the so-called Acts of God, such as earthquakes or floods—that may hinder performance or render it completely impossible. Or they may be acts of government, such as the declaration of an embargo or quarantine. If the event is not expressly identified in the contract as excusing performance, the seller may claim that it was an implied condition of the contract that its nonperformance would be excused if such an event occurred. Under the Code, this claim is called "excuse by failure of presupposed conditions" and is analyzed under § 2-615, which provides:

> **§ 2-615. Excuse by Failure of Presupposed Conditions.**
>   Except so far as a seller may have assumed a greater obligation and subject to the preceding section on substituted performance:
>   (a) Delay in delivery or non-delivery in whole or in part by a seller who complies with paragraphs (b) and (c) is not a breach of his duty under a contract for sale if performance as agreed has been made impracticable by the occurrence of a contingency the non-occurrence of which was a basic assumption on which the contract was made or by compliance in good faith with any applicable foreign or domestic governmental regulation or order whether or not it later proves to be invalid.
>   (b) Where the causes mentioned in paragraph (a) affect only a part of the seller's capacity to perform, he must allocate production and deliveries among his customers but may at his option include regular customers not then under contract as well as his own requirements for further manufacture. He may so allocate in any manner which is fair and reasonable.

> (c) The seller must notify the buyer seasonably that there
> will be delay or non-delivery and, when allocation is required
> under paragraph (b), of the estimated quota thus made available
> for the buyer.

Under the default rule in subsection (a), a seller is not in breach if "performance as agreed has been made impracticable by the occurrence of a contingency the non-occurrence of which was a basic assumption on which the contract was made." Parties frequently contract around this default rule. One uncommon way they may contract around it is found in the introductory language, "[e]xcept so far as a seller may have assumed a greater obligation." This essentially means that a seller is free to agree to assume the risk of an unanticipated event that would otherwise excuse its nonperformance. An example is the eloquently phrased "hell or high water clause," under which a party agrees that it will not claim any excuse no matter what unanticipated events occur. Of course, if the event occurs, the party will not be able to perform, so the phrase really means that the party will not claim that its nonperformance is not breach.

The more common way to contract around the default rule is with a force majeure clause in which the parties enumerate the events that will excuse nonperformance. By operation of the rule of interpretation, *expressio unius est exclusio alterius* ("the expression of one is to the exclusion of another"), the fact that the parties enumerated certain events as excusing means that non-enumerated events are not excusing. The drafter must therefore word the clause carefully. Such a clause might look like this:

> Neither party shall be liable in damages or have the right to terminate this Agreement for any delay or default in performing hereunder if such delay or default is caused by conditions beyond its control including, but not limited to, Acts of God, government restrictions (including the denial or cancellation of any export or other necessary license), wars, insurrections and any other cause beyond the reasonable control of the party whose performance is affected.

The drafter of the sample clause has been careful to use the language "including, but not limited to" before enumerating the excusing events. This technique makes clear that the events listed are merely illustrative and not exclusive. A party would be wise to "time travel" into the future to determine what kind of events might occur that would hinder its performance, and then bargain for their inclusion in the force majeure clause. Inclusion is especially important if the events would not otherwise excuse nonperformance. An example might be a clause excusing performance or mandating modification of the agreement in the event a change in market price makes the cost of performing substantially higher than anticipated.

If the excusing events are not enumerated in the contract, the party seeking excuse must satisfy the elements of § 2-615(a):

> performance as agreed has been made impracticable by the occurrence of a contingency the non-occurrence of which was a basic assumption

on which the contract was made or by compliance in good faith with any applicable foreign or domestic governmental regulation

Some of these elements have proven to be problematic. Let's look at each one. With respect to the language "performance as agreed has been made impracticable," the issue is how burdensome performance has to be to excuse nonperformance. The word *impracticable* suggests something short of impossible, but how hard does performance have to be to be impracticable? Is merely losing profit enough, or does it have to drive the party practically to bankruptcy? The answer is probably somewhere in between. A party should not expect to be excused just because performance is more expensive than it thought; one of the reasons parties enter into contracts is to eliminate risk by securing a certain price for the goods they are buying and selling. On the other hand, a dramatic increase in expenses might be sufficient to excuse. Official Comment 4 seems to want to have it both ways:

> 4. Increased cost alone does not excuse performance unless the rise in cost is due to some unforeseen contingency which alters the essential nature of the performance. Neither is a rise or a collapse in the market in itself a justification, for that is exactly the type of business risk which business contracts made at fixed prices are intended to cover. But a severe shortage of raw materials or of supplies due to a contingency such as war, embargo, local crop failure, unforeseen shutdown of major sources of supply or the like, which either causes a marked increase in cost or altogether prevents the seller from securing supplies necessary to his performance, is within the contemplation of this section.

The issue with the language "the occurrence of a contingency the nonoccurrence of which was a basic assumption on which the contract was made" is often phrased in terms of *foreseeability*. Did the parties foresee the possibility that the event would occur? The problem with phrasing the issue that way is that an event may be foreseeable or actually foreseen, but the parties might still have made a basic assumption that the occurrence of the event would excuse nonperformance. For example, assume a seller of goods asks a buyer, "What if a meteorite destroys my factory?" The buyer laughs and says, "That'll never happen!" The seller says, "I guess you are right," and signs the contract. Two minutes later, a meteorite destroys the factory. It is clear that the possibility of a meteorite was foreseen. Nevertheless, it also appears that its nonoccurrence was a basic assumption on which the contract was made. In other words, the seller did not assume the risk of its occurrence. Similarly, the possibility of drought is always within a farmer's contemplation, but it is still possible that the parties in entering the contract assumed that there would be no drought. Professor E. Allan Farnsworth suggests a helpful test for determining whether the nonoccurrence was a basic assumption. Think of the rule as supplying a term that the parties omitted. That is, the parties did not address what would happen in the event a meteorite or a drought struck. We must therefore go back to the time the parties made the contract and ask whether reasonable people in the shoes of the parties would have put it in the contract as the kind of event that would excuse performance if they had thought about it. If so, it is an excusing event. Our economist friends, like Judge (and former Professor) Richard Posner, suggest a slightly different test. Professor Posner says that the party that is the most efficient risk-bearer should assume the risk of the non-occurrence of an event. For example, a manufacturer may be in a better position than a buyer to purchase insurance to cover the loss of the goods.

Section § 2-615 specifically refers to a *seller* whose performance has become impracticable. Nevertheless, most courts have found that the doctrine of impracticability is available to excuse buyers as well, if the buyer otherwise establishes the applicable elements. Excuse of the buyer is usually called *frustration,* and the elements are the same except that instead of the seller's performance being made impracticable, the buyer's principal purpose must be frustrated. Note, however, that a buyer's principal obligation is usually to pay money. Courts are not sympathetic to a buyer who claims excuse because some event causes it to lack money. Courts address this problem by stating that the impracticability or frustration must be *objective*—that is, the issue is the extent of the frustration any party would face in that situation and not the ability of the particular party to pay an expense.

Two frequent contingencies that parties claim excuses their nonperformance are unexpected increases in costs and failure of a source of supply. In general, increases in costs do not excuse. As one case stated when a buyer claimed impracticability because of a dramatic decline in the market price:

> The tough stance we are taking in this case is in view of the fact that virtually all contracts which are based upon a fixed price could be subject to modification if a change in the market price would occur. Interpreting the law as appellant suggests would invite countless suits by speculators in the market as well as by persons merely disappointed in their bargains. Few contractual agreements would be secure. As stated in comment 4 to [§ 2-615], an increase or decrease in prices, even a radical change, is just the thing that fixed price contracts are designed to protect against.

Lawrance v. Elmore Bean Warehouse, 702 P.2d 930, 933 (Id. App. 1985).

In dealing with the issue of increased costs, it might be helpful to distinguish between a seller faced with a direct inability to perform and a seller faced with performance at a higher cost. It is sometimes said that fluctuation in market prices is foreseeable, but the better view is that a party who agrees to a fixed-price contract takes the risk that the cost of its inputs may fluctuate. For example, if a farmer promised beans from his farm and the farmer is unable to produce beans because of a severe drought, the farmer would probably be excused. However, if a manufacturer of canned beans had promised a supermarket a supply at a fixed price, the manufacturer would probably not be excused if the market price of beans went up due to the drought. The farmer is unable to perform because of the direct consequence of the event. The manufacturer is able to perform, but at a higher cost; thus, for the manufacturer, the consequence of the event is indirect. This example leads to our second point. If the manufacturer had relied on a particular source for its bean supply, then the failure of that source might be an excuse. The seller seeking excuse on that ground should make clear in the contract that it was looking to a particular source of supply. Furthermore, the manufacturer should enter into a contract with that source of supply. Official Comment 5 provides that "[t]here is no excuse under this section, however, unless the seller has employed all due measures to assure himself that his source will not fail."

QUESTION 4. The builder of a highway in Southern California contracts with the owner of a gravel pit to purchase 5,000 cubic feet of gravel from the pit for a price of $3 per cubic foot, the gravel to be removed by the seller. (Quick review: Is this an Article 2 transaction?) After the seller has removed 3,000 cubic feet, the seller discovers that the rest of the gravel is under water. The seller refuses to perform, claiming impracticability. It will cost the seller $4 per cubic foot to remove the remaining gravel. Is this fact likely to satisfy the element that "performance as agreed has been made impracticable"?

A. Yes, where the additional cost would wipe out the seller's profit and cause a small loss on the transaction.

B. Yes, where the seller was not solvent and the loss on this job would drive it into bankruptcy.

C. No, because this is not the kind of event that excuses nonperformance.

D. No, because increased cost alone does not generally excuse nonperformance.

ANALYSIS. The best response is **D**. Official Comment 1 states in part, "Increased cost alone does not excuse performance unless the rise in cost is due to some unforeseen contingency which alters the essential nature of the performance." Here, there is an unforeseen contingency, but it does not alter the essential nature of the performance. Response **B** may seem attractive, but courts take an objective view, looking at whether the event would excuse a reasonable seller, and not a seller in the particular situation.

The review question can be answered by consulting § 2-107(1):

§ 2-107. Goods to Be Severed From Realty: Recording.

(1) A contract for the sale of minerals or the like (including oil and gas) or a structure or its materials to be removed from realty is a contract for the sale of goods within this Article if they are to be severed by the

seller but until severance a purported present sale thereof which is not effective as a transfer of an interest in land is effective only as a contract to sell.

Here, the minerals are to be severed by the seller, so the sale is within Article 2. See Chapter 4.A.

QUESTION 5. The builder of a highway in Southern California contracts with the owner of a gravel pit to purchase 5,000 cubic feet of gravel from the pit for a price of $3 per cubic foot, the gravel to be removed by the seller. After the seller has removed 3,000 cubic feet, the seller discovers that the rest of the gravel is under water. The seller refuses to perform, claiming impracticability. It will cost the seller $4 per cubic foot to remove the remaining gravel. Which of the following is the best argument for the seller in claiming "the occurrence of a contingency the non-occurrence of which was a basic assumption on which the contract was made"?

A. It will cost the seller $4 per cubic foot to remove the remaining gravel, wiping out its profit and causing a small loss on the transaction.
B. The principal purpose of the seller in entering this transaction was to make money, and that purpose was frustrated.
C. The water entered the pit through a fissure caused by an earthquake.
D. It is customary in the gravel business for the seller to test the pit for water before a sale is made, but the seller did not do so.

ANALYSIS.   As we saw in the previous question, response **A** goes to the issue of how much impracticability is required to excuse. We are now moving on to the issue of whether the nonoccurrence of the event was a basic assumption. Response **B** seems foolish to me, but the court actually went for it in the notorious case of *Alcoa v. Essex Group, Inc.*, 499 F. Supp. 53 (W.D. Pa., 1980). Fortunately, that decision has not been followed. Response **D** indicates the kind of evidence that will be used to resolve this kind of problem, for frequently custom and usage determines who bears the risk of unanticipated events. I think it would be likely for a risk like this to be placed on the seller, so this is not a good argument for the seller. Response **C** is probably the best argument, as an earthquake would be the kind of unanticipated event that excuses. Does it make a difference that the contract was being performed in Southern California? I'm not sure that would change the result, even though an earthquake might be foreseeable in Southern California. The issue is not whether it is foreseeable but whether, had they addressed the issue in the contract, the parties would have agreed to excuse the seller in the event of an earthquake. The question is not whether they would have foreseen it happening; the question is whether they would have put the risk of it happening on the seller.

QUESTION 6. A force majeure clause in a contract for the sale of cattle provides:

> Seller's nonperformance is excused in case of Acts of God, war, riots, fire, explosion, flood, strike, lockout, injunction, inability to obtain fuel, power, raw materials, labor containers, or transportation facilities, accident, breakage of machinery or apparatus, or national defense requirements.

Seller is unable to perform because the government orders a quarantine of his cattle due to an outbreak of disease. Is the seller excused?

A. Yes, because the contract impliedly includes other events beyond the seller's control.

B. Yes, because § 2-615(b) includes "governmental regulation or order" as an excusing event.

C. No, because this event is not enumerated in the contract.

D. No, because this event is not a natural occurrence and so would not excuse whether in the contract or not.

ANALYSIS. A drafter has to be very careful when drafting a force majeure clause to ensure that it is appropriate for the transaction. Often drafters make clear that the list of excusing events is nonexclusive by prefacing the list with a phrase such as, "including but not limited to." That phrase is not here, so I don't think it would be implied. Also, I think that when the parties agree to enumerate specific events in a force majeure clause, they are displacing the default rule of § 2-615. Even though quarantine would clearly be an excusing event under that provision, I think the statute does not apply because the parties used freedom of contract to displace the default rule. Therefore, the best response is **C**. Obviously, the seller would have been better off without a force majeure clause than with this one, for without such a clause in the contract, the default rule of § 2-615 would govern.

C.   Notice, allocation, and buyer's options

Finally, let us look at the following aspects of impracticability:

- Notice,
- Allocation, and
- Buyer's options

1. Notice

To rely on the excuse defense, § 2-615(c) requires a seller to seasonably notify the buyer that there will be delay or nondelivery. This is a reasonable requirement, but it might be difficult for a seller to determine whether there will be merely delay, or nondelivery, and if there will be nondelivery in part, what the allocation will be. In terms of the seasonableness of the notification, it seems the answer is, as in most Code situations, for the seller to act in good faith.

2. Allocation

Under § 2-615(b), if an unforeseen contingency, such as a crop failure, affects only a part of the seller's capacity to perform, the seller must allocate production and deliveries among its customers in any manner that is fair and reasonable. For example, assume a farmer has contracted to sell half of his anticipated crop of 100,000 bushels of barley to be grown on specified land to two purchasers. As a result of drought, the farmer only produces 40,000 bushels, and the nonperformance is excused. The farmer must allocate the 40,000 bushels in a fair and reasonable manner among the two purchasers. Note, however, that a "fair and reasonable" allocation does not always mean an equal allocation. For example, a seller might be able to fairly allocate production to old customers at the expense of new customers, or to customers with a greater need at the expense of customers with a lesser need.

3. Buyer's options

Assume now that the buyer has received proper notification from the seller that it will only be able to perform part of its obligation and the allocation is reasonable. The buyer's options are set forth in § 2-616:

> **§ 2-616. Procedure on Notice Claiming Excuse.**
> (1) Where the buyer receives notification of a material or indefinite delay or an allocation justified under the preceding section he may by written notification to the seller as to any delivery concerned, and where the prospective deficiency substantially impairs the value of the whole contract under the provisions of this Article relating to breach of installment contracts (Section 2-612), then also as to the whole,
> > (a) terminate and thereby discharge any unexecuted portion of the contract; or
> > (b) modify the contract by agreeing to take his available quota in substitution.
> (2) If after receipt of such notification from the seller the buyer fails so to modify the contract within a reasonable time not exceeding thirty days the contract lapses with respect to any deliveries affected.
> (3) The provisions of this section may not be negated by agreement except in so far as the seller has assumed a greater obligation under the preceding section.

Under this provision, the buyer is not necessarily bound to accept the allocation. As to any delivery proposed by the seller, the buyer may affirmatively agree to modify the contract. Alternatively, the buyer may terminate the contract. In fact, according to subsection (2), failure of the buyer to affirmatively agree to modification operates as a termination. In addition, the buyer must determine whether the "prospective deficiency substantially impairs the value of the whole contract." This is the same test used in § 2-612 to determine whether there has been a breach of the whole with respect to an installment contract. See Chapter 13.C. If the test is satisfied, then the buyer may take the same steps with respect to the whole contract as it took with respect to any delivery.

> **QUESTION 7.** A law school has ordered 150 shirts from a seller because the law school thinks it would be nice for every member of the entering class to have the same shirt. The seller informs the buyer that due to an unanticipated event, its manufacturing ability has been impaired and it will be able to ship only 100 of the shirts. Advise the law school what it should do.
>
> **A.** Because this deficiency does not substantially impair the value of the whole contract, it must accept the shipment.
> **B.** It must affirmatively notify the seller if it intends to terminate the contract.
> **C.** It does not need to do anything, and the contract will be considered terminated.
> **D.** It does not have to accept the modification because there is no consideration for it.

ANALYSIS.   Under these facts, it would appear that the deficiency (note we don't call it a *breach*, because there is no breach when a party's non-performance is excused) does substantially impair the value of the whole contract. The law school needs a shirt for every student, so nothing less will suffice. Therefore, the law school does not have to accept performance. Although I think it would make sense for the law school to affirmatively notify the seller of that decision, according to § 2-616(2), notification is not necessary. As stated in the Official Comment to this section, "If the buyer does not elect so to modify the contract, he may terminate it and under subsection (2) his silence after receiving the seller's claim of excuse operates as such a termination." The best response is **C**. Note that **D** is not a correct response because under § 2-209(1), a modification does not require consideration.

D.   Closers

QUESTION 8. A seller has promised a buyer 100 widgets to be shipped by truck on June 1 to buyer. The seller delivers the widgets to the trucking company, but en route to the buyer's place of business, the truck is in an accident and 40 of the widgets are destroyed. What is the correct legal view of the situation?

A. The seller is in breach.
B. The seller is not in breach because the risk of loss passed to the buyer.
C. The seller is not in breach because there was a casualty to the goods and the contract is terminated.
D. The seller is not in breach because there was a casualty to the goods and the buyer has the choice of either treating the contract as terminated or accepting and paying for the 60 remaining widgets.

ANALYSIS.   This is a bit of a trick question. You were probably immediately drawn to subsection (b) of § 2-613 because "the loss is partial." First, however, we have to satisfy the elements from the preceding language of that statute, and one of those elements is that the loss occurs "before the risk of loss passes to the buyer." This is a shipment contract (see Chapter 13.D), and under § 2-509(1)(a), "the risk of loss passes to the buyer when the goods are duly delivered to the carrier." Here, the risk of loss had passed to the buyer. Therefore, the correct response is **B**.

QUESTION 9. A seller promises a buyer 300 crates of onions to be shipped from a particular ranch. Because of a government quarantine, the seller is able to ship only 200 crates of the onions, and the seller duly informs the buyer that it is shipping the 200 crates. Is the buyer justified in refusing to accept the 200 crates?

A. Yes, because the seller's breach is material.
B. Yes, because the seller's failure to perform is material.
C. No, because the seller's breach is immaterial.
D. No, because the seller's failure to perform is material.

ANALYSIS.   There are two parts to this analysis—whether the seller has breached or failed to perform, and whether that breach or failure is material. We know that the seller's promise to deliver and the buyer's promise to pay are conditions. If the seller had not performed at all, it would be easy to determine that the buyer's performance is excused. The question is harder when the seller has given some of the promised performance. A useful tool for making this determination is Restatement (Second) of Contracts § 241. This section, titled "Circumstances Significant in Determining Whether a Failure Is Material," is usually used to determine whether a breach is material. As we have seen in this chapter, though, not all failures to perform are breach. Under the facts of this case, the breach or failure is probably material. As to whether it is a breach or a failure to perform, § 2-615(a) provides that a seller is excused "if performance as agreed has been made impracticable . . . by compliance in good faith with any applicable foreign or domestic governmental regulation or order whether or not it later proves to be invalid." A quarantine is such a governmental order that operates as an excusing event. The seller is not in breach, so the best response is **B**. This analysis is strengthened by § 2-616, which authorizes the buyer to terminate the contract when it receives notification of an allocation.

QUESTION 10. A buyer promises to buy 50,000 bushels of corn from a farmer. Because of an unanticipated drought in the area, the crop is completely destroyed and the farmer is unable to perform. What is the best argument by the buyer that the farmer is in breach?

A. The performance is not impracticable because the farmer can obtain corn on the market.
B. The event is not the kind of event that makes performance impracticable.
C. The contract did not contain a force majeure clause that excused the farmer.
D. The farmer notified the buyer that it would not be able to perform.

ANALYSIS. Response **B** is probably not correct because drought is generally considered to be an excusing event. Response **C** is irrelevant; in the absence of a force majeure clause, the farmer would be excused if it satisfied the elements of § 2-615. Response **D** doesn't make sense, for § 2-615(c) provides just the opposite—"The seller must notify the buyer seasonably that there will be delay or nonperformance." Most cases agree with response **A**. Section 2-613 applies "where the contract requires for its performance goods identified when the contract is made." The problem for the farmer is that the contract does not specifically provide that the crops are to be grown on designated land. Using that argument, the buyer may claim that the seller is perfectly capable of supplying the buyer with 50,000 bushels of corn from the market. The lesson here is for the seller to designate where the goods will come from if it expects to be excused if that source fails. This is consistent with the general rule that the failure of a seller's exclusive source of supply does not excuse unless that source of supply was part of the contract.

Burnham's picks

Question 1	**C**
Question 2	**D**
Question 3	**D**
Question 4	**D**
Question 5	**C**
Question 6	**C**
Question 7	**C**
Question 8	**B**
Question 9	**B**
Question 10	**A**

15

Assurances and Reclamation

A. Introduction

The Code often reflects the real world of commercial practice, taking the rules from that world rather than imposing rules on it. Furthermore, the Code wants parties to communicate with each other to try to work out problems. These aspects of Code jurisprudence play out in the Code's approach to the problem of anticipatory repudiation. The right to demand assurances is an interesting concept in the Code, reflecting the Code's practicality and flexibility. Moreover, the Code gives a seller some additional rights before it has shipped the goods, and even after it has shipped them, when it learns that the buyer is a credit risk.

B. Anticipatory repudiation

Anticipatory repudiation is not defined in the Code. We therefore look to the common law for the rule, as I'm sure you recall from our discussion of § 1-103(b) in Chapter 2.A.3. An anticipatory repudiation is usually defined as a clear and unequivocal refusal to perform before the time for performance is due. It is possible that the intention of the Code drafters was to make the rule less strict than at common law, for Official Comment 2 to § 2-610 states:

> 2. It is not necessary for repudiation that performance be made literally and utterly impossible. Repudiation can result from action which reasonably indicates a rejection of the continuing obligation.

The concept of anticipatory repudiation was not always accepted at common law, for logically it is not possible to breach before the time for performance. If a seller is obligated to deliver goods on June 1, and it tells the buyer on May 1 that it will not perform, then logically the seller has not failed to perform because it has not failed to deliver the goods on June 1. However, it will promote efficiency to recognize an anticipatory repudiation as a breach because the nonbreaching party will have more time to prevent losses that might occur from the breach. The Code is clear that when there is an anticipatory repudiation by one party, the other party may take appropriate steps. Section 2-610 provides:

> **§ 2-610. Anticipatory Repudiation.**
>   When either party repudiates the contract with respect to a performance not yet due the loss of which will substantially impair the value of the contract to the other, the aggrieved party may
>   (a) for a commercially reasonable time await performance by the repudiating party; or
>   (b) resort to any remedy for breach (Section 2-703 or Section 2-711), even though he has notified the repudiating party that he would await the latter's performance and has urged retraction; and
>   (c) in either case suspend his own performance or proceed in accordance with the provisions of this Article on the seller's right to identify goods to the contract notwithstanding breach or to salvage unfinished goods (Section 2-704).

This section can be thought of as "breach by anticipatory repudiation" because a repudiation prior to the time for performance is a breach. For example, assume a buyer and a seller have entered into a contract under which the seller is obligated to deliver 1,000 widgets on June 1. On May 1, the seller calls the buyer and says, "The market price of widgets has gone up dramatically since we made our contract. I am not going to deliver the promised widgets to you on June 1." The seller has breached the contract on May 1. The buyer may pursue remedies for breach. In fact, the buyer is obligated to do so after a reasonable time. In a rising market, the buyer should "cover" by ordering the goods elsewhere to mitigate the damages and avoid consequential damages that might arise if the goods are not available on June 1.

It might happen that the seller changes its mind and retracts its repudiation. This situation is addressed in § 2-611:

> **§ 2-611. Retraction of Anticipatory Repudiation.**
>   (1) Until the repudiating party's next performance is due he can retract his repudiation unless the aggrieved party has since the repudiation cancelled or materially changed his position or otherwise indicated that he considers the repudiation final.
>   (2) Retraction may be by any method which clearly indicates to the aggrieved party that the repudiating party intends to perform, but must

include any assurance justifiably demanded under the provisions of this Article (Section 2-609).

(3) Retraction reinstates the repudiating party's rights under the contract with due excuse and allowance to the aggrieved party for any delay occasioned by the repudiation.

These rules seem to reflect common sense. When one party repudiates, the other party might not immediately end the relationship but might attempt to cajole or persuade the other party into performing. That is one reason § 2-610 allows the nonbreaching party to await performance for a "commercially reasonable" time. Eventually, however, the nonbreaching party is going to look for someone else to perform. If the repudiating party retracts after the other party has relied on the repudiation, then the retraction is not effective. Nor is the retraction effective if the nonbreaching party makes clear that the repudiation has been accepted.

> **QUESTION 1.** A buyer and a seller entered into a contract under which the seller is obligated to deliver 1,000 widgets on June 1. On May 1, the seller calls the buyer and says, "The market price of widgets has gone up dramatically since we made our contract. I am not going to deliver the promised widgets to you on June 1." The buyer responds, "I don't deal with dirty contract breakers. I'll never buy widgets from you again." An hour later, before the buyer has had an opportunity to find the widgets elsewhere, the seller calls and retracts the repudiation. Does the buyer have to accept the retraction?
>
> **A.** Yes, because the buyer has not relied on the repudiation.
> **B.** Yes, because the actions of the seller did not amount to a repudiation in the first place.
> **C.** No, because the buyer indicated that he considered the repudiation final.
> **D.** No, because the seller did not offer to pay damages caused by the repudiation.

ANALYSIS. It seems clear that the seller's statement was a clear and unequivocal refusal to perform, so it was a repudiation. Section 2-611(1) provides that "[u]ntil the repudiating party's next performance is due he can retract his repudiation unless the aggrieved party has since the repudiation cancelled or materially changed his position or otherwise indicated that he considers the repudiation final." Here the buyer as the aggrieved party made clear that he considered the repudiation final. Therefore, **C** is the best response. Note that § 2-611(3) provides that if the aggrieved party does accept the retraction, the repudiating party has to pay any damages caused by the repudiation.

C.   Demand for assurances

Sometimes one party takes an action or says something before performance that leads the other party to believe that there may be a repudiation. The common law, which applies in the absence of a Code definition, makes clear that a repudiation has to be clear and unequivocal. Frequently, for example, the seller calls the buyer and says something like, "The market price of widgets has gone up dramatically since we made our contract. I just don't know if I can deliver the promised widgets to you on June 1, because I'll lose a lot of money if I do." Such a statement does not rise to the level of a clear and unequivocal repudiation. If one party resorts to remedies for breach and a court later determines that the other party did not repudiate, the party who jumped the gun may end up as the breaching party.

So how does a party determine whether the other party has repudiated when the repudiation is not clear and unequivocal? The Code's answer is simple—he *asks* him. For example, a seller has a contract under which she allows her customer to pay for the goods 30 days after delivery. The seller hears that other creditors have not been paid by this customer. The seller would be taking a risk if she delivered the goods without a good prospect of payment. On the other hand, she would be taking a risk if she did not deliver the goods, for without a clear and unequivocal repudiation by the buyer, nondelivery would likely constitute a breach.

The seller can resolve this difficult dilemma by seeking guidance from § 2-609:

> **§ 2-609. Right to Adequate Assurance of Performance.**
>
> (1) A contract for sale imposes an obligation on each party that the other's expectation of receiving due performance will not be impaired. When reasonable grounds for insecurity arise with respect to the performance of either party the other may in writing demand adequate assurance of due performance and until he receives such assurance may if commercially reasonable suspend any performance for which he has not already received the agreed return.
>
> (2) Between merchants the reasonableness of grounds for insecurity and the adequacy of any assurance offered shall be determined according to commercial standards.
>
> (3) Acceptance of any improper delivery or payment does not prejudice the aggrieved party's right to demand adequate assurance of future performance.
>
> (4) After receipt of a justified demand failure to provide within a reasonable time not exceeding thirty days such assurance of due performance as is adequate under the circumstances of the particular case is a repudiation of the contract.

The steps each party must take in this situation are outlined in the statute. First of all, there has to be "reasonable grounds for insecurity." What does that mean? It is answered by subsection (2): "Between merchants the reasonableness of grounds for insecurity . . . shall be determined according to commercial standards." This is Code jurisprudence at work. The Code does not supply an answer in the abstract but is confident that an answer will emerge from the facts and circumstances of the particular business and the particular situation. In our hypothetical, if in this business the fact that other creditors are not being paid makes a creditor feel insecure, then our creditor has reasonable grounds for insecurity. Second, there has to be a written demand for assurances. At that point the party demanding assurances may suspend performance. In our hypothetical, for example, the seller would not have to deliver the goods. Then, if she receives adequate assurance, she must perform. What are adequate assurances? We look again to subsection (2): "Between merchants . . . the adequacy of any assurance offered shall be determined according to commercial standards." Obviously the best assurance would be tender of cash in advance; this may be asking too much, however, as it would essentially rewrite the bargain of the parties. On the other hand, assume the buyer merely wrote back stating, "No problem. You will be paid." That does not reasonably assure the seller. If the creditor does not receive adequate assurances within a reasonable time not to exceed 30 days, then subsection (4) provides that there is a repudiation. In that case, the party who suspended performance is not in breach.

The demand for assurances is a win–win situation. If the demanding party does receive assurances, the contract is back on track. If he does not, then he may conclude that there has been a repudiation, and may suspend his performance and sue for breach. Other contexts in which a demand for assurance arises in Article 2 are found in § 2-210, when an obligee is concerned about a delegation of a duty, and in § 2-612, when a party to an installment contract needs to know whether a breach with respect to one installment is a breach of the whole.

QUESTION 2. Before the time for planting, a potato buyer buys a farmer's entire potato crop, to be delivered at harvest time. After a few months, the buyer asks the farmer how the potato crop is looking and the farmer replies that he never planted potatoes because the market for onions looked more promising. Can the buyer sue the farmer for breach at this point?

A. Yes, because there has been an anticipatory repudiation by the farmer.
B. Yes, because the farmer did not respond to the buyer's demand for assurances.
C. No, because the buyer must first demand assurances.
D. No, because the farmer is not in breach.

ANALYSIS. This question is included to make the point that although the demand for assurances is a useful provision, its function is to determine whether there has been an anticipatory repudiation. If there is a clear and unequivocal refusal to perform, as in this case, there is no need to demand assurances. Because the farmer has breached by anticipatory repudiation, the best response is **A**.

D. Right of reclamation

If a seller ships goods to a buyer on credit and then discovers that the buyer is unlikely to be able to pay, it is obviously too late to suspend performance and demand assurances. But all is not lost. Under § 2-702, the seller may have a right to reclaim the goods:

> **§ 2-702. Seller's Remedies on Discovery of Buyer's Insolvency.**
> (1) Where the seller discovers the buyer to be insolvent he may refuse delivery except for cash including payment for all goods theretofore delivered under the contract, and stop delivery under this Article (Section 2-705).
> (2) Where the seller discovers that the buyer has received goods on credit while insolvent he may reclaim the goods upon demand made within ten days after the receipt, but if misrepresentation of solvency has been made to the particular seller in writing within three months before delivery the ten day limitation does not apply. Except as provided in this subsection the seller may not base a right to reclaim goods on the buyer's fraudulent or innocent misrepresentation of solvency or of intent to pay.
> (3) The seller's right to reclaim under subsection (2) is subject to the rights of a buyer in ordinary course or other good faith purchaser under this Article (Section 2-403). Successful reclamation of goods excludes all other remedies with respect to them.

This provision applies only if the buyer is *insolvent*, a term of art under the Code:

> **§ 1-201(b)(23) "Insolvent" means:**
> (A) having generally ceased to pay debts in the ordinary course of business other than as a result of bona fide dispute;
> (B) unable to pay debts as they become due; or
> (C) insolvent within the meaning of federal bankruptcy law. [The Bankruptcy Code, 11 U.S.C. § 101 (32), provides that "insolvent" means that the entity's debts are greater than its assets.]

If the seller finds out the buyer is insolvent prior to delivery, under § 2-702(1) the seller may refuse to extend credit and insist on payment on delivery. If the seller finds out the buyer is insolvent *after* delivery, under subsection (2) the seller may reclaim the goods upon demand within ten days of receipt of the goods, with a longer period if the buyer has made a written misrepresentation of solvency within three months before delivery.

Although this provision is theoretically of value, often the seller will be out of luck. As noted in subsection (3), the right is defeated by a buyer in ordinary course or other good faith purchaser. See Chapter 13.E. Moreover, the right may be defeated by a secured party who has an interest in the goods in the hands of the buyer. As you will learn when you study Secured Transactions—the subject of Article 9 (covered in *The Glannon Guide to Secured Transactions*)— frequently another creditor has a security interest in the buyer's inventory or equipment to secure credit. That security interest attaches to the goods as soon as the buyer has an interest in them and a secured party is a "purchaser" under the Code. If the buyer is in default under the agreement with that creditor, or files for bankruptcy, as insolvent parties often do, then most courts have found that the secured party has priority in the goods the seller seeks to reclaim.

QUESTION 3. *Statute reader.* On June 1, a seller is negotiating the sale of $10,000 worth of widgets to a buyer. The seller is concerned about the buyer's solvency, so the buyer gives the seller specific written assurances of its solvency. The seller then agrees to sell the goods with the understanding that the buyer will pay within 30 days. On June 2, the seller delivers the goods to the railroad, which delivers them to the buyer on June 7. On June 14, the seller discovers that the buyer is insolvent and sends written notice of its right to reclaim the goods to the buyer. When the buyer refuses to return the goods, the seller immediately goes to court. Does the seller have a right of reclamation?

A. No, because it did not demand assurances before it asserted the right.
B. No, because it did not assert the right within ten days from its shipment of the goods.
C. Yes, because it timely asserted the right within ten days.
D. Yes, because the seller had made a misrepresentation of solvency.

ANALYSIS. This one requires close attention to the language of the statute. We can reject response **A** because we are not demanding assurances under § 2-609; it is too late for that, because the goods have been shipped. Under § 2-702, the demand for reclamation must be made "within ten days," but it is ten days "after the receipt [of the goods]." Under our facts, because the goods were received on June 7 and demand was made on June 14, the demand was made within ten days after receipt, so response **C** is correct. You might wonder why response **D** is not correct, for the statute provides that the ten-day rule does not apply if the seller had made a misrepresentation of solvency. This is not as good an answer, however, because you would rather come within the "safe harbor" of the ten-day rule and not have to litigate the issue of whether there had been "misrepresentation of solvency." Note that as a practical matter, although you are told that the buyer is insolvent, the seller will have to prove that as well.

E.   Closers

QUESTION 4. A manufacturer of cash registers promises a fast food company that it will deliver 30 cash registers with an innovative design in ten months. After six months, the manufacturer has not been able to complete a prototype. At a meeting of the parties, the company demands that the manufacturer show progress by a meeting scheduled to take place in 30 days. At that next meeting, the manufacturer has shown no progress, so the company cancels the contract. Is the company justified?

A. Yes, because there was a clear and unequivocal refusal by the manufacturer to perform.

B. Yes, because the company did not receive adequate assurance.

C. No, because the company did not have reasonable grounds for insecurity.

D. No, because the company did not demand adequate assurance in writing.

ANALYSIS.   This question is based on the case of *AMF, Inc. v. McDonald's Corp.*, 536 F.2d 1167 (7th Cir. 1976). Applying § 2-609 to the facts, the court found that McDonald's had reasonable grounds for insecurity and AMF did not timely provide adequate assurance. The only problem was that McDonald's had not demanded the assurances in writing. The court was not concerned about that technicality, reasoning that the Code should be "liberally construed" instead of being applied formalistically. That "liberally construed" language comes from the purposes and policies in § 1-103. Subsection (a) states that "[t]he Uniform Commercial Code must be liberally construed and applied to promote its underlying purposes and policies." Under the facts of *AMF*, the loose reading of the Code seems to make sense. The writing requirement is probably evidentiary in purpose, to make sure there is no misunderstanding about the seriousness of the demand. That requirement was satisfied by the first formal meeting, which left AMF with the clear understanding of what was expected within 30 days. I agree with that reasoning and think that **B** is the best response, but response **D** could well win the day with a more formalistic judge who does not appreciate Code jurisprudence.

> **QUESTION 5.** A seller and a buyer agree that the seller will ship 100 widgets on June 1, with payment by the buyer due 30 days after delivery. Before the seller delivers the widgets, it learns that another seller has received a check from the same buyer that bounced. What would you recommend the seller do?
>
> A. Immediately cancel the contract.
> B. Proceed with the delivery of the goods.
> C. Suspend the delivery and demand written assurances.
> D. Refuse delivery except for cash.

ANALYSIS. The remedy suggested by response **D** invokes the refusal of delivery under § 2-702(1):

> (1) Where the seller discovers the buyer to be insolvent he may refuse delivery except for cash including payment for all goods theretofore delivered under the contract, and stop delivery under this Article (Section 2-705).

However, a condition to the seller's resort to this remedy is that the buyer is insolvent. The fact that one check has bounced is probably not sufficient evidence to conclude that the buyer is insolvent under § 1-201(b)(23). Nevertheless, it is probably sufficient to give the seller "reasonable grounds for insecurity" under § 2-609(1). Under that provision, the seller may suspend its performance and demand reasonable assurances. You might wonder what difference assurances would make, as the best assurance would be payment in cash and the seller might not be entitled to that good an assurance. The answer is that the buyer may have an explanation as to why the check bounced, such as that there was a bank error or that it stopped payment because of breach by the other party, or, if the demand was justified, it might be able to provide adequate assurance in a manner that does not rewrite the contract. The best response is **C**.

 # Burnham's picks

Question 1	C
Question 2	A
Question 3	C
Question 4	B
Question 5	C

16

Seller's Remedies

A. Introduction

1. General principles of contract remedies

Article 2 contains a number of formulas for computing damages. Nevertheless, it is a good idea to take the long view before getting caught up in the details of Code remedies. That is, it is important to recall the basic principles of contract remedies and read them into the Code. This approach can also be helpful if you don't like dealing with numbers; it is the principles that are important, not the numbers. The general principles behind Code remedies are found in Article 1. These principles include the following:

- Expectation
- Compensation
- Reasonable certainty
- Mitigation
- Foreseeability

Section 1-305(a) provides as follows:

§ 1-305. Remedies to Be Liberally Administered.

(a) The remedies provided by [the Uniform Commercial Code] must be liberally administered to the end that the aggrieved party may be put in as good a position as if the other party had fully performed but neither consequential or special damages nor penal damages may be had except as specifically provided in [the Uniform Commercial Code] or by other rule of law.

In the statement that the goal of Code remedies is that "the aggrieved party may be put in as good a position as if the other party had fully performed," we see the principle of *expectation damages*, or the expectancy. This means that the remedy should put the nonbreaching party in the same position it would have been in if the contract had been performed. Another goal of Code remedies is *compensation*: The remedies are intended to compensate the non-breaching party, not to punish the breaching party. Therefore, punitive damages are not available. Official Comment 1 to this section states that a third principle is found in § 1-305:

The third purpose of subsection (a) is to reject any doctrine that damages must be calculable with mathematical accuracy. Compensatory damages are often at best approximate: they have to be proved with whatever definiteness and accuracy the facts permit, but no more.

I'm not sure I see that principle of *reasonable certainty* expressly stated. However, I do not doubt that it should be applied to Code transactions, for according to § 1-103(b), "the principles of law and equity . . . supplement its provisions." Another common law principle that is not expressly stated but that should be read into the Code is *mitigation*. The nonbreaching party has a duty to take reasonable steps that reduce the damages the breaching party must pay. Finally, the Code recognizes the principle of *foreseeability* when it refers to consequential damages.

In terms of the cost of obtaining a remedy, under the common law *American Rule*, each side pays its own attorney's fees whether it wins or loses. There are two exceptions to this rule. First, parties are free to change the rule by contract. Second, some statutes, particularly consumer protection statutes, provide for attorney's fees. The Code, however, is silent on attorney's fees. In a Code transaction, therefore, it is necessary to read the contract and any other relevant statutes carefully to determine whether a prevailing party is entitled to attorney's fees.

QUESTION 1. A buyer breaches a contract by refusing to accept the goods. The seller resells the goods to another buyer for a price that is lower than the market price and attempts to recover the difference between the contract price and the resale price. The buyer claims that the seller failed to mitigate damages because it could have sold the goods at the market price without any difficulty. The seller claims that because the Code is silent on mitigation, it cannot have failed to mitigate the damages. Is the seller right?

A. Yes, because the Code is silent on mitigation.
B. Yes, because mitigation is not required under the common law.
C. No, because § 1-305 expressly includes the principle of mitigation.
D. No, because the principle of mitigation supplements the Code according to § 1-103(b).

ANALYSIS.   The Code is largely silent on mitigation. It could be claimed that the principle of mitigation is impliedly found in § 1-305, because when it says that the goal of Code remedies is compensation, this suggests that the goal is not *overcompensation*. However, that is not expressly stated, so **C** is not the best response. The best response is **D**, because § 1-103(b) states that "the principles of law and equity . . . supplement its provisions," and mitigation is an important principle in the law of contract remedies.

2. Organization of remedies

We examine the remedies available to the seller in this chapter and the remedies available to the buyer in the next chapter. The remedies are organized around each of the four situations that are a function of (1) who is in breach, and (2) who has the goods. These situations are as follows:

- Buyer in breach; buyer has goods
- Buyer in breach; seller has goods
- Seller in breach; seller has goods
- Seller in breach; buyer has goods

We look first at the seller's remedies when the buyer is in breach. Article 2 contains an Overview of Seller's Remedies in § 2-703:

§ 2-703. Seller's Remedies in General.
Where the buyer wrongfully rejects or revokes acceptance of goods or fails to make a payment due on or before delivery or repudiates with respect to a part or the whole, then with respect to any goods directly affected and, if the breach is of the whole contract (Section 2-612), then also with respect to the whole undelivered balance, the aggrieved seller may:
    (a) withhold delivery of such goods;
    (b) stop delivery by any bailee as hereafter provided (Section 2-705);
    (c) proceed under the next section respecting goods still unidentified to the contract;
    (d) resell and recover damages as hereafter provided (Section 2-706);

(e) recover damages for non-acceptance (Section 2-708) or in a proper case the price (Section 2-709);

(f) cancel.

B.   Buyer in breach; buyer has goods

If the buyer has the goods but the buyer is in breach, this must mean that the buyer has accepted the goods but has not paid for them. The seller's remedy in this situation is to recover the price of the goods pursuant to § 2-709(1)(a):

§ 2-709. Action for the Price.

(1) When the buyer fails to pay the price as it becomes due the seller may recover, together with any incidental damages under the next section, the price

(a) of goods accepted or of conforming goods lost or damaged within a commercially reasonable time after risk of their loss has passed to the buyer.

QUESTION 2. A seller and a buyer agree on a contract for the sale of 100 widgets for $10,000, to be delivered on June 1. By June 1, the widget market has gone up and the value of the widgets is $10,500. The seller nevertheless timely delivers the widgets. The buyer has no defense to payment but refuses to pay for the widgets. The seller is compelled to hire a lawyer to bring suit against the buyer. How much can the seller recover?

A. $10,000.
B. $10,500.
C. $10,000 plus reasonable attorney's fees.
D. $10,000 plus reasonable attorney's fees and punitive damages.

ANALYSIS.   Section 2-709(1)(a) provides that the seller may recover "the price of goods accepted." The price of the goods was $10,000. The correct response is **A**. Even though the section provides that the seller may recover incidental damages, incidental damages do not include attorney's fees. In the next section we look at what items are included in incidental damages. Attorney's fees may be recovered only if the contract so provides. Punitive damages may not be recovered for breach of contract.

QUESTION 3. A buyer agrees to buy a widget from a seller for $5,000 payable 30 days after delivery. Assume that the risk of loss passes to the buyer when the goods are put in the hands of the shipper. The goods are lost in shipment. After 30 days, can the seller recover the price from the buyer?

A. Yes, because the risk of loss was on the buyer.
B. Yes, but the seller can only recover its costs and not its profit.
C. No, because the buyer is not at fault.
D. No, because a reasonable time has not passed.

ANALYSIS.   Section 2-709(1)(a) provides that "the seller may recover . . . the price of goods . . . lost or damaged within a commercially reasonable time after risk of their loss has passed to the buyer." Here, the goods were lost, a commercially reasonable time has passed, and the risk of loss was on the buyer. Therefore, the seller may recover the price and the correct response is **A**. The buyer may have a remedy against the shipper, but that does not affect the seller's rights.

C.   Buyer in breach; seller has goods

1. Introduction

There are a number of reasons why the seller might have the goods when the buyer is in breach. The buyer may have repudiated the contract before the goods left the hands of the seller, or the buyer may have wrongfully rejected the goods or wrongfully revoked acceptance and returned them to the seller. By "wrongfully," it is meant that the buyer had no legal right to do so. See Chapter 12.B for a fuller explanation of these concepts. In any of these events, the seller is likely to incur incidental damages under § 2-710, which provides:

> **§ 2-710. Seller's Incidental Damages.**
> Incidental damages to an aggrieved seller include any commercially reasonable charges, expenses or commissions incurred in stopping delivery, in the transportation, care and custody of goods after the buyer's breach, in connection with return or resale of the goods or otherwise resulting from the breach.

The point of incidental damages is to allow the seller to recover out-of-pocket expenses with respect to the goods that it would not have incurred if the buyer had not breached.

QUESTION 4. A seller ships goods to a buyer under their contract. As agreed in the contract, the seller pays the shipping charges. The buyer rejects the goods even though there is nothing wrong with the goods or the tender. The seller incurs the following reasonable costs:

I. $500 to transport the goods to the buyer initially

> **II.** $500 to transport the goods back to the seller after the rejection
> **III.** $700 to store and insure the goods until the seller can find another buyer
>
> Which of these expenses can the seller recover from the buyer as incidental damages?
>
> **A.** None of them.
> **B.** I only.
> **C.** II and III only.
> **D.** All of them.

ANALYSIS. Incidental damages under § 2-710 include expenses incurred "in the transportation, care and custody of goods after the buyer's breach." The seller was required to pay for transportation to the buyer under the contract, so that expense was not incurred because of the breach. In other words, it would have been incurred even if there had been no breach, so the loss did not result from the breach. Transportation back to the seller and storage and insurance costs did result from the breach. Because the expenses enumerated in II and III fit the description of incidental damages, the correct response is **C.**

2. Contract price

In a rare instance, the seller may be able to recover the contract price even though the seller still has the goods. The usual situation, described in § 2-709(1)(b), arises when the seller cannot sell the goods to another buyer:

> (1) When the buyer fails to pay the price as it becomes due the seller may recover, together with any incidental damages under the next section, the price
>
> . . . .
>
> (b) of goods identified to the contract if the seller is unable after reasonable effort to resell them at a reasonable price or the circumstances reasonably indicate that such effort will be unavailing.

> **QUESTION 5.** From a seller of neon signs, a buyer orders a sign that says "Joe's Bar and Grill" at a price of $2,000. The seller is able to make the sign at a cost of $1,600 and will profit $400 from the transaction. When the sign is ready, the buyer decides that the sign is not appropriate for his establishment and repudiates the contract. From past experience, the seller knows that there is no market for this sign. Without making any effort to resell the sign, the seller sues the buyer. What should the seller recover?
>
> **A.** Nothing, because the seller did not make reasonable efforts to resell the sign.
> **B.** $1,600, because that is the amount the seller lost on the contract.

> **C.** $2,000, the contract price.
> **D.** The seller should be awarded specific performance.

ANALYSIS. It seems to me that the circumstances indicate that it would not be reasonable for the seller to try to find another buyer, as the market for a sign that says "Joe's Bar and Grill" is very limited. These circumstances show that an effort to resell the sign will be unavailing. Therefore, under § 2-709(1)(b), the seller may recover the contract price, which is $2,000. The correct response is **C**. You may have noticed that § 2-716 is captioned "*Buyer's* Right to Specific Performance or Replevin." This caption strongly suggests that only buyers have a right to specific performance under Article 2. In any event, even if specific performance were permitted a seller, it is unlikely that a court would compel a buyer to purchase goods it did not want.

What happens to the goods if the seller sues for the price and recovers the money? It won't surprise you that in that event the buyer is entitled to the goods. This rule is stated in § 2-709(2):

> (2) Where the seller sues for the price he must hold for the buyer any goods which have been identified to the contract and are still in his control except that if resale becomes possible he may resell them at any time prior to the collection of the judgment. The net proceeds of any such resale must be credited to the buyer and payment of the judgment entitles him to any goods not resold.

If the buyer pays the contract price, the buyer is entitled to the goods. In our neon sign hypothetical, for example, the seller cannot collect the contract price and keep the sign.

3. Resale

The most common remedy for the seller is to resell the goods and then recover from the buyer the difference between the contract price and the resale price. Note that this rule, called the *resale* measure of damages, gives the seller its expectation by putting the seller in the position it would have been in if the buyer had performed. This rule is stated in 2-706(1):

§ 2-706. Seller's Resale Including Contract for Resale.
> (1) Under the conditions stated in Section 2-703 on seller's remedies, the seller may resell the goods concerned or the undelivered balance thereof. Where the resale is made in good faith and in a commercially reasonable manner the seller may recover the difference between the resale price and the contract price together with any incidental damages allowed

under the provisions of this Article (Section 2-710), but less expenses saved in consequence of the buyer's breach.

. . . .

The omitted subsections of this provision contain rules for the sale that follows the breach. These rules are similar to those found in Article 9, for they try to maximize the amount recovered through resale. These rules are a good example of the principle of mitigation. For example, assume a buyer repudiated a contract to buy a widget for $20,000, and then the seller resold it to another buyer for $16,000. Under the statute, the seller is entitled to recover $4,000 from the breaching buyer. Note how this recovery gives the seller the expectancy. If the contract had been performed by the buyer, the seller would be out the widget but would have $20,000. When the seller resells, the seller is out the widget and has $16,000. To put the seller where it would have been if the buyer had not breached, we need to give the seller an additional $4,000. That computation assumes that "the resale is made in good faith and in a commercially reasonable manner." One aspect of good faith is mitigation. If the buyer can prove that the seller could have reasonably sold the widget for $18,000, then the damages will be computed as if the seller had done so—the seller will recover only $2,000.

The provision can be restated as the following formula:

Contract price – resale price + incidental damages (2-710) – savings

We have already looked at an example that involved the first two parts of the formula. Let's now add some additional facts that require use of the rest of the formula.

QUESTION 6. A buyer and a seller entered into a contract for the sale of a widget for $20,000. Under the contract, the seller was obligated to pay the cost of shipping the goods to the buyer, which would have been $500. When the buyer repudiated, the seller had to reasonably spend $200 insuring and storing the widget while it looked for another buyer. It then found a buyer who was willing to pay the reasonable price of $16,000 and who agreed to pick up the widget at the seller's place of business. How much should the seller recover from the buyer?

A. $4,000.
B. $4,200.
C. $3,700.
D. $16,300.

ANALYSIS.   In this problem, the contract price is $20,000, the resale price is $16,000, the seller has reasonable incidental damages of $200, and the seller has $500 of "expenses saved in consequence of the buyer's breach" because it does not have the shipping expense under the resale contract. Plugging these figures into the formula, we get:

$$\text{Contract price [\$20,000] } - \text{ resale price [\$16,000] } + \text{ incidental damages (2-710) [\$200] } - \text{ savings [\$500]}$$

The result of the calculation is $3,700, so the correct response is **C**.

Again, I urge you not to think in terms of formulas but in terms of the principles involved. Under the principle of the expectancy, our goal is to put the seller where it would have been had the buyer performed. Had the buyer performed, the seller would have received $20,000 but would have had the shipping cost of $500, so it would have ended up with $19,500. Because of the breach, it received $16,000, but had expenses of $200, so it has $15,800. The amount it will take to bring the seller from where it is now ($15,800) to where it would have been ($19,500) is $3,700, so that is the measure of expectancy damages.

4. Market

The principal alternative to the resale measure of damages is the "market" measure of damages found in § 2-708(1). It follows the same formula as § 2-706(1) but substitutes "market price" for "resale price." The section provides:

§ 2-708. Seller's Damages for Non-acceptance or Repudiation.

(1) Subject to subsection (2) and to the provisions of this Article with respect to proof of market price (Section 2-723), the measure of damages for non-acceptance or repudiation by the buyer is the difference between the market price at the time and place for tender and the unpaid contract price together with any incidental damages provided in this Article (Section 2-710), but less expenses saved in consequence of the buyer's breach.

This provision will be applicable in many cases where there is no actual resale, but the damages are calculated on the basis of a hypothetical resale based on the market price at the time and place for tender. For example, I have a car that has a market value of $4,800, but you have agreed to pay me $5,000 for it. You realize you had made a bad bargain and repudiate the contract. I decide not to sell the car after all. Have I lost anything? Yes, I lost the benefit of the bargain, because if you had completed the purchase, I would have had an increase in my wealth of $200 when I sold something with a market value of $4,800 for $5,000. I am entitled to recover that expectancy.

The same principle works in commercial cases. A seller of commodities might not resell the goods for a number of reasons. For example, a seller of wheat agrees to sell wheat in the future to a buyer at a fixed price. The market price falls and the buyer repudiates. The seller does not in reality identify a particular lot of wheat that it was going to sell to that buyer. Rather, the seller can calculate how much it lost because the buyer repudiated the contract.

The provision can be restated as the following formula:

Contract price – market price + incidental damages (2-710) – savings

---

QUESTION 7. *Statute reader.* A seller has a contract with a buyer for the sale of a widget on June 1 for $1,000. On June 1, the market price of widgets is $800. The buyer decides to buy the widget on the market for $800 rather than buy it from the seller for $1,000, so the buyer breaches. The seller could have sold the widget for the market price of $900 on June 3 but does not. Assuming the seller incurs no additional expenses because of the breach, how much should the seller recover as damages for the breach under § 2-708?

A. $1,000.
B. $200.
C. $100.
D. $0.

ANALYSIS. Focus on the seller's expectancy. If the contract had been performed on June 1, as promised, the seller would have sold something with a market value of $800 for $1,000, so the seller would have had an increase in wealth of $200. This is the result obtained if we use the Contract price – Market price formula of § 2-708(1). If you carefully read the text of § 2-708(1), you will see that you use the market price "at the time and place for tender" because that is the expectancy. In our example, if the contract had been performed as promised, it would have been performed on June 1, so that is the time and place for tender. Here, the contract price was $1,000 and the market price "at the time and place for tender" was $800, so the damages are $200. The correct response is **B**.

QUESTION 8. A seller of wheat in Minneapolis has agreed to sell 10,000 bushels of wheat to a buyer in New York for $2.00 a bushel. The wheat is to be tendered in Minneapolis on October 1, and it will cost the seller five cents a bushel to ship it to New York. After the contract is made, the price begins to fall, and on October 1, the price of wheat is $1.90 a bushel in Minneapolis and $1.85 a bushel in New York. The buyer repudiates. How much can the seller recover?

A. $0.
B. $500.
C. $1,000.
D. $1,500.

ANALYSIS.   In this problem, the contract price is $20,000, the market price "at the time and place for tender"—which is October 1 in Minneapolis—is $19,000, the problem mentions no incidental damages, and the seller has $500 of "expenses saved in consequence of the buyer's breach" because it does not have the shipping expense. Plugging these figures into the formula, we get:

$$\text{Contract price [\$20,000]} - \text{market price [\$19,000]} + \text{incidental} \\ \text{damages [\$0]} - \text{savings [\$500]}$$

The result of the calculation is $500, so the correct response is **B**.

5. Lost profits

Section 2-708(2) is a provision about which there is a lot of contention, so we are going to keep it simple. It provides an alternative to the measures we have been discussing and is called the *lost profits* measure of damages. The section provides:

> (2) If the measure of damages provided in subsection (1) is inadequate to put the seller in as good a position as performance would have done, then the measure of damages is the profit (including reasonable overhead) which the seller would have made from full performance by the buyer, together with any incidental damages provided in this Article (Section 2-710), due allowance for costs reasonably incurred and due credit for payments or proceeds of resale.

The following example explains the usefulness of this section as an alternative method of computing damages. Assume Bob agrees to buy his friend Sarah's car for $10,000. Bob repudiates, and five minutes later, Brenda agrees to pay Sarah $10,000 for the car. Under the resale formula of § 2-706, Sarah has suffered no damage. Now assume that instead of buying a car from Sarah, Bob had gone to Bitterroot Motors, a new car dealer. Bob picks out a model with particular features and agrees to pay $25,000 for it. Then Bob repudiates. Five minutes later, Brenda agrees to pay Bitterroot Motors $25,000 for the same model. Bob claims that under the resale formula of § 2-706, Bitterroot Motors has suffered no damage because it sold the car to Brenda at the contract price, just as Sarah did. Is he right?

Bitterroot will claim that it is in a different position from Sarah. The difference is that unlike Sarah, it is a volume seller and could have sold cars to *both* Bob and Brenda. If that is true, then its sale to Brenda did not compensate it for the loss caused by Bob's breach. Bitterroot Motors claims that in compensation for Bob's breach, it should recover the *profit* it would have made on the sale to Bob. Although Official Comment 2 states that "the normal measure there would be list price less cost to the dealer," calculating lost profit is not that simple. For example, if Bitterroot produced an invoice showing that it paid the manufacturer $20,000 for the car, it might claim that its cost was $20,000, so it lost $5,000 in profit when Bob failed to pay $25,000 for the car. However, Bob could claim that there were other costs, like the fixed expenses of running the business, that reduce the profit on each car sold. If he could prove additional costs of $2,000, then the lost profit would be only $3,000.

QUESTION 9. Retail Marine, a retailer of boats that is able to get a supply of boats from manufacturers, agrees to sell Neri a boat for $12,587. Before the date for delivery, Neri repudiates the contract. After several weeks, Retail Marine is able to sell the boat to another customer for $12,587. Retail Marine is able to prove that it incurred reasonable expenses of $674 in connection with the resale, and that its profit on the sale would have been $2,587. How much should Retail Marine recover as damages from Neri?

A. $13,261, the sale price plus the expenses incurred.
B. $3,261, the lost profit plus the expenses incurred.
C. $2,587, the lost profit.
D. $674, the expenses incurred in connection with resale.

ANALYSIS.   Under the resale formula of § 2-706, Retail Marine would be entitled to:

$$\text{Contract price } [\$12,587] - \text{resale price } [\$12,587] + \text{incidental damages } [\$674] - \text{savings}$$

This calculation comes to $674. However, Retail Marine would claim that it is a "lost volume" seller under § 2-708(2), because it could have sold a boat to both Neri and the other customer. This seems persuasive, so Retail Marine is entitled to $3,261, the lost profit plus the expenses incurred. The correct response is **B**. See *Neri v. Retail Marine Corp.*, 285 N.E.2d 311 (N.Y. 1972).

Section 2-708(2) serves in another situation. Suppose a buyer orders widgets from a seller at a contract price of $12,000. Before the seller has a chance to assemble the widgets ordered by a buyer, the buyer repudiates the contract. The market price under § 2-708(1) is $11,000, so under that formula, the damages resulting from the breach is $1,000. However, the seller has some costs associated with this order, including the cost of materials and labor plus fixed costs. These costs come to $5,000. In addition, the seller would have made $1,000 in profit on the transaction. Under § 2-708(2), the seller is entitled to claim this $6,000 as an alternative measure of damages. One complication, however, is that the buyer can now claim that the seller should have completed the goods and resold them to mitigate the damages. If, under these facts, the seller could have completed the goods and sold them for $7,000, then the damages would have been only $5,000 under § 2-706(1) (contract price of $12,000 − resale price of $7,000).

QUESTION 10. A buyer orders widgets from a seller at a contract price of $12,000. Before the seller has a chance to assemble the widgets ordered by a buyer, the buyer repudiates the contract. The market price under § 2-708(1) is $11,000. The seller has some costs associated with this order, including the cost of materials and labor plus fixed costs, that come to $5,000; in addition, the seller would have made $1,000 in profit on the transaction. The seller believes it has a claim under § 2-708(2) for $6,000 as an alternative measure of damages. The seller also reasonably believes that it can complete production of the widgets and sell them for $7,000, so that the buyer's damages will be $5,000, which is less than the damages would be if it did not complete production. It goes ahead and completes production, but by the time it has done so, the market has fallen so that the market price is only $4,000. The seller sells them at that price. What should the seller recover as damages from the buyer?

A. $1,000, the amount under the market price formula of § 2-708(1).
B. $5,000, the amount the seller thought the damages would be if mitigated.
C. $6,000, the amount under the lost profit formula of § 2-708(2).
D. $8,000, the amount it actually lost after it attempted to mitigate.

ANALYSIS. I think the best response here is **D**. The $8,000 figure is arrived at using the resale formula of § 2-706(1) (contract price of $12,000 − resale price of $4,000). Even though this damage award is greater than the damages would have been if the seller had not tried to mitigate, we should reward a party for attempting to mitigate by taking actions that seemed reasonable at the time, even if they didn't work out in hindsight. This policy will best serve the goal of reducing costs overall, even if they do not reduce costs in a particular instance.

D.   Closers

QUESTION 11. Seller is a homeowner who has a boat for sale. Buyer 1 contracts to buy the boat for $12,587. Before the date for delivery, Buyer 1 breaches. Seller puts an ad in the paper and a week after the breach, Seller is able to sell the boat to Buyer 2 for $12,587. Of the following expenses incurred by Seller, which one is not included as incidental damages under § 2-710?

A. $20 for the ad in the paper.
B. $250 to consult an attorney about Buyer 1's breach.

C. $25 for insurance and storage costs between the time of the breach and the resale.

D. $12 interest lost on the $12,587 because it was not paid a week earlier.

ANALYSIS. Section 2-710 provides:

§ 2-710. Seller's Incidental Damages.

Incidental damages to an aggrieved seller include any commercially reasonable charges, expenses or commissions incurred in stopping delivery, in the transportation, care and custody of goods after the buyer's breach, in connection with return or resale of the goods or otherwise resulting from the breach.

All of the expenses appear to fit the description of incidental damages. The ad was taken out in connection with the resale of the goods. The insurance and storage costs were incurred in the care and custody of the goods after the breach. Interest payments resulted from the breach because they would put the seller where it would have been if the contract had been performed. It has been argued that a seller should not be allowed to recover interest because it is not an expense related to the goods, like the others described in the statute. Nevertheless, most courts have held that it is an expense "otherwise resulting from the breach." Although the attorney's fees resulted from the breach, the policy is not to allow attorney's fees to be recovered as damages. The correct response is **B**.

QUESTION 12. A seller contracts with a buyer to sell 1,000 widgets for $2,000. The seller agreed to pay the $40 cost of shipping to the buyer. Because of a change in the buyer's customers' needs, the buyer does not need the widgets, so the buyer repudiated the contract before delivery. After the seller incurred storage and insurance costs of $100, the seller found a new purchaser at a price of $1,000, the best price it could get. The new purchaser was willing to come to the seller's place of business to pick up the widgets. What are the seller's damages?

A. $1,060.

B. $1,140.

C. $2,860.

D. $3,140.

ANALYSIS. In this problem, the contract price is $2,000, the resale price is $1,000, the seller has reasonable incidental damages of $100, and the seller has $40 of "expenses saved in consequence of the buyer's breach" because it does not have the shipping expense under the resale contract. Plugging these figures into the § 2-706(1) formula, we get:

$$\text{Contract price [\$2,000]} - \text{resale price [\$1,000]} + \text{incidental damages [\$100]} - \text{savings [\$40]}$$

The result of the calculation is $1,060, so the correct response is **A**.

QUESTION 13. A seller has a contract to sell 1,000 widgets to a buyer for $2,000. The buyer repudiates, and the seller resells for a total resale price of $1,000. However, the market price at the time of delivery and the time of resale is $1.50, so the seller could just as easily have resold for a total resale price of $1,500. What damages may the seller recover?

A. $2,000, the contract price under § 2-709.
B. $1,000, the difference between the contract price and the resale price under § 2-706.
C. $500, the difference between the contract price and the market price under § 2-708.
D. Nothing, because the seller failed to mitigate.

ANALYSIS. Under § 2-706, the seller can recover the difference between the contract price and the resale price only "[w]here the resale is made in good faith and in a commercially reasonable manner." Here, the resale was not reasonable because the seller failed to mitigate by selling at the highest available price. If it had mitigated, the seller would have sold the widgets for the market price. Therefore, we can compute the seller's damages under § 2-708(1) as contract price minus market price, which would be $2,000 − $1,500 = $500. The correct response is **C**.

 # Burnham's picks

Question 1	**D**
Question 2	**A**
Question 3	**A**
Question 4	**C**
Question 5	**C**
Question 6	**C**
Question 7	**B**
Question 8	**B**

Question 9   **B**
Question 10   **D**
Question 11   **B**
Question 12   **A**
Question 13   **C**

17

Buyer's Remedies

A.   Introduction

Article 2 contains an Overview of Buyer's Remedies in § 2-711:

§ 2-711. Buyer's Remedies in General; Buyer's Security Interest in Rejected Goods.

(1) Where the seller fails to make delivery or repudiates or the buyer rightfully rejects or justifiably revokes acceptance then with respect to any goods involved, and with respect to the whole if the breach goes to the whole contract (Section 2-612), the buyer may cancel and whether or not he has done so may in addition to recovering so much of the price as has been paid

(a) "cover" and have damages under the next section as to all the goods affected whether or not they have been identified to the contract; or

(b) recover damages for non-delivery as provided in this Article (Section 2-713).

(2) Where the seller fails to deliver or repudiates the buyer may also

(a) if the goods have been identified recover them as provided in this Article (Section 2-502); or

(b) in a proper case obtain specific performance or replevy the goods as provided in this Article (Section 2-716).

(3) On rightful rejection or justifiable revocation of acceptance a buyer has a security interest in goods in his possession or control for any payments made on their price and any expenses reasonably incurred in their inspection, receipt, transportation, care and custody and may hold such goods and resell them in like manner as an aggrieved seller (Section 2-706).

We break our analysis down to two situations:

- The seller is in breach, and the seller has the goods.
- The seller is in breach, and the buyer has the goods.

B.   Seller in breach; seller has goods

1. Specific performance

Historically, the remedy at law that is available for breach of contract is money damages. The equitable remedies of specific performance and injunctive relief are available only when the remedy at law is inadequate. When it awards specific performance, the court orders the breaching party to perform. The Article 2 provision on specific performance is found in § 2-716:

§ 2-716. Buyer's Right to Specific Performance or Replevin.

(1) Specific performance may be decreed where the goods are unique or in other proper circumstances.

(2) The decree for specific performance may include such terms and conditions as to payment of the price, damages, or other relief as the court may deem just.

(3) The buyer has a right of replevin for goods identified to the contract if after reasonable effort he is unable to effect cover for such goods or the circumstances reasonably indicate that such effort will be unavailing or if the goods have been shipped under reservation and satisfaction of the security interest in them has been made or tendered.

The Official Comment to this section states that "this Article seeks to further a more liberal attitude than some courts have shown in connection with the specific performance of contracts of sale." That more liberal attitude is conveyed by the statutory language "in other proper circumstances." The suggestion is that there are circumstances that supplement the common law rule that specific performance is available "where the goods are unique." In spite of that language, specific performance under the Code is fairly rare, for there is often a market in which replacement goods can be found.

QUESTION 1. A seller agrees to sell a buyer a particular Rembrandt painting that the buyer intends to hang in her living room. The seller breaches and the buyer sues for specific performance. Is specific performance available to the buyer under Article 2?

A. Yes, because the goods are unique.
B. Yes, because this is an example of "other proper circumstances."
C. No, because the buyer can find another Rembrandt on the market.
D. No, because this is not an Article 2 transaction as the buyer is not a merchant.

ANALYSIS. We know that response **D** is incorrect because § 2-102 states that Article 2 applies to "transactions in goods." A few provisions apply only to merchants, but § 2-716 is not one of them. This is the classic situation in which specific performance is appropriate. Money damages are not adequate because the buyer cannot go to the market and buy the same painting. A good working definition of *unique* is that there is no market in which the buyer can find the goods. Therefore, response **A** is correct.

QUESTION 2. A buyer contracts to buy a supply of oil over a term of 12 years. At the end of the third year, the contract is not profitable for the seller and it breaches. The buyer finds that oil is readily available from sellers on a short-term basis, but because of volatility in the market, no seller will enter into a long-term agreement similar to the one the buyer had with the seller. Is specific performance available to the buyer under Article 2?

A. Yes, because the goods are unique.
B. Yes, because this is an example of "other proper circumstances."
C. No, because the buyer can buy oil on the market.
D. No, because the seller can't be compelled to perform a losing contract.

ANALYSIS. This is an interesting situation. On the one hand, oil is not unique and is available on the market. On the other hand, the buyer did not lose a specific quantity of oil but lost a contract to have a supply of oil for another nine years, and the buyer cannot obtain that on the market. It is therefore arguable that this is a situation where specific performance is appropriate, as it is the only way to give the buyer the expectancy. Note also that if a court awarded damages for the breach, it would be very difficult to calculate the damages that the buyer would suffer because it was unable to get oil under the contract for another nine years. If the court ordered specific performance, however, the parties might be able to negotiate a settlement. See *Walgreen Co. v. Sara Creek Property Co.*, 966 F.2d 273 (7th Cir. 1992). The best response is **B**.

Can a seller obtain specific performance? It is unlikely that a court would order a buyer to pay money. The remedy for failing to obey an order of specific performance is contempt and courts do not like to jail people for failing to pay money, for that would signify the return of debtors' prison. Also, the section is titled "*Buyer's* Right to Specific Performance." That limitation is not found in the substance of the provision. As a general rule, the titles to statutes are not part of the statutes because the legislature does not enact them. Uniform Laws present an exception, however, for the title is enacted along with the rest of the statute. The rule is found in § 1-107, which provides, "Section captions are part of the Uniform Commercial Code."

2. *Cover*

a. Introduction.   Once you have an understanding of the seller's remedies, it is easy to understand the buyer's remedies, for they are the mirror image of the seller's remedies. When the buyer was in breach for not accepting the goods, the resale remedy for the seller under § 2-706 was to find another buyer. Similarly, when the seller is in breach, the buyer generally looks to find another seller, a remedy the Code calls "cover" in § 2-712:

> **§ 2-712. "Cover"; Buyer's Procurement of Substitute Goods.**
> (1) After a breach within the preceding section the buyer may "cover" by making in good faith and without unreasonable delay any reasonable purchase of or contract to purchase goods in substitution for those due from the seller.
> (2) The buyer may recover from the seller as damages the difference between the cost of cover and the contract price together with any incidental or consequential damages as hereinafter defined (Section 2-715), but less expenses saved in consequence of the seller's breach.
> (3) Failure of the buyer to effect cover within this section does not bar him from any other remedy.

The formula for recovery of damages in this provision is:

Cover price – contract price + incidental damages (§ 2-715(1)) + consequential damages (§ 2-715(2)) – savings

Note that although this formula is very similar to the seller's resale formula in § 2-706, there is one significant difference. Under the Code, a buyer can recover consequential damages but a seller cannot. The justification for the difference is that as a result of the buyer's breach, the seller usually does not receive payment. The law does not want to get into the problem of determining the consequences that arise when a seller does not get paid. On the other hand, the law does not like absolute rules, so there may be cases in which a seller may recover consequential damages. Before we get into this formula, let's explore the concepts of incidental and consequential damages from the point of view of the buyer.

b. Incidental damages.   The rules for the buyer's incidental damages are found in § 2-715(1):

> **§ 2-715. Buyer's Incidental and Consequential Damages.**
>   (1) Incidental damages resulting from the seller's breach include expenses reasonably incurred in inspection, receipt, transportation and care and custody of goods rightfully rejected, any commercially reasonable charges, expenses or commissions in connection with effecting cover and any other reasonable expense incident to the delay or other breach.

We looked at the seller's incidental damages in Chapter 16. The concept in this chapter is identical, except now the expenses are incurred by the buyer. The buyer might have expenses in connection with the storage and shipment of rejected goods, and with effecting cover to obtain the goods from another seller when the original seller does not perform.

QUESTION 3. Pursuant to a contract between them, a seller ships a widget to the buyer. The contract price of the widget is $10,000. After inspection, the buyer determines that the widget appears to be defective. The buyer incurs expenses of $500 in hiring an expert to inspect the widget, and after receiving the expert's report that the widget is damaged beyond repair, the buyer incurs an expense of $300 shipping it back to the seller. The buyer then pays a commission of $200 to a broker to find a replacement widget, and buys one at a cost of $11,000. Which of the expenses can the buyer not recover as incidental damages?

A. The $500 expense to have an expert inspect the widget.
B. The $300 expense of shipping the widget back to the seller.
C. The $200 expense of paying a broker to find a replacement widget.
D. The $1,000 difference between the price of the original widget and the replacement widget.

ANALYSIS.   *Note on test taking.* This question asks you in effect to choose the wrong answer, the one that is *not* incidental damages.

Responses **A**, **B**, and **C** all describe expenses that result from the breach and that were "reasonably incurred in inspection, receipt, transportation and care and custody of goods rightfully rejected, [and] any commercially reasonable charges, expenses or commissions in connection with effecting cover," as described in § 2-715(1). These are all incidental damages. It might appear that the $1,000 expense was incurred in connection with effecting cover, but it was not incidental. As we shall shortly see, this is the direct damage that resulted from the breach. The correct response is **D**.

c. Consequential damages.   The rules for buyer's consequential damages are found in § 2-715(2):

> **§ 2-715. Buyer's Incidental and Consequential Damages.**
>
> . . . .
>
>   (2) Consequential damages resulting from the seller's breach include
>
>   (a) any loss resulting from general or particular requirements and needs of which the seller at the time of contracting had reason to know and which could not reasonably be prevented by cover or otherwise; and
>
>   (b) injury to person or property proximately resulting from any breach of warranty.

The concept of consequential damages for a buyer takes us back to the rule in *Hadley v. Baxendale,* 156 Eng. Rep. 145 (Ex. Ct. 1854). In that case, the court held that a reasonable shipper of a millshaft would not know that the mill could not operate without the millshaft, because there might be a spare millshaft available or the mill might be down for some other reason. In fact, the language of § 2-715(2)(a) sounds very similar to the language of *Hadley:* The seller is liable for "any loss resulting from general or particular requirements and needs of which the seller at the time of contracting had reason to know." This is often referred to as the requirement of *foreseeability.* Note that the test for whether a loss is foreseeable is an objective one—the seller is liable if he "had reason to know" of the buyer's needs. The seller has reason to know either because he has actual knowledge, usually because the buyer told him, or because he has imputed knowledge because a reasonable person would know from the circumstances.

QUESTION 4. A manufacturer of soft drinks orders a ton of sugar from a seller to be delivered on June 1. The seller is late in making the shipment and the manufacturer has to close its assembly line, losing profits because it could not make the drink without the sugar. The manufacturer asks you whether you would advise him to make a claim against the sugar supplier for consequential damages. Is he likely to recover consequential damages?

A. Yes, because he was told that the sugar was needed to keep the assembly line operating.

B. Yes, because a reasonable person would know that the sugar was needed to keep the assembly line operating.

C. No, because the late delivery of the sugar did not cause the assembly line to cease operation.

D. No, because the seller would not reasonably know that the sugar was needed to keep the assembly line operating.

ANALYSIS. These facts are close to the facts of *Hadley*. In that case, the court held that a reasonable shipper of the millshaft would not know that the mill could not operate without the millshaft. Similarly, although a reasonable person would know that sugar is needed to manufacture the soft drinks, a reasonable person would not know that the buyer did not have an adequate supply on hand to keep the assembly line in operation. If he expected the seller to know this, the buyer should have told him. The best response is **D**.

Section 2-715(2)(a) contains the only express reference to mitigation in Article 2. It states that the buyer cannot recover for any loss "which could not reasonably be prevented by cover or otherwise." In other words, a buyer cannot recover consequential damages for a loss that it could have prevented by buying the goods elsewhere.

QUESTION 5. A manufacturer of soft drinks orders a ton of sugar from a seller to be delivered on June 1. The manufacturer tells the supplier that if it does not deliver the sugar on time, it will have to close its assembly line. On May 31, the supplier calls the manufacturer and says that it will be unable to deliver the sugar until June 5. The manufacturer ran out of sugar on June 3 and closed its assembly line, losing profits because it could not make the drink without the sugar. The manufacturer asks you whether you would advise him to make a claim against the sugar supplier for consequential damages. Is he likely to recover consequential damages?

A. Yes, because he was told that the sugar was needed to keep the assembly line operating.

B. Yes, because a reasonable person would know that the sugar was needed to keep the assembly line operating.

C. No, because the manufacturer did not make efforts to find substitute sugar after it knew the seller would not deliver.

D. No, because the seller would not reasonably know that the sugar was needed to keep the assembly line operating.

ANALYSIS. Note how this question differs from the previous question. Here, the seller had knowledge that without the sugar the assembly line would cease to operate. This would appear to make the seller liable for consequential damages under § 2-715(2)(a). However, the buyer apparently made no effort to obtain sugar after he was told that the supplier would not be delivering the sugar. Because he could have prevented the consequential damages by obtaining the sugar elsewhere, he will be barred from trying to recover them. The correct response is **C**.

Section 2-715(2)(b) is a difficult provision to understand, because it seems to dispense with the foreseeability requirement of § 2-715(2)(a). That section provides that consequential damages include "injury to person or property proximately resulting from any breach of warranty." It appears from this provision that to recover consequential damages for breach of warranty, causation is a required element, but foreseeability is not. For example, a rancher sells hay to another rancher, who feeds it to horses. The horses become sick because the hay was diseased. The buyer claims that the seller is liable for the loss. Assuming the seller is a merchant with respect to hay, there is a warranty that the hay is fit for the ordinary purposes for which the goods are used. So it appears there is a breach of warranty. It also appears that the breach is the proximate cause of the injury to the buyer's property. It would seem that all the elements of § 2-715(2)(b) are satisfied. However, it seems to me that we still have to inquire into foreseeability: Would a reasonable person in the position of the seller have known at the time of contracting that the buyer would feed the hay to horses? Official Comment 5 to this provision suggests that the purpose of this provision is to add the requirement of proximate cause, and not to subtract the requirement of foreseeability:

> 5. Subsection (2)(b) states the usual rule as to breach of warranty, allowing recovery for injuries "proximately" resulting from the breach. Where the injury involved follows the use of goods without discovery of the defect causing the damage, the question of "proximate" cause turns on whether it was reasonable for the buyer to use the goods without such inspection as would have revealed the defects. If it was not reasonable for him to do so, or if he did in fact discover the defect prior to his use, the injury would not proximately result from the breach of warranty.

Reasonable minds can differ over the interpretation of this section. For example, White and Summers, *Uniform Commercial Code* § 10-4, says:

> Note that an action brought under 2-715(2)(b) has one major advantage over actions brought under paragraph (a): paragraph (b) contains no foreseeability requirement. Thus, a seller is liable for injury to person or property even if the seller did not know or have reason to know of the buyer's intended use.

Nevertheless, it seems unlikely that the drafters intended to write the common law requirement of foreseeability out of the Code, so I would read it into this provision.

d. Applying the cover formula.   Now that we have looked at incidental damages and consequential damages in more detail, let's return to the § 2-712 formula. The formula for recovery of cover damages is:

Cover price – contract price + incidental damages (§ 2-715(1)) + consequential damages (§ 2-715(2)) – savings

In a typical situation, the buyer will "cover" by purchasing the goods from another seller. The principle of mitigation is implied here because the buyer must make reasonable efforts not to increase the damages that the seller is obligated to pay. If the buyer pays too much to cover, then the damages should be calculated as if the buyer had paid the market price. Note also that any savings that resulted from the breach are deducted from the buyer's recovery.

QUESTION 6. A buyer and a seller had a contract under which the buyer ordered 100 widgets for $1,000 and agreed to pay the $50 shipping cost. The seller knew that the buyer had a contract to resell the widgets for $3,000. When the seller breached, the buyer expended $10 to find another seller, who sold the widgets to him for $1,750, shipping included. Because of the delay, the buyer was able to resell the widgets for $2,750. What amount of damages is the buyer entitled to recover?

A. $1,960.
B. $1,010.
C. $960.
D. $210.

ANALYSIS.   The contract price is $1,000, the cover price is $1,750, the incidental damages are $10, the consequential damages are $250 (because the buyer was able to resell the widgets for $2,750 instead of $3,000), and the savings are $50 because of the saved shipping cost. Plugging these numbers into the § 2-712(2) formula for recovery of cover damages, we get:

Cover price [$1,750] – contract price [$1,000] + incidental damages [$10] + consequential damages [$250] – savings [$50]

This calculation comes to $960, so the correct response is **C**.

QUESTION 7. A seller has a contract with a buyer to sell 100 widgets for $2,000. The seller repudiates. At the time of the breach, the buyer could easily buy the widgets at the market price of $3,000, but the buyer decides to buy them from a friend who charges $5,000. How much will the buyer be able to recover in damages?

A. $3,000, under § 2-712.
B. $2,000, the contract price.
C. $1,000, under § 2-713.
D. $0, because the buyer failed to mitigate.

ANALYSIS.   The buyer is not entitled to § 2-712 damages (cover price minus contract price), because the buyer's cover purchase was not reasonable. He did not mitigate. However, the only consequence of not mitigating is that the buyer will recover damages based on the amount he would have been damaged if he had mitigated. If he had mitigated, buyer would have purchased at the market price, so he is entitled to § 2-713 damages. The formula is the market price of $3,000 minus the contract price of $2,000, which is $1,000. The correct response is **C**.

3. *Market*

If the buyer does not cover, the buyer has still lost the benefit of the bargain. As an alternative to cover damages, the buyer can recover based on the market price, the price at which the buyer would have theoretically covered. The recovery, called buyer's market damages, is found in § 2-713, which provides:

> **§ 2-713. Buyer's Damages for Non-delivery or Repudiation.**
>   (1) Subject to the provisions of this Article with respect to proof of market price (Section 2-723), the measure of damages for non-delivery or repudiation by the seller is the difference between the market price at the time when the buyer learned of the breach and the contract price together with any incidental and consequential damages provided in this Article (Section 2-715), but less expenses saved in consequence of the seller's breach.
>   (2) Market price is to be determined as of the place for tender or, in cases of rejection after arrival or revocation of acceptance, as of the place of arrival.

The formula in this section is:

$$\text{Market price} - \text{contract price} + \text{incidental damages (§ 2-715(1))} + \text{consequential damages (§ 2-715(2))} - \text{savings}$$

QUESTION 8. When they made a contract for the sale of widgets for $1,000 in New York, the buyer told the seller that the buyer had a purchaser in Los Angeles who was going to purchase the widgets for $3,000. When the seller did not deliver, the buyer missed the deadline to perform his Los Angeles contract because, despite his best efforts, the buyer could not timely find a seller. When the buyer did not perform the Los Angeles contract, the Los Angeles customer paid $3,250 for the widgets and claimed $250 in damages from the original buyer. Is the original buyer's $250 loss recoverable as consequential damages under § 2-715(2)?

A. No, because the seller did not agree to be liable for the loss.
B. No, because consequential damages are not available when a buyer does not cover.

C. Yes, because it was a loss resulting from a requirement the seller at the time of contracting had reason to know.

D. Yes, because the buyer lost this amount even though he covered when the seller breached.

ANALYSIS.   The formula for the recovery of market damages in § 2-713(1) includes consequential damages. Section 2-715(2)(a) defines consequential damages as "any loss resulting from general or particular requirements and needs of which the seller at the time of contracting had reason to know and which could not reasonably be prevented by cover or otherwise." Under these facts, the buyer has a loss that "could not reasonably be prevented by cover" (that is, by buying the replacement widgets). Because of the breach, the buyer was not able to cover in time to prevent the loss of the $250 from a contract that the seller was aware of. Therefore, even though the buyer elected to recover damages under the market formula, the buyer may recover consequential damages. The buyer did not cover, so response **D** is not factually correct. The correct response is **C**.

QUESTION 9. A buyer and a seller had a contract under which the buyer ordered 100 widgets for $1,000 and agreed to pay the $50 shipping cost. The seller repudiates the contract and the breach costs the buyer $100 in expenses. At the time of tender, the market price of the widgets was $1,250. What are the buyer's damages?

A. $0.
B. $150.
C. $250.
D. $300.

ANALYSIS.   The contract price is $1,000, the market price is $1,250, the incidental damages are $100, there is no mention of consequential damages, and the savings are $50. Plugging these numbers into the § 2-713(1) formula for recovery of market damages, we get:

$$\text{Market price [\$1,250]} - \text{contract price [\$1,000]} + \text{incidental damages [\$100]} + \text{consequential damages [\$0]} - \text{savings [\$50]}$$

This calculation comes to $300, so the correct response is **D**.

C.   Seller in breach; buyer has goods

The fact that the buyer has accepted nonconforming goods does not leave the buyer without a remedy. See Chapter 12.B. This is the situation described by breach of warranty. Buyers who accept the goods with a warranty have a claim if the goods do not conform to the warranty. Section 2-714 fits these situations and provides as follows:

§ 2-714. Buyer's Damages for Breach in Regard to Accepted Goods.

(1) Where the buyer has accepted goods and given notification (subsection (3) of Section 2-607) he may recover as damages for any non-conformity of tender the loss resulting in the ordinary course of events from the seller's breach as determined in any manner which is reasonable.

(2) The measure of damages for breach of warranty is the difference at the time and place of acceptance between the value of the goods accepted and the value they would have had if they had been as warranted, unless special circumstances show proximate damages of a different amount.

(3) In a proper case any incidental and consequential damages under the next section may also be recovered.

Subsection (1) refers to damages for "non-conformity of tender." Recall that under § 2-313, an express warranty must "relate to the goods." However, there may be other promises that do not relate to the goods, such as the time of delivery. If the seller is late delivering, then the buyer may recover damages under § 2-714(1); in addition, § 2-714(3) provides that the buyer making a claim under either subsection (1) or subsection (2) may recover any incidental or consequential damages under § 2-715. That section provides:

§ 2-715. Buyer's Incidental and Consequential Damages.

(1) Incidental damages resulting from the seller's breach include expenses reasonably incurred in inspection, receipt, transportation and care and custody of goods rightfully rejected, any commercially reasonable charges, expenses or commissions in connection with effecting cover and any other reasonable expense incident to the delay or other breach.

(2) Consequential damages resulting from the seller's breach include

(a) any loss resulting from general or particular requirements and needs of which the seller at the time of contracting had reason to know and which could not reasonably be prevented by cover or otherwise; and

(b) injury to person or property proximately resulting from any breach of warranty.

The buyer could then deduct those damages from the purchase price under § 2-717 if it notified the seller it was doing so:

§ 2-717. Deduction of Damages From the Price.

The buyer on notifying the seller of his intention to do so may deduct all or any part of the damages resulting from any breach of the contract from any part of the price still due under the same contract.

> **QUESTION 10.** Hadley orders a millshaft from Baxendale. At the time the contract was formed, Hadley informed Baxendale that one of its mills was going offline on June 1 and the replacement millshaft was needed for another mill to become operational. Baxendale promised that the millshaft would be delivered by June 1. In fact, because of delays by Baxendale, the shaft was not delivered until June 5. Can Hadley claim as damages the profit it lost because the mill was not operational for four days?
>
> **A.** Yes, because there was a nonconformity in tender and Baxendale had reason to know these losses would result from the delay.
> **B.** Yes, because Baxendale breached a warranty.
> **C.** No, because no express warranties were given.
> **D.** No, because even though there was a nonconformity in tender, Baxendale had not agreed that it would be responsible for any losses that resulted from the delay.

ANALYSIS. The delay in delivering the goods is a nonconformity of tender under § 2-714(1). This breach entitles the buyer to damages. According to § 2-714(3), the damages would include consequential damages under § 2-715. These damages include "any loss resulting from . . . needs of which the seller at the time of contracting had reason to know." Under the facts, the seller knew that the buyer needed the millshaft to operate a mill. Knowledge is sufficient for this purpose; acceptance is not required. Because consequential damages are appropriate in this case, the correct response is **A**.

You will note that this hypothetical is loosely based on the facts of *Hadley v. Baxendale,* but it differs in that the *Hadley* court did not find that the shipper knew or should have known that the millshaft in issue was required for the operation of the mill.

In the event of a breach of warranty, § 2-714(2) provides that the measure of damages is "the difference at the time and place of acceptance between the value of the goods accepted and the value they would have had if they had been as warranted, unless special circumstances show proximate damages of a different amount." In addition, the buyer may recover incidental and consequential damages as provided in § 2-715. For example, for $2,000 a person buys a computer that is described as having 20 gigabytes of memory. In fact, as delivered it only has 10 gigabytes of memory. You will recall from Chapter 9.B that an express warranty under § 2-313 is "an affirmation of fact or promise made by the seller to the buyer which relates to the goods." The affirmation of fact that the computer has 20 gigabytes of memory is an express warranty, so there is a breach of warranty. Let's assume that the seller sells a computer with 10 gigabytes of memory for $1,925. Under these facts, the value of the goods accepted is $1,925 and the value they would have had if they had been as warranted is $2,000. Therefore, one measure of the damages for breach of warranty is the difference between $2,000 and $1,925, or $75. Alternatively, the buyer might take the computer to a repair shop and have another 10 gigabytes of memory installed at a cost of $100. This cost of repair is an alternative measure of the damages that would be justified under the statutory language, "unless special circumstances show proximate damages of a different amount."

QUESTION 11. A seller of supercomputers represents that a certain model computer can perform certain specified functions. A buyer buys that model at a price of $25,000. It turns out that although the model is a very good computer, it cannot perform the specified functions. The computer as delivered to the buyer is worth $20,000. If it did have the specified functions, it would be worth $75,000. If the buyer keeps the computer and claims damages, how much can it recover?

A. $0.
B. $5,000.
C. $50,000.
D. $55,000.

ANALYSIS. It may not seem intuitive, but the correct response is **D**. There is an express warranty that the computer can perform the specified functions, and the seller has breached that warranty. The measure of damages for breach of warranty is "the difference at the time and place of acceptance between the value of the goods accepted and the value they would have had if they had been as warranted." Plugging the numbers into that formula, the value of the goods accepted is $20,000 and the value they would have had if they had been as warranted is $75,000, so the difference is $55,000. As I suggested at the beginning of the previous chapter, you can reach that same result by ignoring the Article 2 formula and applying general principles of contract law. Under the principle of expectancy damages, the injured party is entitled to the amount that will bring it from where it is after the breach to where it would have been had the contract been performed. Here, the buyer has a computer worth $20,000 but it would have had a computer worth $75,000, so that amount is $55,000. This hypothetical is based on the case of *Chatlos Systems v. National Cash Register Corp.*, 670 F.2d 1304 (3d Cir. 1982).

QUESTION 12. *Statute reader.* In a department store, a buyer sees a sign that says, "Shirts. $20 value. Sale price $10." The buyer buys one of the shirts, but it proves to be defective and is worth only $5. The buyer brings it back to the seller, who offers a $10 refund. The buyer replies,

"Oh, no. According to UCC § 2-714(2), the measure of damages for breach of warranty is the difference at the time and place of acceptance between the value of the goods accepted and the value they would have had if they had been as warranted. Therefore, I want $15, the difference between the $20 you promised it was worth and the $5 it turned out to be worth." Assuming the sign is part of the bargain, is the buyer entitled to the $15?

A. Yes, because that is the measure of damage for breach of warranty.
B. Yes, because there has been a nonconformity in tender.
C. No, because there was no breach of warranty.
D. No, because the buyer is not a merchant, so Article 2 does not apply to the transaction.

ANALYSIS. This is a bit of a trick question. I told you it was a statute reader, but I didn't tell you which statute to read. The relevant statute is § 2-313(2), which relates to express warranty. It provides:

> (2) It is not necessary to the creation of an express warranty that the seller use formal words such as "warrant" or "guarantee" or that he have a specific intention to make a warranty, but an affirmation merely of the value of the goods or a statement purporting to be merely the seller's opinion or commendation of the goods does not create a warranty.

Here, assuming that the sign is part of the contract, the seller has affirmed that the value of the shirt is $20. However, according to this provision, an affirmation of value does not create a warranty. Therefore, the correct response is **C**.

D. Closers

QUESTION 13. A seller agreed to sell a buyer 100 widgets for $1,000. The buyer planned to resell the widgets for $2,000. When the seller delivered the widgets, the buyer on inspection discovered that they were made from inferior materials. After consulting with an attorney at a cost of $300, the buyer "rightfully rejected" them in the language of § 2-711, sending them back at a cost of $150. The buyer then bought replacement widgets from another seller at a cost of $1,750, but because of the delay, the buyer lost $200 when he resold them. Which of the following represents the buyer's incidental damages under § 2-715?

A. The $750 difference in price.
B. The $200 lost because the buyer did not have the widgets to resell.

> **C.** The $300 reasonably charged by the attorney that the buyer consulted.
> **D.** The $150 cost of shipping the widgets back to the seller.

ANALYSIS. Response **A** represents cover damages as defined in § 2-712(1). Response **B** is consequential damages. Response **C** appears to be a logical choice, but American courts do not award attorney's fees as incidental damages. **D** is the correct response because the $150 expense incurred in transportation fits the § 2-715 definition of incidental damages.

QUESTION 14. *Statute reader.* When they made a contract for the sale of widgets for $1,000 in New York, the buyer told the seller that the buyer had a purchaser in Los Angeles who was going to purchase the widgets for $3,000. The seller breached and the buyer found another seller of widgets, but because of the seller's breach, the buyer was late getting the widgets to Los Angeles, and because of the lateness, the buyer's purchaser was obligated to pay only $2,750. Is the buyer's $250 loss (the difference between the $3,000 she would have had and the $2,750 she got from her purchaser) recoverable as consequential damages under § 2-715(2)?

A. No, because the seller did not agree to be liable for the loss.
B. No, because it was not an expense incident to the delay or other breach.
C. Yes, because it was a loss resulting from a requirement the seller at the time of contracting had reason to know.
D. Yes, because the buyer may recover the difference between the cost of cover and the contract price.

ANALYSIS. Response **B** reflects the rule for incidental damages and Response **D** reflects the rule for cover damages. The call of the question was whether consequential damages may be recovered. According to § 2-715(2), consequential damages include "any loss resulting from general or particular requirements and needs of which the seller at the time of contracting had reason to know." The seller had reason to know that there would be a resale by the buyer. The $250 loss resulted from the breach even though the buyer took reasonable steps to prevent it. The requirement is that the seller knows that the loss might occur, not that the seller agrees to it. Therefore, **A** is not a correct response and **C** is correct.

QUESTION 15. A buyer and a seller entered into a contract under which the buyer ordered 100 widgets for $1,000. On the day of delivery, when the seller does not deliver the widgets to the buyer, the market price is

$1,250 for 100 widgets. The buyer believes that the price of widgets will fall, so the buyer does not immediately buy replacement widgets. The buyer turns out to be right and the buyer later buys 100 replacement widgets for $500. When the buyer sues the seller for breach of contract, will the buyer recover any damages?

A. Yes, $250 under § 2-713.
B. Yes, $500 under § 2-712.
C. No, because the breach saved the buyer money.
D. I cannot come up with a definite answer for this one.

ANALYSIS.   This is an interesting question, because under § 2-713, the buyer is entitled to the difference between the market price at the time of tender and the contract price, which is $250. The buyer covered, however, and actually saved $500 by covering. Therefore, response **B** must be incorrect as there were no cover damages. So the issue is whether we will permit the buyer to recover damages under the market formula in this situation.

On the one hand, § 2-711 provides that the buyer may recover cover damages or market damages, so it sounds like the buyer can elect which remedy to seek. On the other hand, the Code seems to contemplate that the buyer who actually covers will be compensated by the cover damages. Official Comment 5 to § 2-713 states that "[t]he present section provides a remedy which is completely alternative to cover under the preceding section and applies only when and to the extent that the buyer has not covered." Finally, as a basic principle, § 1-305(a) provides that "[t]he remedies provided by [the UCC] must be liberally administered to the end that the aggrieved party may be put in as good a position as if the other party had fully performed." Most courts do not want to award remedies that put the injured party in a better position than performance would have put it.

Putting this all together, I prefer response **C**, but I have to admit there is authority the other way, so **D** is probably the best response.

 # Burnham's picks

Question 1	A
Question 2	B
Question 3	D
Question 4	D
Question 5	C
Question 6	C
Question 7	C

Question 8   **C**
Question 9   **D**
Question 10   **A**
Question 11   **D**
Question 12   **C**
Question 13   **D**
Question 14   **C**
Question 15   **D**

18

Limitation of Remedies

A. Introduction

Parties generally have the freedom of contract to expand or limit the otherwise available remedies. Section 2-719 provides:

(1) Subject to the provisions of subsections (2) and (3) of this section and of the preceding section on liquidation and limitation of damages,

(a) the agreement may provide for remedies in addition to or in substitution for those provided in this chapter and may limit or alter the measure of damages recoverable under this chapter, as by limiting the buyer's remedies to return of the goods and repayment of the price or to repair and replacement of nonconforming goods or parts; and

(b) resort to a remedy as provided is optional unless the remedy is expressly agreed to be exclusive, in which case it is the sole remedy.

In addition to the limitations expressed in that section, there are strong policies that may limit the available remedies. Section 1-305 provides in part that "[t]he remedies provided by the UCC must be liberally administered to the end that the aggrieved party may be put in as good a position as if the other party had fully performed but neither consequential or special damages nor penal damages may be had except as specifically provided in the UCC or by other rule of law." In seeing that the aggrieved party is "put in as good a position," the law is concerned with overcompensating as well as undercompensating the party.

259

We examine the following limitations of remedies:

- Liquidated damages
- Exclusive or limited remedy
- Consequential damages

B.   Liquidated damages

The parties have limited rights to circumvent the default rules on damages found in the Code. They can provide in their contract an amount that they believe reasonably represents the damages that would occur in the event of breach. The damages the parties agree to are called *liquidated damages*, as described in § 2-718:

> **§ 2-718. Liquidation or Limitation of Damages; Deposits.**
>
> (1) Damages for breach by either party may be liquidated in the agreement but only at an amount which is reasonable in the light of the anticipated or actual harm caused by the breach, the difficulties of proof of loss, and the inconvenience or nonfeasibility of otherwise obtaining an adequate remedy. A term fixing unreasonably large liquidated damages is void as a penalty.

Although parties are free to contract for a reasonable estimate of their damages, they are not free to agree to punitive damages because punitive damages are prohibited by the Code. That is why the last line of this provision states that "[a] term fixing unreasonably large liquidated damages is void as a penalty." One issue that frequently arises is whether the liquidated damages clause represents an attempt to ascertain actual damages or represents an attempt to penalize a party for breach. Another issue is whether, if the parties attempted to ascertain actual damages, but the actual damages turn out to be far less than the liquidated damages, the liquidated damages provision should be enforced. The view that the provision should not be enforced, called the *hindsight approach,* is repudiated by the language of the section, which states that the damages may be liquidated "at an amount which is reasonable *in the light of the anticipated or actual harm* caused by the breach." That is, if the amount is reasonable in light of the anticipated harm at the time the contract is formed, it should be irrelevant what the actual harm is at the time of breach. Nevertheless, it seems fair to say that many courts are hostile to liquidated damages and carefully scrutinize them, while many commentators, particularly from the law and economics school, believe that this element of the bargain is best left to the judgment of the parties.

QUESTION 1. A buyer and a seller of widgets agreed to insert a clause providing for liquidated damages in the event of breach by the buyer, but they could not agree on a reasonable estimate of the anticipated damages, so they agreed on the arbitrary amount of $10,000. When the buyer breached, the buyer refused to pay the liquidated damages. The seller proved that the actual damages were $9,000. Is the liquidated damage clause enforceable under § 2-718(1)?

A. Yes, because the court will enforce liquidated damages as a matter of freedom of contract.
B. Yes, because the liquidated damages are reasonable in light of the anticipated harm caused by the breach.
C. Yes, because the liquidated damages are reasonable in light of the actual harm caused by the breach.
D. No, because the liquidated damages are not reasonable in light of the anticipated or actual harm caused by the breach.

ANALYSIS.   Response **A** is not correct. A court will scrutinize liquidated damages to determine whether they are permissible under the statute. There are two ways in which a liquidated damages clause is enforceable under § 2-718(1). The statute provides that the liquidated damages must be "reasonable in light of the *anticipated or actual* harm caused by the breach." Under these facts, the liquidated damages clause was not reasonable in light of the anticipated harm, so **B** is not correct. However, the clause did turn out to be reasonable in light of the actual harm caused by the breach. Because the clause was reasonable in light of the actual loss, the clause is enforceable. The correct response is **C**. The seller will recover the $10,000 liquidated damages, not just the $9,000 actual damages.

QUESTION 2. C & H is in the business of shipping sugar from Hawaii to California for processing. C & H contracts with Sun Ship to construct a large ship. C & H is concerned that if the ship is not ready on time, it will have to pay a premium price to find available ships, so the parties agree on liquidated damages of $100,000 per day, which they believe represents the cost to C & H of finding alternative shipping. Sun Ship delivers the ship 150 days late, and C & H seeks liquidated damages of $15 million. In fact, at the time the ship was to be delivered, there was a large supply of shipping available and C & H suffered no significant financial loss because of the breach. Is the liquidated damages clause enforceable?

A. Yes, because the court will enforce liquidated damages as a matter of freedom of contract.
B. Yes, because the liquidated damages are reasonable in light of the anticipated harm caused by the breach.

C. Yes, because the liquidated damages are reasonable in light of the actual harm caused by the breach.
D. No, because the liquidated damages are not reasonable in light of the anticipated or actual harm caused by the breach.

ANALYSIS. Under § 2-718(1), the amount of liquidated damages must be reasonable in light of either the anticipated or actual harm caused by the breach. Here it was reasonable in light of the anticipated harm even if it was not reasonable in light of the actual harm. Therefore, the correct response is **B**. This is the kind of situation that troubles many courts, for they hesitate to award damages where there were in fact no damages. Most economists would enforce the liquidated damages clause because the parties used their freedom of contract to determine what risks they would assume. This is especially true where the agreement was the result of bargaining between two commercial parties. In the actual case, the clause was enforced. See *C & H Sugar Co. v. Sun Ship, Inc.*, 794 F.2d 1433 (9th Cir. 1986).

Another issue dealt with in § 2-718 arises when a buyer makes a deposit, such as a down payment. If the buyer repudiates the contract, may the seller retain the deposit? Section 2-718(2) makes clear that just because the buyer made a deposit, this sum is not to be considered liquidated damages. Liquidated damages arise by agreement by the parties. If the amount qualifies as liquidated damages under subsection (1), then the seller may keep it. If not, then it must be refunded. However, there is an exception to this rule. Section 2-718(2)(b) provides a "quick and dirty" method for the seller to retain part of the deposit even if the parties did not agree that it represented liquidated damages:

> (2) Where the seller justifiably withholds delivery of goods because of the buyer's breach, the buyer is entitled to restitution of any amount by which the sum of his payments exceeds
>> (a) the amount to which the seller is entitled by virtue of terms liquidating the seller's damages in accordance with subsection (1), or
>> (b) in the absence of such terms, twenty per cent of the value of the total performance for which the buyer is obligated under the contract or $500, whichever is smaller.

There is also an exception to the exception. If the seller can prove that it suffered actual damages equal to or greater than the amount of the deposit, then it is not required to return the deposit. This rule is found in § 2-718(3):

> (3) The buyer's right to restitution under subsection (2) is subject to offset to the extent that the seller establishes

(a) a right to recover damages under the provisions of this Article other than subsection (1), and

(b) the amount or value of any benefits received by the buyer directly or indirectly by reason of the contract.

QUESTION 3. A buyer agrees to buy a widget for $10,000 and gives the seller a down payment of $1,500. The buyer then repudiates the contract. How much of the down payment does the seller have to return to the buyer?

A. None of it, because it is presumed to be liquidated damages.

B. All of it, because the down payment bears no relationship to actual damages.

C. None of it, because under the statutory formula, the seller must give back only an amount that exceeds 20% of the value of the total performance.

D. $1,000, because under the statutory formula, the seller must give back an amount that exceeds 20% of the value of the total performance or $500, whichever is smaller.

ANALYSIS. I have suggested that you try to apply principles rather than formulas, but I must say I couldn't tell you what principle is at work in § 2-718(2)(b), so we will just have to apply the formula. Under the facts, there is only a down payment and no agreement for liquidated damages. The formula provides that the seller must make restitution "of any amount by which the sum of his payments exceeds . . . twenty per cent of the value of the total performance for which the buyer is obligated under the contract or $500, whichever is smaller." Under our facts, the payment is $1,500 and the total performance is $10,000. Therefore, 20% of the value of the total performance is $2,000. $500 is smaller than that amount. So the seller must return the amount by which the sum of the payments ($1,500) exceeds $500. That amount is $1,000. The correct response is **D**. Note that under this formula, if the amount of the total performance is over $2,500, the most the seller can keep is $500; if the amount is under $2,500, the seller can keep 20% of that amount, because then 20% will be the smaller of the two amounts.

C.   Exclusive or limited remedy

We saw in Chapter 9 that parties have a great deal of freedom of contract when creating warranties. In the absence of limitation, the remedies for breach of warranty are found in § 2-714(2) and (3):

(2) The measure of damages for breach of warranty is the difference at the time and place of acceptance between the value of the goods accepted and the value they would have had if they had been as warranted, unless special circumstances show proximate damages of a different amount.

(3) In a proper case any incidental and consequential damages under the next section may also be recovered.

These damages, especially the consequential damages, can constitute a substantial amount of money. A seller could limit the remedies available to a buyer by disclaiming all warranties, but most sellers do not take that approach. Instead, a seller frequently gives a warranty but limits the buyer's remedies under the warranty. For example, the seller may limit recovery to a certain dollar amount, such as the purchase price of the product. Section 2-719, however, places a number of restrictions on the seller who limits remedies. The reason for this policy is stated in Official Comment 1 to § 2-719: "[P]arties . . . must accept the legal consequence that there be at least a fair quantum of remedy for breach of the obligations or duties outlined in the contract."

One of the restrictions is the provision in § 2-719(1)(b) that "resort to a remedy as provided is optional unless the remedy is expressly agreed to be exclusive, in which case it is the sole remedy." This is a drafting matter. For example, the manufacturer of a camera provides this express warranty:

> If your camera is defective in materials or workmanship, we will repair your camera at no extra charge within one year after purchase. No other warranties apply.

Assume the camera proves defective after 14 months. Does the buyer have a claim? The answer is probably yes, because the seller did not effectively disclaim the implied warranty of merchantability. See Chapter 10.C. Because the remedy under the express warranty is not expressly stated to be exclusive, it is not, and other remedies, such as a remedy for breach of the implied warranty of merchantability, remain available.

Frequently a seller gives a "repair or replace" warranty in which the seller agrees to repair or replace any defects for a certain period of time. Sometimes the buyer takes the goods in for repair, the seller fixes them, and then they need repair again. The buyer takes them in for repair, the seller fixes them, and the process repeats itself. At some point, the buyer claims that it is tired of this runaround, but the seller claims that it is living up to the terms of the warranty, because it remains willing to repair any defects. Subsection (2) offers a way for the buyer to get out of this stalemate:

(2) Where circumstances cause an exclusive or limited remedy to fail of its essential purpose, remedy may be had as provided in this Act.

Often courts are satisfied that a limited remedy "fail[s] of its essential purpose" when it does not serve the purpose of giving the buyer what the buyer reasonably expected—goods that would operate without constantly needing repair.

The remedy that is frequently provided is revocation of acceptance in accordance with § 2-608. This provision operates in a manner similar to common law rescission, allowing the buyer to return the goods and get its money back. There may be some restitution awarded to the seller for the use of the goods. See Chapter 12.B.4.

The relief provided in § 2-719(2) is similar to that provided by state *lemon laws.* In most jurisdictions, the lemon law applies only to the consumer purchase of an automobile under warranty. If, after a number of attempts, the manufacturer is unable to repair a significant defect, then the manufacturer must buy the vehicle back from the buyer, often according to a formula dictated in the statute.

QUESTION 4. A buyer bought a mobile home. The purchase agreement had an express warranty that for the first year, the seller would repair or replace any defective parts. Almost immediately, different parts of the mobile home began to fail. As soon as the seller repaired one part, another would fail. The buyer had little use of the home, for it was always in the shop. Finally, the buyer said that he had enough and that the seller could keep it. The seller claimed the buyer had no right to give it up because the seller stood ready to repair every problem. Is the buyer likely to succeed in a claim that he was justified in revoking acceptance?

A. No, because the buyer failed to timely reject the goods on delivery.
B. No, because the seller was performing as it had promised under the warranty.
C. Yes, because the lemon law gave the buyer a remedy.
D. Yes, because the limited remedy failed of its essential purpose.

ANALYSIS. In most jurisdictions, the lemon law would not apply to this transaction because the definition of motor vehicle under lemon law statutes usually excludes mobile homes. Section 2-719(2) provides that "[w]here circumstances cause an exclusive or limited remedy to fail of its essential purpose, remedy may be had as provided in this Act." Here, the "repair or replace" warranty did not serve the purpose of giving the buyer a working mobile home. If it fails, the buyer can avail himself of other remedies under Article 2, such as revocation as provided in § 2-608. The correct response is **D**. For a case on similar facts, see *Murray v. Holiday Rambler, Inc.,* 265 N.W.2d 513 (Wis. 1978).

D.   Limitation of consequential damages

Many warranties provide a remedy that addresses the direct damages for the loss of the goods themselves but the remedy excludes liability for consequential damages, the losses set in motion by the loss of the goods. Section 2-719(3) provides:

> (3) Consequential damages may be limited or excluded unless the limitation or exclusion is unconscionable. Limitation of consequential damages for injury to the person in the case of consumer goods is prima facie unconscionable but limitation of damages where the loss is commercial is not.

In the case of consumer goods, limitation of consequential damages for personal injury is prima facie unconscionable. This means that there is a presumption of unconscionability, but the presumption may be rebutted. Similarly, where the loss is commercial, there is a presumption that the provision is not unconscionable, but that presumption may also be rebutted.

We need to explore one more twist on these possibilities. Assume, as is often the case, that the seller has provided the buyer with a repair or replace warranty that also excludes consequential damages. Because of repeated repairs, the court determines that the limited remedy fails of its essential purpose. The court throws out the repair or replace warranty under § 2-719(2). Should it also throw out the exclusion of consequential damages, or does that remain in place? Courts are divided on this issue, with some courts finding them separate limitations, some finding them linked, and some deciding the matter on a case-by-case basis. Not surprisingly, one factor is whether the limitations resulted from negotiations between sophisticated parties or were put in a contract of adhesion by the party with greater bargaining power. Another factor might be the way the limitations were drafted—were they found in the same paragraph, and thus can easily be excised together, or were they found in separate provisions, so one can be thrown out while the other remains?

QUESTION 5. An office buys accounting software for $799. The warranty provides that the software is warranted against defects, but the recovery is limited to the cost of the product and consequential damages are excluded. The software fails because of a defect and the buyer is required to pay workers many hours in overtime, amounting to $3,000, to restore the records. What can the buyer recover as damages for breach of warranty?

A. $0.
B. $799.
C. $3,000.
D. $3,799.

ANALYSIS.   In Chapter 4.A we discussed the issue of whether software is a good, and noted that most courts treat it as such, either directly or by analogy. This question is a good illustration of why it makes sense to apply Article 2 to software, because the seller modeled its warranty after Article 2 warranties and the analysis of that warranty under Article 2 is also sensible. Can the buyer recover the $799? According to § 2-719(1), the limitation of remedy to the purchase price is permissible. Can the buyer recover the $3,000 loss? This question provides a good review of § 2-715(2)(a). It would seem that there is no causation issue, for the loss was caused by the defective software. Was it foreseeable, though? Would a reasonable person in the position of the seller know that if the software failed, the buyer would have to reconstruct the records by hand? I think the answer is yes. However, the seller excluded liability for consequential damages. According to § 2-719(3), the exclusion of liability for consequential damages is permissible unless it is unconscionable. It is unconscionable only in the event of personal injury, and even then it is only presumptively unconscionable in the case of consumer goods. Here, the goods are not consumer goods and the loss is not a personal injury, so the exclusion is probably effective. The correct response is **B**.

E.   Closers

QUESTION 6. A consumer buys a tire for $200 from a tire store. The tire comes with a warranty that conspicuously states that the seller will repair or replace any defects, but the seller is not liable for consequential damages. While the buyer is driving the car, the tire blows out due to a defect, destroying the tire and causing the car to crash into a tree. The damages to the car cost $2,000 to repair and the driver suffers personal injuries in the amount of $5,000. For which of these losses is the seller liable under the warranty?

    I. The $200 loss of the tire.
    II. The $2,000 damage to the car.
    III. The $5,000 personal injury loss to the driver.

A. None of them.
B. I only.
C. I and III only.
D. All of them.

ANALYSIS.   The direct damage resulting from the breach is the loss of the tire. There is no question that that loss is covered by the warranty. The other losses are consequential damages. It seems that a reasonable seller would know that these losses could result from a defect, so they would be recoverable if not excluded. We are told that the seller did exclude them, but we also know from § 2-719(3) that the exclusion of liability for consequential damages is permissible unless it is unconscionable. It is unconscionable only in the event of personal injury, and even then it is only presumptively unconscionable in the case of consumer goods. Here, the tire is a consumer good. Therefore, the exclusion for a personal injury loss is presumably unconscionable, and I see no reason to rebut the presumption under these facts. The exclusion would apply to the property damage, however. Because the buyer can recover under the warranty for the loss of the tires and the personal injury, the best response is **C**.

QUESTION 7. John buys a minivan to use in his flower delivery business. The car comes with a warranty that conspicuously states that the seller will repair or replace any defects, but the seller is not liable for consequential damages. When a part fails, the car crashes and John is injured. Does he have a claim for breach of warranty?

A. Yes, because a seller may not disclaim liability for consequential damages.

B. Yes, because the disclaimer of consequential damages is not effective in the case of consumer goods.

C. No, because the disclaimer of consequential damages is effective where the loss is commercial.

D. No, because a disclaimer of consequential damages is generally effective.

ANALYSIS.   This is a tough one. The rule is found in § 2-719(3), which provides:

> (3) Consequential damages may be limited or excluded unless the limitation or exclusion is unconscionable. Limitation of consequential damages for injury to the person in the case of consumer goods is prima facie unconscionable but limitation of damages where the loss is commercial is not.

We know responses **A** and **D** are incorrect as overly broad. Here the minivan is ordinarily consumer goods, but in this case it is being used for commercial purposes. This might well be a case where even though the limitation is prima facie unconscionable, the presumption is rebuttable. I think most courts would agree with **B**, but **C** is certainly arguable. See, for example, *Ford Motor Co. v. Tritt*, 430 S.W.2d 778 (Ark. 1968) (holding that even though the goods were inventory in the hands of a remote seller, they are consumer goods for this purpose).

✦ Burnham's picks

Question 1	**C**
Question 2	**B**
Question 3	**D**
Question 4	**D**
Question 5	**B**
Question 6	**C**
Question 7	**B**

19

Assignment and Delegation

A. Introduction

Although assignment and delegation are important parts of commercial life, the topics are often neglected in law school. Fortunately for us, the Code provision on assignment and delegation is very straightforward, and the relevant rules can all be found in it. Section 2-210 provides:

§ 2-210. Delegation of Performance; Assignment of Rights.

(1) A party may perform his duty through a delegate unless otherwise agreed or unless the other party has a substantial interest in having his original promisor perform or control the acts required by the contract. No delegation of performance relieves the party delegating of any duty to perform or any liability for breach.

(2) Except as otherwise provided in Section 9-406, unless otherwise agreed all rights of either seller or buyer can be assigned except where the assignment would materially change the duty of the other party, or increase materially the burden or risk imposed on him by his contract, or impair materially his chance of obtaining return performance. A right to damages for breach of the whole contract or a right arising out of the assignor's due performance of his entire obligation can be assigned despite agreement otherwise.

(3) [Omitted]

(4) Unless the circumstances indicate the contrary a prohibition of assignment of "the contract" is to be construed as barring only the delegation to the assignee of the assignor's performance.

(5) An assignment of "the contract" or of "all my rights under the contract" or an assignment in similar general terms is an assignment of rights and unless the language or the circumstances (as in an assignment for security) indicate the contrary, it is a delegation of performance of the duties of the assignor and its acceptance by the assignee constitutes a promise by him to perform those duties. This promise is enforceable by either the assignor or the other party to the original contract.

(6) The other party may treat any assignment which delegates performance as creating reasonable grounds for insecurity and may without prejudice to his rights against the assignor demand assurances from the assignee (Section 2-609).

The vocabulary in this area is important and easy to master, although as we shall see shortly, many lawyers abuse it. The best place to start is to break the contract down into the rights and duties that each party has under it. For example, if Buyer and Seller have entered into a contract in which Seller agrees to sell 100 widgets to Buyer for $1,000, the parties have the following rights and duties:

Rights: Buyer has a right to the 100 widgets.
    Seller has a right to the $1,000.
Duties: Buyer has the duty to pay $1,000.
    Seller has the duty to tender the widgets.

We now employ the vocabulary that rights are *assigned* and duties are *delegated*. In our example, Buyer might assign to Buyer Two the right to the widgets; Seller might assign to First Bank the right to the $1,000. These parties (or assignees) now possess the rights, and if the assignment is effective, the *obligor* (the party with a duty to perform) must perform for the assignee. Similarly, Buyer might delegate to Buyer Two the duty to pay the $1,000; Seller might delegate to Seller Two the duty to tender the widgets. If the delegation is effective, those parties (or delegates) now have the duty to perform for the *obligee* (the party to whom the duty is owed).

The key question, of course, is whether an assignment of rights or a delegation of duties is effective. The general rule is that rights are freely assignable and duties are freely delegable. These rules and the exceptions are laid out in the statute. Let's examine them.

B.   Assignment of rights

With respect to the assignment of rights, subsection (2) provides:

(2) Except as otherwise provided in Section 9-406, unless otherwise agreed all rights of either seller or buyer can be assigned except where the assignment would materially change the duty of the other party, or increase materially the burden or risk imposed on him by his contract,

or impair materially his chance of obtaining return performance. A right to damages for breach of the whole contract or a right arising out of the assignor's due performance of his entire obligation can be assigned despite agreement otherwise.

When one party has assigned a right to an assignee, the assignee "stands in the shoes of the assignor" and the obligor must perform for the assignee. If a buyer owes money to a seller, and the seller assigns its right to recover to a bank, then the buyer must pay the bank and may assert against the bank any claim it has against the seller up to the amount of the obligation. One exception to free assignability arises when the parties have "otherwise agreed." As is generally the case under the Code, parties can contract around the default rule by providing in their agreement that the assignment of rights is not permitted. However, there is an exception to that exception in Article 9, where § 9-406 provides that a prohibition of assignment of the right to receive money for purposes of security is not effective. For example, assume that the seller and buyer agree that the assignment of rights is not permitted. The seller nevertheless uses as collateral for a loan from First Bank its accounts receivable, including the right to receive $1,000 from the buyer. The seller defaults on its loan and First Bank, claiming that it possesses an assignment of the right, attempts to recover the $1,000 from the buyer. In spite of the prohibition of assignment, Article 9 provides that the seller's assignment to the bank of its right to receive the money from the buyer is effective.

The final exception to free assignability arises "where the assignment would materially change the duty of the other party, or increase materially the burden or risk imposed on him by his contract, or impair materially his chance of obtaining return performance." An example of this might arise in a requirements contract. Assume that a small ice cream manufacturer agreed to purchase "all the milk and cream it requires" from a particular dairy farm. The ice cream manufacturer is then bought out by a giant ice cream corporation, to which it assigns all the rights under its existing contracts. It would obviously be unfair to the dairy farm to have its duty materially altered by the increased demand of the giant corporation.

QUESTION 1. A customer orders a tailor-made suit from a particular tailor. The tailor informs the customer that he would like the customer to make payment to the doctor next door, to whom the tailor owes a substantial sum of money. The customer nevertheless pays the tailor. Does the doctor have a claim against the customer?

A. Yes, because there was an effective assignment to the doctor.
B. Yes, because the duty to pay was effectively delegated to the doctor.
C. No, because the assignment materially changed the duty of the customer.
D. No, because the assignment is for a personal purpose rather than a business purpose.

ANALYSIS.   There are two issues here. The first is whether there is an effective assignment. I believe there is. An assignment does not need to be for a business purpose. There is no burden on the customer, for it is just as easy for him to pay the doctor as the tailor. Note that response **B** is not correct because the tailor has assigned a right and has not delegated a duty. The second issue is whether the doctor has the right to make a claim. The general rule is yes, for the assignee (here, the doctor) stands in the shoes of the assignor (here, the tailor) and has whatever rights the assignor had. By the way, this is also true when the shoe is on the other foot. If the customer has a claim that it could assert against the tailor, like a claim for breach of warranty, then the assignee takes the assignment subject to those claims and defenses. The correct response is **A**.

C.   Delegation of duties

With respect to the delegation of duties, subsection (1) provides:

> (1) A party may perform his duty through a delegate unless otherwise agreed or unless the other party has a substantial interest in having his original promisor perform or control the acts required by the contract. No delegation of performance relieves the party delegating of any duty to perform or any liability for breach.

As with assignment of rights, the first exception to free delegation is "unless otherwise agreed." The other exception is "unless the other party has a substantial interest in having his original promisor perform or control the acts required by the contract." An issue frequently arises as to whether the obligee has a personal interest in performance by the other party to the contract. Conventional thinking sometimes runs up against the strong policy of the law favoring delegation. For example, a buyer could have ordered widgets from a number of manufacturers, but the buyer chose Seller One because of Seller One's good reputation in the industry. Does this mean that the buyer has a substantial interest in having Seller One perform? Probably not. Widgets are widgets, and Seller Two can probably do just as good a job. Furthermore, there are a number of protections for the buyer in the event of the seller's delegation. The last sentence of the subsection provides that "[n]o delegation of performance relieves the party delegating of any duty to perform or any liability for breach." In other words, even though Seller One has delegated the duty to Seller Two, Seller One remains liable in the event of Seller Two's breach. Contrast that with the assignment situation where the assignor drops out of the picture after an effective assignment.

Further protection for the buyer is found in subsection (6):

(6) The other party may treat any assignment which delegates performance as creating reasonable grounds for insecurity and may without prejudice to his rights against the assignor demand assurances from the assignee (Section 2-609).

If the buyer has reasonable grounds for believing that the delegate will not properly perform, he may demand assurances from that party under § 2-609. If he does not receive reasonable assurances, then the delegation is not effective. See the discussion of § 2-609 in Chapter 15.C.

QUESTION 2. A customer orders a tailor-made suit from a particular tailor. The tailor is very busy and informs the customer that it has delegated to another tailor shop the duty to make the suit. Does the customer have to accept performance from the delegate?

A. Yes, because the assignment does not materially change the duty of the customer.
B. Yes, because the customer does not have a substantial interest in having the original party perform.
C. No, because the customer has a substantial interest in having the original party perform.
D. No, because the customer has the right to demand assurances if he is concerned.

ANALYSIS.   Maybe this is a close case, but I think it is significant that this is a specially manufactured good. That seems to suggest that there was a choice of person when the customer chose the seller and that personal relationship should not be disturbed by delegation. The best response is probably **C**. By the way, although there are arguments in favor of responses **B** and **D**, response **A** is not correct because these facts involve a delegation, not an assignment.

QUESTION 3. Jones chooses to buy wrought iron fixtures from Zenith, Inc. because Zenith has the best reputation in the area for reliable service. Jones is shocked to learn that Zenith has delegated the duty to tender the fixtures to Nadir, Inc., a company with which Jones has had bad experiences. Is there anything that Jones can do prior to receiving the fixtures from Nadir?

A. No, because this is a lawful delegation.
B. No, because Jones can be compensated for any damages caused by Nadir's defective performance.
C. Yes, Jones can inform the parties that it refuses to honor the unlawful delegation.
D. Yes, Jones can demand assurances from Nadir.

ANALYSIS. The law favors this delegation. Jones may have had a substantial interest in having Zenith perform the contract, but there is nothing personal about it and if Jones did not want the duty to be delegated, he should have put a term prohibiting delegation in the contract. However, Jones is not entirely out of luck, because he can demand assurances from Nadir under subsection (6):

> (6) The other party may treat any assignment which delegates performance as creating reasonable grounds for insecurity and may without prejudice to his rights against the assignor demand assurances from the assignee (Section 2-609).

If he does not receive reasonable assurances, he can refuse to accept performance from Nadir on grounds that the delegation is not effective. The best response is **D**.

D. Common drafting mistakes

Subsections (4) and (5) anticipate common drafting errors in the area of assignment and delegation. Of course, you will never make this mistake, but some lawyers draft a provision in an agreement that states, "This contract may be assigned." As we know, rights are assigned and duties are delegated, so the drafter has created an ambiguity by stating that the *contract* is assigned—did the drafter mean rights may be assigned, duties may be delegated, or both? The answer is found in subsection (5):

> (5) An assignment of "the contract" or of "all my rights under the contract" or an assignment in similar general terms is an assignment of rights and unless the language or the circumstances (as in an assignment for security) indicate the contrary, it is a delegation of performance of the duties of the assignor and its acceptance by the assignee constitutes a promise by him to perform those duties. This promise is enforceable by either the assignor or the other party to the original contract.

It is clear that when the contract states, "This contract may be assigned," it means that rights may be assigned and duties may be delegated. Of course, because that is the default rule, there is not a lot of reason to put the language in the contract. A drafter is more likely to try to contract around the default rule, and do it badly, by providing, "This contract may not be assigned." Did the drafter intend that rights may not be assigned, duties may not be delegated, or both? The answer is found in subsection (4):

> (4) Unless the circumstances indicate the contrary a prohibition of assignment of "the contract" is to be construed as barring only the delegation to the assignee of the assignor's performance.

According to this subsection, when the contract states, "This contract may not be assigned," the drafter has effectively only prohibited the delegation of duties and not the assignment of rights. Although this may seem inconsistent with the rule from subsection (5), it is actually consistent, for the law favors assignment and delegation, and therefore will construe the ambiguity to further that policy. Also, the goal of interpretation is to carry out the intention of the parties, and it is likely that only prohibition of delegation was intended, for usually a party is more concerned about the other party delegating duties rather than assigning rights.

QUESTION 4. A buyer and seller have a contract in which the seller agrees to sell 100 widgets to the buyer for $1,000. The contract provides, "This contract may not be assigned without the consent of the other party." The buyer tells the seller that he has "assigned" the widgets to another business to which it will be no more burdensome for the seller to deliver the widgets. The seller does not consent. Is the buyer in breach of the agreement?

A. Yes, because the contract prohibits the assignment of rights.
B. Yes, because the contract prohibits the delegation of duties.
C. No, because the contract prohibits the assignment of rights.
D. No, because the contract prohibits the delegation of duties.

ANALYSIS.   There are two steps here: first, to figure out what the buyer has done, and second, to figure out what the contract prohibits. The buyer has assigned to another party his right to receive the widgets. The ambiguous prohibition clause will be interpreted as prohibiting only the delegation of duties. See § 2-210(4). Because the assignment of rights is not prohibited by the contract, the correct response is **D**.

E. Remedies

Another issue is to determine the appropriate remedy if an assignment or delegation violates either a statutory exception or an express prohibition in the contract. The courts are divided. One view is that the wrongful assignment or delegation is nevertheless effective and the injured party is entitled to damages. This strikes me as an insufficient remedy, especially since the obligee is always entitled to damages, even if the delegation is effective. For example, if Seller One wrongfully delegates to Seller Two its duty to perform, under this view the delegation is effective and Seller One is liable to the obligee for any damages Seller Two performs badly. But if the delegation were permissible, the result would be exactly the same, because the delegator remains liable for the performance and breach of the delegate. Therefore, the violation of the prohibition of delegation has no meaningful consequence.

The other view is that a wrongful delegation is not effective and the obligee does not have to accept performance from the delegate. Under this view, if Seller One wrongfully delegates a duty to Seller Two, then the obligee may refuse the tender of performance from Seller Two. This consequence of violating the prohibition of delegation seems more meaningful. In fact, this hypothetical raises another question: If the original obligor breached by assigning or delegating, is that a material breach permitting the obligee to terminate the contract? For example, after refusing the tender of performance from Seller Two, could the obligee then refuse to accept performance from Seller One on the grounds that Seller One had materially breached, discharging the obligee from its obligations under the contract? Rather than leave the issue to a court, the obligee could protect itself by providing in the contract the consequence of a wrongful delegation.

F.   Closers

> **QUESTION 5.** A small ice cream manufacturer has a contract with a dairy to provide "all the cream the buyer requires." The manufacturer sells its business to a big ice cream manufacturer. As part of the sale of the business, the small manufacturer assigns its contract rights and delegates its contract duties to the big manufacturer. The big manufacturer demands that the dairy provide all the cream it requires, which is considerably more than the small manufacturer had ever demanded. Is the dairy in breach if it fails to provide the cream?
>
> **A.** No, because the delegation of duties was not permissible.
> **B.** No, because the assignment of rights was not permissible.
> **C.** No, because the delegation of duties was not permissible.
> **D.** No, because the assignment of rights was not permissible.

ANALYSIS. A good first step is to determine whether this transaction involves an assignment or a delegation. This was an assignment because the buyer had the right to receive the cream. The appropriate rule is found in § 2-210(2):

> (2) Unless otherwise agreed all rights of either seller or buyer can be assigned except where the assignment would materially change the duty of the other party, or increase materially the burden or risk imposed on him by his contract, or impair materially his chance of obtaining return performance.

Because this is a requirements contract (see § 2-306, discussed in Chapter 5.D), the quantity depends on the needs of the buyer. The assignment from the small manufacturer to the big manufacturer has "materially change[d] the duty of the other party, or increase[d] materially the burden or risk imposed on him by his contract." The assignment of rights is not permissible in these circumstances, so the correct response is **D**.

QUESTION 6. A buyer and a seller have a contract in which Seller agrees to sell 100 widgets to Buyer for $1,000. The contract provides that "neither party may delegate duties under this contract without the consent of the other party." Without Buyer's consent, Seller arranges for Seller Two to provide the widgets, which are just as good as widgets that would have been provided by Seller. Is Seller in breach of the agreement?

A. Yes, because the prohibition of delegation is effective.
B. Yes, because the duty is personal.
C. No, because the prohibition of delegation is not effective.
D. No, because the widgets are just as good.

ANALYSIS. I think there is no doubt that the prohibition of delegation is effective. Because Seller breached this term, the correct response is **A**.

QUESTION 7. Under the facts of Question 6, what is the remedy for this breach?

A. Buyer does not have to accept performance from Seller Two.
B. Buyer has to accept performance from Seller Two but may recover damages from Seller.
C. Buyer can avoid the contract.
D. It depends on the jurisdiction.

ANALYSIS. The most obvious remedy is that because the delegation is not effective, Buyer does not have to accept performance from Seller Two. Yet in some jurisdictions, Buyer would have to accept performance from Seller Two, and his remedy would be limited to any damages caused by the unlawful delegation. Another question is whether Buyer would have to accept performance from Seller, because Seller breached the contract by delegating the duty. It was probably not a material breach, however, so even if Buyer did not have to accept performance from Seller Two, he would still have to accept performance from Seller. For the breach to relieve Buyer of his obligations to Seller, the contract would have to expressly provide that the delegation was a material breach. The best response is **D**.

✦ Burnham's picks

Question 1	**A**
Question 2	**C**
Question 3	**D**
Question 4	**D**
Question 5	**D**
Question 6	**A**
Question 7	**D**

20

The Statute of Limitations

A.   Introduction

In general, a statute of limitations is a procedural rule that states the time within which an action must be brought. The goal, of course, is to bar stale claims. In most jurisdictions, a series of code provisions enumerates the different claims and the statute for each claim. Attorneys ignore these statutes at their peril—missing the statute of limitations is the number one basis for malpractice suits. Article 2 has its own statute, found at the very end of the article, in § 2-725:

> **§ 2-725. Statute of Limitations in Contracts for Sale.**
>
> (1) An action for breach of any contract for sale must be commenced within four years after the cause of action has accrued. By the original agreement the parties may reduce the period of limitation to not less than one year but may not extend it.
>
> (2) A cause of action accrues when the breach occurs, regardless of the aggrieved party's lack of knowledge of the breach. A breach of warranty occurs when tender of delivery is made, except that where a warranty explicitly extends to future performance of the goods and discovery of the breach must await the time of such performance the cause of action accrues when the breach is or should have been discovered.

(3) Where an action commenced within the time limited by subsection (1) is so terminated as to leave available a remedy by another action for the same breach such other action may be commenced after the expiration of the time limited and within six months after the termination of the first action unless the termination resulted from voluntary discontinuance or from dismissal for failure or neglect to prosecute.

(4) This section does not alter the law on tolling of the statute of limitations nor does it apply to causes of action which have accrued before this Act becomes effective.

One issue that may arise is whether the action involves the "breach of any contract for sale." In the context of Article 2, this means a contract for the sale of goods. Recall that in Chapter 4.A we discussed the importance of determining whether a transaction, especially a mixed goods and services transaction, is governed by Article 2. An important consequence of that determination is that one statute of limitations will apply to the transaction if it involves the sale of goods, but another will apply if it does not. The importance of determining whether the underlying transaction is a contract for sale may arise in other contexts as well. For example, assume a buyer uses a bank-issued credit card to pay for goods and the credit card company waits five years to pursue the obligation. The underlying contract involved the sale of goods. However, when payment is made by credit card, the bank pays the seller and then makes a claim against the cardholder under its credit agreement. Therefore, the credit card company is not making a claim based on breach of the contract for sale, but based on the debt that arose under the credit agreement. The statute of limitations for that claim is likely to be more than four years.

Assuming that we have determined that our situation involves the sale of goods, we focus on three issues that arise with any statute of limitations:

- What is its duration?
- What event triggers it (starts it running)?
- What events toll it (keep it from running once it has started)?

We will see that Article 2 often does not provide a clear answer to these questions. More clarity is provided by the revision in Amended § 2-725. Recall, however, that Amended Article 2 is not enacted law and has been withdrawn by its sponsors. Nevertheless, it may be useful as persuasive authority that shows how the experts who redrafted Article 2 would have resolved the issue.

B.   What is the duration of the statute of limitations?

A claim based on a written contract generally enjoys a lengthy statute of limitations, often six or eight years, while a claim based on an oral contract usually has a shorter duration. The Article 2 rule may come as a surprise, for the duration is only four years, whether the agreement is written or oral. This fact reinforces the importance of determining, as we did in Chapter 4.A, whether a transaction involves the sale of goods. Also, several states have nonuniform versions of § 2-725, so it is especially important to determine whether the statute is shorter under the applicable law. Note that the parties may have inserted a boilerplate "choice of law" clause that determines the law that governs the contract. Furthermore, according to subsection (1), the parties have a limited freedom of contract to reduce the period to not less than one year but they may not extend it.

A claim based on tort, on the other hand, generally enjoys a short statute of limitations, often three years for negligence and one year for products liability. Often a claim can be brought either as a tort products liability claim or as a breach of warranty claim. In many jurisdictions, the plaintiff has a choice of remedy and the statute applicable to that remedy will apply. That is why you sometimes see a personal injury claim brought as a breach of warranty claim—the plaintiff has missed the statute of limitations in tort and must sue under the Code. In other jurisdictions, however, the claim is seen as purely a tort claim, with the shorter statute applying.

If there is a claim that a product is defective but the only injury is an economic loss rather than a personal injury, most jurisdictions hold that the claim must be brought for breach of warranty and not in tort. In *East River S.S. Corp. v. Transamerica Delaval*, 476 U.S. 858 (1985), a ship's turbine blew up on the high seas, but did not injure anyone. Because warranties had been effectively disclaimed, the buyer was not able to sue for breach of warranty. When it sued in tort on a theory of product liability, the U.S. Supreme Court denied liability, stating, "When a product injures only itself the reasons for imposing a tort duty are weak and those for leaving the party to its contractual remedies are strong." You may wonder why the Supreme Court decided a matter that is usually left to state law. The answer is found in the fact that the injury took place "on the high seas." The Court decided the case under its admiralty law jurisdiction. Although this decision is not mandatory authority for states facing the issue, it has proven highly persuasive.

QUESTION 1. A seller and a buyer enter into a contract for the sale of a widget on October 1 for $10,000. In this jurisdiction, the statute of limitations for a written contract is six years. The written contract provides that in the event of breach, the injured party has six years from the breach to file a claim. The seller never delivers the widget. Approximately five years from the delivery date, the buyer sues the seller. The seller raises the affirmative defense of the statute of limitations. Assuming the jurisdiction has enacted the uniform version of § 2-725, is the defense good?

A. Yes, because the relevant statute of limitations is four years.
B. Yes, because the agreement is void as the parties violated the statute of limitations.
C. No, because the parties agreed to a period of six years.
D. No, because sales of goods are a type of contract, so the six-year contracts statute applies.

ANALYSIS.   Because this contract involved the sale of goods, the relevant statute of limitations is four years according to § 2-725(1). This statute overlaps with the general contracts statute, but the rule of statutory construction is that the narrower statute governs, so the rule applicable to the sale of goods subset of contract law would govern. However, the parties negotiated a change in the limitations period, making it six years. According to § 2-725(1), the parties may not extend the period of limitations. Here, the parties violated that rule. It seems to me that the consequence of violating that rule is not that the agreement would be voided, but that the agreed-upon statute of limitations would not be effective. We would then read in the default rule, which is the four-year period provided in § 2-725(1). The correct response is **A**.

C. What event triggers the running of the statute of limitations?

Section 2-725 purports to answer the question of what event triggers the running of the statute of limitations, but the answers are hazy. Subsection (1) provides that the action "must be commenced within four years after the cause of action has accrued." Assuming the cause of action is breach of a sales contract, subsection (2) provides three rules for when a breach occurs. The general rule is that "[a] cause of action accrues when the breach occurs, regardless of the aggrieved party's lack of knowledge of the breach." An exception for breach of warranty is that "a breach of warranty occurs when tender of delivery is made." An exception to the breach of warranty rule is that "where a warranty explicitly extends to future performance of the goods and discovery of the breach must await the time of such performance the cause of action accrues when the breach is or should have been discovered." Let's look at these rules one at a time.

1. Breach of contract

If there is an issue with respect to tender, then there is a cause of action for breach of contract when the breach occurs. The most obvious claim would be for nondelivery or nonpayment. Obviously the breach occurs when delivery or payment was due and was not made. Recall from Chapter 15.B that if there is a breach by anticipatory repudiation, then the breach occurs within a reasonable time after the repudiation.

QUESTION 2. A seller has promised to deliver goods on October 1, but on August 1 the seller tells the buyer, "I absolutely positively will not deliver on October 1." When does the statute of limitations begin to run?

A. August 1.
B. When a reasonable time for awaiting performance after August 1 has expired.
C. October 1.
D. A reasonable time after October 1.

ANALYSIS.   Some authorities maintain that although there has been repudiation on August 1, the breach does not occur until October 1. Under that view, the statute would begin to run on October 1. The better view, however, is that there has been a breach by anticipatory repudiation on August 1 that permits the nonrepudiating party to either await performance for a commercially reasonable time or to treat the repudiation as a breach at that time. See § 2-610. Any longer delay should be seen as a failure to mitigate. Because the nonrepudiating party can resort to any remedy for breach at that time, the statute should start to run at that time. The best response is **B**. Amended Article 2, which you will recall is only persuasive authority, makes this the rule in § 2-725(2)(b):

> (b) For breach of a contract by repudiation, a right of action accrues at the earlier of when the aggrieved party elects to treat the repudiation as a breach or when a commercially reasonable time for awaiting performance has expired.

2. *Breach of warranty*

According to subsection (2), "[a] breach of warranty occurs when tender of delivery is made." For example, if there is an express warranty, then breach occurs when nonconforming goods are tendered. Note that this is true "regardless of the aggrieved party's lack of knowledge of the breach." This distinguishes warranty from tort claims, which often do not arise until discovery of the tort. Similarly, if there is an implied warranty of merchantability or of fitness for a particular purpose, it is logical to assume that if the goods do not conform to what was promised in the warranty, they must have not conformed when they were delivered. The quarrel with the rule is with the difficulty of discovery of the breach, but even if the problem of discovery was accommodated, there would still have to be some limitation on actions. Amended § 2-725 tried to balance these considerations. It added that the action may be commenced "one year after the breach was or should have been discovered, but no longer than five years after the right of action accrued."

The difficulty of discovery is more problematic with the warranty against infringement in § 2-312(3). The seller probably breached the warranty at the time of the sale, but the buyer could not know this until the third party makes and publicizes the infringement claim. Amended § 2-725(3)(d) balanced the need for repose against the difficulty of discovery. It provided:

> (d) A right of action for breach of warranty arising under Section 2-312 accrues when the aggrieved party discovers or should have discovered the breach. However, an action for breach of the warranty of noninfringement may not be commenced more than six years after tender of delivery of the goods to the aggrieved party.

QUESTION 3. A buyer purchases a laptop computer that is described as having a certain brand of processor that is important to the buyer. The parties agreed in the contract that the period of limitations would be one year. After a year and a half, the buyer has a technician install a chip. In the process, the technician discovers that the processor is not of the stipulated brand. Is the buyer's claim for breach of warranty barred by the statute of limitations?

A. No, because the buyer has four years from delivery to make the claim.
B. No, because the buyer could not reasonably have discovered the breach until the computer was opened.
C. Yes, because the agreed-upon statute of limitations period had run.
D. Trick question—no warranty was given, so there is no claim for breach of warranty.

ANALYSIS.   According to § 2-313, there was an express warranty that the processor would be of a certain brand, and that warranty was breached. According to § 2-725(1), the parties may agree to reduce the period of limitations to a period of not less than a year, so that term is enforceable. According to § 2-725(2), "[a] cause of action accrues when the breach occurs, regardless of the aggrieved party's lack of knowledge of the breach. A breach of warranty occurs when tender of delivery is made." Applying that rule to the facts, the cause of action arose on delivery, and knowledge of the breach does not matter. Because the applicable statute is one year and the claim was not made for a year and a half, the buyer's claim is barred by the statute of limitations. The correct response is **C**.

> **QUESTION 4.** The buyer in the previous question would certainly be upset to hear that he was sold goods that did not conform to what was promised. He may be out of luck on a claim for breach of warranty, but could he revoke acceptance under § 2-608?
>
> A. No, because the claim for revocation would also be barred by the statute of limitations.
> B. No, because revocation must occur within a reasonable time.
> C. No, because the nonconformity does not substantially impair the value of the computer.
> D. Yes, because revocation is not a claim for "breach."

ANALYSIS. This is a tough one. Let's first visit the elements of revocation and then consider the effect of the statute of limitations. The fact that the brand was important to the buyer would probably satisfy the substantial impairment test, because it is a subjective test. Section 2-608(1) speaks to whether the "non-conformity substantially impairs its value *to him.*" It was difficult to discover the nonconformity, as one would be foolish to open up a laptop computer. Looking at § 2-608(2), revocation did occur within a reasonable time after the buyer discovered the ground for it, and there was probably no substantial change in the condition of the goods, as computers do not deteriorate over time. Perhaps the seller could argue that that provision protects a seller by ensuring that the seller will still have most of the original value of the goods on revocation; if that is the case, then it could be argued that the condition of the computer had changed when it depreciated in value. Assuming a right to revoke, I don't think the statute of limitations would be a bar, because § 2-725(1) refers to "an action for breach of any contract for sale." The action for revocation is not an action for breach; it is an action to restore the parties to their pre-delivery situation. Of course, even revocation must be time-barred at some point. It may well be governed by a catch-all statute of limitations, which is likely to be more than a year. With some hesitation, I would venture to say that the correct response is **D**.

3. A warranty explicitly extends to future performance

The final breach is the most complex. Section 2-725(2) contains an exception to the rule that a claim for breach of warranty begins to run on delivery. The exception applies "where a warranty explicitly extends to future performance of the goods and discovery of the breach must await the time of such performance." In that event, "the cause of action accrues when the breach is or should have been discovered." This rule kicks in when there is an express warranty that extends for a period of years. A clear example of such a warranty would state, "Seller warrants that the product will be defect-free for a period of five years." Such a statement suggests that the warranty covers not only defects that existed at the time of delivery, but also defects that manifest themselves during that five-year period. If the warranty states, "guaranteed for five years," the outcome is not as clear. The warranty does seem to extend to the future, but it does not "explicitly extend to future performance." Some courts have held that a term measured by an indefinite period of time, such as a "lifetime" warranty, does not satisfy this exception because there is no specific time period.

QUESTION 5. A gallery selling a painting states that the work was painted by John Singer Sargent. Twenty years later, the buyer discovers that the work was in fact not painted by Sargent. Does the buyer have a claim for breach of warranty?

A. Yes, because the warranty extended to future performance.
B. Yes, because of the difficulty of the buyer discovering the breach.
C. No, because this was not a warranty but an opinion.
D. No, because the warranty did not explicitly extend to future performance and the breach could have been discovered earlier.

ANALYSIS.   This problem is based on the case of *Rosen v. Spanierman*, 894 F.2d 28 (2d Cir. 1990). An express warranty was given, so **C** is not the correct response. The court held that the warranty did not explicitly extend to future performance as required by the statute. That is true, but I think the buyer would not have had a remedy even if the seller had promised something like, "This is a Sargent and it will continue to be a Sargent for 50 years." Even in that case, the second element is not satisfied, that "discovery of the breach must await the time of such performance." The buyer could have discovered that the work was a fake at the time of delivery. It seems reasonable to give the seller repose at some point after the sale. The best response is **D**.

QUESTION 6. A warranty provides that the seller will "repair or replace any defects for two years from purchase." A defect appears in the first year, and the buyer sues four years later. Did the buyer sue before the statute of limitations had run?

A. Yes, because the warranty extended to future performance.
B. Yes, because even if the warranty was breached on delivery, the suit was timely.
C. No, because the promise to repair defects does not extend the time of the warranty.
D. No, because the applicable statute of limitations is six years.

ANALYSIS.   The distinction is subtle, but most courts have found that the repair or replace warranty does not extend to future performance—it merely provides a remedy for existing defects. In *Ontario Hydro v. Zallea Systems, Inc.,* 569 F. Supp. 1261 (D. Del. 1983), the judge expressed the distinction between these two types of warranties as follows:

> [T]he key distinction between these two kinds of warranties is that a repair or replacement warranty merely provides a *remedy* if the product becomes defective, while a warranty for future performance *guarantees the performance* of the product itself for a stated period of time. In the former case, the buyer is relying upon the warranty merely as a method by which a defective product can be remedied which has no effect upon his ability to discover his breach. In the latter instance, the buyer is relying upon the warranty as a guarantee of future performance and therefore has no opportunity to discover the breach until the future performance has been tested.

By this reasoning, there is not a warranty of future performance. Therefore, there was breach on delivery. The applicable statute is four years, so the buyer did not sue before the statute of limitations had run. The correct response is **C**.

Amended § 2-725(2)(c) proposed a rule for this kind of promise, which it called a "remedial promise." It stated:

> (c) For breach of a remedial promise, a right of action accrues when the remedial promise is not performed when performance is due.

If this view had been adopted, then the promise would have been breached when the seller failed to make the repair.

D.   What events toll the statute of limitations?

Section 2-725(4) states that "[t]his section does not alter the law on tolling of the statute of limitations." Tolling is an equitable concept that prevents one party from asserting the statute of limitations as a defense if certain circumstances exist. The Code leaves this matter to the common law. An issue that frequently arises is whether repair attempts by the seller toll the running of the statute of limitations. Courts are divided on this issue. Those that hold that the statute is tolled seem to do so on a reliance theory. One court explained that "the doctrine will only apply under circumstances where the evidence reveals that repairs were attempted; representations were made that the repairs would cure the defects; and the plaintiff relied upon such representations."

> **QUESTION 7.** A buyer and a seller have agreed that the statute of limitations on a sale will be one year. Eleven months after the sale, the goods develop some problems that the buyer believes are covered by the implied warranty. The seller has proven very cooperative in attempting to repair the goods, and has taken them to its shop to work on them. The buyer is concerned that the one-year statute is about to expire but is embarrassed to bring a claim against the seller at this point. Would you advise the client that it should be concerned about the running of the statute of limitations?
>
> **A.** No, because Article 2 provides that the statute will be tolled during the repair period.
> **B.** No, because the one-year statute of limitations is not enforceable.
> **C.** Yes, because the repair attempts might not toll the statute.
> **D.** Yes, because Article 2 provides that the statute will not be tolled during the repair period.

ANALYSIS.   According to § 2-725(1), the parties may reduce the statute of limitations to one year, so **B** is not a correct response. In § 2-725(4), the Code provides that "[t]his section does not alter the law on tolling of the statute of limitations." There is no Code rule, but the Code leaves it to the common law of each jurisdiction. Therefore, the correct response is **C.** As a practical matter, the buyer would not have to sue the seller but could get an agreement extending the time to bring a claim, called a *stand still agreement.*

E.   Third-party issues

As we saw in Chapter 11, sometimes the buyer brings a claim not against the seller, but against a remote seller, such as a manufacturer. It is quite possible that the manufacturer has put the goods into the stream of commerce more than four years before the ultimate purchaser acquired them or before the injury occurs. Should the buyer nevertheless have a claim? On the one hand, perhaps the buyer should have a claim under a warranty made by the manufacturer. On the other hand, there is some point at which the manufacturer should not have to keep records and at which the claim becomes stale. There is no rule on this issue in enacted Article 2, but the rule in most jurisdictions balances the interests of the two parties by providing that the cause of action accrues when the remote purchaser receives the goods. This was the rule in Amended § 2-725(3)(b).

The issue gets even more complicated if the claim is brought by a third-party beneficiary who is entitled to make the claim under § 2-318. Most jurisdictions have held that this claim is a derivative claim based on the purchaser's claim, so the statute begins to run at the same time it would have run for the purchaser.

Finally, if a buyer or third-party beneficiary recovers against a seller, the seller may have a claim against the manufacturer or other supplier of the goods. The principle of indemnity recognizes that a party compelled to pay damages caused by the fault of another may shift the burden of that loss to the responsible party. There is, however, a split of authority on when a claim arising under an indemnity must be filed. Some courts have ruled that the claim for indemnity accrues only after the party seeking indemnity has been damaged, that is, after a judgment has been entered against it. Under this line of cases, the statute of limitations for filing the indemnity claim arises when the judgment (or other determination of liability, such as a settlement agreement) is entered against the party seeking indemnification. Other courts have held that a claim for indemnity must be brought within the statute of limitations governing the underlying claim. This seems to be the better rule, and was the one proposed by Amended § 725(2)(d):

> (d) In an action by a buyer against a person that is answerable over to the buyer for a claim asserted against the buyer, the buyer's right of action against the person answerable over accrues at the time the claim was originally asserted against the buyer.

This rule would have encouraged the parties to bring other parties into the case as early as possible, which seems a more efficient method of resolving the problem.

QUESTION 8. In January 2006, a manufacturer of pajamas delivers to a retail store pajamas that are warranted to be fire resistant. After two years, in January 2008, the retail store sells its remaining stock to a discount seller. After more than two years, in June 2011, the discount seller sells them to a mother who gives them to her daughter. In February 2012, the daughter is injured when the pajamas catch on fire. In most jurisdictions, is the daughter's claim against the manufacturer barred by the statute of limitations?

A. Yes, the statute began to run in January 2006, when the manufacturer first sold the pajamas.

B. Yes, the statute began to run in January 2008, when the retail store sold the pajamas.

C. No, the statute began to run in June 2011, when the mother purchased the pajamas.

D. No, the statute began to run in February 2012, when the daughter was injured.

ANALYSIS.   In most jurisdictions, the answer would be **C**. See *Infante v. Montgomery Ward & Co.*, 49 A.D.2d 72 (N.Y.A.D. 1975), on which this question is based. The court stated:

> It seems apparent that it is not the public policy of this State to insulate manufacturers from liability for defective products which they place in the stream of commerce and which causes injury to remote users.

F.   Closers

> **QUESTION 9.** A buyer purchases a computer from a retail store on December 1, 2008. The computer is sold with an effective disclaimer of implied warranties and an express one-year warranty under which the seller promises to repair or replace any defective part. On November 15, 2009, the computer fails. The buyer is too busy during the holiday season to do anything about it and does not make a warranty claim until January 5, 2009. The store claims that it is not obligated to make any repair because the warranty term has expired. Is the store right?
>
> **A.** No, because the issue of the statute of limitations is different from the issue of the warranty term.
>
> **B.** No, because even though the express warranty has expired, the buyer still has a claim under the implied warranty of merchantability.
>
> **C.** Yes, because the warranty was for one year and the buyer made the claim after a year.
>
> **D.** Yes, because the warranty only covers defects that were apparent at the time of sale.

ANALYSIS.   The first question is whether the buyer has a claim for breach of warranty. The answer to that is yes, under the express warranty, for the defect manifested itself during the covered period of time. The next question is when the statute of limitations began to run. In most jurisdictions, a repair or replace warranty is deemed to be breached on delivery, because the computer must have been defective at that time even if the defect did not manifest itself for a period of time. In the absence of any fact about a different term in the contract, we would assume that the four-year statute of § 2-725 applies, so the buyer had until December 1, 2012, to make a claim. We now see that the store's complaint is not that the defect was not covered by the warranty, and not that the statute of limitations had run, but that the buyer did not give the store timely notice of the breach. What would be considered timely notice? If you have gained an understanding of Code jurisprudence, you know the answer to that question—a reasonable time! Section 2-607(3)(a) provides:

(3) Where a tender has been accepted
    (a) the buyer must within a reasonable time after he discovers or should have discovered any breach notify the seller of breach or be barred from any remedy;

What is a reasonable time? Official Comment 4 suggests that a consumer should be cut some slack in making this determination:

4. The time of notification is to be determined by applying commercial standards to a merchant buyer. "A reasonable time" for notification from a retail consumer is to be judged by different standards so that in his case it will be extended, for the rule of requiring notification is designed to defeat commercial bad faith, not to deprive a good faith consumer of his remedy.

In our hypothetical, it would seem that the buyer has given timely notice. There is a question of fact as to when the defect occurred, but as a matter of law, there is no reason why this claim should be barred. The best response is **A**.

QUESTION 10. A buyer purchases a machine from a seller of goods of that kind. Nothing is said as to warranty. The buyer does not use the machine very often, and after five years it breaks down due to a defective part. An expert convincingly demonstrates that the machine had been used for only 100 hours, and that a machine of this kind ordinarily lasts for more than 1,000 hours. Is the buyer's claim for breach of warranty barred by the statute of limitations?

A. No, because it would be unfair to deprive the buyer of a remedy.
B. No, because the statute did not begin to run until the defect was discovered.
C. Yes, because the four-year statute ran before the claim was made.
D. The buyer does not have any warranty claim, so the statute of limitations is irrelevant.

ANALYSIS. Since the seller is a merchant with respect to goods of the kind, the buyer received an implied warranty of merchantability. See § 2-314. Since the goods were not fit for the ordinary purposes, there was a breach of that warranty. According to § 2-725(2), "[a] cause of action accrues when the breach occurs, regardless of the aggrieved party's lack of knowledge of the breach. A breach of warranty occurs when tender of delivery is made." Applying that rule to the facts, the breach occurred when the goods were tendered. As that was more than four years earlier, the buyer does not have a claim. Therefore, the correct response is **C**. Although this result does not seem fair, it is at least logical. If there is a valid claim that the goods were defective, they must have been defective when they were delivered. The quarrel with the rule is with the difficulty of discovery of the breach, but even if discovery were considered, there would still have to be some limitation on actions. Amended § 2-725 tried to balance these considerations. It added that the action may be commenced "one year after the breach was or should have been discovered, but no longer than five years after the right of action accrued."

 # Burnham's picks

Question 1	**A**
Question 2	**B**
Question 3	**C**
Question 4	**D**
Question 5	**D**
Question 6	**C**
Question 7	**C**
Question 8	**C**
Question 9	**A**
Question 10	**C**

21

Article 2A: Leases of Goods

A.   Introduction

In the 1980s, commercial leasing of goods became widespread. For example, most airlines began to lease, rather than buy, their fleet of airplanes. Leasing became popular for several reasons, including tax and accounting advantages. A comprehensive law of leasing, however, was lacking. Although Article 2 in § 2-102 purports to apply to "transactions in goods," most operative provisions relate only to sales of goods. For example, the definitions of *contract* and *agreement* under § 2-106 are limited to those relating to the sale of goods. To govern leases of goods, the Uniform Law Commission (ULC) promulgated Article 2A in 1987, and amended it in 1990. Currently, 48 states have adopted Article 2A. Look carefully for its enactment in a particular jurisdiction; in California, for example, it is enacted as Article 10. As with Article 2, an Amended Article 2A was drafted and then withdrawn. In addition to regulating leases in general through Article 2A, many states regulate the lease known as a *rent-to-own* transaction through separate consumer protection legislation.

We first distinguish a lease transaction from other transactions. We then look at particular types of leases, namely:

- Consumer leases
- Finance leases
- Rent-to-own transactions

Finally, we compare provisions of Article 2A and Article 2, with an emphasis on available remedies.

B. Definition of lease

There may be many reasons why it is important to determine whether a transaction is in fact a lease. The UCC looks at the substance of the transaction, and not the form of the transaction or what the parties may call it. For example, if a law firm enters into a 24-month "lease" of a copy machine, with the right to purchase the machine for $1 at the end of the term, this will be treated as a sale rather than a lease, regardless of how the parties have characterized the transaction. For purposes of UCC Article 9, it is frequently important to distinguish between a *lease* and a *sale with a reservation of a security interest,* because the rights of the parties and the rights of third parties will vary depending on how the law characterizes the transaction. The problem is that just as a creditor with a security interest in goods may repossess the goods on default, the lessor may take possession of the goods if the lessee defaults on the lease. Unlike the creditor who obtains a security interest, however, the lessor does not have to file notice of its interest to have priority over other creditors or to recover the goods in bankruptcy. It is usually another creditor with an interest in the goods or the bankruptcy trustee who claims that the alleged lease is not a lease. If it is not, then it is most likely a sale with reservation of a security interest, and the parties look to Article 9 to resolve their dispute.

Section 2A-103(1)(j) defines a *lease* as "a transfer of the right to possession and use of the goods for a term in return for some consideration." The crucial factor is that in a true lease, the lessor enjoys a reversionary interest in the property; that is, the lessee must return the goods at the end of the lease. The definition adds that "a sale, including a sale on approval or a sale or return, or retention or creation of a security interest is not a lease." A *sale* is defined at § 2-106(1) as "the passing of title from the seller to the buyer for a price." *Security interest* is defined in § 1-201(b)(35) as "an interest in personal property or fixtures which secures payment or performance of an obligation."

The real work of "sharpening the line between true leases and security interests disguised as a lease," in the words of Official Comment 2, is done at § 1-203, "Lease Distinguished from Security Interest." The overall guidance provided by § 1-203(a) is that "[w]hether a transaction in the form of a lease creates a lease or security interest is determined by the facts of each case." The key facts are those that indicate whether the lessor retains a meaningful residual interest in the goods; that is, whether the lessor gets the goods back while they still have a useful economic life. Section 1-203 establishes a two-prong objective test to make this determination.

The first prong, according to § 1-203(b), is to ask whether "the consideration that the lessee is to pay the lessor for the right to possession and use of the goods is an obligation for the term of the lease and is not subject to termination by the lessee." If the lessee is not bound for the term of the lease, the transaction is a true lease. This issue is easily resolved in the case of the rent-to-own transaction. In the typical rent-to-own transaction, a lessee agrees to rent goods for a certain periodic payment, such as a television set for 52 weeks for $20 a week, and has the right to terminate at any time. This latter fact makes the transaction a true lease. However, if the lessee is contractually obligated to make all payments for the term of the lease, then the lease "is not subject to termination by the lessee" and we move to the second prong, asking whether any one of four factors listed at § 1-203(b)(1) through (4) is present. If one of them is present, then the transaction is probably not a lease, but is instead a sale with reservation of a security interest. Those four factors are as follows:

(1) the original term of the lease is equal to or greater than the remaining economic life of the goods;

(2) the lessee is bound to renew the lease for the remaining economic life of the goods or is bound to become the owner of the goods;

(3) the lessee has an option to renew the lease for the remaining economic life of the goods for no additional consideration or for nominal additional consideration upon compliance with the lease agreement; or

(4) the lessee has an option to become the owner of the goods for no additional consideration or for nominal additional consideration upon compliance with the lease agreement.

Application of those factors requires an analysis of the "remaining economic life" of the leased property and whether the consideration to be paid under a purchase or renewal option is "nominal." As to the first analysis, § 1-203(e) provides that "remaining economic life" and "fair market value" are determined with reference to the facts and circumstances at the time the transaction is entered into. As to the second analysis, § 1-203(d) provides that additional consideration is *nominal* if it is less than the lessee's reasonably predictable cost of performing if the option is not exercised. Additional consideration is not nominal if the renewal rental or optional purchase price is based on predicted fair market values at the time the option is to be performed. Finally, § 1-203(c) sets forth certain factors that do not, in and of themselves, turn a lease into a sale with a retained security interest. For example, if the lessee agrees to assume the risk of loss of the goods, or to pay insurance and maintenance costs during the term of the lease (normally an incident of ownership), these facts alone do not turn a transaction that is otherwise a lease into a disguised sale.

QUESTION 1. As Jim contemplates law school, he decides to acquire his dream computer, which costs $2,400. Because he doesn't have that much cash, he considers a lease under which he will pay a fixed amount for 24 months. Under the terms of the agreement, Jim is responsible for maintenance and for risk of loss. Jim must make all 24 payments, but at the end of the 24-month term, he will have an option to purchase the computer or return it to the dealer. Is this a lease governed by Article 2A, or a sale with reservation of a security interest governed by Articles 2 and 9?

A. Lease, because the lease is not subject to termination by the lessee.
B. Sale, because Jim is responsible for maintenance and for risk of loss.
C. Sale, because Jim has the option to purchase the computer at the end of the term.
D. It depends on whether the option to purchase is for nominal additional consideration.

ANALYSIS. Under the first prong of the analysis in § 1-203(b), Jim must make all 24 payments. The fact that the lease is not subject to termination satisfies that prong, so we must go to the second prong of the analysis. Under § 1-203(c), the fact that Jim is responsible for maintenance and for risk of loss does not make it a sale. Under § 1-203(b)(4), one of the factors that makes it more likely a sale is that "the lessee has an option to become the owner of the goods for no additional consideration or for nominal additional consideration upon compliance with the lease agreement." We are told that the lessee has the option to become the owner of the goods, but we don't know the amount he has to pay to do so. Therefore, response **D** is correct. If he has the option to purchase for $1, for example, it is likely to be nominal consideration, but if he has the option to purchase for the then-remaining value of the computer, it is not.

QUESTION 2. As Jim contemplates law school, he decides to acquire his dream computer, which costs $2,400. Because he doesn't have that much cash, he considers a lease under which he will pay a fixed amount for 24 months. Under the terms of the agreement, Jim is responsible for maintenance and for risk of loss. Jim must make all 24 payments, and at the end of the 24-month term, he must return the computer to the dealer. When entering the transaction, the dealer reasonably thought the computer would have a value of $400 at the end of the lease term. However, because of technological developments, the computer depreciated rapidly and it turned out to have no value at the end of the lease term. Is this a lease governed by Article 2A, or a sale with reservation of a security interest governed by Articles 2 and 9?

> A. Lease, because the lease is not subject to termination by the lessee.
> B. Sale, because the lessee is responsible for maintenance and for risk of loss.
> C. Lease, because the lease is not subject to termination by the lessee and the lessee must return the computer at the end of the term.
> D. Sale, because the economic life is gone at the end of the term, so in fact there is nothing to go back to the dealer.

ANALYSIS.   Under the first prong of the analysis in § 1-203(b), Jim must make all 24 payments. The fact that the lease is not subject to termination satisfies that prong, so we must go to the second prong of the analysis. Under § 1-203(c), the fact that Jim is responsible for maintenance and for risk of loss does not make it a sale. Under § 1-203(b)(1), one of the factors that makes it more likely a sale is that "the original term of the lease is equal to or greater than the remaining economic life of the goods." That is, at the end of the lease term, the computer will have no value. Because there is nothing of value reverting to the lessor, this may appear to be a sale. However, § 1-203(e) cautions us that "[t]he 'remaining economic life of the goods' . . . must be determined with reference to the facts and circumstances at the time the transaction is entered into." Because we are told that, when entering the transaction, the lessor reasonably believed the computer would have some remaining economic life at the end of the term, we can discount this factor. The best response is **C**.

C.   Consumer leases

Once it has been determined that the transaction is a lease, the next step is to determine whether it is a consumer lease. Section 2A-103(1)(e) defines a *consumer lease* as:

> a lease that a lessor regularly engaged in the business of leasing or selling makes to a lessee who is an individual and who takes under the lease primarily for a personal, family, or household purpose [if the total payments to be made under the lease contract, excluding payments for options to renew or buy, do not exceed $_____].

Each state has the option to enact the bracketed language or not, and if it does enact it, to establish a point at which the amount of money involved takes the lease out of being a consumer lease. Many states have not enacted the bracketed language, or have enacted it and filled in the blank with an amount that effectively excepts leases of motor vehicles from the definition. Therefore, if the bracketed language is not enacted, then the lease of a motor vehicle for personal use will be a consumer lease. But if the bracketed language is enacted with the amount set at a figure that is less than the cost of a motor vehicle, then the lease of a motor vehicle for personal use will generally not be a consumer lease.

Why does it matter whether a lease is a consumer lease? Recall that Article 2 makes virtually no mention of consumer transactions. However, there are special rules applicable to consumer leases under Article 2A. The provisions include the following:

- § 2A-106: Choice of law and choice of forum. A choice of the law of a jurisdiction other than where the lessee resides is not enforceable, nor is the choice of a forum that would not otherwise have jurisdiction over the lessee.
- § 2A-108: Unconscionability. Under subsection (2), in a consumer lease unconscionable acts include those in inducing the contract or collecting a claim. Subsection (4) provides for attorney's fees for the consumer if the court finds unconscionability or against the consumer if the court finds the claim was groundless.
- § 2A-109(2): Option to accelerate at will. In a consumer lease, the burden of establishing good faith under this provision is on the party who exercised the power.
- § 2A-503(3): Consequential damages. As with a sale under Article 2, "[l]imitation, alteration, or exclusion of consequential damages for injury to the person in the case of consumer goods is prima facie unconscionable."
- § 2A-504(3)(b): Liquidated damages. There is a limitation of a consumer lessee's liability for payments retained as liquidated damages.
- § 2A-516(3): Notice of infringement. In a consumer lease, failure to give notice of a claim for infringement is not a bar to recovery.

QUESTION 3. In a jurisdiction that has filled in the blank in § 2A-103(1)(e) with $5,000, Jim enters into a 36-month lease for a four-wheeler with Bob's Equipment Rental at $150 per month. Jim intends to use the four-wheeler to herd his cattle a few times a year, and other than that, he intends to use it for recreational purposes on weekends and whenever else he can get away. Is this a consumer lease?

A. Yes, because the lease is primarily for personal purposes.
B. Yes, because the lessor is regularly engaged in the business of leasing.
C. No, because the lease is primarily for business purposes.
D. No, because the payments to be made exceed $5,000.

ANALYSIS. This transaction passes the first two tests of § 2A-103(1)(e): The lessor is regularly engaged in the business of leasing, and the lease is primarily for personal, family, or household purposes. However, it does not pass the test in that jurisdiction that "the total payments to be made under the lease contract, excluding payments for options to renew or buy, do not exceed $5,000."

Jim has promised to make 36 payments of $150, which comes to $5,400. Therefore, this requirement is not satisfied. The correct response is **D**.

QUESTION 4. Jim, who lives in Searchlight, Nevada, leases a four-wheeler for personal purposes from a business located in Las Vegas. Nevada has not enacted the bracketed language in § 2A-103(1)(e). The lease provides that any lawsuit arising out of the lease will (1) be governed by Arizona law and (2) resolved in an Arizona court. The reason for these provisions is that the seller is a branch of a large corporation located in Phoenix, Arizona, and all of the paperwork is handled there. Is either of these provisions enforceable?

A. Both are enforceable because in a commercial lease, the general rule is freedom of contract.
B. Both are enforceable because in a consumer lease, the parties are free to choose the law and the forum.
C. Only the choice of law provision is enforceable because in a consumer lease, the parties may choose the law but may not choose the forum.
D. Neither is enforceable because in a consumer lease, the parties may not choose the law or the forum.

ANALYSIS.   Section 2A-106 provides:

> **§ 2A-106. Limitation on Power of Parties to Consumer Lease to Choose Applicable Law and Judicial Forum.**
> (1) If the law chosen by the parties to a consumer lease is that of a jurisdiction other than a jurisdiction in which the lessee resides at the time the lease agreement becomes enforceable or within 30 days thereafter or in which the goods are to be used, the choice is not enforceable.
> (2) If the judicial forum chosen by the parties to a consumer lease is a forum that would not otherwise have jurisdiction over the lessee, the choice is not enforceable.

This transaction is a consumer lease. In a consumer lease, the parties may not choose the law of a jurisdiction that is not the residence of the consumer, and may not choose as a forum a state that would not otherwise have jurisdiction over the lessee. Here, the lessee is not a resident of Arizona and it is unlikely that Arizona would have jurisdiction over the lessee. Therefore, the correct response is **D**.

Note that if a lessee entered the lease agreement in another state, it is possible that that state could have jurisdiction over the lessee under its long-arm statute. In that case, that state would be a forum that would otherwise have jurisdiction over the lessee, so the choice of forum might be enforceable even if the choice of law was not.

D. Finance leases

Article 2A also defines a special type of lease at § 2A-103(1)(g), called a *finance lease*. As noted in Official Comment (g) to § 2A-103, a typical finance lease involves three parties: (1) the seller ("supplier") of the equipment; (2) a third party, whose purpose is to finance the purchase price of the equipment and who serves as lessor; and (3) the lessee, who selects the supplier and the equipment, and who uses the equipment. In effect, the lessee is relying on the supplier to provide the goods and to stand behind any warranties relating to the goods, and is relying on the lessor as the source of financing of the goods.

Once it is established that there is a valid finance lease, Article 2A limits the ability of the lessee to bring a breach of warranty or other type of claim against the lessor, who is intended to be a financier rather than a supplier of the goods. The warranties are essentially passed down from the supplier to the lessee. Section 2A-209 provides:

> **§ 2A-209. Lessee Under Finance Lease as Beneficiary of Supply Contract.**
>
> (1) The benefit of a supplier's promises to the lessor under the supply contract and of all warranties, whether express or implied, including those of any third party provided in connection with or as part of the supply contract, extends to the lessee to the extent of the lessee's leasehold interest under a finance lease related to the supply contract, but is subject to the terms of the warranty and of the supply contract and all defenses or claims arising therefrom.
>
> (2) The extension of the benefit of a supplier's promises and of warranties to the lessee (Section 2A-209(1)) does not: (i) modify the rights and obligations of the parties to the supply contract, whether arising therefrom or otherwise, or (ii) impose any duty or liability under the supply contract on the lessee.
>
> (3) Any modification or rescission of the supply contract by the supplier and the lessor is effective between the supplier and the lessee unless, before the modification or rescission, the supplier has received notice that the lessee has entered into a finance lease related to the supply contract. If the modification or rescission is effective between the supplier and the lessee, the lessor is deemed to have assumed, in addition to the obligations of the lessor to the lessee under the lease contract, promises of the supplier to the lessor and warranties that were so modified or rescinded as they existed and were available to the lessee before modification or rescission. ,
>
> (4) In addition to the extension of the benefit of the supplier's promises and of warranties to the lessee under subsection (1), the lessee retains all rights that the lessee may have against the supplier which arise from an agreement between the lessee and the supplier or under other law.

> **QUESTION 5.** Samco manufactures refrigerated units for the storage of medicine. The units are specially designed to meet the space requirements and storage needs of each particular hospital that buys its products. Samco agrees to manufacture storage equipment for use by Hospital. To stay within the equipment budget adopted by its Board of Directors, Hospital indicates to Samco that it wants to enter into a lease instead of buying the equipment. Samco, however, needs the money from the sale to finance its expanding operations and isn't willing to enter a lease. Samco has worked in the past with a company that buys hospital equipment for re-lease to hospitals. Accordingly, Samco enters into an agreement to sell the specially manufactured equipment to Finance Company for cash, and Finance Company then leases the equipment to Hospital. How is Finance Company identified in this transaction?
>
> **A.** The "supplier" (§ 2A-103(1)(x)).
> **B.** The "merchant lessee" (§ 2A-103(1)(t)).
> **C.** The "lessor" (§ 2A-103(1)(p)).
> **D.** The "lessee" (§ 2A-103(1)(n)).

ANALYSIS. Section 2A-103(1)(x) defines *supplier* as "a person from whom a lessor buys or leases goods to be leased under a finance lease." Section 2A-103(1)(p) defines *lessor* as "a person who transfers the right to possession and use of goods under a lease." In this agreement, which is a finance lease, Samco is the supplier of the goods, Finance Company is the lessor, and Hospital is the lessee. The correct response is **C**.

> **QUESTION 6.** Assume the transaction is structured as in the previous question. The refrigerated units turn out to be defective. Who is liable to Hospital for breach of warranties?
>
> **A.** Both Samco and Finance Company.
> **B.** Samco only.
> **C.** Finance Company only.
> **D.** Neither Samco nor Finance Company.

ANALYSIS. You can see how practical the law is in this situation. Finance Company is a lessor, and the general rule is that lessors give warranties to the lessee. See, e.g., § 2A-212(1), which provides that "a warranty that the goods will be merchantable is implied in a lease contract." Nevertheless, it does not make sense to make Finance Company responsible for the quality of the goods, for essentially all it did was provide the money for the lease transaction. For that reason, § 2A-212 begins with the ominous words "[e]xcept in a finance lease," and § 2A-209(1) provides:

> The benefit of a supplier's promises to the lessor under the supply contract and of all warranties, whether express or implied, including those of any third party provided in connection with or as part of the supply contract, extends to the lessee to the extent of the lessee's leasehold interest under a finance lease related to the supply contract, but is subject to the terms of the warranty and of the supply contract and all defenses or claims arising therefrom.

These sections work together to make the supplier of the goods, rather than the financier, responsible for the warranties. Furthermore, to have the transaction qualify as a finance lease, the lessee must have sufficient information. One of the alternatives, § 2A-103(1)(g)(iii)(C), provides that:

> the lessee, before signing the lease agreement, receives an accurate and complete statement designating the promises and warranties, and any disclaimers of warranties, limitations or modifications of remedies, or liquidated damages, including those of a third party, such as the manufacturer of the goods, provided to the lessor by the person supplying the goods in connection with or as part of the contract by which the lessor acquired the goods or the right to possession and use of the goods.

These procedures will ensure that the lessee has the same protection against the supplier that it would normally have against the lessor of the goods. The correct response is **B**.

E.   Rent-to-own transactions

In a rent-to-own transaction, the lessee agrees to make a periodic payment to lease the goods, and the contract stipulates that the lessee owns the goods after a certain number of payments are made. A rent-to-own transaction is a true lease because the lessee has no commitment to rent the goods for any particular period. However, there is an incentive to rent for the entire term because at the end of the term, the lessee becomes the owner of the goods. This arrangement makes financial sense in the short term. For example, if a businessperson in town for a three-week stay needs a television set, or if a parent wants to see if her child is interested in a particular musical instrument, it may make sense to lease the goods for a short term. The problem, however, is that if the lessee rents for the full term and thereby purchases the goods, the lessee ends up paying a great deal more for the goods than if they had been purchased on credit. For example, a person may be interested in a $400 television set, but does not have the cash to buy it and does not have access to credit. A rent-to-own store may lease it for $20 a week with the lessee becoming the owner after 52 weeks. Although $20 per week might not sound like a lot, at the end of the year, if the lessee completes the payments required for ownership, the lessee has paid $1,040 for a $400 television set. Even though the Truth-in-Lending Act requires the disclosure of interest paid, these are lease payments rather than credit financing, so no disclosure is required under that act.

Many states have stepped in and regulated the rent-to-own transaction. Some jurisdictions regulate the terms of the transaction, but most require some form of disclosure so that lessees know before they enter the transaction what they are getting into. For example, the Nevada Lease of Personal Property with Option to Purchase Act in NRS 597.030 requires that certain information be conspicuously disclosed, including (among many other items):

- A statement of the cash price of the property
- The total number, the amount, and the timing of all rental payments necessary to acquire ownership of the property
- A statement that the consumer will not have an ownership interest in the property until the consumer has made the total number of rental payments necessary to acquire ownership
- A statement that the consumer is responsible for the fair market value of the property if the property is lost, stolen, damaged, or destroyed.

Courts in jurisdictions that have regulated rent-to-own transactions have tended to read these acts as providing "cumulative" remedies or requirements to those supplied by other statutes, such as the UCC or statutes regulating consumer sales or retail installment contracts. See, e.g., *Miller v. Colortyme*, 518 N.W.2d 544 (Minn. 1994). Thus, an agreement falling under both the UCC (as a consumer lease or as a sale with a retained security interest) and a rent-to-own statute would have to be drafted in a manner that complies with both regulatory schemes.

QUESTION 7. A Nevada rent-to-own agreement conspicuously discloses, among other things, that the retail price of a television set is $400; that the lessee must make 52 weekly payments of $20 to acquire ownership; and that until the amount of $1,040 is paid, the lessee has no ownership interest. Is the lessor in violation for failing to disclose that the effective interest rate is around 250%?

A. Yes, it is a violation of the Lease of Personal Property with Option to Purchase Act.

B. Yes, it is a violation of Article 2A.

C. Yes, it is a violation of both of the above.

D. No, it is not a violation of either of the above.

ANALYSIS.   There is nothing in Article 2A that requires disclosure of an interest rate. Although rent-to-own regulations, such as the Nevada Lease of Personal Property with Option to Purchase Act, require many disclosures, there is no required disclosure of an interest rate. The correct response is **D**. It is readily apparent, however, that if used as a financing mechanism, a rent-to-own transaction can be very costly to the consumer. Even with the required disclosures, many consumers nevertheless enter into this unfavorable transaction because they have no source of credit.

F.   The substance of Article 2A

Most of the provisions of Article 2A are analogous to a comparable provision of Article 2, with changes to accommodate the fact that the article deals with leases rather than sales, and sometimes to update or clarify a provision. A couple of examples of the latter are that the dollar amount to bring a transaction within the statute of frauds in § 2A-201(1) has been increased to $1,000, and the Exclusion of Warranties in § 2A-214 requires that both the disclaimer of the implied warranty of merchantability using the word *merchantability* and the disclaimer using the term *as is* be by a conspicuous writing.

The similarity to Article 2 is by design. The Official Comment to each Article 2A provision begins with a "Uniform Statutory Source" that cites the analogous Article 2 provision. The "Changes" and "Purposes" in the Official Comment typically explain how the sales provision was modified to be applicable to a lease transaction, and the reason for the modification. Finally, the "Cross References" and "Definitional Cross References" typically cite the appropriate Article 2 analogue. For example, the Official Comment to § 2A-201, the statute of frauds, provides in full (omitting the Definitional Cross References to sections other than Article 2):

> **Uniform Statutory Source**: Section 2-201 former Sections 9-203(1) and 9-110.
>
> **Changes:** This section is modeled on Section 2-201, with changes to reflect the differences between a lease contract and a contract for the sale of goods. In particular, subsection (1)(b) adds a requirement that the writing "describe the goods leased and the lease term," borrowing that concept, with revisions, from the provisions of former Section 9-203(1)(a). Subsection (2), relying on the statutory analogue in former Section 9-110, sets forth the minimum criterion for satisfying that requirement.
>
> **Purposes:** The changes in this section conform the provisions of Section 2-201 to custom and usage in lease transactions. Section 2-201(2), stating a special rule between merchants, was not included in this section as the number of such transactions involving leases, as opposed to sales, was thought to be modest. Subsection (4) creates no exception for

transactions where payment has been made and accepted. This represents a departure from the analogue, Section 2-201(3)(c). The rationale for the departure is grounded in the distinction between sales and leases. Unlike a buyer in a sales transaction, the lessee does not tender payment in full for goods delivered, but only payment of rent for one or more months. It was decided that, as a matter of policy, this act of payment is not a sufficient substitute for the required memorandum. Subsection (5) was needed to establish the criteria for supplying the lease term if it is omitted, as the lease contract may still be enforceable under subsection (4).

Cross References:
Sections 2-201, 9-108, and 9-203(b)(3)(A).
Definitional Cross References:
"Sale." Section 2-106(1).

These comments tell you that the principal source for § 2A-201 is § 2-201. Notice that the newer lease provision resolves one of the principal issues that arises with respect to § 2-201, namely, what elements of the contract the writing must contain. Section 2A-201 provides that the writing must "describe the goods leased and the lease term." Also, notice that the confirmation rule of § 2-201(2) is gone because that transaction does not generally occur with respect to leases. On the other hand, the term of the lease is an important element that might be omitted from the writing that evidences the transaction, so a new section, § 2A-201(5), provides for how the term can be supplied when it is missing from the writing. It is crucial when you encounter an Article 2A provision that you use your knowledge of Article 2 to understand it, and enhance that understanding by studying the Official Comments.

QUESTION 8. Section 2-201(3)(c) provides:
> A contract which does not satisfy the requirements of subsection (1) but which is valid in other respects is enforceable . . .
>> (c) with respect to goods for which payment has been made and accepted or which have been received and accepted (Sec. 2-606).

There is no comparable provision in § 2A-201. Why is that?

A. The provision had never been used, so it was deleted to modernize the statute.

B. Payments are not made and accepted in leases, so it would not be appropriate.

C. Payments under a lease are different from payments in a sales transaction.

D. It was probably an oversight on the part of the drafters of Article 2A.

ANALYSIS. The "Purposes" part of the Official Comment to § 2A-201 explains:

Subsection (4) creates no exception for transactions where payment has been made and accepted. This represents a departure from the analogue, Section 2-201(3)(c). The rationale for the departure is grounded in the distinction between sales and leases. Unlike a buyer in a sales transaction, the lessee does not tender payment in full for goods delivered, but only payment of rent for one or more months. It was decided that, as a matter of policy, this act of payment is not a sufficient substitute for the required memorandum.

The correct response is **C**.

G.   Remedies

The remedies provisions of Article 2A are analogous to those of Article 2, but notice that the expectancy of the lessor is to have an income stream in the future and that the expectancy of the lessee is to pay certain rental payments in the future. Thus, the concept of *present value* must be used when computing future losses. Present value is defined in § 1-201(b)(28):

> "Present value" means the amount as of a date certain of one or more sums payable in the future, discounted to the date certain by use of either an interest rate specified by the parties if that rate is not manifestly unreasonable at the time the transaction is entered into or, if an interest rate is not so specified, a commercially reasonable rate that takes into account the facts and circumstances at the time the transaction is entered into.

Think of present value as reverse interest. Assume that a buyer breaches an agreement to pay a seller $1,000 on May 1. The case comes to trial exactly a year later. The seller's expectancy was to get $1,000 a year ago. How can the court give the seller $1,000 a year ago? By giving the seller interest, the amount of money a prudent person would have earned had the person invested $1,000 a year ago. If that amount is 5%, then the judgment will be for $1,050.

Assume now that a lessee breaches an agreement to pay a lessor $1,000 in one year. As permitted under the doctrine of anticipatory repudiation, the lessor brings the claim today and gets judgment. The lessor's expectancy was to get $1,000 in one year. How can the court give the lessor $1,000 in one year? By giving the lessor the present value of $1,000 in a year—the amount of money a prudent person would have to invest to have $1,000 in a year. If a commercially reasonable interest rate would be 5%, that amount would be around $950. Thus, it can be said that $950 is the *present value* of $1,000 in a year. Alternately, we can say that $1,000 in a year is *discounted* to $950 today.

Section 2A-501(1) states that whether a party is in default is determined by the agreement and by Article 2A. More so than in sales transactions, parties to a lease often define events of default in their contract. For example, the lease may provide that it is an event of default if the lessee fails to insure the leased goods, or moves them to a location different from that specified in the lease. Because of the lessor's reversionary interest, these terms can be of great importance to the lessor.

The significant remedy provisions with their Article 2 analogues are as follows.

1. Lessee's remedies

Section 2A-508 [cf. § 2-711] is an overview of Lessee's remedies for Lessor's default.

a. Cover.   Section 2A-518 [cf. § 2-712]. The cover remedy contemplates that if the lessor breaches, then the lessee will obtain a replacement lease. The formula is:

> Present value of rent for the remaining term under the new lease agreement present value of rent for the remaining term of the original lease agreement + incidental and consequential damages – expenses saved

The replacement lease must be "substantially similar" to the original lease. Note that damages are calculated "as of the date of the commencement of the term of the new lease agreement."

b. Market.   Section 2A-519 [cf. § 2-713]. The market remedy contemplates that if the lessor breaches, then the lessee might not enter into a new lease, but is still entitled to the benefit of the bargain it made. The formula is:

> Present value of the market rent for the comparable period present value of rent for the remaining term of the original lease agreement + incidental and consequential damages – expenses saved

Note that damages are calculated by the market rent "as of the date of the default."

c. Breach of warranty.   Section 2A-519(4) [cf. § 2-714]. The implied warranties in a lease are similar to those in a sale. The remedy for breach of warranty is also similar. The formula is:

> Present value if the goods had been as warranted for the lease term present value of the use of the goods accepted + incidental and consequential damages – expenses saved

d. Lessee's incidental and consequential damages.   Section 2A-520 [cf. § 2-715]. If you review buyer's incidental and consequential damages in § 2-715, discussed in Chapter 17.B, you will see that the concepts are similarly applied in Article 2A.

QUESTION 9. On January 1, Lessor leases equipment to Lessee for 12 months at $500 per month. On June 30, Lessor breaches. On August 1, Lessee leases substantially similar equipment for 12 months at $700 per month. What are Lessee's cover damages?

A. $1,200, representing the difference between $700 and $500 payments for six months.
B. $1,000, representing the difference between $700 and $500 payments for five months.
C. The present value of the difference between $700 and $500 payments for six months.
D. The present value of the difference between $700 and $500 payments for five months.

ANALYSIS.   Section 2A-518(2) provides in pertinent part:

> the lessee may recover from the lessor as damages (i) the present value, as of the date of the commencement of the term of the new lease agreement, of the rent under the new lease agreement applicable to that period of the new lease term which is comparable to the then remaining term of the original lease agreement minus the present value as of the same date of the total rent for the then remaining lease term of the original lease agreement, and (ii) any incidental or consequential damages, less expenses saved in consequence of the lessor's default.

The term of the new lease agreement commences on August 1. Therefore, the lessee may recover the difference between the payments that are made under the new lease and those that would have been made under the old lease for the remaining term of the original lease agreement, which is five months. These payments must be reduced to present value, because the lessee would not have had to make them until a future time. The correct response is **D**. No incidental or consequential damages were mentioned in this problem but if there were any, the lessee would be entitled to them.

QUESTION 10. On January 1, Lessor leases equipment to Lessee for 12 months at $500 per month. On June 30, Lessor breaches. Lessee decides not to lease substitute goods. If it had, it would have paid $700 per month. What are Lessee's market damages?

A. $1,200, representing the difference between $700 and $500 payments for six months.
B. $1,000, representing the difference between $700 and $500 payments for five months.

> **C.** The present value of the difference between $700 and $500 payments for six months.
>
> **D.** The present value of the difference between $700 and $500 payments for five months.

ANALYSIS.   Section 2A-519(1) provides in pertinent part:

> the measure of damages for non-delivery or repudiation by the lessor or for rejection or revocation of acceptance by the lessee is the present value, as of the date of the default, of the then market rent minus the present value as of the same date of the original rent, computed for the remaining lease term of the original lease agreement, together with incidental and consequential damages, less expenses saved in consequence of the lessor's default.

The lessee may recover the difference between the payments that would have been made under a market lease and those that would have been made under the old lease for the remaining term of the original lease agreement, which is six months. These payments must be reduced to present value, because the lessee would not have had to make them until a future time. The correct response is **C**. No incidental or consequential damages were mentioned in this problem but if there were any, the lessee would be entitled to them.

2. Lessor's remedies

Section 2A-523 [cf. § 2-703] is an overview of the lessor's remedies for a lessee's breach. Under § 2A-523(2), "the lessor may recover the loss resulting in the ordinary course of events from the lessee's default as determined in any reasonable manner." This is often the lost rent, as provided in § 2A-529, subject to the lessor's obligation to mitigate. Recall the discussion of the seller's action for the contract price in § 2-709, discussed in Chapter 16.C. If the seller has the goods, the seller may recover the price only in those rare instances where the goods are unmarketable. Similarly, if the lessee has the goods, the lessor may recover the rent under the lease, but if the lessor recovers the goods from the lessee, then the lessor must act in a commercially reasonable manner to reduce the amount owed by the lessee under the lease, as explained in the following sections.

a. Repossession and disposition.   Sections 2A-525 to 527 [cf. § 2-706]. On default, the lessor has the right to repossess the goods from the lessee if it can do so without breach of the peace. Alternatively, the lessor may bring an action to recover the goods or for damages. If it repossesses the goods, the lessor may dispose of the goods by lease or sale. If it leases the goods, it may recover damages. The formula is

Unpaid rent + the present value of the total rent for the remaining lease term of the original lease – the present value of the rent under the new lease for the comparable period + incidental damages – expenses saved

Note that incidental damages under § 2A-530 includes expenses of the default and disposition. Note also that consequential damages are not recoverable.

b. Market.   Section 2A-528 [cf. § 2-708]. If after default the lessor decides to retain the goods or disposes of them other than by releasing them, normally by selling them, then it may recover the loss according to the market value of the lease. The formula is

Unpaid rent + the present value of the total rent for the remaining lease term of the original lease – the present value of the market rent for the comparable period + incidental damages – expenses saved

Section 2A-528(2) [cf. § 2-708(2)] provides for "lost profit" for a volume lessor.

c. Action for the rent.   Section 2A-529 [cf. § 2-709]. The present value of the promised rental amount is available under § 2A-529(1)(a) where the lessee has possession of the goods, or the goods have been lost or damaged after the risk of loss passed to the lessee; and under § 2A-529(1)(b) where the lessor is unable to dispose of the goods or the circumstances indicate that effort to do so would be unavailing. The lessor may also recover incidental damages but must deduct expenses saved.

d. Lessor's incidental damages.   Section 2A-530 [cf. § 2-710]. If you review seller's incidental damages in § 2-710, discussed in Chapter 16.C, you will see that the concepts are similarly applied.

QUESTION 11. On January 1, Lessor leases a computer to Lessee for 24 months at $100 per month. After one year, the computer has become obsolete, so Lessee cancels the lease and returns the computer. After spending $150 advertising the sale, Lessor holds a sale of the computer but no one buys it. What are Lessor's damages?

A. $1,200.
B. $1,350.
C. The present value of 12 payments of $100.
D. The present value of 12 payments of $100, plus $150.

ANALYSIS.   Section 2A-529(1)(b) provides in pertinent part:

[T]he lessor may recover from the lessee as damages: ...
(b) for goods identified to the lease contract if the lessor is unable after reasonable effort to dispose of them at a reasonable price or the circumstances reasonably indicate that effort will be unavailing, (i) accrued

and unpaid rent as of the date of entry of judgment in favor of the lessor, (ii) the present value as of the same date of the rent for the then remaining lease term of the lease agreement, and (iii) any incidental or consequential damages allowed under Section 2A-530, less expenses saved in consequence of the lessee's default.

Here, the lessor was unable to dispose of the goods at a reasonable price. Therefore, the lessor may recover the present value of the unpaid rent, plus incidental damages. Section 2A-530 provides that incidental damages include "expenses . . . incurred . . . in connection with return or disposition of the goods." Here, the $150 would qualify as incidental expenses. The correct response is **D**.

QUESTION 12. On January 1, Lessor leases equipment to Lessee for 12 months at $500 per month. On June 30, Lessee breaches. Lessor recovers the goods and on August 1 re-leases them for $400 per month. Lessor spent $600 to recover the goods and to dispose of them. What are Lessor's damages?

A. $600, representing the difference between $500 and $400 payments for six months.
B. $1,200, representing the difference between $500 and $400 payments for six months, plus $600 for expenses.
C. $1,600, representing $500 for lost rent in July, $500 for the difference between $500 and $400 payments for five months, plus $600 for expenses.
D. An amount slightly less than $1,600, representing $500 for lost rent in July, the present value of the difference between $500 and $400 payments for five months, plus $600 for expenses.

ANALYSIS. Section 2A-527(2) provides in pertinent part:

[T]he lessor may recover from the lessee as damages (i) accrued and unpaid rent as of the date of the commencement of the term of the new lease agreement, (ii) the present value, as of the same date, of the total rent for the then remaining lease term of the original lease agreement minus the present value, as of the same date, of the rent under the new lease agreement applicable to that period of the new lease term which is comparable to the then remaining term of the original lease agreement, and (iii) any incidental or consequential damages allowed under Section 2A-530, less expenses saved in consequence of the lessee's default.

Here, "the accrued and unpaid rent as of the date of the commencement of the term of the new lease agreement" is $500, the "present value, as of the same date, of the total rent for the then remaining lease term of the original lease agreement minus the present value, as of the same date, of the rent under the new lease agreement applicable to that period of the new lease term which is comparable to the then remaining term of the original lease agreement" is the present value of five payments of $100, and the "incidental . . . damages allowed under Section 2A-530" are $600. The correct response is **D**.

H. Closers

> **QUESTION 13.** A business wishes to obtain the use of a widget that has a retail market value of $4,000 and an economic life of two years (i.e., it will decline in value until it has no value at the end of two years). Leasco and the business enter into a document called a "lease agreement" under which the business agrees to lease the widget for a year for $300 per month and return it to Leasco at the end of 12 months. Nine months into this agreement, a superwidget is introduced, making the original widget obsolete. There is no longer a market for widgets like this one and its entire economic life is gone after less than one year. Is the transaction a true lease?
>
> A. Yes, because the parties characterized it as a lease.
> B. Yes, because the anticipated economic life was two years and the business agreed to return it to Leasco after one year.
> C. No, because there was nothing of value to return to Leasco at the end of the lease term.
> D. No, because the lessee has an option to renew the lease or to become the owner of the goods.

ANALYSIS. The fact that the parties characterized the agreement as a lease is of no significance. Section 1-203(a) provides that "[w]hether a transaction in the form of a lease creates a lease or security interest is determined by the facts of each case." Therefore, response **A** is not correct. One of the factors that makes a transaction a sale with reservation of a security interest rather than a lease is, according to § 1-203(b)(1), that the lease "is not subject to termination by the lessee, and . . . the original term of the lease is equal to or greater than the remaining economic life of the goods." This factor makes response **C** attractive, because the lease here was not subject to termination by the business and the 12-month term was longer than the 9-month life of the goods. Therefore, even though the business had to nominally return the widget to Leasco, in fact there was nothing of economic value to return. However, § 1-203(e) provides that "the 'remaining economic life of the goods' . . . must be determined with reference to the facts and circumstances at the time the transaction is entered into." At that time, it was believed that the widget had an economic life of two years and that there would be something of economic value to return to Leasco. It was only the later introduction of the superwidget that changed the situation. Therefore, this appears to have been a true lease at the time of its making, so the correct response is **B**.

QUESTION 14. Leasco, a company in the business of leasing, leases a television set to John Smith that John uses in his living room. When there is a dispute about the lease, the court determines that a term in the lease is unconscionable. The court refuses to enforce the unconscionable clause but does not award attorney's fees to John. Is this decision correct?

A. No. If it finds a term unconscionable, it must refuse to enforce the entire contract and not just the term.

B. Yes. The court has the power to refuse to enforce the unconscionable clause, but under the American Rule it may not award attorney's fees.

C. No. If it finds a term unconscionable, the court may refuse to enforce the term, but in that event it must award attorney's fees.

D. Yes. The court has the power to refuse to enforce the unconscionable clause, and under Article 2A it has the discretion to award attorney's fees or not.

ANALYSIS. This is a consumer lease. Section 2A-103(1)(e) defines a *consumer lease* as:

> a lease that a lessor regularly engaged in the business of leasing or selling makes to a lessee who is an individual and who takes under the lease primarily for a personal, family, or household purpose.

Here Leasco is regularly engaged in the business of leasing, and the lessee is an individual who is using the television primarily for a personal purpose. The rule on unconscionability is found in § 2A-108. It provides:

§ 2A-108. Unconscionability.

(1) If the court as a matter of law finds a lease contract or any clause of a lease contract to have been unconscionable at the time it was made the court may refuse to enforce the lease contract, or it may enforce the remainder of the lease contract without the unconscionable clause, or it may so limit the application of any unconscionable clause as to avoid any unconscionable result.

(2) With respect to a consumer lease, if the court as a matter of law finds that a lease contract or any clause of a lease contract has been induced by unconscionable conduct or that unconscionable conduct has occurred in the collection of a claim arising from a lease contract, the court may grant appropriate relief.

(3) Before making a finding of unconscionability under subsection (1) or (2), the court, on its own motion or that of a party, shall afford the parties a reasonable opportunity to present evidence as to the setting, purpose, and effect of the lease contract or clause thereof, or of the conduct.

(4) In an action in which the lessee claims unconscionability with respect to a consumer lease:

(a) If the court finds unconscionability under subsection (1) or (2), the court shall award reasonable attorney's fees to the lessee.

(b) If the court does not find unconscionability and the lessee claiming unconscionability has brought or maintained an action he [or she] knew to be groundless, the court shall award reasonable attorney's fees to the party against whom the claim is made.

(c) In determining attorney's fees, the amount of the recovery on behalf of the claimant under subsections (1) and (2) is not controlling.

As with the unconscionability provision in Article 2, § 2-302, subsection (1) grants the court the power to either refuse to enforce the contract or the unconscionable term. The Article 2A provision differs from the Article 2 provision in providing for attorney's fees. Article 2 is silent on attorney's fees, so under the American Rule, each side pays its own attorney's fees whether they win or lose. Section 2A-108(4), however, has rules that apply only to a consumer lease. Subsection (a) provides that "[i]f the court finds unconscionability under subsection (1) or (2), the court shall award reasonable attorney's fees to the lessee." Note that the operative word here is *shall.* The award of attorney's fees is not discretionary, as it is under many consumer protection statutes, but is mandatory. Therefore, the correct response is **C.**

Note that under subsection (b), the consumer may have to pay the attorney's fees of the lessor if the claim is groundless. In computing the award of attorney's fees, the court should follow subsection (c), which provides that "[i]n determining attorney's fees, the amount of the recovery on behalf of the claimant under subsections (1) and (2) is not controlling." Many courts are reluctant to make an award of attorney's fees that is disproportionate to the recovery. For example, reasonable attorney's fees are based on the amount of time expended and the hourly rate of the attorney. An attorney who bills at $200 per hour who put in 30 hours on a case might request attorney's fees of $6,000. The recovery in a consumer case might be a few hundred dollars. Nevertheless, under subsection (c), the amount of the recovery should not control the determination of a reasonable attorney's fee, and the attorney's fee of $6,000 should be awarded.

Burnham's picks

Question 1	**D**
Question 2	**C**
Question 3	**D**
Question 4	**D**
Question 5	**C**
Question 6	**B**
Question 7	**D**
Question 8	**C**
Question 9	**D**
Question 10	**C**
Question 11	**D**
Question 12	**D**
Question 13	**B**
Question 14	**C**

22

Software Transactions

A. Introduction
B. Scope
C. Standard form transactions
D. Warranties
E. Remedies
F. Closer
✥ Burnham's picks

A.   Introduction

Information technology represents a significant portion of the U.S. economy, and that portion is growing. Yet there is no comprehensive body of law addressing software transactions. The Uniform Law Commission (ULC) promulgated the Uniform Computer Information Transactions Act (UCITA), but it ran into significant opposition and has gained little traction; it has been enacted in only two states: Maryland and Virginia. The American Law Institute published the Principles of the Law of Software Contracts in 2009. The Principles are a useful source for discussion of appropriate rules for software contracts. Although the Principles may guide judges in their decision-making, they do not have the force of law.

On the other hand, there is no need to despair that there is no law governing software transactions. There is always governing law in the form of the common law, so the issue becomes a question of which principles of the common law should be applied to these transactions. One of the first cases to discuss this issue, *Advent Systems Ltd. v. Unisys Corp.*, 925 F.2d 670 (3d Cir. 1991), found that a software transaction is within the scope of Article 2 because "'software' refers to the medium that stores input and output data as well as computer programs. The medium includes hard disks, floppy disks, and magnetic tapes." This statement seems spectacularly wrong. Better-reasoned decisions have concluded that software purchases do not involve the sale of goods, both because the software is not sold but is licensed, and because the software itself is not movable even if the container it comes in is—and of course with direct downloads, it frequently does not come in a container at all. The opinion in *Advent Systems*, however, went on to say that "[a]pplying the U.C.C. to computer software transactions offers substantial benefits to litigants and the courts," which seems to be a very sensible statement. Even if software transactions are not within the scope of Article 2, many software suppliers have modeled their contracts after contracts for the sale of goods, and many courts have applied Article 2 by analogy to software contracts.

This Chapter explores software contracts, with a particular emphasis on the areas in which Article 2 has been applied either directly or by analogy. Throughout this chapter, I refer to the parties to the software transaction as *buyer* and *seller*. Keep in mind, though, that the buyer of software is obtaining something less than title to the product.

B.   Scope

In Chapter 4.A, we looked at mixed transactions, largely from the point of view of a mixed goods and services transaction. But many transactions involve a mixture of goods and software, because we increasingly see "smart goods" having computer information embedded in them. When determining the applicable law in such a case, it seems sensible to apply the "predominant factor" test, considering the software to be part of a goods transaction unless the predominant factor in the transaction is the transfer of software, with goods incidentally attached. If the software is not embedded in goods, but is a separate part of a mixed transaction, then it seems reasonable to apply the law that is appropriate for each part of the transaction, irrespective of which is the predominant factor. In some jurisdictions, the "gravamen" test could be applied. In that case, if the complaint is about the goods, Article 2 would apply; if the complaint is about the software, the common law would apply, which might involve Article 2 used by analogy.

QUESTION 1. Ralph bought a particular microwave oven because one of the key features of the oven is the software program that permits the user to employ many different cooking options. Because of a software malfunction, the oven does not work. The microwave came with a warranty that was modeled after the Article 2 warranty scheme. Should a court treat this transaction as within the scope of Article 2?

A. Yes, because Ralph's principal purpose was to purchase a microwave oven, which is a good.

B. Yes, because the warranty is an Article 2 warranty, which brings the transaction within Article 2.

C. No, because Ralph's principal reason for purchasing this microwave oven was because of its software.

D. No, because the problem was with the software.

ANALYSIS.   All of these responses are arguably correct, but I think that **A** is the best response. The microwave is a "smart good" that has embedded software. Even though Ralph was motivated to buy the oven because of the software, he did not buy software to which an oven was attached; rather, he bought an oven to which software was attached. Furthermore, under the objective theory of contracts, we would probably look at the transaction from the point of view of a reasonable buyer, not from the point of view of this particular buyer. Because the oven is the predominant factor, **C** is not as good a response. We will see in section D below that many software warranties are modeled after Article 2. As a practical matter, this makes it easier to apply Article 2 by analogy, but this does not make it an Article 2 transaction, so **B** is not as good a response. Finally, under the gravamen test, response **D** would be correct, but the gravamen test represents the minority rule. The Principles of the Law of Software Contracts would support this result. See Principles § 1.07, Illustration 1.

QUESTION 2. For $600, Terry bought a digital camera that contained embedded software. The purchase price included a software program for editing the photos on a computer; if purchased separately, the software program would have cost $50. Terry had problems with the software program. Should a court treat this transaction as within the scope of Article 2?

A. Yes, because the predominant factor was the purchase of a digital camera.

B. Yes, because the transaction was for an amount of $500 or more.

C. No, because the software was not embedded in the goods.

D. No, because the problem was with the software program.

ANALYSIS.   This question can be distinguished from the previous question in that the software here was not embedded in the goods but was part of a mixed goods and software transaction. Therefore, even though the predominant factor was the sale of goods, the best response is **C** rather than **A**. The Principles of the Law of Software Contracts would support this result. See Principles § 1.08, Illustration 1. Note that the result would be different if the problem was with the software embedded in the camera. In that case, the rule for software embedded in goods would apply.

Hopefully you weren't misled by response **B**. In determining whether a transaction is within the scope of Article 2, the amount of the purchase price is irrelevant. If the gravamen test were the majority rule, then **D** would make a lot of sense. In fact, you have a good argument that in a context where the software is not embedded in the goods, we are essentially applying the gravamen test. So Article 2 would likely end up being applied by analogy.

C.   Standard Form Transactions

Software contracts tend to be contracts of adhesion, raising the age-old question of the enforceability of terms contained in a form agreement. Moreover, the manner in which software contracts are presented is problematic because the seller often discourages the buyer from reading the terms prior to the purchase. These manners of acceptance have been described as *shrinkwrap, browsewrap,* and *clickwrap*. In a shrinkwrap transaction, the seller presents the terms inside the box or, when there is electronic delivery, on a computer screen visible when the product is first used. Therefore, the buyer can read the terms only after purchasing the software. In a browsewrap transaction, the terms are available on a separate screen from the screen on which the buyer indicates assent; the buyer frequently indicates agreement to the terms without ever going to that screen. The clickwrap agreement is similar, but the terms appear on the same screen as the assent and can be read by scrolling through them; the buyer frequently takes the option of clicking to indicate agreement without reading the terms. While in theory the drafter of these unread terms might have an incentive to include harsh terms, there are a number of factors that militate against this practice, including competition and reputational capital. Furthermore, courts can use the principles of unconscionability and reasonable expectations to police the manner of presentation and the substance of the terms. See Chapter 4.D.

QUESTION 3. Mary desires to use an Internet service. A screen advises her to read the terms and conditions that are available on the screen by scrolling down through them before accepting them. Mary clicks on a checkbox that says "I Accept" without reading through the terms. She later finds that the service has billed her for a large amount of money for services that were not reasonably connected with the transaction. A term buried in the middle of the agreement in ordinary type authorized the service to make the charges. What is Mary's best defense against the enforceability of the term?

A. No contract was formed because Mary did not effectively accept the terms that were offered.

B. The term is not enforceable because of unconscionability.

C. The term was not within her reasonable expectations.

D. Mary has no good defense because she had the opportunity to read the terms prior to giving her assent to the contract.

ANALYSIS.   This is a clickwrap agreement, probably the most direct way to bring the agreement to the attention of the purchaser prior to the transaction. According to the objective theory of assent to a contract, it does not matter that Mary did not read or understand the terms—she manifested her assent to the terms by clicking on the box. Therefore, **A** is not a good response. However, just because a person does not read a contract prior to entering it does not mean that all the terms are enforceable. Therefore, **D** is not a good response.

Two defenses available to a person in this situation are the doctrine of reasonable expectations and the doctrine of unconscionability. Under the doctrine of reasonable expectations, terms that are reasonable may nevertheless not be considered part of a standardized agreement if they are not reasonably brought to the attention of a person who would not expect to find them in the agreement. See Second Restatement of Contracts § 211. Some software sellers construct their presentation of terms to highlight certain terms that they wish the buyer to acknowledge in order to satisfy this requirement. Under the doctrine of unconscionability, terms that substantively shock the conscience of the court may be refused enforcement, particularly when the person agreed to the terms through a procedure that was less than straightforward. See UCC § 2-302 and Principles § 1.11, which adopts the Article 2 rule. Here, the facts better fit unconscionability. It sounds like this is not the kind of reasonable term that only had to be called to Mary's attention to be enforceable. Rather, it is an unfair term that the service should not have inserted. Therefore, **B** is a better response than **C**.

D.   Warranties

Article 2 grants the buyer of goods a warranty against infringement in § 2-312(3) and provides for damages for breach of the warranty in § 2-714(2). Infringement of intellectual property is more likely to be a problem with software sales than with the sale of goods. The Principles of the Law of Software Contracts recommend in § 3.01(b) that the industry move toward an obligation to indemnify the buyer in the event of breach of this warranty, in the hope that sellers would tailor their indemnity obligation rather than disclaiming liability altogether, but this recommendation is unlikely to gain traction. Software sellers are more likely to continue to disclaim any warranty against infringement.

Software providers have generally modeled their warranties on the UCC, taking advantage of the freedom of contract under the Code that allows sellers to disclaim warranties entirely. One interesting provision in the Principles is the language relating to express warranties. Section 3.02(b) provides:

(b) Except as provided in subsection (d), the transferor creates an express warranty to the transferee as follows:

(1) An affirmation of fact or promise made by the transferor to the transferee, including by advertising or by a record packaged with or accompanying the software, that relates to the software and on which a reasonable transferee could rely creates an express warranty that the software will conform to the affirmation of fact or promise.

(2) Any description of the software made by the transferor to the transferee on which a reasonable transferee could rely creates an express warranty that the software will conform to the description.

(3) Any demonstration of software shown by the transferor to the transfer on which a reasonable transferee could rely creates an express warranty that the software will conform to the demonstration.

Recall that the language of § 2-313(1)(a) requiring express warranties to be part of the "basis of the bargain" has been variously interpreted. See Chapter 9.B. In the Principles, that language has been replaced in § 3.02(b) with language that the affirmation of fact or promise must be one "on which a reasonable transferee could rely." This test would not require actual reliance, so the warranty would be given to a buyer who did not learn of the warranty until after completing the transaction. Furthermore, the provision makes clear in (b)(1) that an express warranty could be found in an advertisement.

QUESTION 4. An online advertisement describes Ace Software as "state of the art." Terry downloads the software from the Delta website. When she uses it, she discovers that the software is not as advanced as software offered by another company. Terry had not seen the advertisement prior to purchasing the software. Does Terry have a claim against Ace for breach of express warranty?

A. Yes, because even though Terry did not see the advertisement, and could not have actually relied, a reasonable person would have relied on the affirmation of fact in the advertisement.

B. No, because the statement was made by Ace, the manufacturer, and a claim for breach of express warranty must be brought against the seller.

C. No, because the statement was not an affirmation of fact.

D. No, because the statement was made in an advertisement, not in a warranty.

ANALYSIS. Under Article 2, many courts have found that express warranties can be made in advertisements. See Amended § 2-313B and Official Comment

1. Section 2-313 of enacted Article 2 makes clear that the warranty is broader than a statement that comes with the product. Therefore, **D** is not the best choice. Although Article 2 limits warranties to statements made by the seller, many courts have found that express warranties can also be made by remote sellers, such as the party that first produced the product. Therefore, **B** is not the best choice. Assuming that an affirmation of fact in an advertisement creates a warranty enforceable against the remote seller, the remaining issues are whether this statement was an affirmation of fact and whether a person who did not rely on it can sue for breach of warranty. In Article 2 cases, the courts are split on the issue of whether a person who did not rely can make a warranty claim under the "basis of the bargain" language, so **A** is not necessarily wrong. I think most courts would agree, however, that describing something as "state of the art" is more like puffing than it is like an affirmation of fact. Therefore, even courts that do not require actual reliance would probably not enforce this statement as a warranty because a reasonable person would not have relied on it. The best response is **C**. This result is supported by Principles § 3.02.

With respect to the warranty of merchantability, while the Principles in § 3.03(b)(2) stick to the Article 2 standard that the software must "be fit for the ordinary purposes for which such software is used," they caution that because software frequently contains "bugs," the seller can't be held to a defect-free standard. Case law has not been very good at addressing the question of what standard of performance the software purchaser can expect, largely because software providers have generally disclaimed the implied warranty of merchantability. Official Comment 3(a) to § 403 of UCITA may be helpful in explaining what the warranty of merchantability means in the context of software. It provides in part:

> To be fit for ordinary purposes does not require that the program be the best or most fit for that use or that it be fit for all possible uses. To an extent greater than for goods, computer programs are often adapted and employed in unlimited or inventive ways or ways that go well beyond the uses for which they were distributed. The focus of the implied warranty is on the ordinary purposes for which programs are used. Use of ordinary, mass-market programs in highly sensitive or commercial applications does not change the warranty into one of fitness for purposes of that use.
>
> Merchantability does not require a perfect program, but only that the subject matter be generally within the average standards applicable in commerce for programs having the particular type of use. The presence of some defects may be consistent with merchantability standards. Uniform Commercial Code § 2-314 (1998 Official Text) explains the concept in terms of "fair average," i.e., goods that center around the middle of a belt of quality B some may be better and some may be worse, but they cannot

all be better and need not all be worse. That approach applies here. While perfection is an aspiration, it is not a requirement of an implied warranty for goods, computer programs or any other property. Indeed, a perfect program may not be possible at all.

The implied warranty of fitness may play a larger role in software transactions than it does in goods transactions because sellers of software frequently act as consultants to buyers with little experience, steering them to particular software or developing particular software to meet their needs.

The software industry has generally conformed its disclaimers of warranty to the requirements of Article 2. The Principles generally reiterate this practice. While Article 2 in § 2-316(2) and the Principles in § 3.06 require that disclaimers be conspicuous, this requirement is problematic in the context of online website displays. As discussed above in section C, if the terms of the contract themselves are not readily available, can the disclaimer in that contract be said to be conspicuous? It seems to me that a wise provider of software would include certain important terms, such as disclaimers, in language that has to be acknowledged by purchasers even if other terms are not called to their attention.

E.   Remedies

Courts have generally applied Article 2 remedies in software disputes. However, Article 2 principles may not be applicable in the case of "open source" software. Because this software is usually made available by non-merchants without charge, it would be reasonable for the user to assume all the risks when using this software. See Principles of the Law of Software Contracts, Summary Overview of Chapter 3, Performance. When software is provided for a price, and the buyer does not pay or substantially violates the license terms, the remedies with respect to goods may fall short. For example, a seller of goods does not generally worry about the buyer making unlawful copies of the goods. In such a case, the seller may wish to terminate the right to use the software, which might require more liberal use of injunctive relief than is generally available under Article 2. One remedy that is unique to software is the ability of the seller to electronically disable the software as a self-help remedy. Although UCITA prohibits this remedy, the Principles would permit it under certain circumstances in a negotiated agreement but not in standard form agreements—but only with a court order! See Principles § 4.03. The Principles also resolve a problem that has divided the courts under Article 2, adopting the rule that even if a limited remedy fails of its essential purpose, an exclusion of consequential damages is enforceable unless unconscionable. See Principles § 4.01.

QUESTION 5. A software company licenses to a manufacturer software that is intended to make the manufacturer's assembly line operate more efficiently. The negotiated warranty terms effectively disclaim all express and implied warranties, but contain a promise to repair or replace defective parts as the exclusive remedy. The contract terms also disclaim liability for consequential damages.

After the software was installed, because of a "bug" in it, the assembly line came to a halt. The software company was able to repair the problem after two days, but in the meantime the manufacturer suffered $50,000 in lost profits because its assembly line went down. Can the manufacturer recover this amount?

A. Yes, because this amount is direct damages that resulted from the breach.
B. Yes, because the exclusion of consequential damages is unconscionable.
C. Yes, because the repair and replace warranty failed of its essential purpose, so all remedies become available including consequential damages.
D. No, because this amount represents consequential damages that the parties agreed were excluded.

ANALYSIS. Because the remedies to which the parties agreed are modeled after Article 2 remedies, this analysis follows the Article 2 remedies provisions. Response **A** is not correct because the lost profits from the shutdown of the assembly line are consequential damages set in motion by the defect in the product. A repair or replace remedy generally fails of its essential purpose under § 2-719(2) when the product fails to work after a number of attempts at repair. Here, the remedy was successful, so it can't be said to fail of its essential purpose, and so **C** is incorrect. Furthermore, under the recommendation of Principles § 4.01(c), an exclusion of consequential damages would be effective even if an exclusive or limited remedy failed of its essential purpose. In a negotiated commercial agreement, the exclusion of consequential damages is unlikely to be unconscionable, so **D** is a better response than **B**. See § 2-719(3) and Principles § 4.01, Comment d and Illustration 7.

F. Closer

QUESTION 6. The following is an excerpt from the end user license terms for software:

> 16. LIMITED WARRANTY FOR SOFTWARE ACQUIRED IN THE US AND CANADA. Company warrants that the Software will perform

substantially in accordance with the accompanying materials for a period of ninety (90) days from the date of receipt.

If an implied warranty or condition is created by your state/jurisdiction and federal or state/provincial law prohibits disclaimer of it, you also have an implied warranty or condition, BUT ONLY AS TO DEFECTS DISCOVERED DURING THE PERIOD OF THIS LIMITED WARRANTY (NINETY DAYS). AS TO ANY DEFECTS DISCOVERED AFTER THE NINETY DAY PERIOD, THERE IS NO WARRANTY OR CONDITION OF ANY KIND. Some states/jurisdictions do not allow limitations on how long an implied warranty or condition lasts, so the above limitation may not apply to you.

. . . .

17. DISCLAIMER OF WARRANTIES. The Limited Warranty that appears above is the only express warranty made to you and is provided in lieu of any other express warranties or similar obligations (if any) created by any advertising, documentation, packaging, or other communications. Except for the Limited Warranty and to the maximum extent permitted by applicable law, Company and its suppliers provide the Software and support services (if any) AS IS AND WITH ALL FAULTS, and hereby disclaim all other warranties and conditions, whether express, implied or statutory, including, but not limited to, any (if any) implied warranties, duties or conditions of merchantability, of fitness for a particular purpose, of reliability or availability, of accuracy or completeness of responses, of results, of workmanlike effort, of lack of viruses, and of lack of negligence, all with regard to the Software, and the provision of or failure to provide support or other services, information, software, and related content through the Software or otherwise arising out of the use of the Software. ALSO, THERE IS NO WARRANTY OR CONDITION OF TITLE, QUIET ENJOYMENT, QUIET POSSESSION, CORRESPONDENCE TO DESCRIPTION OR NON-INFRINGEMENT WITH REGARD TO THE SOFTWARE.

18. EXCLUSION OF INCIDENTAL, CONSEQUENTIAL AND CERTAIN OTHER DAMAGES. TO THE MAXIMUM EXTENT PERMITTED BY APPLICABLE LAW, IN NO EVENT SHALL COMPANY OR ITS SUPPLIERS BE LIABLE FOR ANY SPECIAL, INCIDENTAL, PUNITIVE, INDIRECT, OR CONSEQUENTIAL DAMAGES WHATSOEVER (INCLUDING, BUT NOT LIMITED TO, DAMAGES FOR LOSS OF PROFITS OR CONFIDENTIAL OR OTHER INFORMATION, FOR BUSINESS INTERRUPTION, FOR PERSONAL INJURY, FOR LOSS OF PRIVACY, FOR FAILURE TO MEET ANY DUTY INCLUDING OF GOOD FAITH OR OF REASONABLE CARE, FOR NEGLIGENCE, AND FOR ANY OTHER PECUNIARY OR OTHER LOSS WHATSOEVER) ARISING OUT OF

OR IN ANY WAY RELATED TO THE USE OF OR INABILITY TO USE THE SOFTWARE, THE PROVISION OF OR FAILURE TO PROVIDE SUPPORT OR OTHER SERVICES, INFORMATON, SOFTWARE, AND RELATED CONTENT THROUGH THE SOFTWARE OR OTHERWISE ARISING OUT OF THE USE OF THE SOFTWARE, OR OTHERWISE UNDER OR IN CONNECTION WITH ANY PROVISION OF THIS EULA, EVEN IN THE EVENT OF THE FAULT, TORT (INCLUDING NEGLIGENCE), MISREPRESENTATION, STRICT LIABILITY, BREACH OF CONTRACT OR BREACH OF WARRANTY OF COMPANY OR ANY SUPPLIER, AND EVEN IF COMPANY OR ANY SUPPLIER HAS BEEN ADVISED OF THE POSSIBILITY OF SUCH DAMAGES.

19. LIMITATION OF LIABILITY AND REMEDIES. Notwithstanding any damages that you might incur for any reason whatsoever (including, without limitation, all damages referenced herein and all direct or general damages in contract or anything else), the entire liability of Company and any of its suppliers under any provision of this EULA and your exclusive remedy hereunder (except for any remedy of repair or replacement elected by Company with respect to any breach of the Limited Warranty) shall be limited to the greater of the actual damages you incur in reasonable reliance on the Software up to the amount actually paid by you for the Software or US$5.00. The foregoing limitations, exclusions and disclaimers (including Sections 16, 17 and 18) shall apply to the maximum extent permitted by applicable law, even if any remedy fails its essential purpose.

How do these warranty terms compare to the warranty terms that might accompany the sale of goods?

A. Because the product is software, these warranty terms differ substantially from those that might accompany the sale of goods.

B. These warranty terms are substantially similar to warranty terms that accompany the sale of goods.

C. These warranty terms are substantially similar to warranty terms that accompany the sale of goods, except that they do not address the Magnuson-Moss Warranty Act.

D. These warranty terms represent an attempt to comply with Article 2 disclaimers, but the drafter did not use appropriate language.

ANALYSIS. The correct response is **B.** This warranty package begins with an express warranty in ¶ 16. It is called a "limited warranty" and gives an implied warranty during the term of the express warranty in order to comply with Magnuson-Moss. See Chapter 9.F. Paragraph 17 begins with a disclaimer of warranties. It disclaims all other express warranties as per § 2-316(1) and disclaims implied warranties by using the language of both § 2-316(2) (note

the use of the word "merchantability") and § 2-316(3)(a) (note the conspicuous language, "AS IS AND WITH ALL FAULTS"). The last sentence of that
paragraph disclaims the warranties of title and noninfringement, pursuant to
§ 2-312(2). See Chapter 10.E.

Paragraph 18 excludes consequential damages as per § 2-719(3). Note
that, in a nod to the *Hadley* rules, the language provides that these damages are
excluded "even if Company or any supplier has been advised of the possibility
of such damages." Paragraph 19 contains a limited remedy under § 2-719(1)
and attempts to provide that these limited remedies govern even if any remedy
fails of its essential purpose, as provided in § 2-719(2). Language omitted from
¶ 16 provided that this is the user's exclusive remedy, as per § 2-719(1)(b). See
Chapter 18.C and 18.D.

 # Burnham's picks

Question 1	**A**
Question 2	**C**
Question 3	**B**
Question 4	**C**
Question 5	**D**
Question 6	**B**

23

International Sales Transactions

A.   Introduction

Just as uniform law is helpful to facilitate trade between the states within the United States, uniform international law is helpful to facilitate trade between different countries. The United Nations Commission on International Trade Law (UNCITRAL) has been instrumental in developing global standards and rules to govern international trade. UNCITRAL has drafted a number of conventions that numerous countries have agreed to follow, including the United Nations Convention on the International Sale of Goods (CISG), which provides the governing rules for international goods transactions. The CISG has been signed by more than 75 countries, including the United States, Canada, Mexico, China, Japan, and Italy; the United Kingdom is a notable exception. See www.cisg.law.pace.edu.

In the area of private law, the International Institute for the Unification of Private Law (UNIDROIT) has promulgated the UNIDROIT Principles of International Commercial Contracts, which are like a Restatement in the area of international contracts. See www.unidroit.org/english/principles/contracts/main.htm. Parties to international contracts often state that they wish the contract to be governed by the UNIDROIT Principles. Furthermore, the International Chamber of Commerce has promulgated the Incoterms, which provide internationally accepted definitions and rules of interpretation for most common commercial terms. See www.iccwbo.org/incoterms.

B. The United Nations Convention on the International Sale of Goods (CISG)

1. Transactions governed by the CISG

Article 2 of the CISG makes clear that, unlike the UCC, the CISG applies only to commercial parties and not to consumer transactions. While the CISG does not define "goods," it applies a "preponderant part" test for mixed transactions, providing in Article 3(2) that "[t]his Convention does not apply to contracts in which the preponderant part of the obligations of the party who furnishes the goods consists in the supply of labour or other services." This test is similar to the "predominant factor" test described in Chapter 4.A that is used by many U.S. courts to determine whether UCC Article 2 applies.

The CISG applies to a transaction when parties whose places of business are in different States ("States" in the CISG means *countries*) make a contract for the sale of goods. CISG Article 1, Sphere of Application, provides:

> (1) This Convention applies to contracts of sale of goods between parties whose places of business are in different States:
> > (a) when the States are Contracting States; or
> > (b) when the rules of private international law lead to the application of the law of a Contracting State.

Subsection (1)(a) is easy to apply. If the Los Angeles office of a U.S. business makes a contract with the Beijing office of a Chinese company, then the requirement that the places of business are in different States has been satisfied, and the requirement that the States are Contracting States is satisfied because both the U.S. and China have ratified the Convention. If, however, the Los Angeles office of a U.S. business makes a contract with the London office of an English company, then subsection (1)(a) would not apply; because the United Kingdom has not ratified the Convention, both States are not Contracting States.

If both States are not parties to the CISG, we analyze the application of subsection (1)(b). When that provision refers to "the rules of private international law," it means choice of law rules. If the application of choice of law rules concluded that U.S. law applies, then according to that provision, it appears that the Convention would apply to the United States–England transaction because those rules led to the application of the law of a Contracting State, namely the United States. On the other hand, if the application of choice of law rules led to the conclusion that English law applies, then according to that provision, the Convention would not apply to the transaction because those rules led to the application of a State that was not a Contracting State.

However, CISG Article 95 provides that a State may declare that it will not be bound by Article 1(1)(b) of the CISG, and the United States has declared such a reservation. Therefore, under the choice of law analysis in the previous paragraph, if U.S. law applies to the transaction, then the CISG does not apply because of the reservation by the United States. We then have to ask what law would apply. Because there is no formal body of federal U.S. contract law for the sale of goods, the court would likely apply general principles of contract law, including the principles and rules found in the UCC.

These issues arise infrequently because the one thing most U.S. lawyers know about the CISG is how to contract around it. Many international transactions provide for arbitration in an international forum rather than using a court system. If the parties choose to use the court system, recall that the parties are free to include a choice of law clause that specifies the applicable law. However, a drafter who intends to draft around application of the CISG has to be very careful. Suppose, for example, the drafter stated:

The Law of California governs this transaction.

The problem is that the law of California includes applicable federal law that is binding on California courts. Applicable federal law includes treaties such as the CISG, so this drafter attempting to draft out of the CISG may have inadvertently drafted into it! To better contract around application of the CISG, the drafter should state:

The UCC as enacted in California governs this transaction.

or

The Law of California governs this transaction, and the parties expressly exclude application of the United Nations Convention on the International Sale of Goods.

QUESTION 1. A Canadian corporation with its headquarters in Vancouver, British Columbia, entered into a contract for the sale of cedar shakes with a U.S. company that is incorporated in Delaware and has its headquarters in Portland, Oregon. The shakes are to be produced in Canada. The buyer brought a claim in state court in Oregon. What is the applicable law for this transaction?

A. Applicable Canadian law.
B. Oregon UCC.
C. Delaware UCC.
D. CISG.

ANALYSIS. The facts of this question are based on *GPL Treatment, Ltd. v. Louisiana-Pacific Corp.*, 894 P.2d 470 (Or. Ct. App. 1995). The trial court applied the Oregon UCC. Then a dissenting judge on the Court of Appeals woke up and realized that the law applicable to the transaction was the CISG. Because the parties to this commercial contract have the relevant places of business in different States, namely the United States and Canada, and those States are "Contracting States" (countries that have ratified the CISG), then the CISG applies. **D** is the correct response.

Assuming the CISG applies to a transaction, we next look at how some of its provisions differ from provisions of the UCC.

2. Contract formation

Since you are familiar with Article 2 of the UCC, the provisions of the CISG will not seem strange to you. You will recognize most of the rules as being similar to the common law or UCC rules, though some have come from the code-based legal systems used in most of the non-English speaking world.

With respect to contract formation, the CISG seems to require more definiteness than the UCC. Article 14(1) of the CISG states that "[a] proposal is sufficiently definite if it indicates the goods and expressly or implicitly fixes or makes provision for determining the quantity and the price." CISG Article 19 contains a much simpler version of the Battle of the Forms than is found in UCC § 2-207. Subsection (1) essentially contains a statement of the common law mirror-image rule, providing a general rule that a reply to an offer that has additional or different terms is not an acceptance but is instead a counteroffer. However, subsection (2) provides that additional or different terms in the reply that do not materially alter the terms of the offer are part of the contract unless the offeror timely objects to them. This is similar to the rule of UCC § 2-207(2), except that the CISG rule expressly addresses both additional and different terms. Subsection (3) is similar to Official Comment 4 to UCC § 2-207, providing a list of terms that would be held to materially alter the terms of the offer.

QUESTION 2. A buyer in Miami, Florida, orders 1,000 pounds of fresh lettuce from a seller in Montevideo, Uruguay. The purchase order provides for a price of 78 cents per pound, delivery by December 15, and payment within 30 days after delivery. The seller sends an acknowledgment that

provides that payment is due within 10 days after delivery. The parties
perform without objection. What is the term of the contract with respect
to payment?

A. Payment is due in 30 days.
B. Payment is due in 10 days.
C. Payment is due on delivery.
D. Payment is due at a reasonable time.

ANALYSIS. Let's first review how this would play out under the UCC.
The seller's response contains different terms. Under § 2-207(1), a contract
is formed. Section 2-207(2), however, does not say what to do with different
terms. Most states have adopted the "knockout" rule under which the different
terms are knocked out and the default rule is read in. Here, the default rule of
§ 2-511(1) is that payment is due on delivery. To me, this indicates how sense-
less the knockout rule is, because if one party provided for payment in 30 days,
and the other for payment 10 days, why should the supplied term be one that
neither of them contemplated?

However, the governing law with respect to a contract for the sale of goods
between commercial parties in the United States and Uruguay is the CISG
because both countries are signatories. Under the CISG, since the different
term was not objected to, the issue would turn on whether it materially alters
the terms of the offer. CISG Article 19(3) provides that "[a]dditional or different terms relating, among other things, to the price, payment, quality and
quantity of the goods, place and time of delivery, extent of one party's liability
to the other or the settlement of disputes are considered to alter the terms of
the offer materially." So the time of delivery would probably be material and
the different term in the acceptance would not become part of the contract.
Therefore the offeror's term of payment within 30 days would be part of the
contract. The correct response is **A**.

Like the UCC, the CISG respects trade usage and the usages of the parties.
However, the CISG does not have a Statute of Frauds, making the enforceability
of oral agreements a question of fact. CISG Article 11 provides that "[a] contract of sale need not be concluded in or evidenced by writing and is not subject
to any other requirement as to form. It may be proved by any means, including
witnesses." Similarly, the CISG does not have a parol evidence rule, making the
parties' intent to include side agreements also a question of fact. In a famous case
decided under the CISG, *MCC-Marble v. Ceramica Nuova D'Agostino, S.P.A.*,
144 F.3d 1384 (11th Cir. 1998), the plaintiff Florida company bought marble
from the defendant Italian company. When the buyer complained about the
merchandise, the seller claimed these complaints were barred because clause 4
on the back side of the written contract stated in pertinent part:

Possible complaints for defects of the merchandise must be made in writing by means of a certified letter within and not later than 10 days after receipt of the merchandise . . . .

The buyer admitted that it had not timely complained in writing, but maintained that the parties had agreed that the terms on the back of the contract would not be part of the agreement! Needless to say, in a transaction governed by the UCC, if the writing appears to be complete and exclusive, this argument would gain no traction under the parol evidence rule. See § 2-202(b). But the court pointed out that the CISG rule is different:

Article 8(1) of the CISG instructs courts to interpret the "statements . . . and other conduct of a party . . . according to his intent" as long as the other party "knew or could not have been unaware" of that intent. The plain language of the Convention, therefore, requires an inquiry into a party's subjective intent as long as the other party to the contract was aware of that intent.

This analysis doesn't make sense if taken literally, because if a party is aware of a subjective intent, then it must have been made objective. By "subjective," the court must have meant an intent not found in the written agreement. The court held that the plaintiff would be allowed to prove that the defendant knew that the plaintiff intended not to have the terms on the back of the writing be part of the agreement. The court also noted that a party could prevent a result like this by including a merger clause in the written agreement.

QUESTION 3. A Canadian corporation with its headquarters in Vancouver, British Columbia, alleges that it entered into an oral agreement with a U.S. company that has its headquarters in Portland, Oregon, for the sale of cedar shakes for more than $500. The buyer claims that the agreement is not enforceable because it is oral. The seller claims that it complied with the § 2-201(2) exception to the statute of frauds when it sent to the buyer a document called "Order Confirmation," requesting that the buyer sign and return it, and the buyer did not object to the confirmation. Is the oral agreement enforceable against the buyer?

A. No, because it is within the statute of frauds.
B. No, because the document sent by the seller was not a confirmation under § 2-201(2).
C. Yes, because the document sent by the seller was a confirmation under § 2-201(2).
D. Yes, if the seller can prove as a fact that the parties made the oral agreement.

ANALYSIS. These were the facts of *GPL Treatment, Ltd. v. Louisiana-Pacific Corp.*, 894 P.2d 470 (Or. Ct. App. 1995), discussed in Question 1. The court was divided on the issue of whether the document was a confirmation, since a confirmation pursuant to § 2-201(2) does not have to be signed and returned. As we saw when analyzing the earlier question, this case should have been decided under the CISG. Under Article 11 of the CISG, there is no writing requirement for a contract within the Convention. Therefore it is a question of fact whether the parties made the oral agreement, and **D** is the correct response.

3. Contract performance

Remedies for nonperformance under the CISG depend upon the character of the breach of contract. As discussed in Chapter 12.B, the UCC purports to have a "perfect tender" rule that permits the buyer to reject the goods because of any nonconformity. The CISG more sensibly characterizes some breaches as "fundamental," similar to the common law concept of "material breach." CISG Article 25 provides:

> A breach of contract committed by one of the parties is fundamental if it results in such detriment to the other party as substantially to deprive him of what he is entitled to expect under the contract, unless the party in breach did not foresee and a reasonable person of the same kind in the same circumstances would not have foreseen such a result.

If the breach is fundamental, then the other party may avoid the contract under CISG Article 64 and claim damages. If the breach is not fundamental, then the aggrieved party may not avoid the contract, but may seek remedies including damages, specific performance, and adjustment of price. The seller's right to cure is more expansive than the right under UCC § 2-508, because the right is not dependent on the time of performance. CISG Article 48(1) provides:

> Subject to article 49, the seller may, even after the date for delivery, remedy at his own expense any failure to perform his obligations, if he can do so without unreasonable delay and without causing the buyer unreasonable inconvenience or uncertainty of reimbursement by the seller of expenses advanced by the buyer. However, the buyer retains any right to claim damages as provided for in this Convention.

QUESTION 4. A contract is entered into by a New York company and an Italian company for the sale of 100 widgets. At the time for performance, the seller tenders only 95 of the widgets and promises the additional widgets in ten days. Can the buyer refuse the tender of the 95 widgets?

A. Yes, because this is a fundamental breach.
B. Yes, because the seller's tender was not perfect.

C. No, the buyer must accept them and permit the seller to supply the additional widgets.

D. No, the buyer must accept them but can recover money damages rather than accept the additional widgets.

ANALYSIS.   This contract is governed by the CISG, since the United States and Italy are Contracting States. The CISG does not have a perfect tender rule. Under the "fundamental breach" rule of CISG Article 25, there are no facts indicating that the failure to tender 5% of the required goods was a fundamental breach. Therefore, the buyer must accept the goods and obtain a remedy. Unless there is a reason why cover would not be appropriate, the buyer must allow the seller to cure the breach under CISG Article 48(1). Of course, the seller would also have to pay any damages that resulted. The correct response is **C.**

4. Contract remedies

Specific performance is more readily available under the CISG than under the UCC, which is not surprising since specific performance is generally available in the many civil law countries that are parties to the CISG. With respect to breach by a seller, CISG Article 46(1) provides:

> The buyer may require performance by the seller of his obligations unless the buyer has resorted to a remedy which is inconsistent with this requirement.

Similarly, with respect to breach by the buyer, CISG Article 62 provides:

> The seller may require the buyer to pay the price, take delivery or perform his other obligations, unless the seller has resorted to a remedy which is inconsistent with this requirement.

QUESTION 5. A company in New York contracted to sell widgets to a company in Canada. The price of widgets went up after the contract was entered into, and the seller informed the buyer that it was going to sell the widgets on the market, where it could obtain a higher price. Can the buyer obtain an order of specific performance, requiring the seller to tender the widgets to the buyer?

A. Yes, as long as the buyer has not obtained "cover" widgets elsewhere.

B. Yes, even if the buyer has obtained "cover" widgets elsewhere.

C. No, because widgets are not unique, the buyer can purchase them on the market and sue for the difference between the cover price and the contract price.

D. No, because specific performance is never available under the UCC.

ANALYSIS. Response **D** is incorrect under the UCC because specific performance is available where goods are unique. These widgets are not unique, however, since there is a market for them. The remedy under the UCC would be **C**, but that is not the correct response because this contract is governed by the CISG since both countries are Contracting States. Under CISG Article 46(1), if the buyer has covered, then specific performance is not available. Therefore, **B** is an incorrect response. Since specific performance is available under the CISG even if the goods are available on the market, **A** is the correct response.

C. The UNIDROIT Principles

1. Transactions governed by the UNIDROIT Principles

Like the Restatements, the UNIDROIT Principles are not law but are a useful synthesis of legal principles that provide guidance to courts and to parties. The Principles apply to all international contracts, not just contracts for the sale of goods. Like the UCC, the Principles contain official comments that provide guidance as to the application and interpretation of the Principles. Unlike the UCC, but like the CISG, the Principles apply only to commercial parties. There is conscious overlap between the Principles and the CISG, and the two sources often provide the same rules.

Because the Principles are not the law adopted by any country, most drafters desiring to employ them incorporate an arbitration clause and then direct the arbitrator to decide the issues according to the Principles. The Preamble to the Principles provides in a footnote:

> Parties wishing to provide that their agreement be governed by the Principles might use the following words, adding any desired exceptions or modifications:
>
>> **"This contract shall be governed by the UNIDROIT Principles (2010) [except as to Articles . . .]".**
>
> Parties wishing to provide in addition for the application of the law of a particular jurisdiction might use the following words:
>
>> **"This contract shall be governed by the UNIDROIT Principles (2010) [except as to Articles . . .], supplemented when necessary by the law of [jurisdiction X]".**

2. Contract formation

The UCC obligation of good faith in § 1-304 applies only to the "performance and enforcement" of the contract. The Principles go further, providing that good faith is required in the negotiation of the contract as well. Principles Article 2.1.15 (*Negotiations in bad faith*) provides:

(1) A party is free to negotiate and is not liable for failure to reach an agreement.

(2) However, a party who negotiates or breaks off negotiations in bad faith is liable for the losses caused to the other party.

(3) It is bad faith, in particular, for a party to enter into or continue negotiations when intending not to reach an agreement with the other party.

The Principles take a very simple approach to the problem of the Battle of the Forms, addressed in UCC § 2-207 and in CISG Article 19:

Article 2.1.22 (*Battle of forms*)

Where both parties use standard terms and reach agreement except on those terms, a contract is concluded on the basis of the agreed terms and of any standard terms which are common in substance unless one party clearly indicates in advance, or later and without undue delay informs the other party, that it does not intend to be bound by such a contract.

The Principles also contain a provision that embodies the doctrine of Reasonable Expectations, which is absent from the UCC. Principles Article 2.1.20 *(Surprising terms)* provides:

(1) No term contained in standard terms which is of such a character that the other party could not reasonably have expected it, is effective unless it has been expressly accepted by that party.

(2) In determining whether a term is of such a character regard shall be had to its content, language and presentation.

As discussed in Chapter 4.D, reasonable expectations is a very practical concept. Although in theory the parties should read and understand the boilerplate of their contract, in practice they often don't. Under this doctrine, a term that a party would not expect to find in the boilerplate is not enforceable unless it was called to that party's attention.

Unlike Article 2 of the UCC, the Principles contain rules on the defenses to contract formation. While the defense of unconscionability has rarely been applied to commercial contracts under Article 2, the Principles take a more expansive view when there is gross disparity. Note that the Principles also permit the court (or arbitrator) to reform the contract or term to make it more reasonable. Principles Article 3.2.7 *(Gross disparity)* provides:

(1) A party may avoid the contract or an individual term of it if, at the time of the conclusion of the contract, the contract or term unjustifiably gave the other party an excessive advantage. Regard is to be had, among other factors, to

(a) the fact that the other party has taken unfair advantage of the first party's dependence, economic distress or urgent needs, or of its improvidence, ignorance, inexperience or lack of bargaining skill, and

(b) the nature and purpose of the contract.

(2) Upon the request of the party entitled to avoidance, a court may adapt the contract or term in order to make it accord with reasonable commercial standards of fair dealing.

(3) A court may also adapt the contract or term upon the request of the party receiving notice of avoidance, provided that that party informs the other party of its request promptly after receiving such notice and before the other party has reasonably acted in reliance on it.

Like the CISG, the Principles have no counterpart to the Statute of Frauds found in UCC § 2-201. The Principles make clear what many U.S. court decisions have determined—that a merger clause is effective in a negotiated agreement to bar the admission of parol evidence. Principles Article 2.1.17 *(Merger clauses)* provides:

A contract in writing which contains a clause indicating that the writing completely embodies the terms on which the parties have agreed cannot be contradicted or supplemented by evidence of prior statements or agreements. However, such statements or agreements may be used to interpret the writing.

Many rules of interpretation are found in the Principles, including one that enumerates the sources that may be looked to in order to determine the meaning the parties intended. Principles Article 4.3 *(Relevant circumstances)* provides:

In applying Articles 4.1 and 4.2, regard shall be had to all the circumstances, including

(a) preliminary negotiations between the parties;

(b) practices which the parties have established between themselves;

(c) the conduct of the parties subsequent to the conclusion of the contract;

(d) the nature and purpose of the contract;

(e) the meaning commonly given to terms and expressions in the trade concerned;

(f) usages.

QUESTION 6. The parties to an international contract for the sale of aviation fuel agreed to apply the UNIDROIT Principles to their contract. The price in the contract drafted by the seller was stated per "ton." It is customary in the aviation fuel business to measure the fuel in "long tons,"

> but the seller claims that the price should be measured in short tons because a provision in the boilerplate of the agreement stated:
>
> > The parties agree that trade usage does not apply to this agreement, and in particular, "ton" does not mean "long ton."
>
> Should the arbitrator enforce the provision found in the boilerplate?
>
> A. Yes, because it is the buyer's responsibility to read the contract.
> B. No, because the parties are not free to contract around trade usage.
> C. No, because the buyer would not have reasonably expected that provision in the contract.
> D. No, because the provision would be knocked out under the Battle of the Forms rules.

ANALYSIS. Response **D** is not correct because the Battle of the Forms does not apply when the parties' agreement is found in a single form. Response **B** is not correct because parties do have the freedom to contract around trade usage. However, because the trade usage is the reasonably expected term, according to Principles Article 2.1.20 (*Surprising terms*), the seller should not have buried such a term in the boilerplate. The term would have been enforceable if it was reasonably called to the attention of the buyer. For example, the seller could have put it in bold print on the front page of the contract or had the buyer separately sign it to show its express acceptance. The correct response is **C**.

3. Contract performance

The Principles do not provide for express or implied warranties. Nonetheless, where goods are to be supplied, the goods must either conform to the contract or, in the words of Principles Article 5.1.6, be "reasonable and not less than average in the circumstances." This standard seems similar to the implied warranty of merchantability.

In addition, the Principles allow for a right to cure, and do not distinguish between the times before and after performance is due when addressing the right to cure. An aggrieved party who rejects partial performance may terminate the contract in its entirety only when the elements of termination are met. Like the CISG, termination is warranted under the Principles only when there is a *fundamental* nonperformance, which is determined, according to Principles Article 7.3.1(2), by looking at the following factors:

> (a) the non-performance substantially deprives the aggrieved party of what it was entitled to expect under the contract unless the other party did not foresee and could not reasonably have foreseen such result;
>
> (b) strict compliance with the obligation which has not been performed is of essence under the contract;

(c) the non-performance is intentional or reckless;

(d) the non-performance gives the aggrieved party reason to believe that it cannot rely on the other party's future performance;

(e) the non-performing party will suffer disproportionate loss as a result of the preparation or performance if the contract is terminated.

4. Contract remedies

The Principles are broader in scope than UCC Article 2 and govern contracts that pertain to more than just the sale of goods; therefore, separate remedies for buyers and sellers are not distinguished. The remedies are very similar to those under the UCC, except that, like the CISG, the Principles favor specific performance, both for monetary and nonmonetary obligations. Principles Article 7.2.2 *(Performance of non-monetary obligation)* makes clear that unlike the UCC, specific performance is the rule rather than the exception:

Where a party who owes an obligation other than one to pay money does not perform, the other party may require performance, unless

(a) performance is impossible in law or in fact;

(b) performance or, where relevant, enforcement is unreasonably burdensome or expensive;

(c) the party entitled to performance may reasonably obtain performance from another source;

(d) performance is of an exclusively personal character; or

(e) the party entitled to performance does not require performance within a reasonable time after it has, or ought to have, become aware of the non-performance.

QUESTION 7. A buyer in one country has agreed to buy silver from a seller in another country. The parties agreed to have the UNIDROIT Principles apply to their contract. Because of a rise in prices between the time the contract was made and the time for performance, the seller refuses to perform. Silver is a widely traded commodity, and the buyer can obtain it at a lower shipping cost from another seller. The buyer seeks specific performance of the contract. Should the arbitrator award specific performance?

A. Yes, because the goods are unique.

B. Yes, because under the Principles, the nonbreaching party may require specific performance.

C. No, because the nonbreaching party may reasonably obtain performance from another source.

D. No, because the performance is of an exclusively personal character.

ANALYSIS. Although the Principles provide for specific performance in a wider range of situations that the Code, this is not one of them. Principles Article 7.2.2 contains a list of situations where specific performance would not be appropriate and the relevant one is (c)—the party entitled to performance may reasonably obtain performance from another source. The correct response is **C**.

D. Closers

QUESTION 8. Thinking it could supply stewing chicken, a seller in New York who was new to the chicken business made an oral contract to sell "chicken" to a buyer in Switzerland. The parties agreed to have the UNIDROIT Principles apply to their contract. The buyer knew that because such a contract called for the shipment of frying chicken, the seller would lose a lot of money under the contract. When the seller learned of its mistake, the seller sought avoidance of the contract. What should the arbitrator decide?

A. The contract is not enforceable because it is oral.
B. The seller must provide fryers at the contract price because it freely agreed to do so.
C. The only remedy is to avoid the contract.
D. The arbitrator may avoid the contract or adapt the contract by providing a more reasonable price term.

ANALYSIS. Response **A** is incorrect because the Principles do not contain a Statute of Frauds. Although there is freedom of contract to make an unfavorable agreement, there is an exception in a situation of "gross disparity," as described in Principles Article 3.2.7. The buyer here took advantage of the seller's ignorance. As a remedy, the arbitrator may either avoid the contract or adapt it to make it commercially reasonable. The best response is **D**.

QUESTION 9. A U.S. manufacturer approaches a Canadian manufacturer with a proposal to produce a machine together. The parties sign a Memorandum of Understanding (MOU) that commits them to attempt to reach a final agreement but provides that there is no binding commitment until a final agreement is signed. The MOU provides that the UNIDROIT Principles apply. After several weeks of negotiation, when it became clear that the U.S. company had entered the negotiations in order to learn about the Canadian company's manufacturing methods, the Canadian company broke off negotiations and made a claim against the U.S. company. Is the Canadian company likely to be successful in its claim?

A. No, because each side to a MOU takes a risk that the parties will not reach a final agreement.
B. No, because good faith only applies to the performance and enforcement of a contract, and here there was no contract.
C. Yes, because the U.S. company did not act in good faith, the Canadian company can recover damages for breach of contract.
D. Yes, because the U.S. company did not act in good faith, the Canadian company can recover its out-of-pocket costs.

ANALYSIS.   Response **A** is true as far as it goes, but it does not go far enough. Although each party takes a risk that the parties may not reach agreement, this does not necessarily mean a party is free from an obligation to act in good faith. Although the UCC does not address precontractual good faith, the common law is incorporated into the UCC by reference in § 1-103(b), and precontractual liability is a developing area of the law. So it is possible that there could be a recovery under the UCC. Therefore, **B** is not a complete response. The parties here agreed to be bound by the UNIDROIT Principles, and Principles Article 2.1.15 requires that a party conduct negotiations in good faith. Because the remedy is the losses caused by the other party's bad faith, the best response is **D**.

 # Burnham's picks

Question 1 **D**
Question 2 **A**
Question 3 **D**
Question 4 **C**
Question 5 **A**
Question 6 **C**
Question 7 **C**
Question 8 **D**
Question 9 **D**

24

Closing Closers: Some Practice Questions

This chapter is different from the others. It consists of a series of practice questions. There is no text or black-letter law in this chapter, so you have an opportunity to try to spot the issues. The questions are not in any particular order, so the issues could come from any chapter. We are also going to do something different in this chapter—the questions are framed around a typical contract for the sale of goods. The chapter thus provides both a review of the issues covered and an opportunity to test your understanding of what the concepts look like when they appear in a contract.

I have included at the end of the chapter my picks for the best response to each question, but to get full value from your review, first analyze the questions completely yourself before looking at my comments.

Good luck! As with the rest of the material in the book, be sure to let me know if you have any questions or comments.

Here is the contract most of the questions refer to:

AGREEMENT FOR THE SALE OF GOODS

_____ Seller, and _____, Buyer, with addresses as they appear with their names below, agree as follows:

1. Description—Sale of Goods. Seller shall transfer ownership and deliver possession to Buyer, and Buyer shall pay for and accept the following goods: _____.

2. Time of Delivery. Buyer shall have the right to specify the date of delivery, but in no event shall the date specified be before _____ 20_____or after _____ 20_____.

3. Delivery in Lots. Buyer shall have the right to demand all of the goods at one time during the period stated in Paragraph 2, or in portions from time to time.

4. Place of Delivery. The goods shall be delivered at Seller's address as it appears below.

5. Method of Tender. Buyer will give notice to the Seller at least 24 hours before Buyer desires to take possession of the goods. Seller agrees that he will furnish the facilities and manpower for loading the goods on trucks furnished by Buyer.

6. Seller to Package Goods. Seller will package goods in accordance with instruction of Buyer provided instructions are furnished in sufficient time to permit Seller to complete the packaging before delivery. Buyer shall pay Seller the reasonable cost of packaging in addition to the price specified in this contract.

7. Identification—Risk of Loss. Identification of the goods under Section 2-501 of the Uniform Commercial Code shall occur at the moment this agreement is signed by the parties. Risk of loss of the goods shall pass to the Buyer upon identification.

8. Title. Title to the goods shall remain with the Seller until Buyer actually receives possession of the goods.

9. Disclaimer of Express Warranties. Seller warrants that the goods are as described in this agreement, but no other express warranty is made in respect to the goods.

10. Disclaimer of Implied Warranties. THE GOODS SOLD UNDER THIS CONTRACT ARE PURCHASED BY THE BUYER "AS IS" AND THE SELLER DOES NOT WARRANTY THAT THEY ARE OF MERCHANTABLE QUALITY OR THAT THEY CAN BE USED FOR ANY PARTICULAR PURPOSE.

11. Amount of Price. The price to be paid by Buyer shall be that contained on the Seller's price list last published before the date of actual delivery of the goods.

12. Time of Payment. Buyer shall pay for the goods at the time and place of delivery.

13. Right of Inspection. Buyer shall have the right to inspect the goods at the time and place of delivery before paying for them or accepting them.

14. Method of Payment. Payment shall be made in cash or by certified check.

15. Remedies. Buyer and Seller shall have all remedies afforded each by the Uniform Commercial Code.

16. Interpretation—Parol Evidence. This writing is intended by the parties as a final expression of their agreement and is intended also as a complete and exclusive statement of the terms of their agreement. [No course of prior dealings between the parties and no usage of the trade shall be relevant to supplement or explain any term used in this agreement.]

Acceptance or acquiescence in a course of performance rendered under this agreement shall not be relevant to determine the meaning of this agreement even though the accepting or acquiescing party has knowledge of the nature of the performance and opportunity for objection. Whenever a term defined by the Uniform Commercial Code is used in this agreement the definition contained in the Code is to control.

17. Authority of Seller's Agents. No agent, employee or representative of the Seller has any authority to bind the Seller to any affirmation, representation or warranty concerning the goods sold under this agreement, and unless an affirmation, representation or warranty made by an agent, employee or representative is specifically included within this written agreement, it has not formed a part of the basis of this bargain and shall not in any way be enforceable.

18. Modifications. This agreement can be modified or rescinded only by a writing signed by both the parties or their duly authorized agents.

19. Waiver. No claim or right arising out of a breach of this contract can be discharged in whole or in part by a waiver or renunciation of the claim or right unless the waiver or renunciation is supported by consideration and is in writing signed by the aggrieved party.

20. Assignment—Delegation. No right or interest in this contract shall be assigned by either Buyer or Seller without the written permission of the other party, and no delegation of any obligation owed, or of the performance of any obligation, by either Buyer or Seller shall be made without the written permission of the other party. Any attempted assignment or delegation shall be wholly void and totally ineffective for all purposes unless made in conformity with this paragraph.

21. Time for Bringing Action. Any action for breach of this contract must be commenced within 2 years after the cause of action has accrued.

22. Applicable Law. This agreement shall be governed by the Uniform Commercial Code. Wherever the term "Uniform Commercial Code" is used, it shall be construed as meaning the Uniform Commercial Code as adopted in the State of as effective and in force on the date of this agreement.

23. Arbitration. Any controversy or claim arising out of relating to this contract, or the breach thereof, shall be settled by arbitration in accordance with the Rules of the American Arbitration Association, and judgment upon the award rendered by the Arbitrator(s) may be entered in any Court having jurisdiction thereof.

SIGNED _____, 20 _____.

BUYER:_____ Address: _____
SELLER:_____ Address: _____

QUESTION 1. In which of the following situations does UCC Article 2 apply to this contract?

    I. Seller is a giant corporation selling a million ballpoint pens to Buyer, another giant corporation.
    II. Seller is a giant corporation selling a single ballpoint pen to Buyer, an individual who will use the pen in her kitchen.
    III. Seller is an individual who is selling a single ballpoint pen to Buyer, a giant corporation.
    IV. Seller is an individual who is selling a single ballpoint pen at a yard sale to Buyer, her neighbor.

A. I only.
B. I and II only.
C. I, II, and III only.
D. All of the above.

QUESTION 2. If this entire contract merely stated, "Seller shall sell Buyer 100 type-A widgets for $100,000," and both parties signed it, would it be enforceable? Feel free to look at § 2-204(3) before you answer.

A. Yes, because it contains the minimum requirements of price and quantity.
B. Yes, because the missing terms can be filled in with the gap fillers.
C. No, because it is too indefinite.
D. No, because contracts for the sale of goods for $500 or more require a more detailed writing.

QUESTION 3. Assume this was a contract for the sale of 100 type-A widgets. Which of the following would not be a principal purpose of ¶ 1?

A. To identify the parties to the contract.
B. To transfer title to the goods.
C. To state a quantity of goods.
D. To create an express warranty.

QUESTION 4. Look at ¶ 2 of our contract. In the absence of specific time provisions in the contract, what is the time for delivery? Feel free to look at § 2-309 before you answer.

A. Without this provision, the contract fails for indefiniteness.
B. Thirty days from the date the contract is formed.
C. A time to be determined by Seller in good faith.
D. A reasonable time.

QUESTION 5. Assume the parties agreed in ¶ 2: "Buyer shall have the right to specify the date of delivery." There is no provision in the Code that gives the Buyer that right. Are the parties allowed to agree to something that is not in the Code? Feel free to look at § 1-302 before you answer.

A. They may generally do so except where the Code provides otherwise.
B. They may generally not do so except where the Code affirmatively allows it.
C. They may always do so.
D. They may never do so.

QUESTION 6. We quibbled in the previous question by saying that parties can "generally" use freedom of contract to get around the default rules. This suggests that there are exceptions. Which of the following is not an exception to the rule? In other words, which of the following is an area where the parties can agree on a rule different from the rule the Code provides? Feel free to look at § 1-302(b) before you answer.

A. The parties agree to be unreasonable.
B. The parties agree one does not have to act in good faith.
C. A specific Code section says they cannot agree otherwise.
D. The parties agree to ignore trade usage.

QUESTION 7. According to § 1-302(b), while the parties may not disclaim the obligation to be reasonable, they "may determine the standards by which the performance of such obligations is to be measured if such standards are not manifestly unreasonable." Which language from the contract exemplifies the right of the parties to determine reasonable standards?

A. "Buyer shall pay for and accept the following goods: _____."
B. "Buyer shall have the right to specify the date of delivery."
C. "[I]n no event shall the date specified be before _____, 20_____, or after _____, 20_____."
D. "Buyer shall have the right to demand all of the goods at one time during the period stated in Paragraph 2, or in portions from time to time."

QUESTION 8. If the parties had not put ¶ 3 in the contract, what default provision would the Code supply? Feel free to look at § 2-307 before you answer.

A. The same as this provision—it is up to the Buyer.
B. It is up to the Seller whether to deliver in a single lot or in portions.
C. Delivery must be in a single lot.
D. Delivery must be in several lots.

QUESTION 9. Assume again that the parties did not include ¶ 3 in their contract, so the default provision applied. Seller is unable to obtain shipping for all 100 widgets at once, and so she ships them in lots. Is Seller in breach?

A. Yes, because under the default rule, the goods must be tendered in a single delivery.
B. Yes, because Seller did not request Buyer's permission to make delivery in lots.
C. No, because under the default rule, the goods may be shipped in lots.
D. No, because the circumstances gave Seller the right to make delivery in lots.

QUESTION 10. Now assume that the parties included ¶ 3 in their contract. Seller is unable to obtain shipping for all 100 widgets at once, and so she ships them in lots. Is Seller in breach?

A. Yes, because under the default rule, the goods must be tendered in a single delivery.
B. Yes, because the contract provides for a single delivery.
C. No, because under the default rule, the goods may be shipped in lots.
D. No, because the circumstances gave Seller the right to make delivery in lots.

QUESTION 11. If the parties had not put ¶ 4 in the contract, what default provision would the Code supply for the place of delivery? Feel free to look at § 2-308 before you answer.

A. The same as the contract provision—Seller's place of business.
B. Buyer's place of business.
C. A reasonable place.
D. There is no default provision—the omission is fatal to the contract.

QUESTION 12. If a law professor sold a household refrigerator to a law student for $400, where would the place of delivery be? Feel free to look at § 2-308 before you answer.

A. The law professor's home.
B. The student's residence.
C. Trick question—this is not an Article 2 transaction.
D. There is no default provision—the omission is fatal to the contract.

QUESTION 13. Assume the contract was between a Seller in Missoula and a Buyer in Las Vegas and the contract stated, "F.O.B. Missoula." What are Seller's obligations?

A. To hold the goods at Buyer's disposition.
B. To put the goods in possession of a carrier in Missoula to be shipped at Seller's expense.
C. To put the goods in possession of a carrier in Missoula to be shipped at Buyer's expense.
D. To deliver the goods in Las Vegas.

QUESTION 14. The Article 2 risk of loss provisions are found in § 2-509. Which part of § 2-509 applies to ¶ 7 of our contract?

A. Subsection (1)—the seller ships the goods by carrier.
B. Subsection (2)—the goods are held by a bailee.
C. Subsection (3)—a case not within subsection (1) or (2).
D. Subsection (4)—the parties have made their own agreement.

QUESTION 15. In ¶ 7, the parties agree that the risk of loss passes to Buyer upon identification. The parties state that identification occurs "at the moment this agreement is signed." Assuming Seller has an inventory of the widgets, did the parties here adopt the default rule on identification? Feel free to look at § 2-501 before you answer.

A. Yes, because the goods are already existing.
B. Yes, because the goods are designated as the goods to which the contract refers.
C. No, because the goods do not exist.
D. No, because the goods have not been designated as the goods to which the contract refers.

QUESTION 16. In ¶ 8, did the parties adopt the default rule with respect to title? Feel free to look at § 2-401(2) before you answer.

A. Yes, as per the default rule, the seller has title until delivery.
B. Yes, as per the default rule, the seller has title until the goods are identified.
C. No, the parties changed the default rule to provide that the buyer has title when the goods are identified.
D. No, the parties changed the default rule to provide that the buyer does not have title until the goods are paid for.

QUESTION 17. Between the time of identification of the goods and delivery, which of the following best describes Buyer's situation under our contract? Feel free to review ¶¶ 7 and 8 before you answer.

A. Buyer has no risk of loss and does not have title to the goods.
B. Buyer has no risk of loss and has title to the goods.
C. Buyer has a risk of loss and has title to the goods.
D. Buyer has a risk of loss and does not have title to the goods.

QUESTION 18. Assuming all of the following statements are part of the agreement, which one of them would not constitute an express warranty under the Code?

A. The contract states, "Description of goods: 100 type-A widgets."
B. The contract states, "Made of 100% titanium."
C. Prior to entering the contract, a salesman for Seller stated, in language that became part of the contract, "This is the best deal on widgets you will find in this town."
D. Prior to entering the contract, a salesman for Seller stated, "Here is a sample of what our type-A widgets look like."

QUESTION 19. Assume the contract stated: "The goods are type-A widgets. Seller makes no express warranty with respect to the goods." If Seller shipped type-B widgets, would Seller be in breach of warranty? Feel free to read § 2-316(1) before you answer.

A. Seller is not in breach because Seller never made a warranty.
B. Seller is not in breach because Seller made a warranty but effectively negated it.
C. Seller is in breach because a seller cannot disclaim express warranties.
D. Seller is in breach because express warranties that are in the contract and negated are deemed made.

QUESTION 20. Before the contract was signed, Seller said to Buyer, "The widgets will be blue," but that language did not make its way into the written agreement. The writing, however, is held not to be fully integrated. The contract states, "Seller makes no express warranty with respect to the goods." Did Buyer get an express warranty that the widgets would be blue?

A. No, because the statement is not an express warranty.
B. No, because although the statement is an express warranty, it was expressly disclaimed.
C. Yes, because the statement is an express warranty and the disclaimer is not effective to negate it.
D. Yes, because the statement is an express warranty and disclaimer of express warranties is not permitted.

QUESTION 21. A law professor sells a refrigerator that she owns to a student. After the purchase, Sears repossesses the refrigerator from the student because the law professor gave Sears a security interest in it. Assuming it was legal for Sears to do this, which it probably was, does the student have a claim against the professor for breach of warranty? Feel free to review § 2-312(1)(b) before you answer.

A. Trick question! Article 2 doesn't apply to this transaction.
B. Yes, the professor warranted that the goods were free from any security interest.
C. No, because the professor owned the refrigerator, she transferred good title to the student.
D. No, because it is the responsibility of the buyer to check for security interests.

QUESTION 22. Which of the following is not within the description of goods that are merchantable? Feel free to look at § 2-314 before you answer.

A. The goods pass without objection in the trade under the contract description.
B. The goods are fungible and are of fair average quality within the description.
C. The goods are fit for the ordinary purposes for which such goods are used.
D. The goods meet a particular purpose specified by the buyer.

QUESTION 23. A law professor sells a law student a used refrigerator. Does the professor give the student an implied warranty of merchantability?

A. Yes, because there is an implied promise that the goods are fit for the ordinary purposes for which such goods are used.
B. No, because the goods are used.
C. No, because the seller is not a merchant.
D. No, because this is not an Article 2 transaction.

QUESTION 24. Which of the following is not a requirement of an exclusion of the implied warranty of merchantability under § 2-316(2)?

A. It must mention merchantability.
B. It can be written or oral.
C. It must be conspicuous if written.
D. It must use language that calls the buyer's attention to the exclusion of warranties.

QUESTION 25. Does ¶ 10 of the contract satisfy the requirement that a written exclusion must be conspicuous? Feel free to look at the definition of conspicuous in § 1-201(b)(10).

A. Yes, because the heading is in capital letters.
B. Yes, because the language in the body of the text is in larger type than the surrounding text.
C. No, because the heading is not in capital letters.
D. No, because there is nothing that calls attention to the word merchantability.

QUESTION 26. Brenda, a law student, sees that Sally, another law student, is selling word processing software. Brenda says, "I need software to prepare my law review article," and Sally replies, "I'll sell this for $25." Brenda says it's a deal and they make the exchange. Brenda then discovers that although the software is perfectly good in every other respect, it doesn't create footnotes. For which of the following does Brenda have a claim? Feel free to look at §§ 2-314 and 2-315 before you answer.

A. Breach of the implied warranty of merchantability only.
B. Breach of the implied warranty of fitness for a particular purpose only.
C. Both of the above.
D. Neither of the above.

QUESTION 27. Which of the following is effective to disclaim the implied warranty of fitness for a particular purpose? Feel free to look at § 2-316(2) before you answer.

A. Seller orally states, in language that becomes part of the contract, "I am not giving you an implied warranty of fitness for a particular purpose."
B. The contract states, "There is no implied warranty of fitness."
C. The contract states, "THERE IS NO IMPLIED WARRANTY OF FITNESS."
D. The contract states, "THERE IS NO IMPLIED WARRANTY OF MERCHANTABILITY."

QUESTION 28. Which of the following is sufficient under § 2-316(3)(a) to disclaim both the implied warranty of merchantability and the implied warranty of fitness for a particular purpose? Feel free to look at § 2-316(3)(a) before you answer.

A. The goods are sold as is.
B. The goods are sold AS IS.
C. THERE ARE NO WARRANTIES WITH THIS SALE.
D. THERE ARE NO WARRANTIES WITH THIS SALE INCLUDING BUT NOT LIMITED TO THE IMPLIED WARRANTY OF MERCHANTABILITY.

QUESTION 29. A supplier of used cars to used car dealers has made a number of sales to a particular dealer using a contract that contains a disclaimer similar to the one found in ¶ 10 of our contract. The supplier then tells the dealer that he has a certain car available for him for a certain price and the dealer says it's a deal. After the car has been delivered and paid for, the dealer claims there was a breach of the implied warranty of merchantability even though no contract was signed. Was there an effective disclaimer of the implied warranty of merchantability in this transaction?

A. Yes, under § 2-316(2).
B. Yes, under § 2-316(3)(a).
C. Yes, under § 2-316(3)(c).
D. No.

QUESTION 30. Paragraph 11 states that Buyer pays the price on Seller's price list. What keeps Seller from posting a high price on the list and then passing that price on to Buyer? Feel free to look at § 2-305 before you answer.

A. The price charged must be reasonable.
B. The price term cannot be unconscionable.
C. The price must be fixed in good faith.
D. There is nothing in the Code to prevent Seller from doing that.

QUESTION 31. Paragraph 11 states that the Buyer shall pay the price on Seller's price list. What happens if Seller doesn't publish a price list? Feel free to read § 2-305 before you answer.

A. There is no contract.
B. The price is a reasonable price.
C. Buyer may establish the price.
D. Buyer may either cancel the contract or fix a reasonable price.

QUESTION 32. Paragraph 12 provides for time of payment. In the absence of the parties' agreement, what is the default rule for time of payment? Feel free to look at § 2-507 before you answer.

A. Seller must deliver before Buyer pays.
B. Buyer must pay before Seller delivers.
C. Buyer has 30 days from delivery to pay.
D. Buyer pays at the time Seller delivers.

QUESTION 33. Frequently the parties change the default rule to allow the buyer a period of time after delivery, such as 30 days, to make payment. This represents a change in the default rule, for the seller now makes delivery unconditionally, without any obligation for the buyer to pay at the time of delivery. If a buyer does not pay 30 days later, what is the seller's remedy?

A. The seller can take the goods back.
B. The seller can recover the price the buyer was supposed to pay.
C. The seller can recover the price plus attorney's fees.
D. The seller has no remedy.

QUESTION 34. Assume that the contract provides that Seller gives Buyer 30 days after delivery to pay. Just before the time for delivery, Seller hears from other creditors that Buyer has not been promptly paying its bills. Seller calls you for advice. What do you recommend Seller should do? Feel free to read § 2-609 before you answer.

A. Refuse to deliver the goods.
B. Demand that Buyer pay cash on delivery.
C. Demand reasonable assurances from Buyer.
D. Deliver the goods as per the contract.

QUESTION 35. In ¶ 13 of our contract, Seller gives Buyer the right to inspect the goods on delivery. If this term were not in the contract, would Buyer have the right to inspect the goods before paying for them?

A. Buyer has a right to inspect the goods before payment or acceptance.
B. Buyer has the right only to inspect the goods for observable nonconformities.
C. Unless otherwise agreed, Buyer must pay for the goods and then inspect them.
D. Buyer has no right of inspection and the parties cannot contract around this provision.

QUESTION 36. In ¶ 14 of our contract, Seller requires payment in cash or certified check. In the absence of this provision, what manner of payment would Seller be required by the Code to accept? Feel free to read § 2-511 before you answer.

A. Legal tender.
B. Check.
C. Certified check.
D. The method of payment that is normal in that particular business.

QUESTION 37. Assume ¶ 14 was not in the agreement and the default rule of § 2-511 governed. Buyer tenders a check at the time of delivery, but Seller has heard rumors that some of Buyer's checks have bounced. Does Seller have the right to demand legal tender? Feel free to look at § 2-511 before you answer.

A. Yes, Seller can do so unconditionally.
B. Yes, but Seller must give Buyer additional time to come up with the money.
C. No, Seller would be in breach.
D. No, but Seller could demand assurances.

QUESTION 38. A law professor orally agrees to sell a law student his Ted Williams autographed baseball for $1,000. The student emails a friend, "I just made a great deal. I'm buying a Ted Williams autographed baseball from my Contracts professor for $1,000." The friend tells the student that he made a poor deal. Will the student be successful in claiming that the contract is unenforceable because of the Statute of Frauds?

A. Yes, because this is a transaction for the sale of goods for over $500.
B. No, because the transaction is evidenced by a writing signed by the party against whom enforcement is sought.
C. No, because the writing does not sufficiently evidence the transaction.
D. Trick question! This is not a UCC transaction.

QUESTION 39. Assume that the professor and the student agreed in writing that the professor would sell the student the Ted Williams autographed baseball for $1,000, and they also agreed orally that the student could return it in 30 days for any reason. Is there anything wrong with this agreement being enforceable because it is partly written and partly oral?

A. The Statute of Frauds says the agreement must be in writing.
B. The oral agreement may be hard to prove—it's a matter of one party's word against the other.
C. The agreement that is partly written and partly oral is enforceable.
D. The agreement that is partly written and partly oral is not enforceable.

QUESTION 40. Assume that the professor and the student agreed in writing that the professor would sell the student the Ted Williams autographed baseball for $1,000, and they also agreed orally that the student could return it in 30 days for any reason. The writing contained a term that stated "No returns. All sales final." Could the student introduce evidence of their oral agreement?

A. Yes, it would be a question of fact whether the agreement was made.
B. It depends whether they intended their writing to be final and exclusive.
C. No, because of the Statute of Frauds.
D. No, because of the Parol Evidence Rule.

QUESTION 41. Assume that the professor and the student agreed in writing that the professor would sell the student the Ted Williams autographed baseball for $1,000, and they also agreed orally that the student could return it in 30 days for any reason. The writing was silent on the subject of returns. Could the student introduce evidence of their oral agreement?

A. Yes, because the agreement was not their final agreement.
B. Yes, because the evidence does not contradict the writing.
C. It depends whether they intended their writing to be final and exclusive.
D. No, because they intended their writing to be final and exclusive.

QUESTION 42. The parties agree that their writing is intended to be the complete and exclusive statement of the terms of the agreement. In order to supplement the terms of the writing, one of the parties wishes to offer evidence of what these same parties did under earlier agreements. Is the evidence admissible?

A. Yes, because evidence of course of performance that supplements the agreement is admissible even if the writing is complete and exclusive.
B. Yes, because evidence of course of dealing that supplements the agreement is admissible even if the writing is complete and exclusive.
C. No, because when the parties intend the writing to be the complete and exclusive statement of the terms of the agreement, evidence may not be offered to supplement it.
D. No, because when the parties intend the writing to be the complete and exclusive statement of the terms of the agreement, evidence may not be offered to contradict it.

QUESTION 43. Assume that in the widget business it is not customary for a seller to sell widgets with full fuel tanks, but every time Seller has had a contract to supply widgets to Buyer, Seller has filled the fuel tanks. In performing the latest contract, Seller does not fill the fuel tanks. Is Seller in breach?

A. Yes, because of course of performance.
B. Yes, because of course of dealing.
C. Yes, because of usage of trade.
D. No.

QUESTION 44. The third sentence of ¶ 16 of our contract states: "Acceptance or acquiescence in a course of performance rendered under this agreement shall not be relevant to determine the meaning of this agreement even though the accepting or acquiescing party has knowledge of the nature of the performance and opportunity for objection." Assume a paragraph of the agreement says that Seller is to service the widget "regularly." Buyer claims Seller is in breach for not servicing frequently enough. Seller offers evidence that it has serviced the widget every month for five months. What is this kind of evidence called?

A. Express term.
B. Course of performance.
C. Course of dealing.
D. Usage of trade.

QUESTION 45. The last sentence of ¶ 16 states that the Code is a "dictionary" for terms used in the agreement. It provides: "Whenever a term defined by the Uniform Commercial Code is used in this agreement the definition contained in the Code is to control." Assume the parties provided in the agreement: "Seller shall repair defects in the widgets within ten days from when Buyer gives notice to Seller of the defects." Buyer claims Seller is in breach because Buyer sent notice to Seller and the widgets were not repaired within ten days. Seller claims it never received the notice. What should a court that found these facts determine? Feel free to look at § 1-202 before you answer.

A. Seller is not in breach because it didn't receive the notice.
B. Seller is not in breach because Buyer didn't send notice to Seller.
C. Seller is in breach because it received notice.
D. Seller is in breach because Buyer gave notice.

QUESTION 46. Assume the contract specifies a price of $100 per widget. Seller calls Buyer and explains that widget production costs have risen dramatically, that he will lose money at that price, and he requests Buyer to agree to pay his costs, which are $105 per widget. Buyer agrees and they write up the modification. On delivery, Buyer refuses to pay more than $100. Is the modification enforceable? Feel free to look at § 2-209 before you answer.

A. Yes, because the general common law rule is that no consideration is required.
B. Yes, because the Code has dispensed with the requirement of consideration.
C. No, because Seller did not act in good faith.
D. No, because the general common law rule is that consideration is required.

QUESTION 47. Assume the contract specifies a price of $100 per widget. Seller discovers that Buyer needs the widgets or his assembly line will stop running, and no widgets are available from other suppliers. Seller tells Buyer she will still deliver for $150. Buyer agrees and they write up the modification. On delivery, Buyer refuses to pay more than $100. Is the modification enforceable? Feel free to look at § 2-209 before you answer.

A. Yes, because the general common law rule is that no consideration is required.
B. Yes, because the Code has dispensed with the requirement of consideration.
C. No, because Seller did not act in good faith.
D. No, because the general common law rule is that consideration is required.

QUESTION 48. Under our contract, does a modification that is not within the Statute of Frauds have to be reduced to writing to be enforceable? Feel free to look at § 2-209 and ¶ 18 of our contract before you answer.

A. No, because a contract not within the Statute of Frauds is enforceable if oral.
B. No, because the Statute of Frauds does not apply to modifications.
C. Yes, because the Code requires modifications to be in writing.
D. Yes, because the parties' agreement requires modifications to be in writing.

QUESTION 49. Assume that our contract specifies that the time of delivery is not before October 1 or after October 30. Seller puts these dates in a tickler file. On October 15, Seller calls Buyer and asks if it would be all right to deliver on November 2. Buyer says that is not a problem. On November 2, when Seller delivers, Buyer claims that Seller is in breach. Seller says, "But we had an agreement." Buyer says, "Look at the contract. That modification didn't count because it wasn't in writing. You're in breach under the only contract that matters—the written one." What is Seller's best defense to this claim? Feel free to look at § 2-209 and ¶¶ 18 and 19 of our contract before you answer.

A. The requirement that modifications must be in writing is not enforceable.
B. Buyer's admission that they made the modification removes the impediment of the writing requirement.
C. Buyer had a right to insist on a writing but waived that right.
D. Buyer is not acting in good faith.

QUESTION 50. Assume again that our contract specifies that the time of delivery is not before October 1 or after October 30. On October 15, Seller orally requests a change in the delivery date to November 2, and Buyer agrees. Later that same day, Buyer calls Seller back and says, "I changed my mind. I won't give you the additional time. I expect performance by October 30." Which of the following statements best describes the legal situation of the parties? Feel free to look at § 2-209 and ¶¶ 18 and 19 of our contract before you answer.

A. Because of waiver, the modification stands.
B. The modification was never effective.
C. Buyer's retraction is effective because Seller had not yet delivered.
D. Buyer's retraction is effective unless Seller has relied on the modification.

QUESTION 51. Assume that a contract provides that a seller will deliver 100 widgets no later than October 30. The seller delivers the widgets on November 10. If the buyer agrees in writing not to assert a claim against the seller, is the agreement enforceable? Feel free to look at § 1-306 before you answer.

A. No. Because the buyer had no claim against the seller, there is no consideration for the promise.
B. No. Even though the buyer had a claim against the seller, there is no consideration for the promise.
C. Yes. The general rule is that contracts for the settlement of claims do not require consideration to be enforceable.
D. Yes. Under the Code, a written agreement discharging a claim is enforceable without consideration.

QUESTION 52. If the same facts as in the previous question arose under our contract, would the agreement be effective? Feel free to look at § 1-306 and ¶ 19 before you answer.

A. No, because the Code language governs as the parties are not free to change it.
B. No, because the parties did not effectively change the Code language.
C. No, because the parties would be held to have waived this provision by their conduct.
D. Yes, because the parties have freedom of contract to change the Code rules.

QUESTION 53. Buyer and Seller agree that Seller will sell 100 widgets to Buyer for $10,000. What are the respective rights under the contract?

A. Buyer has the right to receive 100 widgets; Seller has the right to receive $10,000.
B. Buyer has the right to receive 100 widgets; Seller has the right to tender 100 widgets.
C. Buyer has the right to pay $10,000; Seller has the right to tender 100 widgets.
D. Buyer has the right to pay $10,000; Seller has the right to receive $10,000.

QUESTION 54. If Seller tells Buyer that XYZ will deliver the widgets and that Buyer should pay XYZ, how would you characterize what has happened?

A. Seller has assigned the contract to XYZ.
B. Seller has delegated the contract to XYZ.
C. Seller has assigned its rights and duties to XYZ.
D. Seller has assigned its rights and delegated its duties to XYZ.

QUESTION 55. Which of the following statements about delegation of duties is not true?

A. In general, parties may delegate their duties.
B. The parties are free to provide that duties may not be delegated.
C. There may be circumstances in which delegation is not permitted.
D. After delegation, the original party is no longer responsible for performance.

QUESTION 56. Assume that the parties take advantage of their freedom of contract and state in the contract: "This contract may not be assigned." What have the parties accomplished?

A. Rights may not be assigned.
B. Duties may not be delegated.
C. Both of the above.
D. Neither of the above.

QUESTION 57. Assume the contract does not prohibit assignment and delegation. Seller delegates to XYZ Manufacturing the duty of providing the goods. Buyer has had bad experiences with XYZ. What should Buyer do?

A. Terminate the contract with Seller.
B. Refuse to accept the goods from XYZ.
C. Demand assurances from XYZ.
D. There is nothing Buyer can do because delegation is permitted.

QUESTION 58. In our contract, the parties have not only effectively prohibited assignment and delegation in ¶ 20, but they have also added this sentence: "Any attempted assignment or delegation shall be wholly void and totally ineffective for all purposes unless made in conformity with this paragraph." What does this language add to the contract?

A. It does not add anything but merely restates the default rule.
B. If one party assigns or delegates, it permits the other to terminate the contract.
C. It discourages assignment and delegation by permitting punitive damages.
D. It puts more teeth into the prohibition of assignment and delegation.

QUESTION 59. Paragraph 21 of our contract, captioned "Time for Bringing Action," states that "any action for breach of this contract must be commenced within two years after the cause of action has accrued." Did the parties change the default rule?

A. No, the statute of limitations under the Code is two years.
B. Yes, the statute of limitations under the Code is four years.
C. Yes, the statute of limitations under the Code is four years and an action must be commenced within four years from the time a party has knowledge that it has a cause of action.
D. Yes, the statute of limitations under the Code is eight years for a written contract and five years for an oral contract.

QUESTION 60. A contract between a seller and a buyer included a one-year warranty against defects. The seller delivered 100 widgets on October 1 and the buyer accepted them. By October 15, a reasonable buyer would have discovered that the widgets were defective. On November 1, the buyer discovered that the widgets were defective, and sent notice to the seller. How long does the buyer have to commence an action for breach of warranty?

A. Five years from October 1.
B. Four years from October 1.
C. Four years from October 15.
D. Four years from November 1.

QUESTION 61. Paragraph 22 of our contract, "Applicable Law," is often called the "Choice of Law" provision in a contract. Assume the parties filled in the blank to say that they wanted the Uniform Commercial Code as adopted in the State of California to govern their agreement. What is the legal effect of that choice?

A. Any claim would be resolved in California.
B. Any claim would be resolved using California law.
C. Both of the above.
D. Neither of the above.

QUESTION 62. Assume a contract was signed in California for the sale of goods between a business in Oregon and a business in China and the parties did not include a Choice of Law clause. What would be the governing law?

A. California UCC.
B. Oregon UCC.
C. China contract law.
D. United Nations Convention on Contracts for the International Sale of Goods.

QUESTION 63. Which of the following is the best language for a drafter to use when it wants the law of California to apply to a contract for the sale of goods between a U.S. company and a Chinese company?

A. This contract is governed by the law of California.
B. This contract is governed by the UNIDROIT Principles, supplemented when necessary by the UCC of California.
C. This contract is governed by the UCC as enacted in California.
D. This contract is governed by the law of California, except for principles of choice of law.

QUESTION 64. How will disputes under this contract be resolved? Feel free to look at ¶ 23 before you answer.

A. They will go to court because of the default rule.
B. They will go to arbitration because the Code requires it.
C. They will go to arbitration because the Federal Arbitration Act requires it.
D. They will go to arbitration because they contractually agreed to it.

QUESTION 65. Just above the signature line, the contract states that it is "signed and sealed." What is the significance of the seal under the Code? Feel free to look at § 2-203 before you answer.

A. Each party must affix its corporate seal for the contract to be enforceable.
B. The Code requires that contracts be evidenced by a seal.
C. The parties have agreed that the signatures must be notarized.
D. The language is traditional, but it has no substantive significance.

> **QUESTION 66.** Two parties used this form contract when they sold software that was delivered on a disk. If a warranty dispute arises, to what extent is a court likely to apply the UCC?
>
> **A.** It will not apply the UCC, because software is not a good.
> **B.** It will apply the UCC, because the software was embedded on a disk, which is a good.
> **C.** It will apply the UCC, because the parties captioned the contract "AGREEMENT FOR THE SALE OF GOODS."
> **D.** It will apply the UCC by analogy, because the parties modeled their warranty terms after the terms in the UCC.

 # Burnham's picks

Question 1. Article 2 applies to transactions in goods. See § 2-102. Goods are defined as movables. See § 2-105(1). A ballpoint pen is a movable. Therefore, it is a good. Therefore, Article 2 applies to its sale. The correct response is **D**.

Question 2. Section 2-204(3) provides that "[e]ven though one or more terms are left open a contract for sale does not fail for indefiniteness if the parties have intended to make a contract and there is a reasonably certain basis for giving an appropriate remedy." Here, the fact that the parties wrote those words and signed the paper evidences an intention to make a contract. The fact that there is a price and quantity provides a basis for giving a remedy. If either party breaches, we can calculate damages.

We then would look to the UCC gap fillers to fill in the missing parts of the contract. There is a gap filler for price, so that is not a required term. Quantity, however, must generally be specified. Therefore, the correct response is **B**.

Question 3. Quantity is a crucial factor in a contract, for a missing quantity usually cannot be supplied by the gap fillers. The description of the goods creates an express warranty. See § 2-313(1). The identity of the specific parties contracting is an important term. Article 2 generally dispenses with the concept of title. Official Comment 1 to § 2-101 states in part: "The legal consequences are stated as following directly from the contract and action taken under it without resorting to the idea of when property or title passed or was to pass as being the determining factor." Therefore, the best response is **B**.

Question 4. Section 2-309(1) provides: "The time for shipment or delivery or any other action under a contract if not provided in this Article or agreed upon shall be a reasonable time." The correct response is **D**.

Question 5.   Section 1-302(a) provides that "Except as otherwise provided in subsection (b) or elsewhere in [the Uniform Commercial Code], the effect of provisions of [the Uniform Commercial Code] may be varied by Agreement." First, remember that provisions in Article 1 govern throughout the UCC. Second, as stated in Official Comment 1 to § 1-302, the Code preserves freedom of contract, allowing the parties to change the rules except where the Code says they cannot. Third, think of the Code as providing "default rules" that apply in the absence of agreement otherwise, just as your word processor uses default settings unless you provide a setting that overrides the default. The correct response is **A**.

Question 6.   Section 1-302(b) provides:

> The obligations of good faith, diligence, reasonableness, and care prescribed by [the Uniform Commercial Code] may not be disclaimed by agreement. The parties, by agreement, may determine the standards by which the performance of those obligations is to be measured if those standards are not manifestly unreasonable.

Putting this together with the general exception in § 1-302(a) ("Except as otherwise provided in subsection (b) or elsewhere in [the Uniform Commercial Code]"), it is apparent that the only exception to the exceptions is response **D**, which is the correct response.

Question 7.   Although Buyer has the right to specify the date of delivery, Buyer has to be reasonable in doing so. By confining Buyer's choice to certain dates, the parties are determining what is reasonable. The correct response is **C**.

Question 8.   Section 2-307 states: "Unless otherwise agreed all goods called for by a contract for sale must be tendered in a single delivery." The correct response is **C**.

Question 9.   Section 2-307 states an exception to the rule of a single delivery: "where the circumstances give either party the right to make or demand delivery in lots the price if it can be apportioned may be demanded for each lot." Here, the circumstances give Seller the right to make delivery in lots. The correct response is **D**.

Question 10.   Seller is now is in breach, for Buyer has the right under the contract to demand all of the goods at one time. Section 2-307 will not aid Seller, for the exception only kicks in "unless otherwise agreed" and here the parties otherwise agreed. The lesson here is to beware of what you promise in your contract. The correct response is **B**.

Question 11.   Section 2-308 states: "Unless otherwise agreed . . . the place for delivery of goods is the seller's place of business." The correct response is **A**.

Question 12.   Section 2-308 states: "Unless otherwise agreed . . . the place for delivery of goods is the seller's place of business or if he has none his residence." Because the law professor is not in the business of selling refrigerators, the place of delivery is his or her house. The correct response is **A**. I am hopeful that you did not choose response **C**. This is a transaction in goods, so Article 2 applies. End of story.

Question 13.   The Code makes a distinction between a *shipment* contract and a *destination* contract. Under a shipment contract, the seller arranges for delivery and delivers the goods to a carrier. In a contract between a seller in Missoula and a buyer in Las Vegas, this could be achieved by the designation "F.O.B. Missoula." See §§ 2-504 and 2-319. Under a destination contract, the seller must deliver the goods to the location specified. In a contract between seller in Missoula and buyer in Las Vegas, this could be designated "F.O.B. Las Vegas." See §§ 2-503 and 2-319. Designating a contract as shipment or destination does not determine who pays for delivery, however. In the absence of an understanding to the contrary, the seller pays to get the goods to the carrier and the buyer pays thereafter. The correct response is **C**.

Question 14.   When subsections 1 and 2 don't apply, usually the general rule in subsection 3 applies—when the seller is a merchant, the risk of loss passes to the buyer on receipt of the goods. However, according to subsection (4), the parties may agree to the contrary. Here, they have stated in ¶ 7 that the risk of loss passes not on receipt of the goods but on identification. The correct response is **D**. This is bad news for Buyer, who should be sure to get the goods insured while they are in Seller's possession.

Question 15.   Section 2-501(1) provides that "identification occurs (a) when the contract is made if it is for the sale of goods already existing and identified; (b) if the contract is for the sale of future goods . . . when goods are shipped, marked or otherwise designated by the seller as goods to which the contract refers." Here, there is not a contract for the sale of goods already existing and identified, for the seller has in no way designated what part of the inventory is the buyer's goods. Therefore, the contract does not adopt the default rule. The correct response is **D**. Note again that Buyer is taking a risk. If, for example, Seller's inventory is destroyed, then Buyer bears the risk of loss.

Question 16.   Paragraph 8 concerns title. Title is generally not important in the UCC as between the buyer and the seller. However, when determining the rights of third parties to the goods, it may be necessary to determine who has title. Therefore, to determine the rights of a third party, it may be necessary to determine whether the seller or the buyer has title. The default rule on title, stated in § 2-401(2), is that the seller retains title until seller delivers the goods, unless the agreement provides otherwise. The contract adopts the default rule. Paragraph 8 provides that Seller has title until delivery. Therefore, response **A** is correct.

Note that in this contract payment is due on delivery. Sometimes when a seller extends credit to the buyer, the seller changes the default rule, as in response **D**, to provide that the buyer does not have title until the goods are paid for. As you will see when you study secured transactions, the transaction is then said to be a sale to the buyer with the reservation of a security interest by the seller.

Question 17.   This is a good example of the freedom of contract that parties have under the Code. Under ¶¶ 7 and 8, Buyer has the risk of loss during this time, and because Buyer does not have title until he receives possession, he has no claim to the goods during this time. The correct response is **D**.

Buyer should make sure he has insurance to cover the goods while in the hands of Seller. The more usual situation, provided for in the Code's default rules, is that a buyer does not have the risk of loss until the buyer receives possession of the goods, for that is when the buyer's insurance usually provides protection.

Question 18.   Paragraph 9 concerns express warranties, which are the subject of § 2-313 of the Code. The language of response **A** is a description of the goods. If they are not widgets or are not type A, Seller is in breach of express warranty. The language of response **B** is an affirmation of fact that the goods are made of 100% titanium. If they are not, Seller is in breach of express warranty. The language of response **C** is not an affirmation of fact or promise, but "puffing" of the goods. Statements like this don't create an express warranty. The language of response **D** is an express warranty created by sample or model. If the goods delivered don't conform to the sample, Buyer has a claim for breach of express warranty. The correct response is **C**.

Question 19.   Seller made a warranty when it described the goods as type-A widgets. Seller also negated express warranties. Section 2-316(1) provides that when words create warranty and other words negate warranty, and the two cannot be read together, then the negation is inoperative. Therefore, the warranty is given. The correct response is **D**. What is the function of the words of negation? Essentially it is saying, "I am not giving you any express warranties other than those found in this writing."

Question 20.   This language would create an express warranty under § 2-313(1)(b). We are told that the writing is not a fully integrated agreement, so the warranty is not barred by the parol evidence rule. Although it is difficult to disclaim an express warranty, it seems to me that this is the kind of statement a seller negates by putting a disclaimer in the contract. The correct response is **B**.

To review, this language when spoken before the contract could be excluded under the parol evidence rule. If it is not, it is effectively disclaimed by the disclaimer. When the language is found in the contract, we have a situation as described in § 2-316(1) where the warranty is both given and disclaimed. It is then deemed to be given.

Question 21. Section 2-312(1)(b) includes a warranty that "the goods shall be delivered free from any security interest or other lien or encumbrance." This is called the *Warranty of Title* and it is implied in every contract for sale (even though it is technically not an implied warranty) unless excluded by specific language. The correct response is **B**.

Question 22. We are now looking at the Implied Warranty of Merchantability, § 2-314. This is the subject of ¶ 10 of the contract, Disclaimer of Implied Warranties. The list of what it means for goods to be merchantable in § 2-314(2) contains the language of responses **A**, **B**, and **C**, but not **D**. Probably the most commonly used definition is (c)—the goods are fit for the ordinary purpose for which the goods are used. The correct response is **D**. This language describes an Implied Warranty of Fitness for a Particular Purpose.

Question 23. You know that response **D** is incorrect, because the transaction involves the sale of goods. According to § 2-314(1), "a warranty that the goods shall be merchantable is implied in a contract for their sale if the seller is a merchant with respect to goods of that kind." Here, it is fair to assume that the law professor is not a refrigerator merchant, so the correct response is **C**. Used goods sold by merchants do come with an implied warranty of merchantability—but the refrigerator must have only as much fitness as can reasonably be expected from a used refrigerator, which might not be much.

Question 24. Section 2-316(2) provides:

§ 2-316. Exclusion or Modification of Warranties.

(2) Subject to subsection (3), to exclude or modify the implied warranty of merchantability or any part of it the language must mention merchantability and in case of a writing must be conspicuous, and to exclude or modify any implied warranty of fitness the exclusion must be by a writing and conspicuous. Language to exclude all implied warranties of fitness is sufficient if it states, for example, that "There are no warranties which extend beyond the description on the face hereof."

Responses **A**, **B**, and **C** all state requirements under § 2-316(2). Response **D** states a requirement under § 2-316(3)(a). The correct response is **D**.

Question 25. Section 1-201(b)(10) provides:

(10) "Conspicuous," with reference to a term, means so written, displayed, or presented that a reasonable person against which it is to operate ought to have noticed it. Whether a term is "conspicuous" or not is a decision for the court. Conspicuous terms include the following:

(A) a heading in capitals equal to or greater in size than the surrounding text, or in contrasting type, font, or color to the surrounding text of the same or lesser size; and

(B) language in the body of a record or display in larger type than the surrounding text, or in contrasting type, font, or color to the surrounding text of the same size, or set off from surrounding text of the same size by symbols or other marks that call attention to the language.

According to § 1-201(b)(10)(A), it would be sufficient if the heading were in capital letters, but that is not the case here. Instead, the text itself is in capitals, which satisfies § 1-201(b)(10)(B). The correct response is **B**. Note that although the text must mention the word *merchantability* to satisfy § 2-316(2), there is no requirement that attention be called to that word.

Question 26. There is no § 2-314 implied warranty of merchantability because the seller, Sally, is not a merchant. There is a § 2-315 implied warranty of fitness for a particular purpose because the buyer, Brenda, communicated a particular purpose—not just word processing software fit for ordinary purposes, but word processing software that would create footnotes—and the seller used her skill or judgment to provide goods that would satisfy that purpose. Note that this warranty can be given by any seller. The correct response is **B**.

Question 27. Section 2-316(2) provides that "to exclude or modify any implied warranty of fitness the exclusion must be by a writing and conspicuous." Unlike disclaimer of the implied warranty of merchantability, it does not have to utilize particular words, but it does have to be in writing and it must be conspicuous. The correct response is **C**, because there is a writing and it is conspicuous.

Question 28. Section 2-316(3)(a) provides an easy way to disclaim the implied warranties of merchantability and fitness (note that under § 2-312(2) the implied warranty of good title must be more specifically disclaimed). Use of phrases like "as is" are sufficient. Even though the statute does not require that the phrase be conspicuous, most courts have read in that requirement. Therefore, **B** is the best response.

Although the language used in response **C** looks as though it would make plain that there is no implied warranty, most courts have found that such language represents a failed attempt to disclaim implied warranties under § 2-316(2) rather than a successful attempt under § 2-316(3)(a). The language of response **D** would probably be sufficient under § 2-316(2), but you were asked to respond with respect to § 2-316(3)(a). Of course, not everyone understands the meaning of "as is," which is why the Federal Trade Commission adopted the Used Car Trade Regulation Rule, which requires sellers of used cars to consumers to place a sticker on the car that makes clear what warranties are included with the purchase.

Question 29. The agreement for the sale of this particular car would incorporate the terms of the previous deals under the concept of course of dealing.

See § 1-303(b). Section 2-316(3)(c) provides that "an implied warranty can also be excluded or modified by course of dealing or course of performance or usage of trade." Their course of dealing included ¶ 10, which contains language that is effective to disclaim the implied warranty of merchantability. The correct response is **C**.

Question 30.   Section 2-305(2) provides that "a price to be fixed by the seller or the buyer means a price for him to fix in good faith." The correct response is **C**.

Question 31.   This situation would probably fall under § 2-305(3), which provides:

> When a price left to be fixed otherwise than by agreement of the parties fails to be fixed through fault of one party the other may at his option treat the contract as cancelled or himself fix a reasonable price.

The correct response is **D**.

Question 32.   The correct response is **D**. The rule of § 2-507 is the same in common law, where it is called the rule of "constructive conditions of exchange." That is, even in the absence of the parties' agreement, payment is a condition of delivery and delivery is a condition of payment. If one party does not perform, the other does not have to.

Question 33.   The correct response is **B**. See § 2-607(1). This is not much of a remedy, so a seller who extends credit should think about building some other remedy into the contract. For example, if the seller takes a security interest in the goods, then it can take the goods back if the buyer does not pay. Recall that the American Rule on attorney's fees is that each side must pay its own attorney's fees whether it wins or loses. A prudent seller would also change this default rule by providing in the contract for the prevailing party to recover attorney's fees.

Question 34.   The Code in § 2-609 has a very practical solution to this problem. If either party (in our problem, Seller) has reasonable grounds for insecurity (here the reports of erratic payment by Buyer), then that party may in writing demand adequate assurances of performance (here from Buyer) and may suspend its own performance until it gets them. If it doesn't get them, it can hold the other party to have breached by anticipatory repudiation. If it does get them, it should be content to continue with the contract as agreed or to make a modification that makes it more secure. Response **A** is not correct because Buyer has not repudiated. Response **B** is not correct because although Seller is entitled to commercially reasonable assurances, it is probably not entitled to rewrite the contract in its favor. The best response is **C**.

Question 35.   Section 2-513(1) provides:

(1) Unless otherwise agreed and subject to subsection (3), where goods are tendered or delivered or identified to the contract for sale, the buyer has a right before payment or acceptance to inspect them at any reasonable place and time and in any reasonable manner.

The correct response is **A**. This is an important right, because the buyer has the right to reject for any nonconformity and it is during inspection that nonconformities are usually discovered.

Question 36.   The correct response is **D**. Section 2-511(2) provides for payment by "any means or in any manner current in the ordinary course of business." In most businesses, checks are the ordinary means of payment. If that is the case here, Seller is being very tough on Buyer by demanding legal tender or certified check.

Question 37.   The correct response is **B**. Section 2-511 states that the seller can demand payment in legal tender but it must give the buyer an extension of time to procure it.

Question 38.   A *Statute of Frauds* is any statute that provides that a certain transaction must be evidenced by a writing to be enforceable. In the UCC, the Statute of Frauds is found at § 2-201. It provides that a contract for the sale of goods for the price of $500 or more is not enforceable unless evidenced by a writing. The statute doesn't require that the contract *be* in writing. It requires that there be "some writing sufficient to indicate that a contract for sale has been made between the parties and signed by the party against whom enforcement is sought." The student's email to a friend satisfies the statute. It is signed by the party against whom enforcement of the contract is sought— the student. Note that the definition of "signed" in § 1-201(b)(37) provides: "'Signed' includes using any symbol executed or adopted with present intention to adopt or accept a writing." For this purpose, the email would be considered a signed writing. The correct response is **B**.

Question 39.   Such an agreement would satisfy the Statute of Frauds as long as the written part was "sufficient to indicate that a contract for sale has been made between the parties and signed by the party against whom enforcement is sought." The statute goes on to say that "a writing is not insufficient because it omits or incorrectly states a term agreed upon." It may be wise for the parties to write down all the terms, but what those terms were is a question of fact. The agreement is perfectly enforceable as a matter of law. The correct response is **C**.

Question 40.   The Article 2 Parol Evidence Rule is found in § 2-202. It provides in pertinent part:

Terms . . . which are . . . set forth in a writing intended by the parties as a final expression of their agreement with respect to such terms as are included therein may not be contradicted by evidence of any prior agreement . . . but may be . . . supplemented . . . by evidence of consistent additional terms. . . .

That basic rule states that a final writing governs over contradictory oral expressions. This makes sense, for parties reading the written contract ought to speak up if it contradicts what they understood from negotiations. Here, the oral agreement offered by the student contradicts a term of the writing and will be excluded under the rule. The correct response is **D**.

Question 41. Note that the evidence here does not contradict the writing; it supplements it. Because it is perfectly acceptable to have an agreement that is partly written and partly oral, the parol evidence rule only excludes supplementary oral terms when the parties intend the writing to be the final and complete statement of their agreement. This is what the last part of § 2-202 provides. It states that the supplementary oral terms are admissible "unless the court finds the writing to have been intended also as a complete and exclusive statement of the terms of the agreement." When the parties intend the writing to be a complete and exclusive statement of the agreement, we say the agreement is *integrated* or the entire agreement is *merged* in the writing. The correct response is **C**.

The issue in parol evidence cases frequently is this: How do you determine whether the parties intended to integrate the entire agreement in the writing? A good starting point, although by no means the final word, is for the parties to state in their agreement that they intend the writing to be the complete and exclusive statement of the terms of the agreement. Such a provision is called a *merger clause* or *integration clause*. A merger clause is found in the first sentence of ¶ 16 of our agreement:

This writing is intended by the parties as a final expression of their agreement and is intended also as a complete and exclusive statement of the terms of their agreement.

Courts are likely to give more weight to a merger clause in a negotiated commercial contract than to one in a contract of adhesion. Paragraph 17 further strengthens the merger clause.

Question 42. Under these facts, evidence of course of dealing is offered to supplement the terms of the writing. According to § 2-202(a), this evidence, along with evidence of course of performance and trade usage, is permitted even if the writing is complete and exclusive. Note that the "unless" clause that modifies "evidence of consistent additional terms" in § 2-202(b) is not found in § 2-202(a). The correct response is **B**.

Note that this is a default rule that can be changed by agreement. In our contract, the bracketed language in ¶ 16 changes this default rule: "[No course of prior dealings between the parties and no usage of the trade shall be relevant to supplement or explain any term used in this agreement.]" Excluding prior dealings and trade usage is dangerous. Because parties often incorporate these usages unconsciously, before adopting this change they must be sure they have not incorporated any trade usages.

Question 43.   Course of dealing refers to the performance under previous contracts between the parties. See § 1-303(b). The facts state that it is not customary to fill the tanks in trade usage, but it is customary in contracts between these parties. In the Code hierarchy, course of dealing governs over usage of trade. See § 1-303(e). Therefore, the course of dealing is part of the contract, so Seller is in breach. The correct response is **B**.

Question 44.   Course of performance refers to performance under the parties' present contract. See § 1-303(a). The correct response is **B**. Note that, as they did with course of dealing and trade usage, the parties to this contract have agreed in ¶ 16 that course of performance evidence is not applicable.

Question 45.   In the hypothetical, the ten days started running from when Buyer gives notice to Seller. According to the way "notifies" is defined in § 1-202(d), a party gives notice when it sends the notice "whether or not the other person actually comes to know of it." Therefore, Seller can be in breach even if it did not "receive" the notice. The correct response is **D**. The drafter must know the Code meanings before agreeing to a provision that states that words are used in their Code sense.

Question 46.   Section 2-209(1) specifically does away with any requirement of consideration. Even modifications of non-Code contracts today are often enforced without consideration. See Restatement (Second) of Contracts § 89. The correct response is **B**.

Question 47.   Even though § 2-209(1) does away with any requirement of consideration, the court can still police the contract to make sure one party has not taken advantage of the other. Official Comment 2 states, "However, modifications made [under subsection 1] must meet the test of good faith imposed by this Act. The effective use of bad faith to escape performance on the original contact terms is barred, and the extortion of a 'modification' without legitimate commercial reason is ineffective as a violation of the duty of good faith." Here, Seller did not act in good faith, but took advantage of Buyer's situation. The correct response is **C**.

Question 48.   According to § 2-209(3), "The requirements of the statute of frauds section of this Article (Section 2-201) must be satisfied if the contract as modified is within its provisions." There is some debate as to exactly what this means (review Chapter 7.D.2), but we have specified that the modification is not within the Statute of Frauds, so this provision is not applicable. If a modification is not within the Statute of Frauds, there is no requirement that the modification be in writing. However, the parties have written their own private Statute of Frauds into the contract in ¶ 18, which provides: "This agreement can be modified or rescinded only by a writing signed by both the parties or their duly authorized agents." Therefore, the correct response is **D**.

Question 49.   No matter what they say in their contract, the fact is that parties often make oral modifications of their written agreements. They might file the contract in a file cabinet and not pay attention to it. They might be down on the factory floor when they work out the modification. Or they might work it out by telephone. Section 2-209(4) deals with this practical situation. It provides that a modification that does not satisfy the requirements of subsection 2—permitting a signed agreement to exclude modification except by a signed writing—can operate as a waiver. Seller had the right to say no to the request, but gave up that right by agreeing. The correct response is **C**.

Response **D** is not correct because it is probably not bad faith to insist on enforcement of a term in the contract. Seller might have an argument that ¶ 19 bars Seller from using the defense of waiver. Most courts, however, find in this situation that a party that freely agreed to a modification in the face of a no oral modification clause waived not only the no oral modification clause but also the no waiver clause. The parties' conduct speaks louder than the forgotten words in their contract.

Question 50.   Section 2-209(5) permits a party to retract the waiver if the performance is executory unless the other party has materially relied on the waiver. The correct response is **D**.

Question 51.   The buyer has a claim for breach under § 2-601 if the tender of delivery fails to conform to the contract. The contract called for delivery by October 31, but the goods were tendered on November 10. The buyer received no consideration for giving up this claim, so the promise would not ordinarily be enforceable. But § 1-306 creates an exception, discharging the claim without consideration if the promise is in writing:

> **§ 1-306. Waiver or Renunciation of Claim or Right After Breach.** Any claim or right arising out of an alleged breach may be discharged in whole or in part without consideration by agreement of the aggrieved party in an authenticated record.

The correct response is **D**.

Question 52.   Compare ¶ 19 with § 1-306 and you will see a good example of the drafter tracking the statute while making the changes. The statutory language "A claim . . . may be discharged . . . without consideration" becomes the contract language "No claim . . . can be discharged . . . unless the waiver or renunciation is supported by consideration." It is good drafting to track the language of a statute so there is no doubt as to the meaning. Their agreement expressly addressed the situation and required not only a writing but consideration. I think their agreement would be enforceable under the general rule of § 1-302 that allows parties to change Code provisions. The correct response is **D**.

Question 53.   When analyzing an assignment and delegation problem, it is important to get the vocabulary right. Here, Buyer has the right to receive the widgets and Seller has the right to receive $10,000. The correct response is **A**. If you were asked what are the respective *duties* under the contract, then Seller has the duty to tender 100 widgets and Buyer has the duty to pay $10,000 for them. Once you understand the concept of rights and duties, remember that rights are *assigned* and duties are *delegated.*

Question 54.   Seller had the duty to deliver the widgets and the right to receive the money. When it entered into the transaction with XYZ, it delegated its duties and assigned its rights. The correct response is **D**.

Question 55.   The correct response is **D**. One of the reasons delegation is generally permitted is because the original party remains liable for performance and for breach. As is usually the case, the Code allows the parties to change the default rule and prohibit delegation. Even if the parties do not prohibit it, there may be times delegation is not permitted; for example, when the contract is personal to the contracting parties. See § 2-210(1). For example, where an "output" contract requires the buyer to purchase the entire output of a seller, the seller could not delegate the duty to a supplier with a larger output.

Question 56.   It may surprise you that the correct response is **B**. This error is so common that the Code drafters provided for it. Section 2-210(4) provides that "[u]nless the circumstances indicate the contrary a prohibition of assignment of 'the contract' is to be construed as barring only the delegation to the assignee of the assignor's performance." This is why it is so important to get the vocabulary right, as the drafters of our contract did in ¶ 20.

Question 57.   This situation should remind you of our old friend § 2-609. The Code does not want Buyer to terminate when there has not yet been a breach, but it does not want Buyer to run a risk either. Section 2-210(6) specifically permits the demand for assurances as a compromise. The correct response is **C**.

Question 58.   As with breach of other provisions in a contract, many courts find that the remedy for breach of the provision that prohibits assignment and delegation is that the assignment or delegation is still effective, but the nonbreaching party can recover damages. That is not much of a disincentive to breach. The provision in our contract provides that the assignment or delegation is not effective, which is stronger than the usual remedy. Responses **B**

and **C** go even further in stipulating remedies, with response **C** going beyond the bounds of the permissible. Thus, response **D** is correct.

Question 59.   The correct response is **B**. Section 2-725(1) provides: "An action for breach of any contract for sale must be commenced within four years after the cause of action has accrued."

Question 60.   Section 2-725(2) provides in part: "A cause of action accrues when the breach occurs, regardless of the aggrieved party's lack of knowledge of the breach. A breach of warranty occurs when tender of delivery is made." Therefore, the correct response is **B**. The explanation is that because the widgets must have been defective when they were delivered, that is when the breach occurred. There is an exception "where a warranty explicitly extends to future performance of the goods," but most courts have held that merely stating a period of time does not explicitly extend the warranty to future performance.

Question 61.   A choice of law clause specifies the law to be applied no matter where the dispute is resolved. The Uniform version of Revised Article 1 § 1-301 initially provided that parties to a commercial contract were free to choose the law of any state, even if the transaction did not bear a relation to that state. But the enacting states refused to adopt this provision, and instead enacted a provision similar to Pre-revision § 1-105, which provided that the chosen law had to bear a reasonable relation to the transaction. The Uniform Law Commission (ULC) has now amended the Uniform version to reflect this view.

You might wonder why it would make a difference which state's version of a uniform law is applied. Recall that the uniform version of the UCC promulgated by the ULC does not have the force of law. When enacted by a state, it becomes law, and the legislature frequently makes changes so that it is not uniform from state to state.

To have dispute resolution take place in California the parties would need to adopt a choice of *forum* clause, specifying that California was to be the forum for dispute resolution. It might look like this:

> It is agreed by and between the passenger and the Carrier that all disputes and matters whatsoever arising under, in connection with or incident to this Contract shall be litigated, if at all, in and before a Court located in the State of California, U.S.A., to the exclusion of the Courts of any other state or country.

This forum selection clause was approved in a consumer contract by the U.S. Supreme Court for purposes of admiralty law in *Carnival Cruise Lines, Inc. v. Shute*, 499 U.S. 585 (1991). Because this contract does not contain a choice of forum clause, the correct response is **B**.

Question 62.   The correct response is **D**. The United Nations Convention on the International Sale of Goods (CISG) is an international treaty, signed by the United States and many nations of the world, governing the commercial sale of goods between those countries. CISG Article 1(1)(a) provides, "This Convention applies to contracts of sale of goods between parties whose places of business are in different States: (a) when the States are Contracting States." Companies in the United States and China are in different States (countries) and both countries are Contracting States; that is, they have both signed the convention. Therefore, it applies to the transaction.

Question 63.   Many U.S. companies prefer to have familiar law apply to their contracts, so they will frequently opt out of the United Nations Convention on the International Sale of Goods (CISG) by utilizing a choice of law clause specifying the law of a U.S. jurisdiction. The CISG permits this in its Article 6, which states that "[t]he parties may exclude the application of this Convention, or, subject to Article 12, derogate from or vary the effect of any of its provisions." Language such as that employed in response **C** would suffice for this purpose. If the parties merely stated, "This contract is governed by the law of California," they would find that they have not opted out of the CISG. The law of California includes treaties that the federal government has entered into that are binding on the states. So the law of California *is* the CISG. Therefore, response **A** is incorrect.

Response **D** would probably be considered the equivalent of **A**, because excepting principles of choice of law does not except the CISG. Response **C** would likely accomplish the purpose. To be clear that the parties did not want the CISG to apply, the drafter could go further, stating, "This contract is governed by the UCC as enacted in California, and the parties expressly disavow application of the CISG." Response **B** is incorrect, because it provides that California law applies only to the extent that UNIDROIT does not have a rule on point.

Question 64.   The general rule is that the parties are entitled to use the court system to resolve their dispute. The exceptions are if a statute or agreement of the parties requires arbitration. Here, they have stipulated to arbitration, so response **D** is correct. The Federal Arbitration Act, 9 U.S.C. §§ 1-15, provides rules for arbitration once a dispute involving interstate commerce goes to arbitration, but it does not get the dispute there.

Question 65.   Section 2-203 eliminates any requirement of a seal. The correct response is **D**. The reference to the seal should probably be eliminated.

Question 66.   A court should not elevate form over substance. The fact that the parties designated their agreement as one for the sale of goods does not make it so. Therefore, **C** is not a good answer. Although some courts have taken this approach, it does not make sense to me to consider a software contract as within the UCC just because the software was delivered on a disk. Therefore, **B** is not a good answer. Since software is not a good as defined in the Code, the UCC does not technically apply. Therefore, there is something to be said for response **A**. However, because the Article 2 provisions, especially the warranty terms, are quite workable when applied to software, many software vendors model their contracts after contracts for the sale of goods. Therefore, **D** is the best answer. Even if the Code is not technically applicable, a court will likely apply it by analogy.

Table of Statutes

Index